Business Law for Insurance Professionals

Business Law for Insurance Professionals

Edited by

Donna Popow, CPCU, AIC

1st Edition • 4th Printing

The Institutes
720 Providence Road, Suite 100
Malvern, Pennsylvania 19355-3433

1st Edition • 4th Printing • August 2016

Library of Congress Control Number: 2010914051

ISBN 978-0-89463-423-9

Foreword

The Institutes are the trusted leader in delivering proven knowledge solutions that drive powerful business results for the risk management and property-casualty insurance industry. For more than 100 years, The Institutes have been meeting the industry's changing professional development needs with customer-driven products and services.

In conjunction with industry experts and members of the academic community, our Knowledge Resources Department develops our course and program content, including Institutes study materials. Practical and technical knowledge gained from Institutes courses enhances qualifications, improves performance, and contributes to professional growth—all of which drive results.

The Institutes' proven knowledge helps individuals and organizations achieve powerful results with a variety of flexible, customer-focused options:

Recognized Credentials—The Institutes offer an unmatched range of widely recognized and industry-respected specialty credentials. The Institutes' Chartered Property Casualty Underwriter (CPCU®) professional designation is designed to provide a broad understanding of the property-casualty insurance industry. Depending on professional needs, CPCU students may select either a commercial insurance focus or a personal risk management and insurance focus and may choose from a variety of electives.

In addition, The Institutes offer certificate or designation programs in a variety of disciplines, including these:

- Claims
- Commercial underwriting
- Fidelity and surety bonding
- General insurance
- Insurance accounting and finance
- Insurance information technology
- Insurance production and agency management
- Insurance regulation and compliance
- Management
- Marine insurance
- Personal insurance
- Premium auditing
- Quality insurance services
- Reinsurance
- Risk management
- Surplus lines

Ethics—Ethical behavior is crucial to preserving not only the trust on which insurance transactions are based, but also the public's trust in our industry as a whole. All Institutes designations now have an ethics requirement, which is delivered online and free of charge. The ethics requirement content is designed specifically for insurance practitioners and uses insurance-based case studies to outline an ethical framework. More information is available in the Programs section of our website, TheInstitutes.org.

Flexible Online Learning—The Institutes have an unmatched variety of technical insurance content covering topics from accounting to underwriting, which we now deliver through hundreds of online courses. These cost-effective self-study courses are a convenient way to fill gaps in technical knowledge in a matter of hours without ever leaving the office.

Continuing Education—A majority of The Institutes' courses are filed for CE credit in most states. We also deliver quality, affordable, online CE courses quickly and conveniently through CEU. Visit CEU.com to learn more. CEU is powered by The Institutes.

College Credits—Most Institutes courses carry college credit recommendations from the American Council on Education. A variety of courses also qualify for credits toward certain associate, bachelor's, and master's degrees at several prestigious colleges and universities. More information is available in the Student Services section of our website, TheInstitutes.org.

Custom Applications—The Institutes collaborate with corporate customers to use our trusted course content and flexible delivery options in developing customized solutions that help them achieve their unique organizational goals.

Insightful Analysis—Our Insurance Research Council (IRC) division conducts public policy research on important contemporary issues in property-casualty insurance and risk management. Visit www.insurance-research.org to learn more or purchase its most recent studies.

The Institutes look forward to serving the risk management and property-casualty insurance industry for another 100 years. We welcome comments from our students and course leaders; your feedback helps us continue to improve the quality of our study materials.

Peter L. Miller, CPCU
President and CEO
The Institutes

Preface

Business Law for Insurance Professionals is the assigned textbook for CPCU 530, one of the required courses for the Chartered Property Casualty Underwriter (CPCU®) designation program.

The goal of CPCU 530 is to enable you to understand and apply principles and concepts of United States law that are relevant to the work of insurance and risk management professionals. The textbook contains ten assignments that support that goal.

Assignment 1 provides an overview of the U.S. legal system; describes the sources of U.S. law; and examines the legal procedures that apply to civil trials, alternative dispute resolution proceedings, and administrative agencies.

Assignment 2 explains the elements of contract law that relate to any type of legal contract, and Assignment 3 shows how these elements apply specifically to insurance contracts.

Assignment 4 examines commercial law, based mainly on the legal rules contained in the Uniform Commercial Code, pertaining to matters such as sales contracts, negotiable instruments, and documents of title.

Assignment 5 considers property law, including subjects such as personal property ownership, bailment, real property ownership and sales, real estate security interests and liens, and the landlord-tenant relationship.

Assignment 6 examines tort law, which is the basis for most liabilities covered by insurance. The major topics covered are negligence, intentional torts, products liability, and recoverable damages.

Assignment 7 explains the elements of agency law that relate to any type of principal-agent relationship, and Assignment 8 shows how these elements apply specifically to insurance agency relationships.

Assignment 9 examines employment law and business entities. Employment law includes the doctrine of employment at will, anti-discrimination laws, labor-management relations, and employee welfare laws. The business entities topic examines the various forms of ownership that a business entity can take, such as corporation, partnership, or limited liability company.

Assignment 10 examines various aspects of the legal environment applicable to companies engaged in international business, whether through foreign trade, foreign contractual relationships, or foreign direct investments.

This textbook was developed in large part with content from The Legal Environment of Insurance, which was previously the assigned textbook for CPCU 530. The persons who participated in developing Business Law for Insurance Professionals are acknowledged on the Contributors page. Although most of those who participated in developing The Legal Environment of Insurance are not named on the Contributors page, The Institutes remain grateful to them for their contributions.

For more information about The Institutes' programs, please call our Customer Success Department at (800) 644-2101, email us at CustomerSuccess@TheInstitutes.org, or visit our website at TheInstitutes.org.

Donna J. Popow

Arthur L. Flitner

Contributors

The Institutes acknowledge with deep appreciation the contributions made to the content of this text by the following persons:

Pamela Lyons, BA, FCIP, CRM

Valerie Ullman Katz, CPCU, MBA, ARM, CBCP, AIM, AIS

Lynn M. Knauf, CPCU, ARP

Kathleen J. Robison, CPCU, ARM, AIC, AU

Martin J. Frappolli, CPCU, FIDM, AIS

Judith Vaughan, AIC

Doug Froggatt, CPCU, AINS

Contents

Assignment 1

Introduction to U.S. Law — 1.1

The U.S. Legal System — 1.3

Sources of U.S. Law — 1.8

Civil Trial Procedures — 1.16

Alternative Dispute Resolution — 1.23

Administrative Agency Procedures — 1.25

Summary — 1.31

Assignment 2

Contract Law — 2.1

Types of Contracts — 2.3

Requirements of an Offer — 2.5

Requirements of a Valid Acceptance — 2.10

Capacity to Contract — 2.13

Consideration — 2.18

Legal Purpose of a Contract — 2.23

Enforceability of a Contract — 2.29

Contract Interpretation — 2.38

Third-Party Contractual Rights — 2.42

Termination of a Contract — 2.46

Breach of Contract — 2.52

Contracts Case Study — 2.57

Summary — 2.63

Assignment 3

Contract Law: Insurance Applications — 3.1

Special Characteristics of Insurance Contracts — 3.3

Insurance Contract Formation — 3.9

Insurance as Third-Party Beneficiary Contract — 3.17

Representations and Warranties in Insurance — 3.21

Waiver, Estoppel, and Election — 3.27

Nonwaiver Agreements and Reservation of Rights Letters — 3.34

Summary — 3.37

Assignment 4

Commercial Law — 4.1

Sales Contracts — 4.3

Negotiable Instruments — 4.13

Documents of Title — 4.18

Secured Transactions — 4.21

Consumer Protection Laws — 4.27

Summary — 4.36

Assignment 5

Property Law — 5.1

Ownership and Possession of Personal Property — 5.3

Bailee's and Bailor's Rights and Duties — 5.7

Real Property Ownership — 5.10

Real Property Sales — 5.14

Real Property Security Interests and Liens — 5.17

Incidental Real Property Rights — 5.21

Land Use Restrictions — 5.25

The Landlord and Tenant Relationship — 5.28

Summary — 5.30

Assignment 6

Tort Law	6.1
Negligence	6.3
Defenses Against Negligence Claims	6.9
Liability of Landowners or Occupiers of Land	6.17
Intentional Torts: Part 1 of 2	6.21
Intentional Torts: Part 2 of 2	6.28
Liability in Extraordinary Circumstances	6.37
Products Liability	6.39
Damages in Tort Suits	6.45
Liability Concepts Affecting Tort Claims	6.48
Summary	6.53

Assignment 7

Agency Law	7.1
Agency Creation	7.3
Agent's Authority	7.6
Agent's Duties and Remedies	7.7
Agency Termination	7.13
Contractual Rights and Liabilities	7.16
Tort Liability of Principal and Agent	7.20
Summary	7.23

Assignment 8

Agency Law: Insurance Applications	8.1
Insurance Producer Classifications	8.3
Producers' Authority	8.4
Extent of Producers' Authority	8.7
Termination of Producer Authority	8.14
Producers' Duties and Liabilities	8.15
Summary	8.31

Assignment 9

Employment Law and Business Entities	9.1
Employment at Will	9.3
Antidiscrimination Laws	9.5
Labor-Management Relations	9.13
Employee Welfare Laws	9.18
Corporations: Formation	9.25
Corporations: Duties and Obligations	9.34
Corporations: Mergers, Dissolution, and Reorganization	9.41
Partnerships	9.45
Unincorporated Associations	9.54
Summary	9.60

Assignment 10

The International Legal Environment	10.1
Methods of Engaging in International Business	10.3
Legal Systems	10.11
International Law	10.17
Multinational Organizations and Agreements	10.19
United States Laws Affecting International Business	10.26
Financial Considerations in International Business	10.29
Non-Legal Factors Affecting International Business	10.36
Summary	10.40

Index	1

Direct Your Learning ▶▶

Introduction to U.S. Law

Outline

The U.S. Legal System

Sources of U.S. Law

Civil Trial Procedures

Alternative Dispute Resolution

Administrative Agency Procedures

Summary

Educational Objectives

After learning the content of this assignment, you should be able to:

▹ Describe the U.S. civil-law and common-law systems and classifications.

▹ Describe the role and usual characteristics of each of the following sources of U.S. law:

- Constitutions
- Legislative bodies
- Courts
- Executive branches
- Administrative agencies

▹ Describe the steps, motions, rules, and other concepts involved in pretrial procedures, trial procedures, and appeals.

▹ Describe each of these alternative dispute resolution procedures:

- Arbitration
- Mediation
- Negotiation

▹ Describe these aspects of administrative agency procedures:

- Rulemaking function
- Adjudicatory function
- Investigative powers
- Judicial review

Introduction to U.S. Law

THE U.S. LEGAL SYSTEM

Insurance and risk management professionals must be familiar with legal principles of insurance, as well as general legal principles. Understanding the prevailing type of legal system in the United States and the common ways of classifying the U.S. legal system is a logical starting point for the study of legal principles.

Ever since ancient people first gathered in groups, people have adopted rules to govern their relations with one another. These rules were handed down orally to succeeding generations and eventually recorded in writing. In Europe, two basic legal systems developed over hundreds of years: the Roman Empire's civil-law system, adopted by continental European countries, and Great Britain's common-law system.

These two systems differ significantly in origin and in form, and both systems exist in the United States. The common-law system is the foundation of the U.S. legal system, although Louisiana bases its law on the civil-law system.

Civil-Law System

The civil-law system, one of the two basic western legal systems, is the foundation of law in continental Europe, Latin America, Scotland, the state of Louisiana, and some other parts of the world. Civil-law systems, such as the French Code of Napoleon, have comprehensive codes of written laws, or statutes, that apply to all legal questions. These systems rely on scholarly interpretations of their codes and constitutions rather than on court decisions, the basis of the common-law system.

Common-Law System

The common-law system is the body of law derived from court decisions as opposed to statutes or constitutions. Beginning as unwritten customs that eventually came to be recognized and enforced by local courts, the common-law system arose in England after the Norman Conquest in 1066. The "law common to all England" developed out of a constantly expanding number of disputes, or cases, settled by English royal courts and tribunals. Over time, the English legal system expanded to include written laws as well as written court cases.

The English common law, brought by English colonists to North America, became the foundation for U.S. law. Today, U.S. law consists of that common-law foundation, the written laws passed by Congress and state legislatures, and the decisions resulting from thousands of U.S. court cases.

Doctrine of stare decisis

The principle that lower courts must follow precedents set by higher courts.

The U.S. common-law system relies on prior case rulings, or precedents. Using this method of resolution, the **doctrine of stare decisis** ("to stand by things decided"), courts follow earlier court decisions when the same issues arise again in lawsuits. This common-law doctrine gives a degree of certainty to the law on which citizens can rely in conducting their affairs. Courts do not necessarily decide all similar cases exactly the same as previous courts have, but they must provide strong reasons to depart from precedents.

In common-law countries, solving a new legal problem in a current case often involves a process called synthesis. The process combines the rulings from several legal authorities into a new rule of law that is applied to the new legal problem. The authorities typically consider relevant statutes, prior cases that interpret the statutes, and prior cases that establish common-law precedents.

When developing a new rule of law using synthesis, courts analyze the reasoning and facts of the relevant prior cases as controlled by the language of a governing statute, if any, and compare the facts of the prior cases to those of the current case. This example illustrates how the common law can evolve through the process of synthesis: If an insured sues an insurer in a state court over a disagreement about a policy provision's meaning, the court analyzes prior cases in which courts have ruled on the meaning of the same or similar provisions. The court first seeks similar cases in its own state or province; if no such cases apply, the court then seeks similar cases in other states or provinces. If no cases on point are found, the court might analyze general contractual principles and court rulings in somewhat similar cases.

Courts often encounter situations for which they can find no prior case or previous law that directly applies. Such unprecedented situations are called "threshold cases" because they present new legal questions. When encountering threshold cases, judges summon all applicable law in an attempt to arrive at fair decisions.

Judicial Influence on Common Law

Methods of selecting judges, as well as individual judges' views and values, can influence judicial decisions. Judicial selection methods include election and appointment, and they vary by state. In some states judges are elected, while in other states elected officials either appoint judges or choose other officials to appoint them.

Although courts strive for objectivity in their decisions, individual judges' political beliefs, views, values, and biases can affect decisions. Newly elected judges can change the direction of a court. Appointed judges can reflect the positions of the political party in power, and court composition can change when the party in power changes. However, some judicial appointments, particularly at the federal level, are for life. For example, U.S. Supreme Court justices are appointed by the president for life terms. Through judicial appointments, a president can influence the law for many years into the future.

The legal system has built-in controls for promoting fair outcomes in disputes. For example, a party that loses in trial court may have grounds to appeal the decision to a higher court, in some cases all the way to the U.S. Supreme Court. Because the Supreme Court is the country's highest court, the views of the court's justices have a profound influence on the law, particularly when justices decide threshold questions.

The Evolution of Common Law

The common law is not an absolute; it reflects the evolution of society's values and attitudes. What was acceptable law in the U.S. a century ago can, in many instances, be unacceptable today. A court can find a prior decision clearly wrong and discard it as precedent.

Courts generally do not follow precedent when the earlier rule of law has lost its usefulness or when the original reasons for the rule no longer exist. Absent those reasons, courts may overrule prior decisions only for sound judicial reasons. This approach helps prevent legal capriciousness and gives stability to society and business. The U.S. Congress or a state legislature can pass new legislation that changes a common-law principle.

The common law also changes through landmark decisions, historic court rulings that significantly change or add to prior law with far-reaching societal effects. One of the most well-known examples is the U.S. Supreme Court decision in *Brown v. Board of Education*,[1] which overruled previous cases condoning racial segregation in schools. Another example is *Miranda v. Arizona*,[2] which requires police to inform suspects in criminal cases of their constitutional right against self-incrimination before questioning them.

The Supreme Court made a landmark decision in 1869 affecting insurance regulation. *Paul v. Virginia*[3] established that insurance is a contract delivered locally and governed by state law rather than federal law. That decision was modified by another landmark insurance decision in 1944, the South-Eastern Underwriters case,[4] in which the Supreme Court ruled that federal law applies to insurance in some cases.

Equity

Common-law courts historically determined legal rights and remedies and awarded money damages. Courts of **equity** arose in England because of the failure of courts of law to provide adequate remedies in some cases. Courts of equity complemented law courts by recognizing many rights that common law courts did not recognize.

Equity

Fairness, or a body of principles constituting what is fair and right.

Equitable remedies seek fair solutions beyond what traditional legal remedies can offer. For example, the usual legal remedy for breach of a contract for the sale of a unique item, such as a one-of-a-kind antique, would be money damages. However, a court of equity would consider money damages inadequate as a remedy because the item, being unique, cannot be replaced. A court of equity might order the breaching party to perform the contract by transferring the antique to the injured party.

Although some states still have separate law and equity courts, many states have unified them into a single system. In some states, one court might sit as a court of equity on one occasion and as a court of law on another. In the federal system and some state systems, the same courts provide both equitable and legal remedies. In civil cases before federal courts, parties are entitled to a trial by jury on questions with which the court is operating as a court of law, but equity court decisions are made by judges.

Classifications of U.S. Law

The U.S. legal system of civil law and common law is subject to classification based on several other factors. Three of the most common ways to classify U.S. law, which can overlap, are these:

- Classification as either criminal or civil law
- Classification by subject matter
- Classification as either substantive or procedural law

Classification as Criminal or Civil Law

Criminal law
The branch of the law that imposes penalties for wrongs against society.

Criminal law applies to acts that society deems so harmful to the public welfare that government is responsible for prosecuting and punishing the perpetrators. This body of law defines offenses; regulates investigating, charging, and trying accused offenders; and establishes punishments for convicted offenders.

Criminal law covers offenses ranging from major crimes, such as murder, to minor offenses, such as traffic violations. A felony is a major crime involving long-term punishment. A misdemeanor is a minor crime punishable by a fine or short-term imprisonment. Summary offenses are crimes that are neither felonies nor misdemeanors under state law; they usually result in fines but not imprisonment. Written laws, such as statutes and ordinances (local laws), specify the nature of crimes and their punishments, whether imprisonment or fines or both. In criminal law, the government acts as the prosecutor, representing the public.

Civil law
A classification of law that applies to legal matters not governed by criminal law and that protects rights and provides remedies for breaches of duties owed to others.

Civil law applies to legal matters that are not governed by criminal law. Civil law basically protects rights and provides remedies for breaches of duties owed to others. The term "civil law" is not, within this classification context, the same as the civil-law system discussed previously.

Civil law protects rights and provides remedies for breaches of duty other than crimes. In a civil action, the injured party usually seeks reimbursement, in the form of money damages, for harm. Cases in equity courts, or those having equitable remedies, also fall under civil law. In a civil equity case, a court can order a specific action—for example, directing an insurance company to honor policy terms.

Another distinguishing factor between civil and criminal law is the burden of proof. A party to a lawsuit has the duty to prove a charge or an allegation. The extent of the proof varies depending on the type of case. The prosecution in a criminal case must establish guilt beyond a reasonable doubt, that is, proof to a moral certainty. The burden of proof in a civil case is less strict. The injured party must establish the case only by a preponderance of the evidence, that is, the evidence supporting the jury's decision must be of greater weight than the evidence against it.

A single act can be both a crime and a civil wrong. In such a case, an injured party can bring a civil suit for money damages, while the government can prosecute a criminal case and seek fines or imprisonment. Suppose an insurance agent has defrauded an insured with misleading information about coverage. This action can constitute both a civil misrepresentation and the crime of fraud and could result in separate civil and criminal trials. The injured party sues for the civil wrong, and the government prosecutes for the crime.

Classification by Subject Matter

Beyond classification as either civil or criminal law, U.S. law can be classified by subject matter. Criminal law is also a subject-matter classification. Subject-matter classifications group cases by type, defined by parties' rights and liabilities. Examples of subject-matter classifications, in addition to criminal law, are contracts, torts, agency, and property law, all of which also fall into the civil law classification. Each type of law has its own rules and precedents.

Classification as Substantive or Procedural Law

Within the classifications of law as civil or criminal, U.S. law is also either **substantive** or **procedural law**.

Substantive law governs the merits of a case, which are based on the facts giving rise to the lawsuit or criminal case. It includes rules of legislative and judicial law that specify what constitutes an enforceable contract, who can own and transfer property, and what forms of conduct are criminal. For example, substantive law is involved in how contract law applies to an insurance policy. Substantive law includes the subject-matter classifications, such as crimes, contracts, torts, agency, and property law.

These two classifications, substantive and procedural, are closely intertwined and are often difficult to distinguish. Procedural law involves the procedures,

Substantive law

A classification of law that creates, defines, and regulates parties' rights, duties, and powers.

Procedural law

A classification of law that prescribes the steps, or processes, for enforcing the rights and duties defined by substantive law.

or mechanics, of court processes and the methods used to enforce substantive law. Criminal and civil actions follow different procedures, called civil procedure and criminal procedure, which specify steps that parties to actions must follow.

Procedural law also specifies the means by which courts can apply substantive law. For example, a state can set a maximum period within which a criminal defendant must come to trial, a procedural rule that enforces a criminal defendant's right to a speedy trial. Substantive law would describe the crime itself and establish the criteria for determining the defendant's guilt. An example of procedural law would be the question of in what court (federal or state, and in which state) an insured should sue an insurer.

SOURCES OF U.S. LAW

The United States federal government and each of the fifty states, Puerto Rico, and the District of Columbia have separate and distinct legal systems, each with its own sources of law. See the exhibit "Source of U.S. Law (Federal and State)."

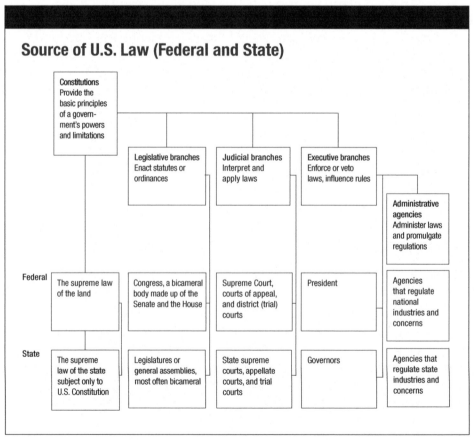

[DA05236]

Each of the legal systems has five sources of law:

- A constitution, which establishes fundamental rights and creates the other branches of government
- The legislative branch—Congress and state legislatures, for example—which enacts statutes
- The judicial branch—courts—which decides cases
- The executive branch—the president and state governors, for example—which enforces law
- Administrative agencies—part of the executive branch—which make and enforce regulations

Constitutions

In the U.S., constitutions lay the groundwork for the legal systems of both state and federal governments. The U.S. (federal) Constitution defines itself as the "supreme Law of the Land." Each state has its own constitution, which is the supreme law of that state, subservient only to the U.S. Constitution.

In the case of a conflict, the U.S. Constitution always prevails over a state constitution. Any law that violates the U.S. Constitution, whether state or federal, is void. Since its adoption in 1789, the Constitution has survived many significant social and economic developments to become the oldest constitution in the world today. In more than 200 years of U.S. history, the Constitution has undergone few changes.

A constitution, whether federal or state, specifies a government's powers and the limitations on those powers. Not all countries have constitutions (England, for example, does not); some countries are developing constitutions. In democratic countries, constitutions not only define governmental powers but also specify individual rights. The U.S. Constitution has served as a model for many countries in specifying individual rights.

Each state has its own constitution. A state can grant broader rights to its citizens than those that federal law or the U.S. Constitution grants as long as the state does not violate the federal Constitution. For example, although the U.S. Constitution does not contain an amendment explicitly prohibiting gender-based discrimination, some state constitutions do.

Separation of Powers

The U.S. Constitution provides for separation of powers among three co-equal branches of government: legislative, judicial, and executive. State constitutions, and most local government charters, follow this model. Inherent in the U.S. legal system is the concept of checks and balances, designed to ensure that no single branch of government can become too powerful. The branches, their powers, and how they check and balance the other branches are summarized in this manner:

- The executive branch (led by the president on the federal level and governors on the state level) has power to recommend, approve, or veto laws and to administer and carry out many laws through administrative agencies. This branch's checks on the other two branches include the power to appoint some judges (those who are not elected at the state level) and the power to veto laws passed by the legislative branch. Administrative agencies are part of the executive branch of government, although some may be independent of executive oversight. These agencies are created by law, and they often develop and enforce regulations to carry out the law.

- The legislative branch (the federal Congress and state legislatures) has the power to pass laws. This branch's checks on the other two branches include its power to approve or deny many of the executive's appointments (judges and heads of administrative agencies, for example) and its ability to pass constitutional laws negating judicial opinions.

- The judicial branch (the courts) interprets, affirms, or negates laws. Supreme courts at both the federal and state levels also interpret their respective constitutions. The judicial branch's checks on the other two branches include the power to declare laws—and sometimes actions or regulations of the executive branch—unconstitutional or unlawful.

Provisions Relevant to Insurance

The U.S. Constitution has several provisions relevant to the insurance business:

- Delegation of powers to Congress
- Commerce Clause
- Due Process Clause
- Equal Protection Clause

The Constitution establishes the express powers of Congress, including the power to regulate commerce, levy and collect taxes, borrow money, and establish uniform laws on bankruptcy. The Constitution also establishes the implied powers of Congress to pass laws necessary to implement all of Congress's express powers. The Constitution delegates to states any powers that it does not specifically reserve for the federal government or forbid states to exercise.

The Constitution's Commerce Clause gives Congress the power to regulate commerce (trade) with foreign nations and among the states (interstate commerce). Interstate commerce includes any commercial activity, whether interstate or intrastate, that has any appreciable direct or indirect effect on trade among states. Any state law or action that interferes with interstate commerce is, therefore, unconstitutional. Commerce includes such activities as underwriting and selling insurance, distributing movies, transacting real estate, gathering news, and playing professional sports. An insurer that conducts business in more than one state is subject to federal law.

The Fifth Amendment's Due Process Clause guarantees notice and a hearing before the federal government can deprive any person of life, liberty, or property. The Fourteenth Amendment extends the same protection in state government actions. An example of a state due process case is an insurer's complaint against the department of insurance for attempting to lower the insurer's premium without notifying the insurer or giving the insurer an opportunity to be heard. The insurer charges that it was adversely affected because it had no opportunity to protect its interests.

The Fourteenth Amendment's **Equal Protection Clause** also addresses individual rights by prohibiting state laws that discriminate unfairly or arbitrarily and requiring equal treatment to all persons under like circumstances and conditions, in terms of both privileges and liabilities. It protects both individuals and corporations. Many state constitutions contain equal protection clauses.

Equal Protection Clause
A part of the Fourteenth Amendment to the U.S. Constitution prohibiting state laws that discriminate unfairly or arbitrarily, and requiring equal treatment to all persons under like circumstances and conditions.

Legislative Bodies

Constitutions delegate the power to make laws to legislative bodies. At practically every level of government, legislative bodies enact laws, or statutes. Major U.S. legislative bodies are Congress and the fifty state legislatures. Local governments also have legislative bodies—for example, city councils, which enact laws that are usually called ordinances.

The U.S. Congress is bicameral—that is, it has two chambers: the Senate and the House of Representatives. Each state has two senators and a number of representatives in the House based on that state's population. Only Congress can enact legislation regarding any powers granted exclusively to the federal government by the Constitution. In the areas that are primarily the concern of the individual states, only the respective states' legislatures can enact legislation.

Most states have bicameral legislatures, or assemblies, mirroring the federal Congressional structure. A few states and U.S. territories have unicameral—single house—legislatures. At the city, county, township, and village levels, thousands of local legislative bodies enact written ordinances governing their citizens. A state or local legislative body can clarify or change the common law and can proscribe unacceptable conduct as long as the laws it enacts do not violate either the U.S. Constitution or federal law or the state constitution and laws.

Questions about whether Congress or a state legislative body has the power to enact a law must be decided by the courts. Courts also interpret statutes and ordinances.

With the federal, state, and territorial governments—as well as thousands of local governments—enacting laws, confusion and conflict can result. Business law can be complicated by laws that vary by state and by local government. To minimize such difficulties, many states have adopted uniform laws. For example, all states except Louisiana have adopted the Uniform Commercial Code (UCC), which regulates the sale of goods and other commercial transactions. The UCC has resulted in uniformity in commercial transactions throughout the country.

Efforts to promote uniformity among state laws have also been made in insurance law. Insurance companies are subject to a multitude of statutes, rules, and regulations in the states. As early as 1871, states recognized the need to establish an organization to promote uniformity in regulation among the states and to exchange regulatory information, resulting in the creation of the **National Association of Insurance Commissioners (NAIC)**. The NAIC pools information to help regulators coordinate responses to changing conditions in the insurance marketplace. The NAIC also develops model laws, regulations, and guidelines.

National Association of Insurance Commissioners (NAIC)

An association of insurance commissioners from the fifty U.S. states, the District of Columbia, and the five U.S. territories and possessions, whose purpose is to coordinate insurance regulation activities among the various state insurance departments.

Courts

In addition to constitutions and legislative bodies, courts are another source of laws. The federal government has its own court system, as does each of the state governments. The state and federal court systems are separate in most respects. A party can appeal from a state to a federal court, but only in cases involving a violation of the U.S. Constitution or a federal statute.

Federal courts have jurisdiction over such cases. Jurisdiction is the power of a court to decide cases of a certain type or within a specific territory. For example, a state trial court has territorial jurisdiction over cases involving state law. Jurisdiction related to types of cases is called subject matter jurisdiction. Courts in which cases are initiated have **original jurisdiction**. Courts that hear appeals from other courts have appellate jurisdiction. Courts that hear a variety of types of cases have general jurisdiction.

Original jurisdiction

The power of a court in which cases are initiated to hear those cases.

Federal Court System

The U.S. Constitution provides that "the judicial power of the United States shall be vested in one Supreme Court, and in such inferior courts as Congress may from time to time ordain and establish." Congress has provided for many U.S. district courts, which are federal trial courts, and for courts of appeal in twelve multi-state judicial circuits and a federal circuit. Special federal courts, including the U.S. Customs Court, Bankruptcy Courts, Patent Appeals Court, and the Court of Military Appeals, hear particular kinds of cases. Federal courts handle cases raising federal questions, such as those involving the U.S.

Constitution, federal laws, and the United States as either plaintiff or defendant. Original jurisdiction also rests with federal courts in these kinds of cases:

- Cases involving admiralty and maritime law
- Lawsuits in which citizens of different states claim land under grants by different states
- Cases involving a legal minimum amount in damages between citizens of different states or between citizens of one state and of a foreign state

The U.S. District Courts are the trial courts of the federal system. For example, a person accused of a federal crime stands trial in a U.S. District Court. District courts hear lawsuits for damages involving federal law and also try cases involving **diversity jurisdiction**, such as a case between an insured in one state and an insurer in another state. A small state may have one federal district court. Larger states have more than one. See the exhibit "Federal Court System."

Diversity jurisdiction

The authority of federal district courts to hear cases involving parties from different states that involve amounts in controversy over a legal minimum.

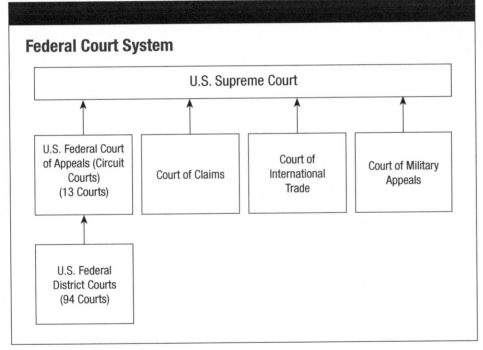

Federal Court System

[DA05237]

A party who is dissatisfied with the outcome in a case before a federal district court, and who has a properly preserved appealable issue, can appeal to the appropriate U.S. Circuit Court of Appeals. For example, a party who loses a lawsuit in the U.S. District Court in Maine can appeal to the U.S. Circuit Court of Appeals for the First Circuit, which serves as the federal appellate court for Maine, Massachusetts, New Hampshire, Puerto Rico, and Rhode Island.

There are eleven circuits, each covering more than one state or territory, a circuit for the District of Columbia, and a federal circuit, which has nationwide jurisdiction to hear appeals in specialized cases. In early U.S. history, federal appeals judges "rode the circuits" on horses or in carriages over a large area, holding court in different places. The federal appeals courts have retained the name "circuit courts." Appeals courts at any level of government are also called appellate courts.

A party who does not prevail on appeal in a circuit court of appeals, and who has a properly preserved legal issue, can take the case to the U.S. Supreme Court by filing a petition for a **writ of certiorari**, a request for the Supreme Court to consider a case. The U.S. Supreme Court grants review solely within its discretion, and it is not required to explain its reasons for granting or denying a petition for a writ of certiorari.

Writ of certiorari

An appellate court's order directing a lower court to deliver its record in a case for appellate review.

The Supreme Court is the final avenue of appeal in the U.S. legal system for the parties involved in a case. Because the Court does not consider most cases, the Circuit Courts' decisions usually stand as the law for their circuits.

State Court Systems

The state court systems are similar to the federal court system. However, no uniformity exists in the use of court names at various levels among the states and territories.

The highest appellate court in each state is usually called the supreme court. Exceptions include the highest Massachusetts court, which is the Supreme Judicial Court, and the highest New York court, the New York Court of Appeals.

Most states have an intermediate appellate-level court, which hears appeals from trial courts. For example, Pennsylvania has two intermediate appellate courts: the Commonwealth Court, which hears all appeals involving the state, local governments, and regulatory agencies, and the Superior Court, which hears appeals involving all other parties. Cases with properly preserved appealable issues can be appealed from either of these courts to the Pennsylvania Supreme Court.

A state's trial courts in which most litigation starts are courts of general jurisdiction. States have various names for this court, including court of common pleas, superior court, and district court. The term "superior court" can mean a trial court in some states but an appellate court in others.

A state's trial court system also includes courts of limited jurisdiction, which hear specific types of cases. Examples are probate courts, county courts, and municipal courts. Probate courts hear primarily estate cases; municipal courts might hear cases involving only limited amounts of money. The lowest courts may be called municipal, small claims, or mayor's courts, depending on local custom. Judges in these courts can be justices of the peace or magistrates. See the exhibit "State Court Systems."

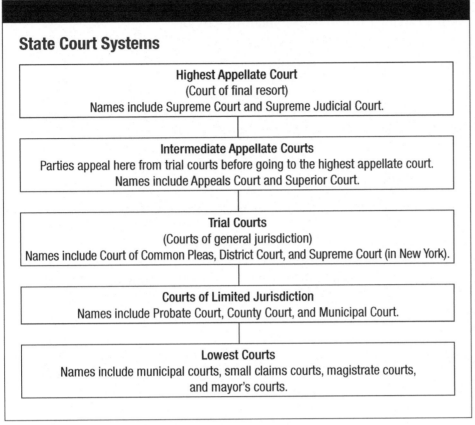

State Court Systems

Highest Appellate Court
(Court of final resort)
Names include Supreme Court and Supreme Judicial Court.

Intermediate Appellate Courts
Parties appeal here from trial courts before going to the highest appellate court.
Names include Appeals Court and Superior Court.

Trial Courts
(Courts of general jurisdiction)
Names include Court of Common Pleas, District Court, and Supreme Court (in New York).

Courts of Limited Jurisdiction
Names include Probate Court, County Court, and Municipal Court.

Lowest Courts
Names include municipal courts, small claims courts, magistrate courts,
and mayor's courts.

[DA05238]

Conflicts of law often arise about which states' law should apply when a dispute is subject to the laws of two or more jurisdictions. In tort cases (cases that involve wrongs between parties), the law in force where the injury occurred generally applies. Courts in contract cases, in contrast, use the center of gravity rule, applying the law of the state with the most significant relationship to the case. To attempt to avoid conflicts of law, the parties to a contract may include in their contract an agreement on which state's laws will apply if a dispute arises.

Conflicts of law
A body of law that resolves questions when states' laws conflict.

Executive Branches

An additional source of law, along with constitutions, legislative bodies, and courts, is executive branches of government, which include chief executives, such as the U.S. president and state governors, and administrative agencies. A president, governor, or mayor can either recommend, approve, or veto laws after the legislative body enacts them but before they become effective. The executive can also appoint the heads of administrative agencies to assist in enforcing the laws. Some of these appointments require legislative approval.

The executive branch can influence the numerous rules and regulations that administrative agencies issue. For example, a state governor may appoint the insurance commissioner. Through this appointment power in some states, a governor can influence insurance industry activities.

Administrative Agencies

Administrative agencies, although part of the executive branch, can be considered a separate source of law. The legislative branch, whether Congress or a state legislature, creates administrative agencies by statute. These agencies implement and enforce governmental functions. At the federal level, more than 150 regulatory agencies administer laws affecting thousands of organizations and all citizens.

The federal regulatory system arose to regulate certain large and powerful industries, such as railroads and banking. The federal government has since created agencies to regulate particular functions across all industries, such as equal employment, financial disclosure, worker health and safety, and environmental concerns. Agencies regulate specific areas, such as taxation, health, and labor, and they vary in the scope of their functions, purposes, and powers. However, they all generally have the power to make rules and to prescribe behavior.

Administrative law

The statutory laws that grant power to administrative agencies to act and the body of law that is created by administrative agencies themselves.

Agency rules, regulations, and rulings have the full force of law and constitute the body of **administrative law**. Federal agencies promulgate thousands of rules every year; that is, they initiate and finalize formal rules and make them known through formal public announcements. The legislative delegation of rulemaking power to an administrative agency is constitutional as long as it meets these three conditions:

- The legislation carefully defines the scope of the delegated power.
- The agency exercises its rulemaking power within the defined scope.
- The rules are subject to court (judicial) review.

Few businesses, if any, escape administrative agency supervision. To be valid, business regulations must apply uniformly to all members within the same business class. The federal government can impose regulations on any aspect of business necessary for the nation's economic needs. The states can regulate business as long as they do not impose unreasonable burdens on interstate commerce or on any federal government activity.

CIVIL TRIAL PROCEDURES

When individuals or businesses cannot resolve their differences privately, they can go to court for resolution. Procedures are prescribed for every stage of the legal process. While jurisdictions vary in procedure and terminology, it is useful to understand the procedures followed in most federal and state courts.

Litigation is extremely costly and time consuming and often proceeds for several years. Its complex legal process can involve meticulous pretrial preparation by lawyers, carefully plotted trial tactics, and procedural complexities. At any point during litigation (the process of carrying on a lawsuit), parties can settle a case by agreeing to terms. The legal system encourages out-of-court settlements.

Pretrial Procedure

Although trials are the most prominent stage of the legal process, lawyers do substantial pretrial preparation to gather as much information as possible about all **allegations** and evidence the parties might present. See the exhibit "Pretrial Procedure."

A party, whether an individual or an organization, starts a lawsuit by filing a **complaint** in the court that has jurisdiction over the dispute. The party who files the complaint is the plaintiff, and the party against whom the plaintiff files a complaint is the defendant. The complaint is the first **pleading** filed with the court. The complaint sets out the plaintiff's allegations, explains why the plaintiff has a **cause of action** against the defendant, and states what remedy the plaintiff requests. The complaint also tells the court why it has jurisdiction over the matter.

In small claims or municipal courts that handle cases involving small amounts of damages, parties can usually file a complaint without a lawyer's assistance. In courts of general jurisdiction, lawyers are usually needed to file pleadings. Pleadings follow prescribed forms that have developed over many years, and lawyers have pleading forms that they can adapt to individual cases.

After a complaint has been filed, the court issues a summons notifying the defendant of the lawsuit, with a copy of the complaint attached. The summons specifies how long the defendant has to file an **answer** to the complaint. The answer can include **counterclaims**. Alternatively, the defendant can file an entry of appearance, which neither admits nor denies any allegations in the complaint; it only states that the defendant will appear in court.

After receiving the defendant's answer, the plaintiff files a reply. Taken together, all pleadings—the complaint, the answer, and the reply—constitute a written dialogue between the parties that informs the court about the substance of the dispute. Given that information, the parties can respond by filing **motions**.

For example, the defendant might file a **motion to dismiss**. An example of a procedural defect is the failure of the plaintiff to state a legally recognized cause of action. A motion for judgment on the pleadings is a request made after the pleadings but before trial for a judgment on the pleadings based on the admissions in the pleadings. At the close of discovery, but before trial, the plaintiff or the defendant can file a **motion for summary judgment**, arguing that the other side has failed to meet the legal standard to submit the case to a judge or jury to decide. Courts apply strict standards when reviewing a motion for summary judgment because if the motion is successful, the nonmoving

Allegation

A claim made in the complaint by the plaintiff, specifying what the plaintiff expects to prove to obtain a judgment against the defendant.

Complaint

The allegations made by a plaintiff in a lawsuit.

Pleading

A formal written statement of the facts and claims of each party to a lawsuit.

Cause of action

A plaintiff's legal grounds to sue a defendant.

Answer

A document filed in court by a defendant responding to a plaintiff's complaint and explaining why the plaintiff should not win the case.

Counterclaim

A complaint brought by the defendant against the plaintiff.

Motion

A formal request for the court to take a particular action.

Motion to dismiss

A request that a court terminate an action because of settlement, voluntary withdrawal, or procedural defect.

Motion for summary judgment

A pretrial request asking the court to enter a judgment when no material facts are in dispute.

Pretrial Procedure

Action	Acting Party	Purpose/Result
Complaint	Plaintiff	• Sets out allegations. • States cause of action. • Requests remedy.
Summons	Court	• Notifies defendant of lawsuit. • Contains copy of complaint. • Sets out time frame for defendant to answer.
Answer	Defendant	• States why plaintiff should not win. • May include counterclaims. • In the alternative, may be only "entry of appearance," which neither admits nor denies allegations.
Reply	Plaintiff	• Responds to defendant's answer.
Motions		
• To dismiss	Defendant	• Asserts that plaintiff has failed to state a claim for which the court can grant relief.
• For judgment on the pleadings, or summary judgment	Defendant	• Admits the allegations but questions whether the law provides a remedy.
		Granted motion ends lawsuit.
Pretrial conference	Both parties, with judge	• Parties may stipulate some or all of the facts. • Judge encourages settlement.
		Settlement ends lawsuit.
Discovery	Both parties	• Parties elicit evidence, using depositions, interrogatories, and motions to produce evidence.

[DA04607]

party is deprived of a jury trial. To grant a summary judgment motion, the court must find that there are no genuine issues of material fact in dispute and that the moving party is entitled to judgment as a matter of law. Many cases end when the court grants one of these motions and never proceed to trial.

Another pretrial option for either party is to request a pretrial conference with the judge. At the pretrial conference, the plaintiff and defendant stipulate, or agree, to the truth of some or all of the facts in the pleadings. Courts use pretrial conferences to encourage settlements—agreements between both parties to end a case rather than to proceed to trial. Stipulations can also shorten a trial by reducing the amount of evidence presented.

The pretrial stage also includes **discovery**. In cases involving complex business questions, such as insurance antitrust cases, discovery can span months or even years and can involve tedious examination of thousands of documents and records. Parties to lawsuits use the discovery tools of **depositions**, **interrogatories**, **subpoenas**, and motions to compel compliance with discovery requests.

Parties must provide everything requested in discovery. A party can object to a request for discovery and ask the court to rule on whether the evidence is required. Discovered information enables the parties to know as much as possible before trial and prevents surprises. If testimony at trial contradicts an earlier deposition or an answer to a written interrogatory, lawyers can use the pretrial evidence to challenge the evidence presented at trial. Discovery can sometimes lead to settlement; once the parties know all the evidence, they may decide to settle rather than go to trial.

Trial Procedure

Although the legal system encourages settling disputes at each step of litigation, many cases still go to trial. Trials are costly but often provide the best means to determine truth and provide justice. A trial gives a judge or jury the opportunity to observe witnesses, hear subjective arguments, and evaluate those factors (in addition to written or other tangible evidence) in reaching a decision. See the exhibit "Trial Procedure."

A jury is a group of people who hear and consider the evidence in a case and decide what facts are true. In a jury trial, the jury decides all questions of fact, and the judge decides all questions of law. If the parties choose not to have a jury, the judge makes all decisions about both facts and law. For example, a question of law in an insurance coverage case is whether the insurance policy covers the loss. A question of fact in the same case might be whether the insured actually bought the policy.

Parties to a lawsuit (usually their lawyers) select jurors from a pool. Each party can exclude potential jurors by using challenges. A challenge for cause can be used to exclude any number of jurors for apparent bias. Each party also has a specified number of peremptory challenges to eliminate jurors for no stated cause.

The trial begins with opening statements. In trials with a jury, opening statements occur after the jury has been selected and sworn in. First, the plaintiff's lawyer summarizes the facts of the case and explains why the plaintiff should

Discovery

A pretrial exchange of all relevant information between the plaintiff and defendant.

Deposition

A pretrial discovery tool involving oral examination of a witness to produce a written verbatim record.

Interrogatories

Specific written questions or requests raised by one party to a lawsuit that the opposing party must answer in writing.

Subpoena

A legal order to a witness to appear at a certain place and time to testify or to produce documents.

Trial Procedure

Action	Acting Party	Purpose/Result
Jury selection (if parties choose to have a jury)	Both parties	• Parties' lawyers select jury members.
Swearing-in of jury	Judge	• Jury members take oath.
Opening statements	Plaintiff, followed by defendant	• Presents summary of what the party expects to prove.
Direct examination	Plaintiff	• Questions witnesses to establish allegations.
Cross-examination	Defendant	• Questions witnesses to challenge testimony or to bring out evidence favorable to defendant.
Direct examination	Defendant	• Questions witnesses to establish defense.
Cross-examination	Plaintiff	• Questions witness to challenge testimony or bring out evidence favorable to plaintiff.
Closing arguments	Plaintiff, then defendant	• Summarizes evidence.
Instructions to jury	Judge	• Instructs the jury about applicable law.
Deliberation and delivery of verdict (if no jury, judge delivers verdict)	Jury	• Confers to reach a verdict and delivers it to court.
Alternatively, judge can end trial at any point by declaring one of the following:	Judge	
• Directed verdict		• Tells the jury what verdict to reach.
• Mistrial		• Ends trial because of error or event that would make it impossible for the jury to reach a fair verdict, or because the jury cannot reach a verdict.
• Nonsuit		• Ends trial because the plaintiff has failed to present a sufficient case or has not complied with a court order.

[DA04608]

prevail. The defendant's lawyer follows with an opening statement summarizing the defendant's position.

Next, the lawyers present the evidence, starting with the plaintiff's case. The plaintiff's attorney calls and examines witnesses to present the facts to establish the case against the defendant. Questioning of witnesses is called **direct examination**. The defendant's attorney can then conduct **cross-examination** of each of these witnesses. When the plaintiff finishes presenting evidence, the defendant follows the same procedure to establish the facts of the defense.

The attorneys follow the rules of evidence in presenting their evidence and in challenging the evidence and testimony presented by the opposing party. Lawyers must be alert during trials to recognize when evidence might violate evidentiary rules and to object immediately. Rules of evidence require that evidence be relevant, material, and competent. Trial courts exclude evidence that does not meet these conditions, meaning that it cannot be considered either by the judge or the jury when reaching a decision in the case.

Evidence must have **relevance** to the case. For example, evidence of the dollar limits of a defendant's liability insurance, or even the existence of such an insurance policy, is irrelevant to determining whether a defendant was negligent in an auto accident case. Insurance coverage is not relevant as to whether an accident occurred, whether the defendant was at fault, or whether the plaintiff suffered damages.

Evidence also must be material, a concept closely related to relevance. A fact can be relevant but might have no **materiality** in a case, rendering it immaterial. For example, evidence that the car in an automobile accident was a recent model is immaterial unless that model had a defect that might have caused the accident.

Evidence must have **competence**. Many objections related to competence are based on the **hearsay rule**. Such evidence is presented by witnesses who repeat the statement but who have no personal knowledge of whether the statement is true. Hearsay can be either a spoken statement or a written document containing the statement. For example, Wilma testifies about actuarial figures in a book that someone else prepared and about which Wilma has no personal knowledge. John testifies about a conversation he overheard. Both witnesses' testimony is inadmissible hearsay unless it falls under an exception set out in the rules of evidence. A lawyer who perceives hearsay testimony during a trial must object and provide a sound reason for that objection for the court to rule that the evidence is not admissible.

Opinion evidence, in general, can also be challenged on the basis of competence. An expert in a particular area can give opinion testimony within that area of expertise. For example, an expert in insurance might testify about underwriting practices or policy coverage. First, however, the expert's credibility as an expert witness must be established in court. This process usually involves detailed questioning about the witness's background and qualifications.

After both sides have presented their evidence, they make closing arguments to the jury to summarize their evidence. The judge instructs the jury about the law applicable to the case, and the jury retires, or confers, to reach its final

---

Direct examination

Questioning one's own witness during a legal proceeding.

Cross-examination

Questioning an opposing party during a legal proceeding to bring out information favorable to the questioner's own position or to challenge the witness's testimony.

Relevance

A quality of evidence that suggests the evidence is more or less likely to be true.

Materiality

A quality of evidence that tends to establish a particular element of the claim that has legal significance.

Competence

A quality of evidence that suggests the source is reliable and the evidence is adequate to justify admission in court.

Hearsay rule

The rule of evidence that prevents the admission of out-of-court statements not made under oath by a person who is unavailable to testify.

General verdict

A kind of verdict that entails a complete finding and a single conclusion by a jury on all issues presented.

Special verdict

A kind of verdict reached by a jury that makes findings of fact by answering specific questions posed by the judge. The judge then applies the law to the facts as the jury has found them.

Res judicata

A doctrine that bars parties to a lawsuit on which final judgment has been rendered from bringing a second lawsuit on the same claim or on related transactions.

decision, or verdict. Jurisdictions may allow either a **general verdict**, a **special verdict**, or both. The judge can decide to take the case from the jury using any one of these actions:

- Issuing a directed verdict telling the jury how to decide the case
- Declaring a mistrial because of an egregious error, an extraordinary event, or the jury's inability to reach a decision
- Declaring a nonsuit if the plaintiff has failed to present a sufficient case or has not complied with a court order

All lower-court decisions can be appealed to higher courts. However, parties cannot relitigate claims in the lower courts based on transactions or on issues already decided by a lower court. Two doctrines evolved in the common law to prevent parties from relitigation:

- The doctrine of **res judicata** (sometimes called claim preclusion) prevents parties from raising, in a subsequent lawsuit, issues or facts that could have been, but were not, included in the first lawsuit. For example, if judgment was against Marie in her lawsuit against Danford Plumbing for negligence that caused damage to her kitchen, she cannot bring another lawsuit against Danford for the same act of negligence that caused damage to her living room at the same time the kitchen was damaged. Nor can she sue Danford Plumbing for intentional destruction of property, having failed on the negligence claim.
- Collateral estoppel (sometimes called issue preclusion) bars parties from relitigating an issue on which a court has already ruled, even if the second lawsuit differs significantly from the first. For example, if a court has ruled that Marco's insurance policy did not cover fire damage to his outbuilding, Marco cannot sue the insurer for loss from a later fire in the same building under the same policy.

Appeals

An appeal is a request to a higher court for a review of a case. The appellant is the losing party in a court case who appeals the case to a higher court. The nonappealing party, usually the winner of the original lawsuit, is the appellee. Appeals must be filed to the appropriate court within a prescribed period. Appeals courts do not conduct new trials but decide whether law has been applied appropriately to a case in the lower court.

To decide whether the trial court's decision was correct, the appeals court relies on a transcript of the lower-court proceedings and on briefs and arguments made by the lawyers for both parties. A brief is a lawyer's written statement submitted on appeal to establish legal and factual arguments and provide supportive authoritative sources, such as statutes and case precedents. Briefs are mandatory in appeals, and courts prescribe their format and content. Many appellate courts base their decisions on the briefs in most cases; they hear oral arguments only in a few cases.

Any objection by either party before, during, or after a trial that is overruled by the court is a potential ground, or basis, for appeal. An appellate court can affirm the trial court outcome, reverse it, or send the case back (remand it) to the trial court for a new trial. For example, if an appellate court finds that the trial court improperly admitted evidence prejudicial, or harmful, to the appellant's case, the court can send the case back to the lower court for a new trial. However, an appellate court might determine that evidence, although improperly admitted at trial, did not prejudice the appellant.

A new trial is not necessarily a victory for the appellant because it can reach the same result as the first trial. The time involved in the appeal process also can jeopardize the appellant's case by making testimony stale or unavailable. Losing parties in lawsuits often decide not to appeal after they weigh the probability of an ultimate victory against the high costs of appeal.

ALTERNATIVE DISPUTE RESOLUTION

As the number of lawsuits filed in the U.S. continues to increase, congested court dockets (calendars), long delays, and additional costs result. While the judicial system handles thousands of disputes, most controversies are resolved by compromise or settlement agreements.

Out-of-court settlements offer the advantages of economy, greater speed of resolution, less hostility between the parties, and some degree of privacy. **Alternative dispute resolution (ADR)** procedures, including arbitration, mediation, and negotiation, are methods that help settle disputes without litigation.

Alternative dispute resolution (ADR)

Procedures to help settle disputes without litigation, including arbitration, mediation, and negotiation.

Arbitration

One ADR method, arbitration, involves taking a dispute to an impartial third party (an arbiter or arbitration panel) for a decision the parties agree will be final and binding. Arbitration has become a major means of dealing with disputes in contracts, labor-management relations, and insurance. Some states' laws and court rules mandate court-administered arbitration for some types of cases.

Arbitration is frequently used for settling insurance disputes. Many insurance policies specifically provide for arbitration. For example, uninsured motorist coverage in automobile policies may include a provision requiring arbitration of policy disputes. Insurers use special arbitration agreements to allocate costs of settlements when coinsurers are involved and to resolve disputes resulting from overlapping coverages. Use of arbitration has also increased under no-fault automobile statutes, under which people involved in automobile accidents seek benefits payments from their own insurers.

Most states have enacted laws that cover all aspects of arbitration procedures. Both the Uniform Arbitration Act, drafted by the National Conference of

Commissioners of Uniform State Laws, and the Federal Arbitration Act, passed in 1925, provide specific remedies if one of the parties refuses to arbitrate or denies the existence of an arbitration agreement.

The American Arbitration Association, which provides arbitration services, designs arbitration systems, and provides training about ADR, has developed the following procedure for selecting an arbitrator: Each party receives a list of proposed arbitrators and has ten days to select several preferred arbitrators from the list. The association then appoints an arbitrator acceptable to both parties. Alternatively, each party can appoint an arbitrator, and those arbitrators, in turn, can appoint a third arbitrator.

Most states allow parties to call witnesses in arbitration proceedings, but strict adherence to rules of evidence and procedure is not required. An arbitrator's award or judgment is filed with the appropriate court and is as valid and enforceable as any court judgment. Parties have limited grounds for appealing an arbitrator's award and must do so within a legally prescribed period.

Mediation

Mediation

An alternative dispute resolution (ADR) method by which disputing parties use a neutral outside party to examine the issues and develop a mutually agreeable settlement.

Another ADR procedure is **mediation**. The mediator is a neutral third party who acts as a catalyst to help parties analyze their dispute, consider possible solutions, and devise a compromise formula. Mediation is nonbinding. Judges often try to mediate during settlement conferences in court cases, but formal mediation involves submitting a dispute to an outside mediator. Mediators are often experienced trial lawyers or retired judges.

Negotiation

Using the ADR procedure of negotiation, parties to a dispute discuss all issues and determine a mutually satisfactory resolution. Negotiation is often the most direct route to dispute resolution. Because negotiations can end at any time, they do not limit opportunities to pursue other dispute resolution methods.

Private mini-trials and court-sponsored mock summary jury trials can lead to negotiation of major disputes. In a mini-trial, lawyers or others familiar with the dispute present evidence and arguments to a panel that may include business executives or other professionals. A neutral party, such as a retired judge or another expert, can act as mediator or issue an advisory opinion after the presentation of evidence and arguments. Because the mini-trial presents the issues to both parties in a dispute, it can encourage negotiation and settlement. Summary jury trials are brief mock trials before juries. The parties can accept the jury's advisory verdict, or the verdict can provide the basis for further negotiations toward settlement.

ADMINISTRATIVE AGENCY PROCEDURES

Administrative law is pervasive in the activities of people and organizations. The legislative output of administrative agencies far exceeds that of legislatures, and the number of administrative decisions far exceeds the thousands of court decisions.

The legal procedures of administrative agencies entail these matters:

- Agencies' rulemaking function
- Agencies' adjudication function
- Agencies' investigative powers
- Judicial review

Role of Administrative Agencies

Legislators at the federal and state levels delegate responsibilities to administrative agencies in much the same way that a supervisor delegates responsibilities to an employee. Legislators do not have the time to pass all the rules and regulations necessary to implement legislation; to develop expertise in every area regulated; or to settle disputes arising from legislation, rules, and regulations. For example, a state legislature that passes a law prohibiting excessive insurance rates delegates the power to administer and enforce the law to its state department of insurance (DOI), which has the insurance expertise to set standards for and examine insurance rates.

Courts generally have upheld legislative delegation to administrative agencies. Although legislators cannot delegate their ultimate power and responsibility, they can delegate the duty to fill in the details of legislation by allowing agencies to make rules and regulations and to resolve disputes. "Enabling legislation" creates an administrative agency and states its purpose.

Administrative agencies have two primary functions: rulemaking and adjudication. Rulemaking is the process by which agencies promulgate rules to implement legislative policies. Adjudication is the process by which agencies decide cases and settle disputes.

To illustrate DOI rulemaking and adjudication, after a state legislature passes a law prohibiting excessive insurance rates, the DOI makes rules about insurance rate review and creates guidelines to determine whether rates are excessive. The insurance commissioner, a private citizen, or a group of citizens might contest an insurance rate as excessive. The DOI then holds a hearing to adjudicate the rate in question. This adjudication affects only the insurer involved and the insureds who would pay the new rate.

Agencies' Rulemaking Function

Agencies promulgate three types of rules:

Legislative rule

A type of substantive administrative agency rule that comes from a statutory delegation of authority and that has the same force as a law enacted by Congress or a legislature.

Interpretative rule

A type of administrative agency rule that interprets statutes, providing guidance for agency staff or regulated parties, but that lacks the force and effect of law and therefore is not binding on individuals.

Procedural rule

A type of administrative agency rule that prescribes procedures for agency operations, legislative rulemaking, and adjudication proceedings.

- **Legislative rules** (substantive rules) come from a statutory delegation of authority and have the same force as a law enacted by Congress or a legislature. The development and passage of legislative rules require adherence to rulemaking procedures.

- **Interpretative rules** interpret statutes, providing guidance for agency staff or regulated parties. However, these rules lack the force and effect of law, and, therefore, are not binding on individuals.

- **Procedural rules**, primarily internal, prescribe procedures for agency operations, for legislative rulemaking, and for adjudication proceedings.

The Administrative Procedure Act (APA) prescribes the procedure for administrative agency rulemaking at the federal level. Most states follow the rulemaking procedures of the Model State Administrative Procedure Act (MSAPA), which requires agencies to adhere to three basic steps:

1. Publish a notice of intent to adopt a regulation
2. Provide opportunity for public comment
3. Publish the final regulation

Federal agencies publish notices of proposed regulations in the weekly *Federal Register*. States usually have similar publications for state agency notices. Notice in one of these official publications usually suffices as official notice to all interested parties that the agency is considering an action that will affect them. For example, a state DOI notice of its plan to adopt a regulation about an aspect of the insurance business, published in the state's official publication for agency notices, is legally sufficient notice to insurers and consumers.

Typically, the published notice of a proposed regulation invites comments by a certain date, usually within a month. Public hearings are required for some, but not all, proposed regulations. The MSAPA requires a public hearing if either a governmental agency or twenty-five interested individuals request it. If no hearing is required, interested organizations and individuals can submit written comments on a proposed regulation.

Interested individuals and representatives of organizations can speak at public hearings; comments can also be submitted in writing. A presiding hearing examiner usually has discretion about who testifies. If large groups of people attend, the examiner can require that only their chosen representatives testify.

If the proposed regulation is controversial, the examiner can require advance registration of those who will testify. After the agency has reviewed all comments about the proposed rule, it can take one of these actions:

- Adopt the originally proposed rule
- Make minimal or extensive changes
- Nullify the proposed rule

If the agency decides to adopt the rule, it must publish the final version. A rule usually becomes effective thirty days after publication, giving affected parties time to conform to the new rule or to challenge its legality. Agencies can publish emergency rules with immediate effective dates when necessary for the public health and welfare.

Agencies' Adjudicatory Function

In addition to rulemaking, agencies have an adjudicatory function. Adjudicatory proceedings are similar to court cases. They affect the rights of an individual or a limited number of people. As in court, people in an agency adjudicatory process have a constitutional right to due process of law. The specific requirements for due process can vary by the nature of the proceeding.

The Due Process Clause of the U.S. Constitution grants parties whose rights are affected by an agency decision the right to be heard. Not every case requires a hearing. However, the agency must provide reasonable notice of the opportunity for a fair hearing. If the party does not waive the right to a hearing, the agency must hold a fair hearing and must render a decision supported by the evidence. Denying due process can be grounds for reversing a decision if the party was harmed by denial.

Appropriate notice is essential to due process, and improper notice can result in nullification of an entire proceeding. Appropriate notice has several factors:

• Statement of the hearing time, place, and nature

• Statement of the hearing's legal authority and jurisdiction

• Reference to the particular statute or rule involved

• A short, clear statement of the matters at issue

The test of appropriate notice is whether it informs the interested party fairly and sufficiently about the case so that the party can respond adequately at the hearing.

Many disputes, such as pension or Social Security claims, do not warrant full hearings and are too numerous to make formal proceedings practical. However, any party faced with deprivation of an alleged property or liberty right can demand a hearing before action is taken. Such hearings are often informal. Agencies can use informal hearings when time, the nature of the proceedings, and the public interest permit. Adjudication, complete with a full hearing, is necessary only if the law specifically requires it or if either party demands one. A hearing examiner or an administrative law judge (ALJ), who is usually both an agency employee and a lawyer, presides.

Generally, any person compelled to appear before an agency and every party to a dispute have the right to counsel. Counsel need not be a lawyer but can be a qualified representative, that is, any trusted person. The government is not required to provide counsel to a party for an administrative hearing.

As in court proceedings, expert witnesses can testify in agency cases. Generally, the rules governing witnesses in court proceedings apply in agency hearings, but agency rules are not as strict. Agency cases do not have juries; the hearing examiner decides factual and legal matters. Generally, evidence in an agency hearing must be relevant, but the rules of evidence are much more relaxed than in a court trial.

Counsel in an adjudicatory hearing can make arguments relating to both fact and law. Most arguments are relatively short and often written instead of oral. Parties have no inherent right or duty to present formal written briefs arguing the law. The hearing examiner or ALJ considers the parties' arguments and makes findings of fact and law. Such decisions may accept, reject, or modify the parties' arguments.

To illustrate an adjudication, a hearing examiner's findings in a case challenging an insurer's rates might be one of these:

- The insurer kept statistics properly.
- The insurer interpreted those statistics properly.
- The statistics indicated the insurer had a loss ratio of 35 percent.
- Insurers can make a profit with a loss ratio of 50 percent.

From these facts, the hearing officer could conclude that the 35 percent loss ratio was too low and that the proper loss ratio should be 50 percent. The hearing officer's decision, based on a statute prohibiting excessive rates, could be to require the insurer to lower rates by a stated percentage to produce a 50 percent loss ratio.

Agencies can impose fines or grant, revoke, or suspend licenses. Enabling legislation for an agency usually defines appeal rights and whether they involve a court or the agency. Most agencies have at least one, and sometimes three or four, tiers of appeal. Once a case has gone through all levels of the agency adjudication and appeals process, the party has exhausted all administrative remedies and can seek judicial review in a court of law.

Administrative agencies can give advisory opinions, unlike courts, which, with very limited exceptions, do not indicate in advance how they would decide a case based on a given set of facts. Although agency advisory opinions are not binding either on the agency or on any parties, the recipient of an advisory opinion can usually rely on it.

Agencies' Investigative Powers

Many federal and state laws contain provisions authorizing agency investigations, which typically relate to rulemaking, ratemaking, adjudicating, licensing, prosecuting, establishing general policy, or recommending legislation.

Agencies may need information and evidence for administrative proceedings and may use subpoenas to gather such information. A subpoena is a legal order to a witness to appear at a certain place and time to testify or to produce documents. Those who disobey subpoenas are subject to penalties.

Agencies receive the power to use subpoenas from legislation. Not all agencies are given the power. If authorized by law, an agency can issue a subpoena on its own behalf or at a party's request. For example, a policyholder alleging an insurer's discriminatory practice can request the DOI to subpoena the insurer's records for a hearing that resolves the dispute.

A party to a dispute has the right not only to testify personally, but also to obtain relevant testimony and records from others. If the other parties refuse to cooperate, then due process requires compelling them to cooperate by subpoena. A subpoena to compel a witness to testify is a subpoena *ad testificandum* (command to testify), usually termed, simply, a subpoena. A subpoena to compel production of documents or records is a subpoena *duces tecum* (literally, a command to "bring things with you").

Violations of constitutional rights can defeat an investigation. The U.S. Constitution places the following limitations on agency investigations:

- Fourth Amendment protection against unreasonable searches and seizures
- Fifth Amendment protection against self-incrimination

In administrative law, the Fourth Amendment prohibition against unreasonable searches and seizures applies primarily to inspecting records. Records demanded must be relevant to the investigation. However, the connection between the requested records and the subject of the investigation can be slight; courts usually find such records relevant and require their production.

For example, a government agency may ask an insurer for all automobile insurance accident records for the past twenty years, even though these records might be voluminous and might require many hours to produce, as long as the agency demonstrates a need for the records. Some courts have held that, when record retrieval and production are very expensive, the burden is on the agency to establish the records' relevance. Sometimes a regulatory agency has no specific purpose but is "fishing" through the records for a possible legal violation.

The Fifth Amendment states that no person "shall be compelled in any criminal case to be a witness against himself." Court decisions have broadened the term "criminal case" to mean almost any type of investigation or proceeding from which legal sanctions might arise. The term "witness" includes not only oral testimony but also the production of records and documents.

A legislative body can require firms to keep certain records and can delegate the power to enforce this requirement to an agency. Inspection power is not limited to records required by law but extends to other relevant records. Agencies do not have a general unlimited right to investigate beyond what is necessary, and any agency request must be reasonably relevant to the investigation.

The Privacy Act and Freedom of Information Act protect the public from agency misuse of the vast amounts of information they collect, including insurance information. The Privacy Act prohibits the government and its agencies from releasing any information that would violate individual privacy. The Freedom of Information Act guarantees public access to some government and agency records and documents to prevent abuse of information collection.

Judicial Review

Generally, federal courts review actions of federal agencies, and state courts review actions of state agencies. As the actions of agencies increasingly affect personal interests, the courts seek to protect those interests more vigorously by insisting on strict judicial scrutiny of agency action. Judicial review is available as long it is not precluded by statute or as long as the action reviewed is not left by statute solely to administrative agency discretion. Judicial review is not limited to agency adjudications but also can apply to agency rulemaking.

Standing to sue

A party's right to sue, as one who has suffered or will suffer a legal wrong or an adverse effect from an action.

To take an administrative action to a court for judicial review, a plaintiff must have **standing to sue**. A party who seeks judicial review of a rulemaking procedure must show that the rule or its application would impair or interfere with that party's legal rights or privileges. If an adjudicatory hearing is involved, the party usually must be "aggrieved," that is, the order has substantially affected his or her personal rights.

Judicial review of a case can occur only after two requirements have been met:

Final order

An administrative agency's final conclusion or disposition of any material private right of a party, terminating an agency proceeding.

- The agency has issued a final order in the case. This **final order** is the basis of the appeal.
- The doctrine called **exhaustion of administrative remedies** has been satisfied: a party can appeal to the courts only after having taken the case through all possible administrative procedures and appeals. A court will make exceptions to this doctrine only when the available administrative remedy is inadequate or when it would be futile to require the party to exhaust administrative remedies.

Exhaustion of administrative remedies

The completion of all possible administrative procedures and appeals in a case; required before a party can appeal an agency action to a court.

A court can set aside agency action on these grounds:

- The action was arbitrary and capricious, an abuse of discretion, or otherwise unlawful.
- The action was unconstitutional.
- The action violated statutory authority.
- The action violated agency procedural rules or was the result of illegal procedures.
- The action is unsupportable by substantial evidence in the record.

A court can review the law and substitute its own interpretation for the agency's interpretation, just as appellate courts review lower court decisions. Courts review facts only to determine whether substantial evidence supports an agency's action. Courts do not set aside agency actions unless they are clearly erroneous.

On appeal, parties often allege that an administrative agency's action was arbitrary and capricious or an abuse of discretion. An action is arbitrary and capricious if it is so clearly erroneous that it has no rational basis or if it is willful and unreasonable. Generally, courts give great deference to agency conclusions on questions of fact because of the agencies' assumed special knowledge and expertise. If a reviewing court determines that it needs more facts to make a judgment, it can send a case back (remand it) to the agency for another hearing.

SUMMARY

The U.S. legal system had its origins in the English common-law system. The foundation of the common-law system is the doctrine of stare decisis, the application of precedents to current court cases. The common-law system differs from the European civil-law system, founded exclusively on codified laws rather than case law.

U.S. law can be classified several ways, including:

- As either criminal or civil law
- In subject matter classifications
- As either substantive and procedural law

Sources of U.S. law include these:

- Constitutions
- Legislative bodies
- Courts
- Executive branches
- Administrative agencies

Court legal procedures fall into different phases, including pretrial, trial, and appellate procedures. Substantial pretrial preparation provides parties with information about allegations and evidence and gives them an opportunity to settle. If a case goes to trial, the evidence presented must be relevant, material, and competent. After a verdict has been reached, the appellant may appeal to a higher court for a review of the case, although the losing party must decide whether the potential for a favorable appellate decision outweighs the high cost of an appeal.

Alternative dispute resolution (ADR) methods, such as arbitration, mediation, and negotiation, are ways to resolve disputes more efficiently than through the overloaded court system.

Administrative agencies have investigatory powers but are also subject to Constitutional limitations. Administrative agencies promulgate legislative, interpretative, and procedural rules. Agency adjudicatory procedure is similar to court procedures, requiring notice, hearing, and adjudication. Judicial review of agency decisions involves issues of standing to sue and exhaustion of administrative remedies, as well as standards of review, such as determining the existence of agency abuse of discretion.

ASSIGNMENT NOTES

1. *Brown v. Board of Education*, 347 U.S. 483 (1954).
2. *Miranda v. Arizona*, 384 U.S. 436 (1966).
3. *Paul v. Virginia*, 8 Wall. 168 (1869).
4. *South-Eastern Underwriters Association, et al.* 322 U.S. 533 (1944).

2

Contract Law

Educational Objectives

After learning the content of this assignment, you should be able to:

▷ Contrast the following types of contracts:

- Bilateral and unilateral

- Executed and executory

- Express and implied

- Void and voidable

▷ Describe the requirements of a valid offer.

▷ Describe the requirements of a valid acceptance.

▷ Describe the circumstances in which each of the following has the capacity to contract:

- Minor

- Insane person

- Intoxicated person

- Artificial entity

▷ Describe consideration for a contract in terms of the following:

- Types of consideration

- Situations in which a contract is enforceable despite a lack of consideration

▷ Given a contract, determine whether it has a legal purpose.

▷ Explain how each of the following may render a contract unenforceable:

- Fraud

- Mistake

- Duress

Outline

Types of Contracts

Requirements of an Offer

Requirements of a Valid Acceptance

Capacity to Contract

Consideration

Legal Purpose of a Contract

Enforceability of a Contract

Contract Interpretation

Third-Party Contractual Rights

Termination of a Contract

Breach of Contract

Contracts Case Study

Summary

2

- Undue influence
- Innocent misrepresentation
- Statute of frauds
- Parol evidence rule

▷ Paraphrase the rules on contract construction that courts commonly use to interpret contracts.

▷ Describe the circumstances in which a third party would have enforceable rights under a contract.

▷ Describe the various ways in which the contractual obligations of the parties to a contract can be terminated.

▷ Describe breach of contract in terms of the following:

- Types of breach
- Remedies for breach

▷ Given a case, determine whether a described contract would be legally enforceable.

Contract Law

2

TYPES OF CONTRACTS

A contract is a legally enforceable agreement. People enter into agreements for many purposes, but not all agreements are legally enforceable contracts.

A **contract** must have four elements to be legally enforceable: agreement, capacity to contract, consideration, and legal purpose. Each party to a contract may be both a **promisor** and a **promisee**.

When two or more parties enter into a contract, they are said to be in **privity of contract**. Ordinarily, a party cannot sue for breach of contract without being in privity of contract with the other party. However, contracts frequently involve third parties' interests. A **third-party beneficiary** of a contract has a legal right to enforce the contract in the case of a **breach of contract** by either of the contracting parties.

A contract may be bilateral or unilateral, executed or executory, express or implied, void or voidable.

Bilateral and Unilateral Contracts

A contract is either a **bilateral contract** or a **unilateral contract**. Most contracts are bilateral. For example, Jay's promise to pay Tony $500 in exchange for Tony's promise to paint Jay's garage creates a bilateral contract in which each party becomes both a promisor and a promisee. If a default occurs, either party may enforce the other's promise in a legal action.

In a unilateral contract, if Jay promises to pay $500 if Tony paints the garage, a binding contract requiring Jay to pay Tony arises only when Tony has painted the garage. The performance of an act, painting, is required in exchange for the promise, payment. Tony does not breach a contract by failing to paint the garage.

Executed and Executory Contracts

A contract is either an **executed contract** or an **executory contract**. When a contract is executed, nothing else is required of either party. For example, one party has bought and paid for clothes that another party has delivered.

A fire insurance policy is an example of an executory contract. The insurer's promise to perform is an executory promise conditional on the occurrence of a fire. As long as no fire occurs, the contract remains executory.

Contract
A legally enforceable agreement between two or more parties in which each party makes some promise to the other.

Promisee
The party to a contract to whom a promise is made.

Promisor
The party to a contract making a promise.

Privity of contract
The relationship that exists between the parties to a contract.

Third-party beneficiary
A person who is not a party to a contract but who benefits from it and has a legal right to enforce the contract if it is breached by either of the contracting parties.

Breach of contract
The failure, without legal excuse, to fulfill a contractual promise.

Unilateral contract
A contract in which only one party makes a promise or undertakes the requested performance.

Bilateral contract
A contract in which each party promises a performance.

Express and Implied Contracts

Executed contract

A contract that has been completely performed by both parties.

Executory contract

A contract that has not been completely performed by one or both of the parties.

Implied contract

A contract whose terms and intentions are indicated by the actions of the parties to the contract and the surrounding circumstances.

Express contract

A contract whose terms and intentions are explicitly stated.

Implied-in-fact contract

A contract that is not express but that the parties presumably intended, either by tacit understanding or by the assumption that it existed.

Implied-in-law contract

An obligation that is not an actual contract but that is imposed by law because of the parties' conduct or some special relationship between them or because one of them would otherwise be unjustly enriched.

Voidable contract

A contract that one of the parties can reject (avoid) based on some circumstance surrounding its execution.

Contracts are either **express contracts** or **implied contracts**. An insurance agent and insurance producer who agree either orally or in writing on an insurance premium rate of $1,000 per year create an express contract.

Implied contracts can be either **implied-in-fact contracts** or **implied-in-law contracts**. If Bill, who has a credit account at the local hardware store, picks up an item, shows it to the store owner without comment, and leaves the store with the item, he has made an implied-in-fact contract to pay for the item. Implied-in-fact contracts often arise through, and are subject to, trade customs, prior relations between parties, and community customs known to all parties.

Implied-in-law contracts are not actual contracts and are sometimes called quasi-contracts. These are obligations that do not arise from the parties' apparent intentions but from courts' notions of justice and equity in particular cases.

Voidable Contracts and Void Contracts

Some contracts are **voidable contracts**, and some agreements are called **void contracts** (although they are not valid contracts).

A voidable contract is a valid contract that can continue in force, and the parties can execute it completely unless an innocent or injured party chooses to avoid it. For example, a minor who has entered into a contract can avoid it at any time during minority or within a reasonable time after reaching legal age. However, the minor may also choose to fulfill his or her promise under the contract and can hold the other party to it.

The behavior of one of the contracting parties, such as an act of fraud or illegal deceit, also can make a contract voidable. An example of fraud is a party's intentional misrepresentation of an important fact relating to a contract. Similarly, a party who has entered into a contract as the result of duress, a form of compulsion, can avoid the contract within a reasonable time. However, an injured party can ratify, or affirm, a voidable contract. For example, if fraud or duress has occurred, the innocent party can nevertheless elect to abide by the agreement and can hold the other party to the contract.

Other agreements are automatically void. Even though the term "void contract" is contradictory because the parties never really create a contract in the first place, courts use it to describe agreements that the parties intend to be contracts that never actually become contracts. Void contracts are not legally enforceable or binding. An agreement to commit a crime, for example, is void and unenforceable because it is made for unlawful purposes.

REQUIREMENTS OF AN OFFER

The first element of an enforceable contract is an agreement between the parties. An agreement comprises an offer and an acceptance.

For contract purposes, an **offer** is valid if it includes these requirements:

- Intent to contract
- Definite terms
- Communication to the other party

If an offer with these requirements is accepted, a contract is created.

Intent to Contract

The first essential requirement of an offer is the intent to contract. The **offeror** must intend, or appear to intend, to create a legally enforceable contract if the **offeree** accepts the offer. The offeror's language is the most important factor indicating whether a communication is an offer. Because an offer is a promise, words of promise indicate the offeror's intent to make an offer. Without specific words of promise, the communication is only a general statement of intention or an invitation for an offer.

A key question in each case involving contractual intent is whether, by words or conduct, a party has shown an intent to be immediately bound. The test of whether the intent has been shown is based on how a reasonable person would interpret the intent, not the party's actual intent.

A general statement of intention that conveys no promise is not an offer. If Anne says to Miguel, "I am going to sell my car for $5,000," and Miguel replies, "All right, I'll pay $5,000 for your car," Anne and Miguel have not created a contract. The test is whether, under the circumstances, a reasonable person would conclude that Anne intended to promise to sell the car specifically to Miguel. A reasonable person would not draw that conclusion in this case. Anne's statement only expresses an intention to sell the car in the future and does not make an explicit offer to Miguel.

If Anne says to Miguel, "I will not sell my property for less than $20,000," and Miguel replies, "I accept your offer," no contract results. A reasonable person would not conclude that Anne's statement of a minimum price was a promise to sell at the figure mentioned.

Some communications are intended to induce others to respond with offers. These communications are not in themselves offers because they express no present intent to contract. Most advertisements, catalogs, and sales letters meet this description; they are invitations to negotiate or to make an offer.

However, some advertisements do constitute offers that would be bound by a customer's acceptance. For example, an advertisement that indicates that the first customer to enter the store can buy specific goods at a specific price has

Void contract

An agreement that, despite the parties' intentions, never reaches contract status and is therefore not legally enforceable or binding.

Offer

A promise that requires some action by the intended recipient to make an agreement.

Offeror

The party to a contract who promises to give something in return for a promise or an act by another party.

Offeree

The party to a contract who makes a promise or acts in return for something offered by another party.

spelled out the conditions of acceptance. When the first person who enters the store agrees to buy the goods, a contract arises. In this case, the advertiser has used words of promise and described specific circumstances under which a customer could purchase the goods, giving rise to a contract based on the advertiser's legally enforceable contractual intention.

A party that asks for offers is free to accept them or reject them. In construction, for example, a project owner asking for bids can elect to accept one bid or to reject all of them. Any bidder can withdraw the bid at any time before its acceptance. A party calling for bids can accept any bid, whether or not it is the lowest one (unless the law requires acceptance of the lowest bid).

Examples of statements that are not offers and that would not lead to valid contracts if accepted because they lack intent to contract include these:

- Social invitations
- Predictions
- Offers made in excitement or jest

For example, if a person withdraws a social invitation or cancels a social event, the invitation's recipient has no legal remedy. If a doctor has predicted that a patient will be in the hospital only a few days and the period of hospitalization turns out to be much longer, the doctor's prediction is not an enforceable promise. If a reasonable person would recognize that a statement was made in jest or in the heat of anger, then acceptance of the statement does not create a contract. However, whether a statement is made in excitement or jest is not always easy to recognize, and a contractual obligation can arise in some cases. Courts consider all the circumstances in a case to determine whether a statement could reasonably be considered an offer. See the exhibit "First Element of a Contract: Agreement."

First Element of a Contract: Agreement

1. Offer
   - Intent to contract
   - Definite terms
   - Communication to offeree
2. Acceptance
   - By offeree
   - Unconditional and unequivocal
   - Offeree's communication of acceptance

[DA06327]

Definite Terms

The second requirement of an offer is definite terms. Definite terms make an agreement enforceable and make it possible to determine whether the parties have fulfilled their promises. They can also allow for calculation of damages in the event of a breach of contract.

An offer's terms must be stated with at least a reasonable degree of certainty. Reasonable certainty generally means identifying the contracting parties, the contract's subject matter, the price, and the time of performance. The absence of one or more of these terms, however, does not necessarily invalidate the offer.

To determine reasonable certainty, courts may ask whether the offer's terms are clear enough to provide a basis for a remedy if default occurs. If necessary and possible, the courts supply such missing terms as price or time of performance. For example, if the parties do not designate a time for performance, courts usually find an implication that performance is to occur within a reasonable time, considering the subject matter involved. If the offer is definite enough to determine the parties' intent, then a court will enforce the offer even though it might be necessary to imply some terms. However, inability to identify the parties to, or the subject matter of, an agreement, makes the offer indefinite and therefore impossible to accept.

Contracts to deal with one supplier, called requirement contracts, are usually enforceable even though the need for the goods might never arise. For example, Allen's promise to buy "all steel required" from Anu is definite enough to enforce. Allen promises to buy all steel required from Anu, and Anu promises to sell Allen the steel. In contrast, if Anu promises to sell "all such steel as I want to supply" to Allen, then the agreement is illusory and too indefinite to provide a remedy in court. The indefiniteness stems from the possibility that Anu might not wish to supply any steel.

Communication to Offeree

The third requirement of an offer is communication to the offeree. An offeree cannot accept a proposal before knowing about it. For example, a newspaper advertisement offers "$100 to anyone who will enter the 100-yard dash on July 4 and beat David." Matt, unaware of the advertisement or offer, enters the race and beats David. No contract exists because Matt could not accept an offer of which he had no knowledge.

However, an offer can be valid if the offeree has begun performance before learning of the offer. For example, Jerry, a burglary victim, has offered a reward for information leading to the burglar's conviction. Paul has already investigated the burglary and has determined that Donna was the burglar. After learning about the reward, Paul reports Donna to the authorities. If Donna is convicted, Paul can collect the reward from Jerry even though part of his effort occurred before he learned of Jerry's offer. The crucial fact is that Paul knew of the offer when he reported Donna as the burglar, that is, when he completed performance.

Duration and Termination

Duration and termination are key to determining whether an offer is binding. Factors considered include the following:

- Lapse of time
- Operation of law
- Offeree's rejection
- Counteroffers
- Offeror's revocation

Lapse of Time

Offers do not remain open indefinitely. An offer ceases to be binding when the time the offer specifies expires or, absent a specific time, when a reasonable amount of time passes. What is reasonable depends on considerations such as the contract's subject matter and the general commercial setting. For example, in an offer to sell perishable goods, the time the goods stay fresh is a key factor.

Once an offer is terminated, any attempted acceptance becomes a counteroffer, which the original offeror can either accept or reject.

Operation of Law

Any one of several events occurring before acceptance can terminate an outstanding offer by operation of law. "Operation of law" means that rules of law apply automatically to a situation without any act by the parties. For example, an offer is terminated if performing a contract becomes illegal after the offer is made. If a law is passed that makes it unlawful to sell certain goods, then a preexisting offer to sell those goods would be automatically terminated by the enactment of the law. Similarly, if the subject matter of an offer is destroyed before acceptance, the offer terminates at the time of destruction, even if the offeree does not know about the destruction.

Also, if an offeror or offeree dies or is formally declared insane before an offer is accepted, the law automatically terminates the offer. For example, Andre writes to Angela to offer to sell her his home. Andre dies before the letter reaches Angela. Andre's offer automatically terminates on his death.

Once a contract arises, death or insanity will not terminate it unless it involves the deceased or insane party's personal or professional service. A contract not involving personal or professional services is enforceable against the deceased party's estate.

Offeree's Rejection

The offeree's rejection of the offer terminates it. A rejection occurs when the offeree notifies the offeror of an intention not to accept. An offeree may reject an offer either by expressly refusing to accept it or by making a new offer to the offeror, called a counteroffer.

Like the offer, the offeree's rejection is not effective until communicated to the offeror. Once the rejection is communicated, the offeree cannot attempt to accept the offer. Any such attempt is considered a new offer.

Counteroffers

A **counteroffer** is not the same as a request for more information, and a request for information is not a rejection of the offer. For example, if Gene offers to sell Patrick a television set for $200 and Patrick says, "I'll give you $150 for it," Patrick's reply is a counteroffer. It automatically rejects Gene's original offer, and Patrick cannot later accept the original $200 offer. If Patrick had replied to Gene's offer by inquiring, "Will you accept $150?", his question is not a counteroffer or a rejection; it is an inquiry. If Gene had responded to the inquiry that $150 was unsatisfactory, Patrick could still accept the $200 offer.

Counteroffers do not terminate an offer that includes a statement that the offer will remain open beyond any counteroffers. Similarly, an offer remains open if the offeree makes it clear that the counteroffer does not reject the original offer.

Counteroffer

A proposal an offeree makes to an offeror that varies in some material way from the original offer, resulting in rejection of the original offer and constituting a new offer.

Offeror's Revocation

Generally, an offeror can revoke, or withdraw, an offer any time before acceptance. As in the case of the offer itself, the revocation is effective only when communicated, in this case to the offeree, and only when the offeree actually receives it. Similarly, if the offeror mails a revocation but the offeree accepts the offer by telephone before receiving the mailed revocation, a contract exists.

Offerors must revoke offers to the general public through the same means of communication they used in making the original offers. For example, one who has offered a reward in an advertisement can revoke it only through another advertisement. The revocation, once advertised, is effective even if someone who has not seen the revocation tries to accept the original offer.

The offeror's statement that the offer is irrevocable for a specific period is not usually sufficient to remove the right of revocation; generally, the offeror can revoke the offer anyway.

If, in a unilateral contract offer, the offeree has partially performed the acts requested by the offer, most courts hold that the offer is irrevocable. For example, Marie promises to pay John $2,000 if John excavates Marie's property.

John has completed one-third of the excavation when Marie attempts to revoke the offer. The revocation is ineffective. Most courts require a substantial performance, more than just preparation to make a revocation ineffective. Once a substantial start occurs, the offeree has reasonable time to perform the entire acceptance. Whether substantial performance has begun is a question of fact, not law, in a trial.

REQUIREMENTS OF A VALID ACCEPTANCE

A contract is a legally binding agreement. To be able to determine whether a contract in fact exists, it is necessary to determine whether one party's offer has been accepted in the required manner by the other party.

The first element of an enforceable contract is an agreement between the parties. The parties must mutually agree to the same terms. Establishing this agreement involves two steps:

1.   The presentation of an offer by the offeror
2.   An acceptance of that offer by the offeree

Acceptance

The assent to an offer that occurs when the party to whom an offer has been made either agrees to the proposal or does what has been proposed.

Understanding what constitutes a valid **acceptance** helps differentiate legally binding contracts from simple agreements.

To create an enforceable agreement, an acceptance must meet three requirements:

* The acceptance must be made by the offeree.
* The acceptance must be unconditional and unequivocal.
* The offeree must communicate the acceptance to the offeror by appropriate word or act.

Acceptance by Offeree

Only the offeree can accept an offer. The offeror has the right to choose with whom to contract. For example, if Dan dies after receiving an offer from Alan, the executor of Dan's estate cannot accept the offer. The offer's language and circumstances determine the identity of the offeree. For example, Janet promises to sell and deliver books to Lisa if Lisa's father promises to pay $100 for the books. Lisa's father is the offeree; therefore, only he can accept the offer by making the return promise.

An offer can be made to one person, to a group or class of people, or to the public. When made to a particular group, any member of the group can accept it. If an offer is made to the public, as in the case of a reward advertisement, anyone can accept it. Once someone accepts the offer, no one else can accept it.

An acceptance expresses the offeree's consent to the offer's terms. Use of the word "accept" is not necessary to bind the offeree; any language showing that the offeree agrees to the proposal suffices as long as it meets all three requirements for a binding acceptance. See the exhibit "First Element of a Contract: Agreement."

First Element of a Contract: Agreement

1. Offer
   - Intent to contract
   - Definite terms
   - Communication to offeree
2. Acceptance
   - By offeree
   - Unconditional and unequivocal
   - Offeree's communication of acceptance

[DA06327]

Unconditional and Unequivocal Acceptance

Acceptance must be unconditional and unequivocal. If the acceptance deviates from the offer's terms, it becomes a counteroffer. An offeree must comply strictly with provisions in an offer regarding time, place, or manner of acceptance.

Acceptances sometimes contain wording that appears to be conditional but that is, in fact, not. For example, a real estate buyer's acceptance that states "Good title must be passed" is an unconditional acceptance. The law implies good title (legal ownership) in real estate transactions. Good title would pass regardless of whether the parties say so.

Some acceptances include wording such as "details will be worked out." Whether this constitutes unconditional acceptance depends on the details. If they are routine clerical matters, this constitutes unconditional acceptance. In contrast, a reply that leaves essential terms undefined, which a court could not determine and therefore could not deem to be implied, cannot be a valid acceptance. For example, an offer to build a house and a reply that accepts the offer "subject to details to be worked out" does not create a binding agreement because too many essential elements are missing.

In addition to being unconditional, an acceptance must be unequivocal, or clear rather than vague. An equivocal response is not an acceptance, a counteroffer, or an outright rejection. For example, an expression of hope, such as "I hope to have the cash for you next Friday morning," does not constitute an acceptance, but neither is it a counteroffer or a rejection.

Offeree's Communication of Acceptance

The offeree must communicate the acceptance to the offeror by appropriate word or act. If an offer specifies certain means of acceptance, the acceptance must comply. Otherwise, customary means used in similar transactions or those reasonable under the circumstances are permissible.

Some situations do not require formal acceptance. For example, if an offer to sell contains the words, "This proposal becomes a contract when an executive officer of the company accepts and approves it," the acceptance occurs when an executive indicates acceptance on the document by signing it. However, some courts still require the offeree to inform the offeror of an acceptance within a reasonable time.

A complaint does not negate an acceptance. For example, a contract results even if an offeree replies to an offer by writing, "Your price is unfair. If I didn't urgently need the property, I would never accept at this price. Enclosed is my check for the unreasonable amount you demand."

An offeree's silence is not an acceptance, and language in an offer cannot circumvent this rule. However, the parties' prior dealings may impose a duty to reject a current offer. For example, if the parties' custom has been for the seller to send goods and the buyer to pay for them later, the buyer receiving an unrequested and unwanted additional shipment would have to reject it. In this case, silence would indicate acceptance.

What the offeree must communicate depends on the type of contract offer. Most offers are bilateral in the sense that they contemplate a return promise from the offeree. When it is unclear whether the parties intended a unilateral or a bilateral contract, courts usually find that the intent of the offer was for a bilateral contract. For bilateral contracts, acceptance is not complete until the offeree gives the offeror the appropriate return promise. The offeror can revoke the offer at any time until the offeree communicates the return promise to the offeror or to the offeror's agent.

While the usual response to a bilateral contract offer is a return promise, the offeree can choose to perform the act requested instead. For example, Jill writes to Barry, "I'll pay you $1,000 if you'll promise to paint my garage by June 1." Barry does not reply to the letter but proceeds to paint Jill's garage, with her knowledge, and completes the work before June 1. A court would likely conclude that a bilateral contract resulted.

Forbearance

The act of giving up or the promise to give up a legal right.

Substantial performance

The performance of the primary, necessary terms of an agreement.

For unilateral contracts, the offeror seeks either performance or **forbearance** from the offeree. The offeree need not communicate acceptance because presumably the offeror will learn of the offeree's compliance. However, in some cases, an offer specifies that the offeree must give notice of performance.

Problems arise when the offeree begins to perform and the offeror revokes the offer before performance is completed. Most courts hold that an offeree's **substantial performance** suspends the offeror's right to revoke the offer. In court, what constitutes substantial performance is a question of fact, not law. Generally, preparations for performance are not substantial performance. A unilateral contract offer includes the understanding that if substantial performance occurs, the offeree can complete performance within the prescribed time.

An acceptance in a manner invited by an offer is effective as soon as it leaves the offeree's possession. The acceptance is effective even if it never reaches the offeror, so long as the offeree has intended it to go directly to the offeror. However, if the offeree simply tells a third person about accepting the offer, the acceptance is ineffective.

If an offer specifies acceptance by return mail, it generally requires that the acceptance be mailed the same business day as receipt of the offer. If no time is specified, acceptance must occur within a reasonable time. Acceptance is effective when the letter is mailed and creates a legally binding contract when it leaves the offeree's possession.

This rule also applies to other communication services not under the offeree's control. A contract is created when an acceptance is delivered to a private messenger or faxed, for example. In all such cases, the offeree must accurately address the acceptance to the offeror. If an incorrectly addressed acceptance arrives at the wrong address, it is effective only when the offeror actually receives it. Courts have yet to establish clear rules governing an offeree's acceptance by e-mail.

An offeror can expressly state that an offer is conditional upon the receipt of the acceptance. For example, Amy mails an offer to lease land to Victor, stating, "Send me a yes or no answer. If I do not hear from you by noon on Wednesday, I will conclude that your answer is no." Victor mails an acceptance, but Amy does not receive the letter until after noon on Wednesday. Victor and Amy have not formed a contract because Amy did not receive the acceptance within the period she prescribed.

An offeree cannot withdraw or revoke an acceptance once made. That the offeree conceivably can reclaim a mailed acceptance from the post office does not prevent the acceptance from taking effect when sent.

CAPACITY TO CONTRACT

Some parties are considered incapable of entering into legally binding contracts. However, under certain circumstances there may be exceptions to this general rule. Because insurance policies are contracts, it is important for insurance professionals to understand the situations in which these exceptions arise.

Competent party

A party to a contract who has the basic or minimal ability to do something and the mental ability to understand problems and make decisions.

Only a **competent party** can enter into a legally binding contract. Parties who may lack capacity to contract include these:

- Minors
- Insane persons
- Intoxicated persons (under the influence of alcohol or drugs)
- Artificial entities (such as insurers) that are restricted by law or corporate charter from entering into certain contracts

Competent Parties

A valid offer and a valid acceptance form an agreement, but for that agreement to qualify as a contract, the parties to it must have legal capacity to contract. Capacity refers to one's ability to sue or be sued or to enter into an enforceable contract. Capacity includes the ability to understand the consequences of one's actions.

A party who lacks legal capacity to contract is considered incompetent under the law. A party deemed competent to contract is one who has the mental ability to understand problems and make decisions. An incompetent person who enters a contract can challenge its validity by arguing that the agreement is a voidable contract. The term that describes a successful challenge of a contract is "avoiding" the contract.

Minors' Contracts

Each state has its own statute that sets the age of majority for contracts. The most common age of majority today is eighteen. The law protects minors from disposing of their property while they are underage.

Generally, minors can assert their minority as a defense against liability in contracts. Even if a minor misrepresents his or her age to induce another party to enter into a contract, the minor can avoid the contract. In this case, however, the other party can also avoid the contract, on the grounds of misrepresentation.

Although minors can avoid contracts during minority, they cannot confirm contracts during minority. A minor can avoid a contract by any expression of intent to renounce the agreement. In addition, any act inconsistent with the contract constitutes avoidance. For example, a minor who contracts to sell property to one person but sells it to another immediately after reaching the age of majority has effectively avoided the original contract. If a minor has not avoided a contract within a reasonable time after coming of age, most courts hold that the minor has ratified the contract. What constitutes a "reasonable time" is a decision for the court.

Restitution

The return of specific property by court order.

Most courts require a minor to make **restitution** of any benefits received before avoiding a contract. A minor cannot challenge a contract and at the same time retain contract benefits. A minor who has purchased an item and then trades it for something else must return the same or a comparable item available upon rejecting the contract.

Unlike most contracts that minors enter into, a minor's contract to purchase necessaries is not voidable, and minors must fulfill their obligations under such contracts. A minor is liable only for the reasonable value of necessaries actually received—for example, the reasonable value of necessary clothing purchased. Necessaries include anything related to a minor's health, education, and comfort appropriate to the minor's standard of living. This exception to the general rule is intended to protect minors. If contracts for necessaries were easily voidable, people would be discouraged from entering into them. Consequently, minors whose parents are unwilling or unable to provide for them would have difficulty obtaining what they need. The exception may not apply to minors whose parents supply the necessities of life; contracts that those minors enter into for necessaries may be voidable.

The concept of necessaries usually does not apply to items used for business purposes. Courts have held minors not liable under contracts for fire insurance and life insurance because these contracts are not for necessaries. However, when a vehicle is one of a minor's necessaries, mandatory auto insurance could arguably be necessary for that minor.

Contracts involving minors are nonvoidable in several other circumstances. For example, if a minor has married, has assumed the obligation of a bail bond, or has the duty of child support, overriding public policy considerations require binding the minor to those commitments. Similarly, if a court has approved a contract for performance of services by a child, such as a child actor, the court will enforce the contract against the minor. In some jurisdictions, minors actively engaged in business pursuits are liable for contracts involving the conduct of those pursuits—for example, matters involving transferring stock, handling bank accounts, and obtaining loans for higher education.

A parent is generally not liable for a minor child's contracts. For a court to hold otherwise would permit indirect enforcement of a minor's agreement. For example, if a minor contracts to purchase a boat and a parent has not become a party to the agreement by signing or otherwise promising to assume the obligation, then the parent is not liable if the minor defaults. In contrast, a parent who has cosigned a minor child's contract is personally liable if the child fails to perform the contract obligations. The parent's liability is the same as that imposed on any other cosigner who assumes liability for another's default.

However, the law does impose liability on a parent for a minor child's contracts in several other situations. For example, the parent is liable if a child has acted on the parent's behalf in a transaction or if a parent has directed a child to sign a contract for the parent's benefit. Similarly, if a parent has neglected or refused to pay for necessaries for a child and the child contracts to purchase them, the contracting party can take legal action against the minor or the parent to recover the reasonable value of the necessaries.

Insane Persons' Contracts

Any agreement an insane person enters into is void. For purposes of contractual liability avoidance, the law recognizes two classes of insane people:

1. Those adjudged insane
2. Those who claim insanity or mental incompetence

A person can be adjudged, or formally declared, insane by a court. A court's adjudication is conclusive and voids any contract that person has entered into while insane, regardless of whether anyone challenges it.

Some people attempt to avoid liability under their contracts by claiming that they were insane or otherwise mentally incompetent at the time they entered into the contracts. Contracts of people who claim insanity, but whom courts have not adjudicated insane, are voidable; they remain in full force and effect until avoided by the parties claiming insanity.

To avoid a contract, a person claiming insanity but not adjudged insane must prove one of these conditions:

*   The person did not know that a contract was forming.
*   The person did not understand the legal consequences of acts purporting to form the contract.

That a party experiences delusions or intervals of insanity, or is eccentric, does not affect a contract in the absence of one of those two conditions. It is not necessary to show that a person is permanently insane, only that the individual was insane at the time of contract formation. Contracts made by mentally ill people during lucid intervals are binding. A person confined to or receiving treatment in a mental institution could be competent to contract, if neither adjudged insane nor meeting one of the two conditions.

Only the incompetent or insane party has the power to avoid a contract. If the insane person has a guardian, then the guardian can avoid the contract. An insane party who has regained competency can affirm a previously made contract. An insane party who has avoided a contract must make full restitution if the other party acted in good faith and was unaware of the insanity.

Insane persons' liability for contracts for necessaries is the same kind of liability as that for minors. To determine what constitutes necessaries, courts examine the individual's station in life, including the need for nursing and medical attention. For example, if the person is institutionalized, legal services to obtain release from custody can be necessary.

If an agreement benefits an insane person and the other party is unaware of the infirmity, the insane person cannot avoid the contract. The party to a contract with an insane person can enforce the contract by proving these facts:

- The sane party lacked knowledge of the insanity.
- The contract benefits the insane person.

For example, an insane person contracts to have her house painted. The other party, who does not know about the insanity, paints the house. The painter has a right to compensation for those services, and the insane person cannot disaffirm the contract. However, if the contracting party knew or should have known of the person's insanity at the time the parties created the contract, the insane person is not liable if the contract has not yet been performed (executory). In such a case, a court will try to achieve fairness for both parties.

Intoxicated Persons' Contracts

Generally, a person who was intoxicated, by use of either alcohol or drugs, when entering a contract cannot avoid the contract. The law usually does not protect people from their own follies. Case law has tempered this rule, however, and exceptions have developed making contracts voidable if the person's judgment was impaired, using the same conditions applied to cases of insanity:

- The person did not know that a contract was forming.
- The person did not understand the legal consequences of acts purporting to form the contract.

Additionally, if one party to a contract has purposely caused the other party to become intoxicated to obtain an unfair advantage, the innocent party can avoid the contract.

In most states, courts can adjudge people as habitual drunkards, just as they can adjudge them insane. Adjudication is a matter of public record and serves as notice to the public that contracts such a person attempts to make are void. In such cases, the other party to the transaction cannot claim lack of knowledge of the party's condition. Conversely, if a contracting party has no knowledge of the other party's intoxication, the contract may be enforceable.

A person whose judgment was impaired because of intoxication when entering into a contract can either avoid or ratify the contract upon becoming sober. However, the other party can claim lack of knowledge of the person's condition to avoid the contract. The party who avoids a contract cannot later retract the avoidance and must return any items of value received.

Artificial Entities' Contracts

Corporations, although artificial creations of the state, are people in the eyes of the law. They can hold property, sue and be sued, commit crimes and torts, and enter into contracts. The extent of a corporation's competence to enter into contracts depends on the scope of the power its charter grants.

Most states permit corporations to engage in any lawful business and do not restrict the types of contracts they can make. However, specially licensed and controlled corporations, such as those in insurance, banking, and transportation, are subject to different restrictions.

Traditionally, an attempted contract that was not within corporate powers was voidable as an *ultra vires* contract, meaning a contract "beyond its power." Either party could avoid such a contract while it was fully executory (still unperformed). If either party had performed its part of the contract, however, the other party must perform. As for a fully executed contract, neither party could avoid the agreement even though an *ultra vires* act was involved. Most states have abolished the defense of *ultra vires*, but courts often use the term when discussing corporate concepts in written decisions.

CONSIDERATION

One element of an enforceable contract, in addition to agreement and capacity to contract, is consideration. Not all types of consideration, however, are sufficient to form a legally binding contract. To determine whether a binding contract exists, an insurance professional must be able to correctly evaluate the consideration associated with the agreement.

Consideration
Something of value or bargained for and exchanged by the parties to a contract.

For the element of **consideration** to be sufficient to create a valid contract, the promisor must receive a legal benefit, such as money, or the promisee must suffer a legal detriment, such as inconvenience, loss, or relinquishment of something of value. The consideration necessary to make a promise enforceable can be one of the following:

- A return promise
- An act performed
- A forbearance from acting

Types of Consideration

Five types of consideration are sufficient to form an enforceable contract:

- Valuable consideration
- Forbearance
- Present consideration
- Future consideration
- Binding promises

Good consideration
Consideration based on natural love or affection, or on moral duty, that is not sufficient to support a contract.

Valuable consideration
The consideration necessary and sufficient to support a valid contract.

Each type of consideration has its own set of legal rules.

Valuable Consideration

The law distinguishes between two types of consideration: **good consideration** and **valuable consideration**. For example, a father signs this written promise:

"For and in consideration of the love and affection I have for my daughter, I will transfer my property to her on November 1." This expression of love and affection is good consideration but not the valuable consideration that can create an enforceable contract. The father's promise is merely a **gratuitous promise**.

Courts generally do not inquire into the adequacy of valuable consideration. Attempts to weigh the fairness of the numerous bargains in business would result in excessive litigation. Courts are not concerned if people are willing to pay $50 for a $20 item.

In some situations, courts do review the value of consideration. For example, a court could find an agreement unconscionable if a large seller charged an excessively high price to a small buyer that had no alternative but to deal with the seller. See the exhibit "Adequacy of Consideration."

Gratuitous promise

A promise not supported by valuable consideration and, therefore, not binding.

Adequacy of Consideration

Mike has written a book and has given it to Bridget to read. Bridget, thinking the book is publishable, offers Mike $10,000 for the manuscript. Mike accepts the offer. Before paying Mike, Bridget attempts to find a publisher but is unsuccessful. Mike sues for the $10,000, and Bridget defends on the basis that she received no consideration because the manuscript was not worth $10,000. A court would rule Bridget's defense invalid because adequacy of the consideration is not an issue. The manuscript was sufficient consideration; that it proved unpublishable is immaterial. Bridget must pay the $10,000.

[DA06287]

Forbearance

Forbearance is sufficient consideration to support a contract and is commonly seen in cases of compromise. For example, a person injured in an automobile accident may have a right to sue for damages. A promise to refrain from suing in return for the other party's promise to pay a sum of money constitutes valuable consideration. However, if the injured person has no cause of action, then a promise to forbear from suing is not valid consideration because it surrenders no right.

Forbearance can be valuable consideration even if it benefits the forbearing party. For example, if a grandfather promised to give $5,000 to his sixteen-year-old granddaughter if she would refrain from smoking, drinking, or gambling until age twenty-one, a court might hold the granddaughter's forbearance sufficient consideration to enforce the promise.

Present and Future Consideration

To constitute valuable consideration, an act or a promise must involve a present or a future commitment. Many state courts and legislatures have created exceptions to this rule. Most jurisdictions enforce a new promise to pay an existing obligation that has become unenforceable for one of the following three reasons:

- One of the parties is a minor.
- The promisor is bankrupt.
- The time for payment has ended.

Although no new consideration supports the new promise, some courts hold that the new promise couples itself to the preexisting debt, and that, therefore, valuable consideration supports the promise. Other courts find renewal promises enforceable because of a preexisting moral obligation sufficient to support the new promise.

To illustrate: When she was seventeen, Francine promised to buy a car from Joy for $200. Francine's promise was unenforceable because she was a minor. Upon reaching eighteen, the age of majority, and having paid none of the purchase price, Francine promises to pay $100 for the car. Although Joy could have disaffirmed the contract entirely and therefore owed no duty of performance (delivery of the car), Francine's new promise to pay $100 is enforceable. However, Joy cannot legally collect the $200 Francine promised initially as a minor.

A new promise to pay a debt previously unpaid due to bankruptcy is enforceable without any additional consideration. The promisor must clearly express the promise to pay, and some states require renewal promises to be in writing. A mere acknowledgment of the debt or partial payment, without an express promise to pay all or part of the preexisting obligation, is not sufficient to create a binding renewal promise to pay. A new promise to pay a debt barred by a statute of limitations is also enforceable.

Binding Promise

To be a valid consideration, a promise must be binding. For example, one party's promise to pay for any work it might request of another party is not binding because the promisor might ask for no work. A promisor who requests work can be bound to pay for it, but the promisee cannot claim that the promisor is legally obligated to request any work.

Courts generally use a different approach for requirements contracts and output contracts. For example, a promisor's agreement to buy from the promisee all the coal the promisor requires during a specified period is a binding promise. Similarly, a company's promise to sell all the coal it produces, or outputs, to a particular promisee is a binding promise.

In each case, the question is whether any requirements or outputs are involved. If some level of previous output has been furnished or expected requirement fulfilled between the parties, then the promise to continue meeting those requirements or providing the output is sufficient consideration. If the promisor does not anticipate any need for coal, then the promise is illusory and is not consideration. See the exhibit "Consideration in Insurance Contracts."

Consideration in Insurance Contracts

The insurance contract, like any other contract, requires valuable consideration. The insurer's consideration is its promise to indemnify or pay on behalf of an insured for loss resulting from a covered occurrence. The insured's consideration is the premium payment or the promise of premium payment.

An insured's obligation to pay a property-casualty insurance premium differs from the obligation to pay a life insurance premium. In property-casualty insurance, prepaying the premium is not a condition necessary to make the contract valid. In life insurance, the application or the policy itself usually provides that the insurance will not take effect until the purchaser pays the first full premium.

In property-casualty insurance, if an insured suffers a loss before paying a premium at the outset of a policy period, an insurer cannot refuse to pay based on lack of consideration. Payment of the entire premium becomes an obligation as soon as the coverage begins. However, parties can agree, for example, that the insured will pay the premium for an annual policy on a monthly basis. Even so, the premium is generally due and payable at the beginning of the agreed-on period. Any premium owed becomes the insured's debt. Canceling the policy during the coverage period requires an appropriate adjustment for collecting earned premium or refunding unearned premium.

In life insurance, the policyholder has no duty to pay premiums after payment of the first premium, but nonpayment of premiums can result in forfeiture of policy rights. The insurer may have the right to avoid the life insurance policy. If the policyholder has paid premiums for a number of years, the insurer might have to return any accumulated cash values to the insured at policy termination.

[DA06288]

What Is Not Valid Consideration?

Three types of consideration are insufficient for forming a binding contract:

- Past consideration
- Promises to perform existing obligations
- Compromise and release of claims

Past Consideration

Past consideration is insufficient to support a contract. For example, if a person mows a lawn without the property owner's knowledge, the owner's subsequent promise to pay for the work is not enforceable. Similarly, if a person finds a wallet and returns it to its owner, who then promises to pay a reward, the consideration exchanged for the owner's promise (the return of the lost wallet) represents a past consideration and is not sufficient to create an enforceable agreement.

Promise to Perform an Existing Obligation

A promise to perform an act that the promisor is already legally required to perform is not consideration. For example, a police officer's promise to the public to arrest a criminal is not enforceable because the arrest is the officer's job. However, if someone offers a firefighter a reward to enter a burning building to retrieve property at great risk, and beyond the firefighter's duty, that performance supports a claim for the reward.

Compromise and Release of Claims

Generally, partial payment of money owed is insufficient consideration to discharge an original obligation. When a debtor owes $100 and promises to pay $50 if the creditor will accept that amount as full payment, the promise is not binding. However, in some situations a promise to accept less than the amount of the original debt can be binding:

- In *bona fide*, or good faith, disputes about the amounts of money owed, the parties believe that their claims are just. Many such claims involve damage to property or injury to people. Each party's promise to surrender a claim for the amount in question is sufficient consideration for the return promise.

- A debtor may pay an amount less than a debt's total before the debt is due. If the creditor has led the debtor to believe that an early payment would discharge the entire obligation, then the promise to accept the lesser amount is binding on the creditor.

- **Accord and satisfaction** allows for payment of less than the original debt. For example, if the debtor makes partial payment and also offers additional consideration in some form other than money, the creditor's agreement to accept is binding.

- One debtor may have many creditors. When several creditors join and each agrees to take a certain percentage of the original obligation owed, they form a composition of creditors. The resulting composition agreement is binding on the assenting creditors and completely extinguishes the original debt. Each creditor's agreement to accept a percentage of the full debt is sufficient consideration for the other creditors' same promise.

Accord and satisfaction

An agreement (accord) to substitute performance other than that required in a contract and the carrying out of that agreement (satisfaction).

Exceptions to the Consideration Requirement

In some cases, contracts are enforceable despite the lack of consideration. These promises are enforceable for equitable or public policy reasons or because state laws make specific exceptions. For example, contracts without consideration are enforceable when one of these concepts or exceptions applies:

- Promissory estoppel
- Charitable subscriptions

Promissory Estoppel

Promises to make gifts, called gratuitous promises, do not involve payment and are therefore generally unenforceable. Inequities resulting from application of this rule led courts to develop the concept of **promissory estoppel**. The principle applies when the following three elements are proven:

- A party has made a promise expecting another party to act, or to forbear from acting, in reliance on that promise.
- The other party has justifiably relied on the promise to his or her detriment and acts or forbears from acting.
- Only enforcement of the promise would achieve justice.

Promissory estoppel involves questions of fact to be determined by a judge or jury. Generally, evidence that the plaintiff will suffer substantial economic damage if the promise is not enforced is necessary for a court to enforce the promise. Under the doctrine of promissory estoppel, a court seeks to grant whatever remedy is necessary to prevent injustice.

For example, Nancy promised to employ Barry for an indefinite term. Barry, who lived a thousand miles away, incurred considerable expense to move closer to Nancy's company because of her promise. When Barry arrived at Nancy's office to accept the job, Nancy reneged on her promise. Barry can sue Nancy for damages even though he provided no valuable consideration in exchange for Nancy's promise.

Promissory estoppel

A legal principle that permits enforcement of a promise made without consideration in order to prevent injustice.

Charitable Subscriptions

When a person makes a subscription or otherwise pledges money to a charitable organization that depends on voluntary contributions, the obligation involves more than a gratuitous promise to make a gift. The commitment is as fully binding on the pledging party as if consideration had supported it. In this situation, some courts apply the doctrine of promissory estoppel on the basis that the organization has relied on the pledge to its detriment by undertaking projects the pledge would support and that injustice would result if the promise were not enforced. However, in practice, many pledge solicitations include statements that the pledge is not legally binding.

LEGAL PURPOSE OF A CONTRACT

An agreement between competent parties, supported by consideration, requires a final element to be an enforceable contract. It must have a legal purpose. To determine whether a contract is legally binding, one must understand what types of contracts are illegal.

A contract is illegal when either its formation or its performance is a crime or a tort. Ordinarily, an illegal contract is void. Consequently, the parties to an illegal contract can neither recover damages for breach of contract nor seek recovery for the value of any partial performance they have made. Although this rule can result in a wrongdoer's unjust enrichment, it deters parties from entering into illegal contracts.

Several exceptions apply to the legal purpose requirement based on overriding considerations of equity or public policy.

Types of Illegal Contracts

Contracts may be illegal either because they are contrary to constitutional, statutory, or case law or because they are against public policy. An agreement that is illegal at the outset does not become enforceable by a subsequent change in the law that makes similar agreements legal. Conversely, if a contract is legal at the outset but later becomes illegal as the result of a statute or court decision, the parties need not perform further. In this situation, referred to as supervening illegality, the parties could recover the value of performance while the contract was still legal. No recovery is available for acts the parties perform after the declaration of illegality.

Illegal contracts fall into nine categories:

- Contracts to commit crimes or torts
- Contracts harmful to the public interest
- Usury contracts
- Wagering contracts
- Contracts with unlicensed practitioners
- Contracts to transfer liability for negligence
- Contracts in restraint of marriage
- Contracts in restraint of trade
- Unconscionable bargains

Contracts to Commit Crimes or Torts

Any agreement under which one party consents to commit a crime or another wrongful act (tort) is illegal and therefore is a void contract. For example, contracts to cause another's injury or death, to induce a breach of contract, or to violate a patent right or copyright are illegal, unenforceable agreements.

Like all contracts, insurance contracts must involve legal subject matter. Insurance coverage of illegally owned or possessed goods is invalid. For example, a property insurance policy covering illegal drugs or illegal weapons is void and unenforceable. However, if the insurance is only incidental to an illegal purpose, then the contract is enforceable. For example, a property insurance policy on a building housing illegal gambling or prostitution is still enforceable because the coverage is on the building, not the activity. However, business interruption insurance on an illegal gambling activity or a house of prostitution would be void and unenforceable.

A legal insurance contract can become unenforceable because of the insured's wrongful conduct. For example, if an insured intentionally burns down his house, the insurance policy on the property does not permit recovery. The insured's illegal act precludes any right to insurance proceeds. In many states, if the insured sues for payment, the insurer must establish by a preponderance of evidence that the insured committed arson. Some states apply a fraud standard to arson, requiring the insurer to prove arson by clear and convincing evidence. A criminal conviction of arson is not necessary. In fact, an acquittal on the criminal charge does not preclude a civil lawsuit based on intentional damage for insurance proceeds. Although the insured who caused the damage could not recover, a majority of states allow an innocent insured spouse to receive a fair share of the insurance proceeds.

Similar issues apply in life insurance. When the beneficiary has caused the insured's death, courts in many states limit the conditions under which the beneficiary can recover policy proceeds. Generally, a beneficiary who has willfully caused or contributed to the death cannot recover, and any proceeds go to the deceased insured's estate or to a secondary beneficiary. In most states, a beneficiary who has accidentally caused an insured's death does not forfeit life insurance proceeds. A beneficiary who has killed an insured in self-defense or when insane also can recover benefits.

If a beneficiary obtained a life insurance policy with the intent to kill the insured for the proceeds and does in fact kill the insured, the insurer can avoid payment. Both the beneficiary's illegal intent and fraudulent concealment are bases for avoidance of the contract, and the policy is entirely void with no benefits payable to anyone.

Contracts Harmful to the Public Interest

Courts have found agreements illegal because they harm the public interest. One example is an agreement to buy or sell a public office. Similarly, agreements to procure government contracts illegally and agreements to contribute amounts exceeding legal limits to political campaigns are contrary to public policy and therefore void.

Agreements to interfere with or obstruct legal processes are also illegal. For example, agreements to bribe witnesses or to suppress evidence impede the administration of justice and are against the public interest. Likewise, agreements that stir up unnecessary litigation are illegal and unenforceable.

In insurance contracts, public policy requires that the insured have an **insurable interest** in any property or life to be covered by the policy. Policies not covering an insurable interest are illegal and void. They are considered

Insurable interest

An interest in the subject of an insurance policy that is not unduly remote and that would cause the interested party to suffer financial loss if an insured event occurred.

wagering contracts because they gamble on others' lives or property. Such contracts increase the likelihood of intentional harm or destruction.

In property-casualty insurance, the insurable interest must exist at the time the loss occurs. The insurable interest in a life must exist at the time the applicant obtains insurance coverage. People can purchase life insurance on their own lives. They have an insurable interest in another's life only if they receive economic benefit from the relationship with the covered person. Relationship by blood or marriage is generally sufficient.

Usury Contracts

Usury

The charging of an illegally high rate of interest on a loan.

Laws in each state limit the amount of interest that lenders may charge for loans. Any contract allowing a lender more than the maximum legal interest is a **usury** contract and is illegal. In most states, a lender that has charged an illegal rate is barred from collecting interest on the loan but can still recover the principal amount loaned. Other states permit recovering interest up to the maximum legal rate.

Wagering Contracts

Wagering (gambling) contracts are contracts entirely for sport, and their performance depends on the occurrence of an uncertain event. A bet placed on the outcome of a sporting event is an example of a wager. Most states have statutes making wagering contracts illegal.

Determining whether a contract involves wagering is difficult in some situations. Futures contracts in the commodity markets are an example. Under these contracts, a seller promises to sell goods, usually agricultural products, that he or she does not currently own. Futures contracts generally include hedging transactions, making simultaneous contracts to purchase and sell particular commodities at a future date. The intention is that a gain on one transaction will offset a loss on another transaction. These contracts protect against market price fluctuation and are not considered wagering contracts because they protect legitimate business profits.

Contracts With Unlicensed Practitioners

State statutes require people engaged in particular trades or occupations to have licenses. These laws are designed to protect the public against unqualified and incompetent people performing specialized services. Licensees must meet minimum levels of competence established by the state. Most states require lawyers, doctors, dentists, pharmacists, barbers, insurance producers, and architects to have licenses.

If a person engages in an occupation without a required license, the recipients of that person's services can refuse to pay for them because the contract was illegal. The licensing laws that apply are those in place in the state in which services are performed. For example, a surveyor licensed in one state cannot sue to recover a fee for work performed under contract in another state because the license does not extend to other states.

Contracts to Transfer Liability for Negligence

Another type of illegal contract involves the attempt to relieve a party of its own **negligence**. Courts narrowly interpret **exculpatory clauses** against the parties attempting to limit their liability. Courts often declare exculpatory clauses illegal because they are contrary to public policy, especially when the other party is at a bargaining disadvantage. An example of an exculpatory clause is a term in a residential lease excusing the owner from liability if the building burns down because of the owner's negligence. In most situations, courts would not enforce such a clause.

Common carriers, such as trains, airplanes, and buses, attempt to restrict their liability for negligence, as do certain public utilities and other monopolies. Such limits are prohibited unless permitted by statute, administrative agency ruling, or international agreement. The lack of equality of bargaining power between a large and powerful entity and the relatively powerless consumer is an important consideration in determining the legality of limits to liability. See the exhibit "Liability Transfer in Bailments."

Negligence

The failure to exercise the degree of care that a reasonable person in a similar situation would exercise to avoid harming others.

Exculpatory clause (exculpatory agreement)

A contractual provision purporting to excuse a party from liability resulting from negligence or an otherwise wrongful act.

Liability Transfer in Bailments

When the owner of personal property (bailor) temporarily gives that property to another person (bailee), the transaction is a bailment. For example, a customer (bailor) entrusting car keys to a parking attendant (bailee) or a coat to a checkroom attendant are bailments.

Bailees' attempts to disclaim liability for negligence raise illegal contract issues. The bailee of the goods generally has a duty to exercise reasonable care under all circumstances. Many bailees attempt to limit their liability for negligence in such places as parking lots or coat checkrooms by placing notices disclaiming liability for lost or damaged property on the receipts for the goods. Some courts hold these clauses to be illegal because the limitations could encourage all bailees to attempt to restrict liability, a result contrary to public policy.

[DA06326]

Contracts in Restraint of Marriage

Contracts restraining the freedom to marry are contrary to public policy and therefore illegal. Examples include these:

- Contracts between two persons to bring about or prevent the marriage of a third person
- Marriage brokerage contracts restraining the freedom of choice in entering into marriage

Restraints on marriage incidental to another legitimate purpose may be valid under some circumstances. People who promise not to marry until age twenty-one can enforce such contracts against parties who have promised to pay them to delay marriage. However, contracts not to marry that have no time limits are unenforceable.

Contracts in Restraint of Trade

Under statutory and common law, contracts that unreasonably restrain trade or stifle competition are illegal and void. Reasonable limits on trade or competition in contracts are legal if they impose no undue hardship on the restricted party and only if they are necessary to protect the parties. Restraint of trade issues often arise in the sale of businesses and in employment contracts.

Often in the sale of a business, a contract provision requires the seller to refrain from opening a new business within a certain distance and time to compete with the buyer. Whether such a restriction is legal depends on its extent. If the restriction bars the seller from ever again competing in the same business or in a particular area, the restriction is unreasonable and invalid. If the restriction prohibits the seller from competing with the buyer for one year and within two miles from the business sold, the restriction is probably enforceable. Similarly, **noncompete agreements** are generally enforceable if the restriction is necessary to protect the employer and is reasonable regarding the time and distance constraints on the employee.

Courts generally look more favorably on contracts not to compete that relate to the sale of a business than on those that apply to employment. Businesses generally have greater bargaining power than individuals in employment situations.

Unconscionable Bargains

Courts would not enforce contracts containing provisions so harsh and unfair that they cause undue suffering to the party resisting performance. Some state laws incorporate this common-law approach for sales contracts by permitting courts to refuse to enforce, or limit the application of, a contract or clause found to be unconscionable when created. For example, a contract provision that requires the seller to provide goods for free if the goods are delivered after a specified date could be considered unconscionable. Courts can revise such sales contracts to include more reasonable terms.

Noncompete agreement

An agreement between an employer (the principal) and an employee (the agent) to protect the employer's customers, trade secrets, confidential information, and other items for a specific period after an employee relationship has been terminated.

Exceptions to the Legal Purpose Requirement

A contract that might be illegal can still be totally or partially enforceable under three types of conditions, each involving overriding considerations of equity or public policy:

- When a specific group is protected by law, an illegal contract might be enforceable. For example, when a corporation issues a type of stock that it is prohibited by law from issuing, the stock's purchaser can sue to recover money paid under the illegal transaction. Similarly, an insurer that issues an illegal policy cannot use its own wrongdoing to defend itself in an insured's lawsuit to collect policy proceeds. The policy's illegal nature does not prevent someone from asserting the right to protection under the policy.

- In the case of **in pari delicto agreements**, if both parties are equally at fault, the contract is not enforceable. However, if the parties bear a significantly unequal degree of fault, an illegal contract might be enforceable against the party at greater fault. Courts apply the concept of *in pari delicto* only in cases involving a clear disparity of fault between the contracting parties.

- In a **severable contract**, failure to perform one promise does not necessarily put the promisor in breach of the entire contract. When contracts contain both legal and illegal provisions, courts can enforce the legal parts. Enforcement is at the court's discretion and occurs only in cases in which the legal and illegal parts are readily separable. If the illegal provisions have tainted the entire transaction, a court can void the contract entirely.

Courts will not enforce illegal contracts, and they do not aid a party who has knowingly entered an illegal contract to recover any loss. However, some courts permit a party to repent before the completion of an illegal contract and to obtain return of any consideration paid. A person electing to repent an illegal act before consummating it can recover any money or goods transferred under the contract—but only if repentance occurs before the contract is performed.

ENFORCEABILITY OF A CONTRACT

An agreement based on offer and acceptance, contractual capacity of the parties to the agreement, consideration, and a legal purpose can still be unenforceable. Ascertaining whether both parties actually intended to enter willingly into a contract is essential to determining whether that contract is enforceable.

Genuine assent in a contract is the demonstration that the parties have actually intended to form a legally binding agreement, breach of which has legal consequences. An innocent party who has not given genuine assent can generally avoid the contract.

In pari delicto agreement
An illegal transaction in which both parties are equally at fault.

Severable contract
A contract that includes two or more promises, each of which a court can enforce separately.

Genuine assent
Contracting parties' actual assent to form a contract or their indication of intent to contract by their actions and words.

Genuine Assent

An apparently valid contract may be unenforceable if either party has not given genuine assent to contract. Genuine assent may be lacking if a party was induced to enter a contract by any of five factors:

- Fraud
- Mistake
- Duress
- Undue influence
- Innocent misrepresentation

In these five situations, courts do not uphold the contracts and sometimes award monetary damages to the wronged parties.

Fraud

Fraud by one party to a contract can result in a lack of genuine assent on the part of the other party. Fraud is a tort, and it can also be a crime. When one party to a contract has committed fraud, the contract is voidable and the innocent party may choose to repudiate it.

In a lawsuit alleging fraud, the plaintiff must prove six elements. Courts will generally rescind a contract if the first five elements of fraud are proven. In a suit for damages, the plaintiff must also prove the sixth. The legal definition of fraud is divided into these six elements:

- a false **representation**
- of a **material fact**
- knowingly made
- with intent to deceive
- on which the other party has placed justifiable reliance
- to his or her detriment.

If fraud is proved, the plaintiff can seek one of two remedies:

- The plaintiff may seek **rescission**. If the court rescinds the contract, the plaintiff has no further duties under it and is entitled to reimbursement of all payments made to the defendant. The plaintiff also must return anything of value received under the contract. The court attempts to put the parties back to the condition they were in before they entered the contract.
- If rescission would not make the plaintiff whole, the plaintiff can sue for damages in a tort action, usually called an action in deceit. The plaintiff can seek compensatory damages for quantifiable harm and punitive damages to punish the defendant and deter future, similar fraudulent actions. The plaintiff must prove the extent of the loss or detriment.

Fraud
An intentional misrepresentation resulting in harm to a person or an organization.

Representation
A statement of fact or opinion made by the insured when applying for insurance, usually in response to a question from the insurer.

Material fact
In insurance, a fact that would affect the insurer's decision to provide or maintain insurance or to settle a claim.

Rescission
A legal action that voids a principal's bid.

In insurance contracts, each party is expected to deal with the other party in the utmost good faith. However, in some cases, applicants for insurance misrepresent or conceal material facts. See the exhibit "Fraud in Insurance Contracts."

Fraud in Insurance Contracts

A person fraudulently induced to make or sign an insurance application can rescind the contract and recover any premium paid. The insurer also has the right to cancel an insurance policy because of fraud by the insured. Any fraudulent action or statement by the insured in procuring the policy, if material, permits the insurer to avoid it.

In cases of alleged fraud, the concealment defense is very important in both property and life insurance. The insurer relies on the applicant's full disclosure to determine acceptability, appropriate coverage, and premium. Most courts impose a duty on the insured to reveal material facts to the insurer. The insured's failure to do so can constitute concealment. For example, an applicant who knows that the property to be insured is subject to an unusual hazard must reveal that information to the insurer. Failure to do so could constitute concealment and avoid the policy.

Fraudulent concealment is generally a question of fact to be determined by a jury. To assert the concealment defense, the insurer must prove two things:

- The insured knew that the fact concealed was material.
- The insured concealed the fact with the intent to defraud.

Courts find intent to defraud only when the facts are clearly and obviously material. They agree that any fact that is the subject of a specific inquiry by the insurer is generally material. An exception to this would be a question on an insurance application that concerns a possibility of loss not covered by the policy applied for.

Standard insurance applications may not include questions about all possible loss exposures. When the insured is aware of an unusual loss exposure not addressed in the application, the test of materiality is whether the information would influence the insurer's decision to enter into the contract. In this case, courts use the reasonable person standard to determine materiality.

Courts have also considered whether previous losses or claims must be disclosed in the absence of a specific question about loss history on an insurance application. Courts have found that such information is not material and have affirmed insurance policies, even when insureds have failed to reveal prior claims.

Most courts agree that an insurance applicant must be reasonably diligent in notifying the insurer of material facts that come to the applicant's knowledge after applying and up to the time the contract becomes effective. The effective date of policy inception, therefore, is crucial.

[DA06349]

Mistake

Like fraud, a **mistake** in a contract can also result in lack of genuine assent. People can make mistakes regarding the facts of a transaction or the law affecting an agreement. Mistakes can involve errors in typing, in arithmetic,

Mistake
A perception that does not agree with the facts.

Bilateral mistake

A perception by both parties to a contract that does not agree with the facts.

Unilateral mistake

A perception by one party to a contract that does not agree with the facts.

or in the value of property in question. While some mistakes do not affect the parties' rights, others make the agreement voidable or unenforceable. Mistakes can be either **unilateral mistakes** or **bilateral mistakes**.

A unilateral mistake ordinarily does not affect a contract. For example, if an offeree accepts an offer that was mistakenly transmitted, a contract is formed because only the offeror was mistaken. However, courts do not permit one party to knowingly exploit another's mistake. For example, if a contract bid is so low that it is obvious that a clerical or mathematical mistake has occurred, the offeree cannot take advantage of the error by accepting the offer.

In certain situations in construction bids, parties can avoid a contract because of a unilateral mistake of fact. A contractor who has made a material mistake in a bid on a public works project can retract the bid if both of these events occur:

- The contractor makes the retraction promptly after discovery.
- The governmental agency involved has done nothing more in reliance on the bid than accept it.

Ordinarily, however, one party's mistake of fact does not affect the other party's rights.

Bilateral mistakes occur when both parties to a contract make the same mistake of fact. Under these conditions, contracts are generally voidable. The mutual mistake must relate to a material fact. Mistakes about collateral considerations, not crucial to the contract, are not grounds for avoidance.

Bilateral mistakes about the subject matter's value do not make a contract voidable. For example, if parties contract for the sale of a jewel, neither knowing the jewel's true value nor making value a condition of their contract, they cannot avoid the contract if the jewel has a different value than either party or both parties anticipated. Courts do not remake such bargains. However, if the mistake is about the jewel's identity, the parties can rescind the contract. For example, parties might mistake a relatively inexpensive cubic zirconium for a diamond. See the exhibit "Mistakes in Insurance Contracts."

Duress

Duress

The use of restraint, violence, or threats of violence to compel a party to act contrary to his or her wishes or interests.

A party who enters a contract under **duress** may not have given genuine assent. The question is whether the wrongdoer deprived the plaintiff of free will in entering the agreement. The court considers the victim's physical health, mentality, experience, education, and intelligence.

Threats of bodily harm to a person or to his or her close relatives constitute sufficient duress to justify contract avoidance. Similarly, a threat to burn down a person's home or to destroy other valuable property belonging to a person constitutes duress. A threat to prosecute someone for a crime also constitutes duress, as could threat of eviction or of damage to one's credit standing.

Mistakes in Insurance Contracts

Of the thousands of insurance policies issued each year, a considerable number contain mistakes. The correction of mistakes over one party's protest can create legal problems. The law does not correct mistakes in judgment or relieve a party of the unforeseen consequences of an act. However, courts do correct errors in expression by interpreting ambiguous policy language or reforming the contract. Court interpretation and reformation are two remedies for mistakenly worded insurance policies.

When interpreting an ambiguity or incorrect description in an insurance policy, courts focus on the parties' intent when entering the contract. The court's ability to interpret the policy is limited to some extent by the restrictions of the parol evidence rule, which prohibits the use of oral evidence to show that the contract terms were different from those in the written policy. However, several exceptions apply to the parol evidence rule.

Courts grant the remedy of reformation only on proof of mutual mistake or of unilateral mistake of which one side was aware. For example, if both the applicant and the insurance producer understood when entering a contract that particular coverage applies but that coverage is not included in the policy, the court can reform the policy in keeping with the contract.

Mistakes of law, whether unilateral or bilateral, do not affect the binding nature of a contract, particularly when the law is not clear. Court decisions can change the law after parties form a contract. For example, both parties to an insurance contract mistakenly believe that property insurance obtained in an individual partner's name protects the partnership's interest in the property. After a loss occurrence, the court could correct the policy to cover the partnership's interest, even though the belief was a mistake of law.

[DA06350]

A court might find duress if one party would suffer irreparable loss under the contract. However, the threat of economic loss or the threat of a civil lawsuit is not generally sufficient to deprive a reasonable person of free will. Similarly, the threat to cease doing business with a person does not constitute duress sufficient to avoid a contract. A threat to withhold payment for work already done unless additional work is performed free of charge is not duress. In such cases, the fear of force imposed on the person is not sufficient to avoid the contract.

Undue Influence

Undue influence can also result in lack of genuine assent to a contract. Undue influence can occur in relationships such as parent and child, nurse and invalid, attorney and client, doctor and patient, and guardian and ward. In contracts between such individuals, the law will assist the victim of undue influence.

Undue influence
The improper use of power or trust to deprive a person of free will and substitute another's objective, resulting in lack of genuine assent to a contract.

Most cases of undue influence concern gifts and wills made by people, often recently bereaved spouses who may be temporarily infirm or elderly persons suffering from physical ailments or dementia.

Innocent Misrepresentation

A person who has reasonably relied on an innocently misrepresented material fact can later avoid a resulting contract because of lack of genuine assent. Even when no intent to defraud exists, the materiality and reasonable reliance elements of fraud also apply to misrepresentation. Misrepresentation is easier to prove than fraud because the plaintiff need not prove intent to deceive. The victim of an innocent misrepresentation asks a court to rescind the contract. Courts do not award monetary damages for innocent misrepresentation.

Statute of Frauds and Parol Evidence Rule

Forms of contracts, as well as rules for interpretation, breach, and discharge of contracts, are determined by the common law, state or federal statutes, court interpretations, and the Uniform Commercial Code (UCC). Statutes of frauds also have significant effects on contracts, and they may permit parol (oral) evidence if needed to interpret a written contract.

Statute of Frauds

Statute of frauds

A law to prevent fraud and perjury by requiring that certain contracts be in writing and contain the signature of the party responsible for performing that contract.

Early common law enforced oral contracts if the parties could establish their terms in court. Even today, most contracts are oral and, if provable, are enforceable. Each state's **statute of frauds** changed common law. All states have enacted statutes of frauds, designed to provide certainty with respect to contractual obligations and reduce the possibility of fraud by requiring written proof of intentions. The usual statute of frauds provision states that "no action shall be brought unless the agreement, or some memorandum or note thereof, shall be in writing, and signed by the party to be charged therewith...."

While state statutes of frauds sometimes include additional provisions, most of them name six situations in which contracts must be written to guarantee enforceability:

- Contracts for the sale of land or any interest in land
- Contracts that cannot be performed within one year
- Contracts to pay another's debt
- Contracts in consideration of marriage
- Contracts by executors of decedents' estates to pay estate debts from executors' own funds
- Contracts for the sale of goods for $500 or more

Some contracts fall into more than one of these categories.

Contracts related to the sale of **real property** or legal interests in real property must be in writing. Legal interests in real property can be complete, such as actual ownership, or partial, such as a renter's interest. Oral contracts for the sale of these interests are generally unenforceable. However, courts have qualified some statute of frauds requirements relating to real estate contracts. For example, when the purchaser of real property has taken possession of the property and made substantial improvements in reliance on an oral contract to sell, most courts enforce the oral contract in the interest of fairness. Under these conditions, the case is "outside the statute of frauds," and the contract may be enforceable. The judge or jury must decide what constitutes substantial improvements.

Real property (realty)
Tangible property consisting of land, all structures permanently attached to the land, and whatever is growing on the land.

The statute of frauds does not allow rescission of a contract but only serves as a defense to a suit for breach of contract. A party who has purchased or sold land under an oral contract, therefore, cannot obtain a refund of money or a return of the deed to land.

Oral contracts not complying with the statute of frauds are not void, but are merely voidable. Either party may use lack of compliance with the statute as a procedural defense in a lawsuit to enforce the contract, but if neither party raises that defense, the contract can be carried through to completion.

Disputes over the terms of long-term oral contracts arise frequently. For this reason, statutes of frauds usually require written evidence of contracts that cannot be performed within one year from the date of their formation. This one-year provision applies only to bilateral contracts. Unilateral contracts that are made orally and are not capable of being performed within one year are enforceable.

Statutes of frauds require one party's promise to another person to pay the debt of a third person to be in writing. For example, if Bob owes Carol money and Annie promises Carol that she will pay Bob's debt if he fails to do so, Annie's promise must be in writing to be enforceable.

Another area subject to fraud and abuse involves promises made in consideration of marriage. The statute of frauds requires that promises to pay money or property if someone marries or promises to marry a person must be in writing to be enforceable.

Oral promises to pay debts against a decedent's estate are enforceable. Such promises may be made by executors or administrators. Most contracts an executor or administrator makes in settling an estate need not be in writing. However, any promise made by an executor or administrator to pay an estate debt from his or her personal funds must be in writing to be enforceable. This rule applies only to promises to pay debts against the estate that arose during the decedent's life. Generally, an executor or administrator would have no legal obligation to pay the decedent's debts out of personal funds. Therefore, a writing is the only way to make such a commitment binding.

Uniform Commercial Code (UCC)

A model code that has been adopted in whole or in part by each state and whose purpose is to provide a consistent legal basis for business transactions throughout the United States and its territories.

Many states have enacted all or part of the **Uniform Commercial Code (UCC)**. The UCC provides that a contract for the sale of goods for $500 or more is not enforceable unless it is in writing. The $500 limit applies to the total price of all the goods the contract purports to sell. If several items, each with a value under $500 but totaling more than $500, are the subject of one contract, then the contract must be in writing.

The writing required as evidence of a contract under the statute of frauds may be a simple note or memorandum. No formal written contract is necessary. The writing can be in any form and can consist of several communications, so long as it provides evidence of the contract's existence.

The statute of frauds requires that the writings be signed by the parties against whom contracts are to be enforced. Signings can consist of signatures, initials, typewritten names, electronic signatures, or any marks that appropriately identify the parties acknowledging the memorandum or communication as their writings. Similarly, signatures, in any of those forms, of representatives who have authority to execute such contracts for others will satisfy the statute's requirement of signed writings. An example is a producer with authority to sign on behalf of an insurance agency. See the exhibit "Insurance Contracts."

Insurance Contracts

Oral insurance policies are valid and enforceable. The customary statute of frauds provisions do not apply to insurance policies. While it is desirable that insurance policies be in writing, the hardship of enforcing this requirement would fall on insureds, and courts therefore do not require written contracts.

In virtually all insurance policies, the contract eventually becomes a written policy, which generally stands by itself as the best evidence of the contract between insurer and insured.

Of the six situations to which the statute of frauds applies, courts have considered applying only two to insurance contracts:

- Policies that are contracts that cannot be performed within one year

- Policies that are promises to answer for another's debt

Courts have held that neither of these statute of frauds provisions applies to insurance contracts.

[DA06352]

Parol Evidence Rule

The parol evidence rule is based on the assumption that all prior negotiations, conversations, and agreements were merged into the final, written contract, which then becomes the complete statement of the parties' agreement. While it does not, on its own, make contracts unenforceable, it has important implications for contract interpretation, because once the parties have reduced any agreement to writing, no oral evidence may be admitted to contradict its terms. Words spoken by the parties before or at the time of contracting, and letters or memoranda they might have prepared before the drafting of the final contract, cannot alter the written words of the contract, and therefore any provisions they contained are unenforceable. The written contract is the only admissible evidence of the agreement.

The parol evidence rule applies to all written documents. In addition to ordinary contracts, it applies to such writings as deeds, wills, leases, insurance policies, releases, and similar legal instruments. The rule serves three purposes:

- To carry out the parties' presumed intention
- To achieve certainty and finality as to the parties' rights and duties
- To exclude fraudulent and perjured claims

For example, Roy sells a boat to Steve. The bill of sale indicates the boat's price, make, model, and year. Steve later claims in a lawsuit that Roy had promised to include other items, such as communications equipment, in the sale. Steve attempts to support his claim in court with a letter Roy wrote and signed before the date of the final bill of sale, in which he promised to include the claimed items. Under the parol evidence rule, the court will not admit the letter into evidence because its terms were not part of the final contract, the bill of sale.

A contract can consist of a series of letters or other documents. The possibility that several documents can constitute a contract can give rise to uncertainty concerning the contractual terms. Parties to a contract can avoid such uncertainty by including the entire agreement in the final contract and not relying on other documents or conversations.

The parol evidence rule applies only to prior or contemporaneous statements and not to oral or written agreements the parties make subsequent to the written contract. Evidence of subsequent agreements is admissible to show that, after entering into the written agreement, the parties agreed to modify or cancel their written contract.

Oral evidence is always admissible to help interpret or explain a written agreement, but not to alter its terms. Legal decisions have established a number of exceptions to the parol evidence rule. They permit the admission of oral evidence of prior or contemporaneous agreements in these situations:

- When an essential contract term is missing, parol evidence is admissible in court to prove that term. For example, Sharon orally agreed to sell her city condominium and her beach house to Tom for $350,000 each. She prepares the agreement of sale for $700,000, which she and Tom both sign, but which does not refer to the beach house. In an action to reform the contract, Tom can introduce evidence of their oral agreement.

- If the written contract contains ambiguous language, oral evidence is admissible to clarify the parties' intent. For example, Isabel provides in her will for payment of money "to my nephew, Bill." If Isabel has two nephews named Bill, after her death, parol evidence can be admitted to determine which nephew Isabel intended to receive the money.

- When fraud or illegality taints a transaction, oral evidence can be admitted to support an allegation of wrongdoing. For example, if one of the parties intentionally substituted the wrong document for the other party's signature, oral testimony is allowed to prove fraudulent conduct. The parties' oral testimony also can show mistakes resulting from the writing process, such as typographical errors.

- Parol evidence is admissible to show that a written document that appears to be a contract never became a contract because of failure of some **condition precedent** to the agreement. For example, if delivery is a condition required before performance, oral evidence can be used to show that delivery did not occur.

Condition precedent

An event that must occur before a duty of performance arises in a contract.

The UCC also makes exceptions to the parol evidence rule.

CONTRACT INTERPRETATION

When the wording of a contract is unclear, it can be difficult to accurately ascertain the obligations of the parties to the contract. In the case of a suit involving an ambiguous contract, a court will interpret the contract based on a set of legal guidelines. Understanding these guidelines helps predict how a court might interpret a contract.

Courts consider a number of factors when interpreting contracts, and they apply certain standards:

- Words are understood in their plain meaning.
- The goal is effectuation of the parties' intent.
- Contracts are classed as entire or divisible.
- Clerical errors and omissions are corrected.
- Contradictory terms are prioritized.
- Ambiguities are interpreted against the writer of the document.
- The parties' own interpretations are considered.
- The court seeks a legal and fair interpretation.
- Trade usage, course of dealings, and performance are considered.

Plain Meaning

When the language of a contract is ambiguous or obscure, courts apply established maxims of construction to ascertain the parties' intent. Maxims of construction are not strict legal rules but well-accepted guidelines for interpretation. They do not make a new contract or rewrite an old one. Courts apply them only to resolve doubts and ambiguities in a contract.

A fundamental standard of contract interpretation is that words are to be understood in their plain and usual meaning. This standard applies even though the parties who agreed to the wording might not have anticipated the consequences. For technical language, courts apply technical meanings, and legal terms are given their established legal meaning.

The law of the location where the contract was made controls the formation of the contract. A court looks at contract language within the context of the contract's subject matter, nature, objectives, and purposes. In every case, the circumstances under which the parties entered into the contract are relevant, whether the contract was oral or written. The circumstances of the agreement, the subject matter, the parties' relationship, and the subject of the agreement all can be considered in determining the meaning of the agreement and in giving effect to the parties' intent. In interpreting the words and conduct of the parties to a contract, a court seeks to put itself in the positions of the parties at the time they made the contract.

Although the plain meaning standard can help ascertain the intention of both parties to a contract, it might not apply when only one party's intention is unclear. For example, a life insurance applicant names his beneficiary as "my wife." At the time the insured obtained the policy, he was living with a woman who was not his legal wife because he had gone through a ceremony of marriage with her without divorcing his first wife. Because the plain meaning of the term "my wife" clearly conflicts with the insured's actual intention, a court can ignore the plain meaning and apply the insured's intention.

Effectuation of Intent

When interpreting a contract, courts apply the interpretation that best carries out the parties' intentions. To ascertain those intentions, a court reads the contract as a whole. If several documents relate to the transaction, a court considers all of them together.

Courts interpret individual clauses and specific words in relation to the main purpose of the contract. The intention expressed in the contract applies, not the subjective intention of one of the parties. If the intention appears clear from the words used, courts have no need to go further.

Courts do not attempt, under the pretext of interpretation, to make new contracts for the parties. Neither do they change written contracts to make them express intentions different from those the parties expressed in the contractual language. Courts generally presume that people mean what they say. Courts do not make agreements for the parties, but they ascertain what the parties' agreements were.

Entire and Divisible Contracts

In an entire contract, one party must complete performance to be entitled to the other party's performance. For example, unless a contract states otherwise, delivery of goods is necessary before payment. In contrast, in a divisible contract, the performance of a portion of the contract entitles the performing party to immediate payment.

A contract is divisible if each party's performance can be divided into two or more parts and if it appears that the parties to the contract contemplated separate compensation for each installment of the performance. Failure to perform one installment is not failure to perform the entire agreement. However, if the division of the contract into parts is only to provide periodic payments applicable toward the amount due upon contract completion, the contract is entire and not divisible. Whenever possible, courts prefer to interpret contracts as divisible to avoid hardships that can result from delaying payments under the contract until full performance has been completed.

Clerical Errors and Omissions

Courts correct obvious clerical errors or mistakes in writing and grammar in contracts. If necessary, courts may transpose, reject, or supply words to clarify language to reflect the parties' intent—unless the error or omission makes it impossible to determine the parties' intent.

Courts consider some contractual terms implied if needed to carry out the parties' intent. In these instances, the unexpressed or implied obligations are those the court believes to be inherent in the transaction. The parties must abide not only by what they expressly intended, but also by intentions the court presumes the parties would have had if they had given more thought to the matter. For example, courts generally presume that payment under a contract is not to be in foreign currency or in a substitute for money. In service contracts, courts find the implication that the parties will render the service with reasonable care and skill. If the parties do not specify the time of performance, it must occur within a reasonable time. If it is customary in the trade to extend credit, a court will read that trade practice into the contract. Therefore, the parties do not need to set forth every contractual provision.

Contradictory Terms

If clauses in a contract conflict but can be interpreted in a way that makes them effective, a court will adopt that interpretation. When the parties have made typewritten or handwritten changes in a printed contract form, courts apply a system of priorities:

- Handwriting prevails over typewriting.
- Typewriting prevails over printing.
- Words prevail over figures.

This is a common-sense approach because parties usually make handwritten changes last. If a document is printed, it is safe to assume that any typing on the document occurred later. For example, words written on a check prevail over figures.

Ambiguity

Ambiguity is uncertainty of meaning, or the capability of being understood in two or more ways. In contract law, ambiguity appears in two different forms:

- A contractual provision can be reasonably interpreted in more than one way.
- The meaning of a provision cannot be determined even by application of all the tools of interpretation.

If a provision can have more than one reasonable meaning, courts adopt the interpretation least favorable to the party who put the provision into the contract and most favorable for the party who assented to it. For example, a court interprets an insurance policy against the insurer that created it. Similarly, courts interpret words in offers against the offerors and words in acceptances against the acceptors. The principle for this rule is that people are responsible for ambiguities in their own expressions.

If a provision is so ambiguous that its meaning cannot be determined with the usual tools of interpretation, the court can admit evidence from outside the contract. For example, a court will permit evidence of prior or contemporaneous agreements to help determine the meaning of ambiguous language.

The **parol evidence rule** does not apply to the introduction of evidence to explain ambiguities. The purpose of this evidence is to clarify what the parties intended the final contract to mean. Evidence to clarify ambiguities explains but does not contradict. Therefore, evidence of the course of performance under the contract, of the parties' prior course of dealings, or of the usages of trade is all admissible to assist the court in determining contractual meaning.

Parol evidence rule

A rule of evidence that limits the terms of a contract evidenced by a writing to those expressed in writing.

Parties' Own Interpretation

The interpretation that the parties have placed on their contract, as shown by their subsequent conduct, has great weight in determining the meaning of doubtful terms. The parties know best what they meant by their words, and their actions under the agreement are some of the best indications of what they meant. However, if a court finds no ambiguity in the contract, and the meaning of its terms is clear, the parties' subsequent conduct placing an unreasonable and erroneous interpretation upon the contract does not prevent a court from enforcing it according to the contractual terms. A court will not remake the contract for parties who have acted in a manner contrary to its provisions.

Legal and Fair Interpretation

If both a legal and an illegal contractual interpretation are possible, the courts assume that the parties intended the legal interpretation. If the court has a choice, it will interpret a contract as reasonable and fair rather than unreasonable and harsh to one of the parties. With that approach, courts adopt interpretations that avoid forfeitures of property when possible. If the terms of the contract itself leave its meaning in doubt, courts attribute to the parties the intent to enter into a fair agreement and therefore interpret the contract equitably.

Trade Usage, Course of Dealings, and Performance

In interpreting contract language, courts give common words their ordinary meanings and technical terms their technical meanings. They also consider local, cultural, and trade usage meanings. In attempting to establish the parties' intent, courts consider their prior course of dealings and their performance under the contract.

A course of dealings relates to similar transactions between the parties before the contract in question. Course of performance involves the performance of the contract that has occurred without either party's objection. If the parties' intent is not clearly expressed in the terms of the agreement, the parties' prior course of dealings takes precedence over usage of the trade in establishing the meaning of the contract. Courts admit evidence on these questions.

THIRD-PARTY CONTRACTUAL RIGHTS

The general rule of contract law is that only the parties to a contract have rights under that contract. There are, however, exceptions to this rule. Understanding these exceptions helps identify contractual situations in which a third party's interests need to be considered.

Third parties have enforceable rights under contracts others have made in two situations:

- An assignment of a contract, by which one party transfers rights arising under a contract to a third party
- Third-party beneficiary contracts, in which one party contracts with another party to confer a benefit on a third party

Contract Assignments

Assignment of contracts is common. Contractual assignments involve transfers of contractual performance rights to other people. For example, creditors often assign the right to receive money from debtors to third parties, such as banks. In this example, the creditor is the **assignor**, and the bank is the **assignee**. If the nonassigning party, in this case the debtor, does not honor the assignment, the assignee may sue the nonassigning party just as though the assignee were a party to the original contract.

When a contract has been assigned, the assignor no longer has any right to performance by the nonassigning party. If that party fails to perform, the right to sue to recover rests solely with the assignee.

Assignment
The transfer of rights or property.

Assignor
The party to a contract who makes an assignment.

Assignee
The individual or entity to whom property, rights, or interests have been transferred.

Just as contract rights can be assigned, obligations under a contract can be delegated to third parties. Unlike with assignment, which eliminates the assignor's rights under an assigned contract, delegation does not relieve the delegating party from the duties under the original contract. Delegation also does not give enforceable contract rights to any third party.

Rights Assignable

Most contract rights are assignable. A seller can assign the right to receive payment for the sale of goods to a third person. The party owing the obligation to pay for the goods, the obligor, then must pay the assignee. Ordinarily, any right to collect a debt is assignable because it is usually no more difficult for a debtor to pay the assignee the amount owed than it would have been to pay the original assignor.

Rights Not Assignable

Notwithstanding the general rule that contract rights are assignable, certain contractual rights are not assignable. These are the most common situations in which contract rights are not assignable:

- Laws restrict prior assignment of such rights as veterans' disability benefits, government pensions, wages, inheritances, and workers compensation benefits.

- The parties to an agreement might specify that they cannot, under the contract, assign the rights. For example, the standard fire insurance policy prohibits insureds from assigning it to new owners of the insured property without the insurer's consent.

- Personal rights are not assignable. For example, a person who contracts to receive the services of a personal trainer cannot assign a third party the right to those services.

- When an assignment materially alters or varies the obligor's performance, a court usually will not uphold it. For example, if Bob contracts to deliver oil to Nancy's house, Nancy cannot assign the right to receive oil delivery to Daniel, who lives in a distant location.

- When a judgment is pending in a personal injury case, generally the injured person cannot assign a claim for damages resulting from the injury. A final judgment, however, is assignable, as is the right to sue to recover for property loss or damage. These assignments involve the right of subrogation, which enables the insurer to obtain damages.

Forms of Assignment

To be effective, an assignment requires neither formality nor writing. Any words or actions that indicate the assignor's intention to transfer contractual rights effects a valid assignment. Assignments are transfers and need not be contracts.

However, an assignment involving subject matter covered by a statute of frauds, such as an assignment of rights under a land sale contract, must be in writing to be enforceable. Statutes of frauds in all states require that transfers of interests in land be in writing.

Although an assignment is a transfer and not a contract, a promise to make an assignment is enforceable only if it is a valid contract. Therefore, if Alphonse (assignor) promises to assign a contract right to Bob (assignee), all of the elements of a valid contract, including consideration, must be present for Bob to enforce Alphonse's promise.

Assignee's Rights

As a general rule, the assignee's rights are those of the assignor and do not extend beyond them. If a party assigns contract rights to an assignee, but a third party to the contract has a defense against the assignor, the third party can assert that same defense against the assignee. For example, if the assignor obtained the original contract through fraud or duress, this defense can be valid against the assignee.

Many consumer sales contracts provide that, if the seller assigns the contract, usually to a finance company or bank, the buyer agrees not to assert any defenses against the assignee that might be valid against the seller-assignor. Adding such provisions to a sales contract makes the contract more marketable to third parties because it places the assignee in a favored position. For the most part, however, people who receive assignments of sales contracts accept them subject to any defenses that would be valid against the assignor.

Notice of Assignment

A valid assignment is effective immediately, even though the assignor has not yet advised the obligor of the assignment. The assignee should nevertheless notify the obligor of the assignment to ensure that the obligor pays the assignee rather than the assignor, thus defeating the original assignor's right to demand the obligor's payment or performance. In such a case, the assignee might have a right to sue the assignor for refusal to, in turn, pay the assignee.

An assignee's notice of assignment to the obligor on the contract also protects additional parties who might take subsequent assignments from the assignors. An assignor would not have the right to make a second assignment but might do so nevertheless, and the original obligor might pay the second assignee. To illustrate, John assigns his contractual rights with George to Dennis. Subsequently, John assigns the same contractual rights to Howard. If Dennis has not given George notice of his own first assignment, George has no reason to know about it and might pay Howard instead. Therefore, it would be to Dennis's benefit to let George know of the first assignment at the outset.

Third-Party Beneficiaries

Formerly, at common law, only the parties to a contract could enforce it. Those were the parties who gave or received consideration or who were in privity of contract. Today, third parties that benefit from contracts may also have enforceable rights under those contracts.

Types of Third-Party Beneficiaries

Third-party beneficiary contracts benefit three types of beneficiaries:

- Creditor beneficiaries
- Donee beneficiaries
- Incidental beneficiaries

Donee and creditor beneficiaries have enforceable rights against the original promisor, but an incidental beneficiary has no enforceable rights.

For example, Henry owes Chuck $500. Henry sells his car to Jeremy for $1,000. Henry receives $500 in cash and Jeremy's promise to pay $500 to Chuck. If Henry's intent in obtaining the promise from Jeremy was to discharge his obligation to Chuck, Chuck is a **creditor beneficiary**. It is the promisee's intent that governs these situations. The promisor's or the third-party beneficiary's intent is not the decisive factor.

If Chuck does not receive payment, he has two possible remedies:

- To proceed as a creditor beneficiary against Jeremy
- To proceed against Henry under the original $500 debt

As another example, Henry wishes to make a $500 gift to Chuck. Henry sells his car to Jeremy for $500 and obtains Jeremy's promise to pay Chuck the $500 price for the car. Chuck is a **donee beneficiary** of Jeremy's promise to pay $500. If he does not do so, Chuck can sue Jeremy for $500.

As a final example, Middletown contracts with Water Company to maintain sufficient water pressure at Middletown's hydrants for fire protection. A Middletown citizen's house burns down because of insufficient water pressure. The citizen is an **incidental beneficiary** and has no enforceable rights under the contract between Middletown and Water Company. Any duty to the citizen is, at best, indirect.

The legal distinction between creditor and donee beneficiary contracts is becoming less important. They are often treated as one class, intended beneficiaries, who are third-party beneficiaries to whom a benefit was intended by the contracting parties. For instance, Chuck contracts to purchase land from Jeremy, breaches the contract, and forfeits a deposit to Jeremy. Helen wants to buy the land, but finds out about Chuck's forfeited deposit. She does not know Chuck but believes that Jeremy should not keep Chuck's deposit. She agrees to purchase the land only if Jeremy promises to repay Chuck's deposit. Jeremy agrees. Helen intended to benefit Chuck, and, regardless of her motive,

Third-party beneficiary contract

A contract between two parties that benefits a third party.

Creditor beneficiary

A third-party beneficiary owed a debt that is to be satisfied by performance of a contract.

Donee beneficiary

A third-party beneficiary who receives the benefit of a contract's performance as a gift from the promisee, with the intent of the contracting parties.

Incidental beneficiary

A third-party beneficiary who has no contractual rights but benefits from a contract even though that is not the intent of the parties to the contract.

Chuck is an intended beneficiary with a right to obtain the forfeited deposit from Jeremy in some jurisdictions.

When a person claims beneficiary status, the court must decide whether the contracting parties intended to confer a benefit upon that person. Unless the claimant can show a direct interest in the performance of the contract about which the contracting parties are aware, the third party is an incidental beneficiary only.

Characteristics of Beneficiary Contracts

Certain rules apply to third-party beneficiary contracts:

- A binding contract must exist between the promisor and promisee.
- The parties to the contract must intend that the third party receive benefits and acquire rights under the contract. Some courts have held that the promisee must have the intention only to benefit the third party.
- The parties must take care in each case to clarify to whom the performance is due. If the parties owe performance to a third party, the third party can sue to enforce it. If, however, performance is due solely to the promisee, only the promisee can sue, and a third party has no rights against the promisor.
- The beneficiary is always subject to defenses the promisor might have against the promisee, including the usual defenses in contract actions, such as lack of consideration, illegality, and fraud.

Beneficiaries' Rights

In general, a beneficiary under a contract—whether creditor, donee, or intended—can enforce the contract. Suppose, however, that the original parties—the promisor and the promisee—agree to annul or change the contract and to eliminate or reduce the beneficiary's rights.

Parties may agree in a contract either to retain or not to retain the right to eliminate or modify the promisor's duty to the third-party beneficiary. The modern legal trend is to permit the original parties in all cases to cut off the beneficiaries' rights unless the beneficiaries can prove that their positions have changed materially in reasonable reliance on the contracts.

TERMINATION OF A CONTRACT

Once a contract has been established, parties to it have contractual obligations to discharge. Understanding the ways in which those obligations can be discharged is essential to identifying whether a breach of contract may have occurred.

The end of contract obligations discharges a contract, terminating the parties' contractual duties. Parties can discharge their contractual obligations in many ways, including these:

- Complete performance of contractual obligations
- Agreement of the parties
- Substitution of a new contract, by waiver, novation, accord and satisfaction, or other agreements
- Impossibility of performance, such as the destruction of the contractual subject matter
- Fraudulent alteration
- Contractual conditions

Performance

Performance discharges most contracts. When each party fulfills all promises, no obligations remain and the contract ceases to exist. Performance under a contract can occur in a number of ways:

- Payment of a debt discharges the contract.
- Rejection by the other party of a **tender** to perform discharges that obligation. However, rejection of a tender of payment of a debt does not discharge the debt.

  Tender

  An offer to perform one's duties under a contract.

- When contractual obligations are difficult to perform entirely, courts may consider substantial performance sufficient to discharge the contract if the party performed in good faith.
- If a contract promises or guarantees satisfaction, unless the promisor can show bad faith on the promisee's part, obligations are not discharged until the promisee experiences personal and subjective satisfaction. Courts apply an objective standard to determine personal satisfaction relating to utility, fitness, or value.
- If a contract fails to specify a time of performance, each party has a reasonable time to perform. Whether performance occurs within a reasonable time is a question for a court to decide.

Discharge of contractual obligations by rejection of a tender can affect damages and defenses in lawsuits for breach of contract, as well as the amount that can be collected on a debt. See the exhibit "Tender of Performance or Payment."

> ### Tender of Performance or Payment
>
> In a contract for the sale of goods, if the seller attempts to deliver the goods and the other party refuses delivery, the refusal discharges the seller from performance. However, refusal to accept the goods permits the tendering party to sue the refusing party for breach of contract. It also allows the tendering party to defend a later action by the refusing party alleging breach of contract for failure to deliver.
>
> In contrast, if the performance due is the payment of money, a refusal to accept an offer to pay the money will not discharge the debt. A valid tender, however, stops any interest from accruing on the debt, and the most the creditor can collect is the amount due on the date of the tender. For the tender to be valid, it must include the entire amount of the debt.

[DA06396]

Agreement of the Parties

The parties to a contract can agree in advance that a certain event will discharge their obligations to one another. For example, Arthur agrees to paint Josh's house unless Josh sells the house by June 1. If Josh sells the house before June 1, Arthur is discharged from the obligation. The occurrence of that contractual condition (the sale of the house) relieves the parties of performance.

Just as the parties can agree to form a contract, they also can agree to rescind it. Unless the original contract requires that any modification or rescission be in writing, the rescission can be oral. Even if the contract requires written rescission, an attempted oral rescission can be effective as a waiver of the writing requirement. The effectiveness of such a waiver can depend on whether the contract is for the sale of goods or for the sale of land.

Substitution

The parties to a contract can agree to substitute a new contract for a previous one. The decision to replace an old contract with a new one is subject to the same rules that apply to rescission of agreements.

Novation
The substitution of a third party for one of the original parties to a contract, releasing the original party from rights and obligations under the contract.

One type of substitution in contractual agreements is **novation**. For the substitution to be effective, all parties must agree to it. The remaining party must agree to accept the new party and must release the withdrawing party. The latter must consent to withdraw and to permit substitution of the new party. The presence of these essentials discharges the withdrawing party from the contract.

To illustrate, Sean contracts to perform cleaning services for Jennifer. Later, Jennifer and Sean agree that Toby will perform Sean's obligations, and Jennifer expressly releases Sean from the original contract. Toby's agreement to replace Sean discharges Sean from the contract. If Jennifer does not expressly release Sean, no novation occurs. Sean has merely delegated performance to Toby and remains liable under the contract.

An accord and satisfaction is used to discharge a debt. For example, if Bill owes John $200, and they agree that Bill will paint John's home in satisfaction of the debt, an accord exists. Bill's painting the home is the satisfaction that discharges the obligation because the accord and satisfaction are complete.

If Joe owes Lisa $500, Lisa's agreement to accept less than $500 in full payment is not binding unless Lisa receives consideration for the promise to discharge Joe. However, Lisa can agree to discharge the debt for a lesser sum in return for payment before the due date or in return for a lesser sum plus an item of value. The value of the additional item may or may not equal the amount of the unpaid debt. The parties have agreed to performance other than that required by the contract (accord), and performance has occurred (satisfaction).

Impossibility

A promisor's duty to perform is discharged if, after the contract has been formed, performance becomes objectively impossible. If the objectively impossible performance was the major undertaking of the contract, both parties are discharged from all contractual duties. For example, an insurance producer has promised an applicant to place a homeowners insurance policy only with a specific insurer, but that insurer becomes insolvent. Performance is impossible, and the producer is not liable to the applicant.

Three similar terms related to contract performance are sometimes confused—frustration, impracticability, and impossibility:

- Frustration is the prevention of the attainment of a goal. To excuse a party's nonperformance of a contract, frustration must arise from an unforeseeable and uncontrollable circumstance that causes a fundamental change and that is the fault of neither party.

- Impracticability is an excuse for nonperformance of a contractual duty the performance of which, though possible, would be extremely or unreasonably difficult.

- Impossibility is the condition of not being able to occur, exist, or be done, excusing performance.

Impossibility may be either objective or subjective. Objective impossibility means that a promisor cannot conceivably perform. An example would be a one-of-a-kind antique that is destroyed by fire after a contract for its sale is entered. Subjective impossibility means that the promisor will not perform even though performance is conceivable. Most courts hold that only objective impossibility excuses the promisor's performance. Subjective impossibility does not discharge the obligation.

Changes in circumstances affecting contract parties and subject matter can lead to impossibility of performance. Several circumstances may make performance of a contract impossible:

- If a change in law or a governmental act makes performance of an existing contract illegal, the promisor's performance is excused.

- The death or incapacitating illness of a specific person necessary to perform a personal service discharges the duty to perform. Ordinary contracts of production and sale are not personal, so the death or illness of one or both parties does not affect them.

- If the specific subject matter of the contract is destroyed or becomes nonexistent after contract formation without the promisor's fault, impossibility of performance discharges the promisor's duty. Exhaustion of an oil well, for example, discharges a contract to furnish oil.

- If the other party's act prevents the performance of a contract, a court will excuse performance. For example, if a contract requires the promisor to cut trees on the promisee's land, and the promisee prevents entry to the land, the promisor cannot perform and a court will discharge the contract.

Impossibility may affect less than the entire performance of a contract. It may be temporary or partial, or it may arise after the contract has been partially performed. Temporary impossibility suspends, but does not discharge, the promisor's duty. After the impossibility has ended, the duty to perform renews.

If performance is only partially impossible, a court will excuse the duty to perform only to the extent that it is impossible. The promisor must perform the balance of the duty regardless of added expense or difficulty. Impossibility of performance often becomes apparent only after partial performance. The performing party is entitled to payment for reasonable value of all the work performed and other expenses.

A mere additional burden does not constitute legal impossibility. The destruction of a partially completed building, for example, does not make performance impossible. Performance still is possible by starting construction anew, although the cost is greater than anticipated, and the owner must bear the additional cost.

Frustration of purpose can discharge a contract that is possible to perform, when a supervening event destroys the purpose or value of the contract, provided that both parties are aware of that purpose or value. For example, Richard's house is on a street where a parade is scheduled to pass. Richard rents a room to Ashley for the day knowing that she intends to view the parade. If the parade does not pass Richard's house, the frustration of purpose excuses Ashley's performance of the contract.

Fraudulent Alteration

If a party to the contract intentionally makes a material alteration to the contract, the contract is discharged. For example, if the payee on a check fraudulently increases the amount payable, the material alteration discharges the liability of the check's maker to the payee.

Contractual Conditions

Failure to fulfill a contract condition may alter, limit, or discharge contractual obligations. For example, if a party does not deliver goods on the specific day required by the contract, the buyer can treat the nondelivery as a breach of condition that extends the duty to pay to a later date.

Contracts contain three types of conditions:

- Nonfulfillment of a condition precedent can discharge a contractual obligation. For example, filing a notice of loss under an insurance policy is a condition precedent to claim payment. Although it is not a promise, until the insured files a claim, the insurer has no duty to perform its contractual obligation.

- If a contract expressly or impliedly provides that both parties are to perform at the same time, then each party's performance is a **condition concurrent**. For example, a sale of goods contract includes a condition for cash payment upon delivery. If the goods are delivered and the buyer cannot pay, the seller can retain the goods because the buyer cannot perform under the contract. This condition is a promise, and the seller can sue for breach.

Condition concurrent
An event that must occur at the same time as another condition in a contract.

- Occurrence of a **condition subsequent** terminates contractual rights. For example, a store lease in a mall provides that the mall owner is to receive a certain amount of rent plus a percentage of the store's gross sales. If the store's sales drop below a set dollar amount per month (condition subsequent), the lease terminates at the mall's option. If the sales do not reach a set dollar amount per month within a year (condition subsequent), the lease terminates at the mall's option. If either of the conditions subsequent occur, the mall can terminate all lease rights and duties. Neither condition is a promise.

Condition subsequent
An event that, if it occurs, discharges a duty of performance in a contract.

Many contracts contain several conditions that can affect the parties' rights. To determine the legal consequences of the conditions, it is important to know whether they exist as conditions precedent, concurrent, or subsequent. See the exhibit "Insurance Policy Conditions."

> ### Insurance Policy Conditions
>
> The insurance policy is an example of a contract containing multiple conditions, and it is not always easy to determine whether the parties to the policy intended a condition to be precedent or subsequent to liability. Examples of insurance policy conditions include:
>
> - The premium payment is a condition precedent to liability under a policy.
>
> - A loss is a condition precedent to an insurer's liability under a policy.
>
> - A condition that an insured must sue within one year from the date of a loss is a condition subsequent.
>
> - The requirement that an insured submit a notice of loss within sixty days of the loss is either a condition precedent to an insurer's liability or, depending on the wording of the condition, a condition subsequent to the insured's loss. For example, a policy can state, "The insurer's obligation will be discharged if no notice of loss is given within sixty days."
>
> Determination of the intent and legal effect of a condition in an insurance policy often requires careful scrutiny by a court.

[DA06397]

BREACH OF CONTRACT

The parties to a contract do not always fulfill their obligations. What happens in such a case? What options are available to the innocent party who suffers a loss as a result?

A breach of contract can be total or partial and may occur when a party fails to perform acts promised, hinders or prevents performance, or otherwise indicates an intention not to fulfill the contract. The nonbreaching party has legal remedies against a breaching party.

Types of Breach

The remedy for breach may depend on its timing in relation to performance and on its effect on complete performance. Types of breach include those made in repudiation or anticipation, and material and minor breaches.

Repudiation

Repudiation
A party's refusal to meet obligations under a contract.

Repudiation of a contract must be positive and unequivocal to constitute a breach. A statement of inability to perform in the future is not repudiation. For example, Marcus and John formed a contract requiring performance on November 1. If, on October 15, Marcus says to John, "I doubt that I can perform the contract—and, the way prices are going up, I don't think I want to anyway," Marcus has not repudiated the contract and John may not sue for breach. John cannot sue successfully for breach until the time for performance has arrived and Marcus has failed to perform. A party must give a positive repudiation by words as well as by conduct. If, on November 1, Marcus says, "I cannot perform," he has repudiated the contract.

Anticipatory Breach

The concept of **anticipatory breach** developed to avoid "enforced idleness" on the part of an aggrieved party, who must wait until the time of performance to sue for breach, and to make it unnecessary for that party to tender performance at the time stated in the contract to prove the other party's breach.

Anticipatory breach
A party's unequivocal indication before contract performance is due that he or she will not perform when performance is due.

The concept gives the nonbreaching party the option of not waiting until the actual date of performance to determine whether the other party will breach the contract. The aggrieved party can treat the repudiation as a present total breach and can sue immediately if two requirements are present:

- The contract is an executory, bilateral contract entailing mutual and dependent conditions.
- The promisor has made a clear expression of his or her intention not to perform.

For example, Millie promises to sell her land, and Tina promises to buy it, for $150,000 on December 1. On November 15, Tina says to Millie, "I cannot and will not go through with our contract." Tina's statement is a breach of contract by anticipatory repudiation. Millie need not wait until December, but may sue immediately for damages for breach of contract.

Anticipatory breach does not apply to a unilateral contract because the promisee has the option to perform an act and to become entitled to compensation. If the promisee does not perform the act, the promisor has no basis to sue.

Material Breach

Many courts distinguish between **material breach of contract** and minor breach. A material breach allows the nonbreaching party to sue the breaching party for damages. The materiality of the breach is a question of fact. Several circumstances affect the materiality of a breach, including these:

Material breach of contract
Violation of the agreement that would justify an owner's termination of the contract.

- The extent to which the breaching party has performed
- The willfulness of the breach
- The extent to which the nonbreaching party has obtained benefits and can receive adequate compensation

One party's material breach excuses the other party's performance and immediately gives rise to remedies for breach of contract. In contrast, a minor breach causes only slight delay in performance or a slight deviation in quantity or quality. A minor breach can have these effects:

- It may temporarily suspend any duty of performance by the nonbreaching party that would have arisen on proper performance.
- It may give the aggrieved party a basis to sue for damages for the breach—usually an offset to the agreed price—but not for remedies for breach of the entire contract.

Remedies for Breach

If a contract is breached, the injured party can seek a legal remedy by suing to collect money damages. An injured party in a breach of contract for the sale of goods can sue either for money damages or for the price of the goods. Alternatively, an injured party can ask a court for one of two equitable remedies to correct the situation: specific performance of the contract or injunction.

Damages

Damages in breach of contract lawsuits fall into five categories:

- Compensatory
- Consequential
- Punitive
- Extracontractual
- Liquidated

Compensatory damages

A payment awarded by a court to reimburse a victim for actual harm.

Consequential damages

A payment awarded by a court to indemnify an injured party for losses that result indirectly from a wrong such as a breach of contract or a tort.

Punitive damages (exemplary damages)

A payment awarded by a court to punish a defendant for a reckless, malicious, or deceitful act to deter similar conduct; the award need not bear any relation to a party's actual damages.

The most frequent remedy for breach of contract is money damages. **Compensatory damages** are intended to give the injured party the "benefit of the bargain," that is, to place the injured party in approximately the position he or she would be in if the breaching party had performed the contract. Compensatory damages comprise the difference between the value of the promised performance and the plaintiff's cost of obtaining that performance elsewhere. They include losses caused by the breach and gains the breach prevented.

In addition to the standard measure of compensatory contract damages, a breaching party may also be liable for any **consequential damages**. Recoverable losses are those that the defendant, as a reasonable person, should have foreseen at the time of contract formation. A plaintiff can recover consequential damages only when the defendant was aware of the probable occurrence of the loss. See the exhibit "Foreseeable Consequences and Consequential Damages."

Punitive, or exemplary, damages punish a defendant for a reckless, malicious, or deceitful act. To establish their value, courts seek a reasonable ratio of punitive damages to actual damages. Courts more commonly award punitive

Foreseeable Consequences and Consequential Damages

A manufacturer orders a supply of raw materials for delivery on a certain date. The seller does not deliver until after that date, and the manufacturer cannot obtain the materials anywhere else and must shut down the plant. The manufacturer then demands as part of the damages the loss incurred because of the plant shutdown.

Although that loss flowed directly from the breach, the manufacturer cannot successfully sue for these damages because manufacturers usually order raw materials for delivery in advance of actual need. Additionally, raw materials are usually available from substitute sources. The seller, therefore, has no reason to believe that delayed shipment will cause a shutdown. However, if the manufacturer had informed the seller of the critical need and the seller, with that knowledge, promised to deliver on the given day, delayed delivery would make the seller liable for the foreseeable loss arising from the shutdown.

[DA06394]

damages in tort actions, such as for an unprovoked and malicious assault and battery. One purpose of punitive damages is to deter such conduct.

Punitive damages are not appropriate in most contract cases because the purpose of contract damages is to give the plaintiff the benefit of the bargain. However, if a seller of personal property has committed fraud or misrepresentation, punitive damages can be appropriate, based on the fraud rather than on breach of contract. An insurer that has unreasonably delayed a claim payment or contested a claim without reasonable grounds can, by statute, be liable for the insured's attorney's fees as a penalty.

In an insurance case alleging **bad faith,** a court can award **extracontractual damages,** also called excess damages and excess-liability damages. See the exhibit "Extracontractual Damages."

Bad faith (outrage)

An intentional or reckless act, extreme or outrageous in nature, causing severe emotional distress that results in physical injury; generally applied in suits for breach of insurance contracts.

Extracontractual damages

A payment awarded by a court that exceeds the usual contract damages for a breach of contract.

Extracontractual Damages

These are the grounds for assessing extracontractual damages:

- Breach of the insurer's duty of good faith and fair dealing in insurance contracts
- Intentional infliction of emotional distress on the insured by the insurer's extreme and outrageous conduct

Extracontractual damages for either of these causes can include both consequential damages for such things as physical and mental suffering and distress, loss of assets, and attorney fees; and punitive damages. In most cases, extracontractual damages far exceed contract damages resulting from the breach.

Laws relating to bad faith and extracontractual damages vary from state to state and continue to evolve. It is important that practitioners keep current in this area and ensure that they clearly understand relevant law.

[DA06395]

Mitigation of damages
A duty owed by an injured party to a claim to take reasonable measures to minimize or avoid additional injury or loss.

Liquidated damages
A reasonable estimation of actual damages, agreed to by contracting parties and included in the contract, to be paid in the event of a breach or for negligence.

The nonbreaching party to a contract is responsible for **mitigation of damages**. When the buyer breaches a contract for the sale of goods, the seller must dispose of the goods elsewhere at the best price possible. If a seller delivers a defective product and the buyer knows that the product is dangerous and could cause injury, the buyer must not permit its use.

The parties can agree on an amount for **liquidated damages** in the contract. To be valid, the clause must specify a sum determined by the parties' good faith effort to estimate actual damages that probably would result from a breach. A court will not enforce a liquidated damages provision if it finds the damages to be a penalty. In that case, the injured party then must prove actual damages. In either case, a court considers whether the contract involved subject matter that would make damages difficult to ascertain and whether the amount the parties agreed on represented a reasonable estimate of the damages that might actually result from breach.

In a contract for the sale of goods, the seller has two remedies for breach: damages and contract price. The first remedy, damages, is available if the seller appropriately resells the goods and receives less than the contract price. The difference between the contract price and the price on resale is the damages. If the seller receives more than the agreed price, the excess need not go to the buyer and belongs to the seller.

A seller of goods will sue for the agreed contract price only in certain circumstances:[1]

- When the buyer has received and kept the goods
- When the goods are destroyed or damaged after the buyer has assumed the risk of loss
- When the buyer has wrongfully rejected delivery and the goods cannot be sold after reasonable effort to sell them at a reasonable price

Equitable Remedies

In cases involving the sale of goods subject to the Uniform Commercial Code (UCC), a suit for damages is not always an effective remedy. Often, when the burden of loss has passed to the buyer, only equitable remedies can make the nonbreaching party whole. Examples of situations that often give rise only to equitable remedies are these:[2]

- When the buyer has accepted the goods
- When a carrier has tendered the goods to the buyer if the contract requires the seller to ship them to the buyer
- When the seller has delivered the goods to the carrier if the contract provides only for delivery to the carrier and not to the destination
- When a third party holds the goods for delivery without moving them

- When the buyer has received a document indicating the buyer's right to the goods
- When the third party acknowledges the buyer's right to possession

Courts order the equitable remedy of **specific performance** when money damages would be inappropriate or inadequate. To determine whether money damages would be adequate, courts consider these factors:

- The difficulty of valuing the subject matter of the contract
- The existence of sentimental and aesthetic qualities of the subject matter that make it unique
- The difficulty or impossibility of obtaining a duplicate or substantial equivalent of the subject matter

Lawsuits requesting specific performance of a contract occur most frequently in contracts for the sale of real estate, which is unique. A court will order a seller to perform the contract and transfer title to an injured party.

Specific performance is an appropriate remedy for breach of a contract to sell personal property only if the item is in some way unique, such as an antique or a painting.

Courts do not direct specific performance of personal service contracts or any other contracts that would require court supervision to ensure that the performance is adequate.

If the services agreed to under a personal service contract are truly unique, a court can issue an **injunction** to prevent the promisor from performing elsewhere during the term of the contract. For example, a court might enjoin an important soloist who breached a contract from singing elsewhere but probably would not impose that remedy on a singer in an opera chorus who broke a contract, because the latter's performance would not cause loss to the other party.

Commercial contracts containing negative agreements are enforceable by injunction. If an owner sells a business and promises not to compete with the buyer in a given area for a certain time, the restriction is legal. If the seller breaches the provision, the buyer can request an order enjoining the seller from competing.

Injunction is an appropriate remedy in both of these cases because money damages would be inadequate. A court has no way to assess the money value of the soloist's performance, and a series of lawsuits for damages resulting from the illegal competition would be too burdensome on the buyer.

CONTRACTS CASE STUDY

Individuals and organizations often enter into agreements with other parties. Being able to ascertain whether an agreement is a legally enforceable contract

Specific performance
A court-ordered equitable remedy requiring a party to perform a certain act, often—but not always—as a result of breach of a contract.

Injunction
A court-ordered equitable remedy requiring a party to act or refrain from acting.

is essential to determining what an injured party's options are, if any, in the event of a breach of that agreement.

This case study involves an agreement between a builder and the co-owners of a restaurant. Based on the facts provided, these questions are examined:

- Was a valid contract formed?
- Is the contract enforceable?
- Was the contract breached, and, if so, what is the remedy?

Case Facts

Jake and Marta are co-owners of Le Garde-Manger, a popular French-style bistro. The restaurant is located in the town's historic district and backs onto a river. The bistro is especially busy during the summer tourist season, and guests often have to wait for a table. Jake and Marta have decided to build a large deck overlooking the river to allow for more space during the busy summer months. Their goal is to double the bistro's seating capacity.

Jake and Marta contact a number of building contractors. Several visit the site to discuss the project with the owners. Three return with rough sketches and preliminary estimates that range from $16,000 to $30,000. The fourth, Paul, makes an appointment to see the owners the following week and arrives at the meeting with detailed drawings of the proposed deck specifying dimensions, materials, and construction details. Paul's proposal also includes a description of the work to be done and a listing of the labor and materials required to complete the project. He indicates that he has time for the project and would like to do the work for them. See the exhibit "Proposal: Le Garde-Manger Deck Project."

Jake and Marta take several days to consider Paul's proposal and check his references. They discover he has all the required licenses, proper insurance coverage, and an excellent reputation for doing quality work and meeting deadlines. They agree to hire Paul to do the work and arrange to meet with him to discuss the proposal in detail. They make no changes to the original drawings Paul provided. Jake tells Paul, "We like your proposal and we'd like to contract you to do the work." Both he and Marta sign the proposal, as does Paul. They write Paul a check for $5,000 as a deposit payment and agree to pay the balance within thirty days of receipt of the final invoice from Paul.

The parties agree that work will start April 15 and that Jake and Marta will select the stain color that afternoon. On the following day, they e-mail Paul with the stain manufacturer's name and the number of the color they have selected. Paul acknowledges the color selection by return e-mail and informs them that the building inspector approved the drawings that morning.

Work on the deck progresses on schedule. Jake and Marta are excited at the thought of having the work completed in time for the beginning of their summer rush and anticipate that the prospect of dining outdoors overlooking

Proposal: Le Garde-Manger Deck Project

From: Paul Vaughan Construction

To: Jake Olidad and Marta Schweiger
        Co-owners, Le Garde-Manger Bistro

Re: Deck Construction Project

Projected start date: April 15, 20XX
Projected finish date: May 15, 20XX

Project Description: To construct deck, according to all applicable building code requirements for a licensed restaurant establishment, as per the attached drawings with pressure-treated substructure and red cedar decking. Balusters to be black metal. Railing to be cedar. Deck to be sanded and stained with water-based stain in owner's color choice. Owner to provide color choice by April 30, 20XX.

Items included: Repair to existing building as required, compressor and breaker rental, and cost of the building permit.

Projected Costs

Construction:
Materials	$ 18,751
Labor	$ 4,000
Subtotal	$ 22,751

Sanding and Staining:
Materials	$ 160
Labor	$ 500
Subtotal	$ 660
Total Cost	$ 23,411
Deposit	$ 5,000

Signature (Paul Vaughan Construction)

_____

Signatures (Co-Owners, Le Garde-Manger Bistro)

_____

[DA06393]

the river will draw many new customers into the bistro. The building portion of the project is completed on May 4. All that remains is to have the railings sanded and the deck and railings stained.

Paul and his employees do not arrive at the jobsite for several days. On May 8, Paul comes to the bistro and explains that three of his employees were badly injured in an auto accident on the way to work several days earlier, and that he has been called for jury duty. Paul tells Jake and Marta, "I have another really big job starting in a week, and I just don't have enough people available at the moment to finish the sanding and staining on the deck. I'm sorry, but there's nothing I can do."

Jake and Marta are frustrated that Paul is going to repudiate the contract. They insist that the work be completed by the date specified in the agreement and point out that it will hurt their business if they have to wait until later and then close down what they expect to be a popular spot for several days to have the staining done. On the other hand, they can appreciate Paul's predicament. They decide to discuss the situation with their attorney.

Was a Contract Formed?

The first step in resolving this case is determining whether Paul and the owners of Le Garde-Manger have actually formed a contract.

The first element required to establish a contract is agreement—this requires a valid offer and valid acceptance. Three elements make an offer valid:

- Intent to contract
- Definite terms
- Communication to offeree

In this case, Jake and Marta invited several contractors to make an offer to construct the deck. Because Paul is a contractor by profession, his offer to do work for Jake and Marta can be reasonably interpreted as indicating intent to contract. By providing detailed drawings, a project description, and projected labor and materials costs, he outlines clearly and definitely the terms of the offer. Moreover, in both his written proposal and the subsequent meeting, he communicates his offer clearly to Jake and Marta.

Three elements are required to make an acceptance valid:

- It must be made by the offeree.
- It must be unconditional and unequivocal.
- The offeree must communicate the acceptance to the offeror by appropriate word or act.

In this case, Paul made his offer to Jake and Marta as co-owners of the bistro, and they accepted the offer. Their acceptance was unconditional and unequivocal—the details of the project were clearly defined, and they accepted them as proposed. They communicated verbally to Paul both their acceptance of the offer and their intent to contract. They demonstrated acceptance in their actions by making a deposit payment and promptly providing Paul with their choice of stain color.

Certain parties are considered incompetent to contract under most circumstances. These include minors, insane persons, intoxicated persons, and in some situations artificial entities. Paul, Jake, and Marta are all adults, mentally competent, and were not intoxicated at the time that the agreement was reached.

To create an enforceable contract, consideration is required. That consideration must be valuable consideration or forbearance, present or future consideration, and involve a binding promise. In this case, the valuable consideration exchanged for the deck's construction is $23,411. The deposit payment represents present consideration. In addition, the promise to pay the outstanding balance is a binding promise of future consideration because Jake and Marta have contracted with Paul to perform a specific task—to build the deck.

Illegal contracts are unenforceable and fall into nine categories: contracts to commit crimes or torts, contracts harmful to the public interest, usury contracts, wagering contracts, contracts with unlicensed practitioners, contracts to transfer liability for negligence, contracts in restraint of marriage, contracts in restraint of trade, and unconscionable bargains. The agreement between Paul and the owners of Le Garde-Manger does not relate to crimes or torts. The building of a deck is not harmful to the public interest. Paul has all the licenses required to pursue his occupation, and the agreement does not appear to be an unconscionable bargain.

Because, in this case, the offer and acceptance are valid, the parties have legal capacity to contract, valuable consideration is being exchanged, and the agreement is not illegal, a contract has been formed.

Is the Contract Enforceable?

An apparently valid contract may be unenforceable if either party has not given genuine assent to contract. Genuine assent may be lacking if a party was induced to enter a contract by fraud, mistake, duress, undue influence, or innocent misrepresentation.

Fraud is legally defined as a false representation of a material fact knowingly made with intent to deceive on which the other party has placed justifiable reliance to his or her detriment. Material misrepresentation in this situation might involve such actions as Paul's intentional misleading of the bistro owners with regard to his qualifications to do the work or Jake and Marta's intentionally misleading Paul as to their financial condition and ability to pay for the work. In this case, all parties to the agreement acted honestly and in good faith.

As an experienced contractor, Paul demonstrated his competence in preparing drawings that met applicable building codes and in accurately estimating construction work. The proposal and drawings contained no typographical or mathematical errors, and the building inspector approved the drawings. Jake and Marta considered the proposal carefully and willingly agreed to contract with Paul under no duress or undue influence. Neither party has innocently misrepresented material facts to the other. In this case, it would appear that the contract is enforceable.

Was the Contract Breached, and, if so, What Is the Remedy?

The attorney Jake and Marta have consulted regarding Paul's stated intention not to complete the work explains that the concept of anticipatory breach applies to their situation. In anticipatory breach, the aggrieved party can treat the repudiation as a present total breach and can sue immediately if two requirements are present:

- The contract is an executory, bilateral contract entailing mutual and dependent conditions.
- The promisor has made a clear expression of his or her intention not to perform.

Because the contract they have with Paul is bilateral and has not been completely performed, and because Paul has indicated that he intends not to complete the work, Jake and Marta have a cause of action against Paul for breach of contract. They could bring a lawsuit against Paul seeking compensatory damages. For example, if the cost to have the deck stained by another contractor is substantially more than the $660 Paul has quoted, they can recover the difference between those two amounts. In addition, they may be able to sue for consequential damages for such things as loss of income resulting from the breach.

Jake and Marta ask the attorney whether a court could force Paul to complete the work. The attorney explains that courts typically order that remedy, specific performance, only when monetary damages would be inappropriate or inadequate. In this case, monetary damages would be more appropriate, particularly considering the reasons for the breach.

The attorney also points out that, when contractual obligations are difficult to perform entirely, courts may consider substantial performance sufficient to discharge the contract if the party performed in good faith. It appears that Paul has performed in good faith and that, given the relatively small cost of the staining, his work to date might constitute substantial performance. In that case, Jake and Marta would incur the cost of a lawsuit without obtaining any benefit.

The attorney inquires about the relationship between the restaurant owners and the builder, and Marta concedes that it had been very good until this disagreement. The attorney discourages Jake and Marta from pursuing a court action and suggests an alternative. If Jake, Marta, and Paul can agree to new terms, they have the option to amend their original agreement. One option would be to amend the contract to include only the deck construction at the original quoted value for that work of $22,751. Alternatively, they could agree to novation and simply release Paul Vaughn Construction from the original contract and substitute another firm to complete the project.

After discussing the situation, Jake and Marta approach a painting contractor about the project. The painter inspects the site and offers to do the staining work for $600. Jake and Marta indicate that they would like to discuss the situation with Paul before accepting his offer, and the painter agrees. Jake and Marta meet with Paul and propose amending the contract to include only the deck construction at the original quoted value for that work of $22,751. Paul is relieved to reach cooperative agreement in what for him has been an embarrassing situation. He makes handwritten changes to both his copy and the owners' copy of the original agreement, and all parties initial the changes and date and re-sign the amended contract. Paul is relieved from further performance under the original contract, and Jake and Marta are free to contract the alternative painting contractor.

In this case, because there has been a valid offer and acceptance, the parties have legal capacity to contract, valuable consideration is being exchanged, and the agreement is not illegal, a contract has been formed. Genuine assent is present because none of the parties were induced to enter the contract by fraud, mistake, duress, undue influence, or innocent misrepresentation. Because the contract is bilateral and executory, and Paul has indicated that he intends not to complete the work promised, Jake and Marta have a cause of action against Paul for breach of contract. In court, they could seek compensatory damages and perhaps consequential damages. Specific performance would not be an appropriate remedy in this case. Alternatively, Jake, Marta, and Paul can agree to amend the terms of their original agreement or to execute a novation.

SUMMARY

A contract may be bilateral or unilateral, executed or executory, express or implied, void or voidable.

A valid offer to contract requires that the offeror intend to enter into a legally binding contract, that the offer includes definite terms, and that the offer be communicated to the offeree. Duration and termination are key to determining whether an offer is binding, and the factors considered include lapse of time, operation of law, the offeree's rejection, counteroffers, and the offeror's revocation.

A valid agreement to contract requires the presentation of an offer by the offeror and an acceptance of that offer by the offeree. To create an enforceable contract, acceptance must meet three requirements:

- The acceptance must be made by the offeree.
- The acceptance must be unconditional and unequivocal.
- The offeree must communicate the acceptance to the offeror by appropriate word or act.

Minors, insane persons, and intoxicated persons generally cannot enter into legally binding contracts because they are not considered competent to do so. Under some circumstances, however, these parties can contract. Artificial entities, such as corporations, can generally contract, but their ability to do so may be limited by their charter.

Five types of consideration are sufficient for forming an enforceable contract: valuable consideration, forbearance, present consideration, future consideration, and binding promises. Each type of consideration has its own set of legal rules.

Three types of consideration are not considered sufficient for forming a binding contract: past consideration, promises to perform existing obligations, and compromise and release of claims.

In some cases, contracts are enforceable for equitable or public policy reasons despite the lack of consideration. Contracts without consideration are enforceable when promissory estoppel applies or in some cases involving charitable subscriptions.

The nine categories of illegal contract are: contracts to commit crimes or torts, contracts harmful to the public interest, usury contracts, wagering contracts, contracts with unlicensed practitioners, contracts to transfer liability for negligence, contracts in restraint of marriage, contracts in restraint of trade, and unconscionable bargains. Although courts generally do not enforce illegal contracts, they may do so when a specific group is protected by law, in the case of *in pari delicto* agreements, or in severable contracts that contain legal provisions.

Genuine assent may be lacking if a party was induced to enter a contract through fraud, mistake, duress, undue influence, or innocent misrepresentation. When genuine assent is lacking, the innocent party has the right to avoid the contract. In these cases, courts do not uphold the contracts and sometimes award monetary damages to the wronged parties.

Under state statutes of fraud, some contracts must be in writing to be enforceable. Generally, when a contract is in writing, oral evidence cannot be used to change the terms of the agreement. However, oral evidence can be used to prove missing contract terms, clarify ambiguities, support an allegation of wrongdoing, or demonstrate the failure of a condition precedent.

When courts are interpreting ambiguous or unclear contracts, words are understood in their plain meaning. The goal is effectuation of the parties' intent. Contracts are classed as entire or divisible, clerical errors and omissions are corrected, contradictory terms are prioritized, ambiguities are interpreted against the writer of a document, and the parties' own interpretations are considered. Courts seek a legal and fair interpretation, and trade usage, course of dealings, and performance are considered.

A third party ordinarily does not have any rights under contracts made by other parties. However, in two situations third parties do have enforceable rights under contracts others have made: assignment and third-party beneficiary contracts.

Although most contract rights are assignable, some are not. To be effective, an assignment needs neither formality nor writing. A primary obligation to perform usually remains with the assignor. In general, if a party assigns rights to the assignee, the third party can enforce against either the assignee or the assignor, but not against both.

Third-party beneficiary contracts benefit creditor beneficiaries, donee beneficiaries, and incidental beneficiaries. Donee and creditor beneficiaries, referred to as intended beneficiaries, have enforceable rights against the original promisor, but an incidental beneficiary has no enforceable rights.

Parties can discharge their contractual obligations by complete performance, agreement of the parties, substitution of a new contract, impossibility of performance, or operation of law. In addition, failure to fulfill a contract condition may alter, limit, or discharge contractual obligations.

A breach of contract can occur through repudiation or anticipatory breach, and breaches can be either material or minor. In the case of a breach of contract, the nonbreaching party can sue for compensatory damages, consequential damages, and in some cases for punitive damages. Extracontractual damages can be awarded against insurers. Parties to a contract can also agree on an amount of liquidated damages when the contract is formed. When money damages are an inappropriate or inadequate remedy for breach of contract, a nonbreaching party can seek equitable remedies including specific performance and injunctions.

Given the facts of a particular case, in order to determine whether a contract is legally enforceable it is necessary to establish two things.

- Was a valid contract formed?
- Is the contract enforceable?

If a contract is legally enforceable and a breach occurs, remedies and other options are available to the innocent party injured by the breach.

ASSIGNMENT NOTES

1. UCC, § 2-709.
2. UCC, § 2-509. *See also* UCC, § 2-510.

Direct Your Learning ▶▶

Contract Law: Insurance Applications

Educational Objectives

After learning the content of this assignment, you should be able to:

▷ Describe these characteristics of insurance contracts:

- A conditional contract
- A contract involving fortuitous events and the exchange of unequal amounts
- A contract of utmost good faith
- A contract of adhesion
- A contract of indemnity
- A nontransferable contract

▷ Describe the unique characteristics of insurance contract formation with regard to these aspects:

- Agreement
- Content
- Delivery

▷ Describe under what circumstances a third party can benefit from an insurance contract.

▷ Explain how representations and warranties affect the creation and voidability of an insurance contract.

▷ Explain how the following concepts legally prevent an insurer from reviving a defense it has forfeited earlier:

- Waiver
- Estoppel
- Election

▷ Explain how nonwaiver agreements and reservation of rights letters affect insurers' and insureds' rights.

Outline

Special Characteristics of Insurance Contracts

Insurance Contract Formation

Insurance as Third-Party Beneficiary Contract

Representations and Warranties in Insurance

Waiver, Estoppel, and Election

Nonwaiver Agreements and Reservation of Rights Letters

Summary

Contract Law: Insurance Applications

SPECIAL CHARACTERISTICS OF INSURANCE CONTRACTS

Insurance contracts must contain all the necessary elements of a legally enforceable contract and are in many ways similar to other contracts. However, insurance contracts have distinctive features and their own body of law.

In addition to having the four essential elements of all contracts, insurance contracts have certain special characteristics:

- They are conditional.
- They involve fortuitous events and the exchange of unequal amounts.
- They are contracts of utmost good faith.
- They are contracts of adhesion.
- They are contracts of indemnity.
- They are nontransferable.

Conditional Contract

An insurance policy, in addition to having the four essential elements of all contracts, is a **conditional contract**. Whether the insurer pays a claim depends on whether a covered loss has occurred. Additionally, the insured must fulfill certain duties before a claim is paid, such as giving prompt notice to the insurer after a loss has occurred. See the exhibit "Elements of a Contract."

Conditional contract
A contract that one or more parties must perform only under certain conditions.

Elements of a Contract

A contract must have each of these elements to be legally enforceable:

- Agreement
- Capacity to contract
- Consideration
- Legal purpose

[DA06178]

A covered loss might not occur during a particular policy period, but that fact does not mean the insurance policy for that period has been worthless. In buying an insurance policy, the insured acquires a valuable promise—the promise of the insurer to make payments if a covered loss occurs. The promise exists, even if the insurer's performance is not required during the policy period.

Contract Involving Fortuitous Events and the Exchange of Unequal Amounts

While noninsurance contracts involve an exchange of money for a certain event, such as the provision of goods or services, insurance contracts involve an exchange of money for protection upon the occurrence of uncertain, or fortuitous, events. Insurance contracts involve an exchange of unequal amounts. Often, there are few or no losses, and the premium paid by the insured for a particular policy is more than the amount paid by the insurer to, or on behalf of, the insured. If a large loss occurs, however, the insurer's claim payment might be much more than the premium paid by the insured. The possibility that the insurer's obligation may be much greater than the insured's makes the insurance transaction a fair trade.

For example, suppose an insurer charges a $1,000 annual premium to provide auto physical damage coverage on a car valued at $20,000. Three situations may occur:

- If the car is not damaged while the policy is in force, the insurer pays nothing.
- If the car is partially damaged, the insurer pays the cost of repairs, after subtracting a deductible.
- If the car is a total loss, the insurer pays $20,000 (minus any deductible).

Unless, by chance, the insurer's obligations in a minor accident come to exactly $1,000, unequal amounts are involved in all three of these cases. However, it does not follow that insureds who have no losses—or only very minor losses—do not get their money's worth or that insureds involved in major accidents profit from the insurance.

The premium for a particular policy should reflect the insured's share of estimated losses that the insurer must pay. Many insureds have no losses, but some have very large losses. The policy premium reflects the insured's proportionate share of the total amount the insurer expects to pay to honor its agreements with all insureds having similar policies.

Contract of Utmost Good Faith

Utmost good faith
An obligation to act in complete honesty and to disclose all relevant facts.

Because insurance involves a promise, it requires complete honesty and disclosure of all relevant facts from both parties. For this reason, insurance contracts are considered contracts of **utmost good faith**. Both parties to an insurance contract—the insurer and the insured—are expected to be honest and forthcoming in their dealings with each other.

The insured has a right to rely on the insurer to fulfill its promises. Therefore, the insurer is expected to treat the insured with utmost good faith. An insurer that acts in bad faith, such as denying coverage for a claim that it knows is clearly covered, could face serious penalties under the law.

The insurer also has a right to expect that the insured will act in good faith. An insurance buyer who intentionally conceals certain information or misrepresents certain facts does not act in good faith. Because an insurance contract requires utmost good faith from both parties, an insurer could be released from a contract because of concealment or misrepresentation by the insured.

Concealment is an intentional failure to disclose a material fact. Courts have held that the insurer must prove two things to establish that concealment has occurred. First, it must establish that the failure to disclose information was intentional, which is often difficult. The insurer must usually show that the insured knew that the information should have been given and then intentionally withheld it. Second, the insurer must establish that the information withheld was a material fact. In the case of an auto insurance applicant, for example, material facts include the use of the applicant's autos, the identity of the drivers, and the ages and driving records of the drivers. If an insured intentionally conceals the material fact that her sixteen-year-old son lives in the household and is the principal driver of one of her cars, the insurer could avoid (reject) the policy based on that concealment.

Insurers carefully design applications for insurance to include questions regarding facts material to the underwriting process. The application includes questions on specific subjects, which the applicant must answer. These questions are designed to encourage the applicant to reveal all pertinent information.

In normal usage, a misrepresentation is a false statement. As used in insurance, a **misrepresentation** is a false statement of a material fact on which the insurer relies. The insurer does not have to prove that the misrepresentation is intentional.

Misrepresentation
A false statement of a material fact on which a party relies.

For example, assume an applicant for auto insurance has had two speeding tickets during the eighteen months immediately before he submitted his application for insurance. When asked whether any driving violations have occurred within the past three years (a question found on most auto insurance application forms), an applicant giving either of these answers would be making a misrepresentation:

- "I remember having one speeding ticket about two years ago."
- "I've never been cited for a moving violation—only a few parking tickets."

The first response provides incorrect information, and this false statement may or may not be intentional. The false statement made in the second response is probably intentional. The direct question posed in the application requires a full and honest response from the applicant because the insurer relies on the information. Anything less is a misrepresentation, whether intentional or not. As with concealment, if a material fact is misrepresented, the insurer could choose to avoid the policy because of the violation of utmost good faith. The laws regarding concealment and misrepresentation can vary by jurisdiction. An insurance practitioner should consult with competent legal counsel before attempting to avoid an insurance contract.

In insurance, it is customary for the parties to agree that they will not contest the validity of the contract after a certain period even if the contract is based on a material misrepresentation or the concealment of a material fact. This agreement in an insurance contract, the **incontestable clause**, is required by all states in life, accident and health, and group life insurance policies.

Incontestable clause

A clause that states that the insurer cannot contest the policy after it has been in force for a specified period, such as two years, during the insured's lifetime.

Unique to insurance, the incontestable clause is contrary to one of the basic maxims in contract law: that "fraud vitiates [negates] consent." Genuine assent cannot be based on fraud. In life insurance and accident and health insurance, the maxim is that "fraud vitiates consent, except in an insurance contract after the contestable period has expired." Therefore, an insurer cannot assert material misrepresentation, concealment, or fraud in connection with life insurance applications when the policy has been in force longer than the **contestable period**, usually two years, during the insured's life. The contestable period is a period during which an insurer can challenge the validity of a life insurance policy. The insurer agrees to waive these defenses after this period. Incontestable clauses are considered valid because the insurer has reasonable opportunity to investigate an applicant's statements during the contestable period.

Contestable period

A period during which an insurer can challenge the validity of a life insurance policy.

Although the incontestable clause applies to fraud, if the fraud is particularly vicious, a court can permit proof of fraud even after the contestable period has expired and can find the policy was invalid at the outset. For example, when one purchases a life insurance policy to profit from the murder of the insured, or when another person takes the insured's medical examination, the incontestable clause will not prevent the insurer from legally refusing to pay insurance proceeds. The public policy against these flagrant wrongs outweighs the reasons for the incontestable clause.

Contract of Adhesion

The wording in insurance contracts is usually drafted by the insurer (or an insurance advisory organization), enabling the insurer to use preprinted forms for many different insureds. Because the insurer determines the exact wording of the policy, the insured has little choice but to "take it or leave it." That is, the insured must adhere to the contract drafted by the insurer. Therefore, insurance policies are considered to be **contracts of adhesion**, which means

Contract of adhesion

Any contract in which one party must either accept the agreement as written by the other party or reject it.

one party (the insured) must adhere to the contract as written by the other party (the insurer). This characteristic significantly influences the enforcement of insurance policies.

If a dispute arises between the insurer and the insured about the meaning of certain words or phrases in the policy, the insured and the insurer are not on an equal basis. The insurer either drafted the policy or used standard forms of its own choice; in contrast, the insured did not have any say in the policy wording. For that reason, if the policy wording is ambiguous, a court will generally apply the interpretation that favors the insured.

Contract of Indemnity

The purpose of insurance is to provide indemnification—that is, to indemnify an insured who suffers a loss. To indemnify is to restore a party who has had a loss to the same financial position that party held before the loss occurred. Most property and liability insurance policies are **contracts of indemnity**.

Property insurance generally pays the amount of money necessary to repair covered property that has been damaged or to replace it with similar property. The policy specifies the method for determining the amount of the loss. For example, most auto policies, both personal and commercial, specify that vehicles are to be valued at their actual cash value (ACV) at the time of a loss. If a covered accident occurs that causes a covered vehicle to be a total loss, the insurer will normally pay the ACV of the vehicle, less any applicable deductible.

Liability insurance generally pays to a third-party claimant, on behalf of the insured, any amounts (up to the policy limit) that the insured becomes legally obligated to pay as damages due to a covered liability claim, as well as the legal costs associated with that claim. For example, if an insured with a liability limit of $300,000 is ordered by a court to pay $100,000 for bodily injury incurred by the claimant in a covered accident, the insurer will pay $100,000 to the claimant and will also pay the cost to defend the insured in court.

A contract of indemnity does not necessarily pay the full amount necessary to restore an insured who has suffered a covered loss to the same financial position. However, the amount the insurer pays is directly related to the amount of the insured's loss. Most policies contain a policy limit that specifies the maximum amount the insurer will pay for a single claim. Many policies also contain limitations and other provisions that could reduce the amount of recovery.

For example, a homeowners policy is not designed to cover large amounts of cash. Therefore, most homeowners policies contain a special limit, such as $200, for any covered loss to money owned by the insured. If a covered fire destroys $1,000 in cash belonging to the insured, the homeowners insurer will pay only $200 for the money that was destroyed.

Contract of indemnity

A contract in which the insurer agrees, in the event of a covered loss, to pay an amount directly related to the amount of the loss.

Principle of indemnity

The principle that insurance policies should provide a benefit no greater than the loss suffered by an insured.

Insurance policies usually include certain provisions that reinforce the **principle of indemnity**. For example, policies generally contain an "other insurance" provision to prevent an insured from receiving full payment from two different insurance policies for the same claim.

Insurance contracts usually protect the insurer's subrogation rights. Other insurance provisions and subrogation provisions clarify that the insured cannot collect more than the amount of the loss. For example, following an auto accident in which the insurer compensates its insured when the other driver is at fault, the subrogation provision stipulates that the insured's right to recover damages from the responsible party is transferred (subrogated) to the insurer. The insured cannot collect from both the insurer and the responsible party.

Another factor enforcing the principle of indemnity is that a person usually cannot buy insurance unless that person is in a position to suffer a financial loss. In other words, the insured must have an insurable interest in the subject of the insurance. For example, property insurance contracts cover losses only to the extent of the insured's insurable interest in the property. This restriction prevents an insured from collecting more from the insurance than the amount of the loss he or she suffered.

Likewise, a person cannot buy life insurance on the life of a stranger, hoping to gain if the stranger dies. Insurers normally sell life insurance when there is a reasonable expectation of a financial loss from the death of the insured person, such as the loss of an insured's future income that the insured's dependents would face. Insurable interest is not an issue in liability insurance because a liability claim against an insured results in a financial loss if the insured is legally responsible. Even if the insured is not responsible, the insured could incur defense costs.

Valued policy

A policy in which the insurer pays a stated amount in the event of a specified loss (usually a total loss), regardless of the actual value of the loss.

Some insurance contracts are not contracts of indemnity but instead are **valued policies**. For example, a fine arts policy might specify that it will pay $250,000 for the loss of a particular painting or sculpture. The actual market value of the painting or sculpture may be smaller or greater than $250,000, but the policy will pay $250,000 in either case. In most valued policies, the insurer and the insured agree on a limit that approximates the current market value of the insured property.

Nontransferable Contract

The identities of the persons or organizations insured are extremely relevant to the insurer, which has the right to select those applicants with whom it is willing to enter into contractual agreements. After an insurance policy is in effect, an insured may not freely transfer, or assign, the policy to some other party. If such a transfer were allowed to take place, the insurer would be legally bound to a contract with a party it might not wish to insure. Most insurance policies contain a provision that requires the insurer's written permission before an insured can transfer a policy to another party.

Traditionally, insurance textbooks used the language that "insurance is a personal contract" to indicate its nontransferable nature and have cited clauses in property policies to illustrate the principle. The policy language does differ between typical property and liability policies, but in both types, the intention is to prohibit the insured from transferring the policy to another party without the insurer's consent.

INSURANCE CONTRACT FORMATION

An insurer and insured form an insurance contract, by which the insurer provides protection if the insured suffers specified losses. When the insurance contract becomes a formal written document, it is an insurance policy.

An insurance contract has unique characteristics with regard to these aspects:

- Agreement, including issues concerning offer and acceptance, effective date, and silence or delay
- Content, which can be oral or informally written, must include necessary terms, can include implied terms, and must include insurer designation
- Delivery, which is the placement of the policy in the insured's control

Agreement

Insurance sales are almost always handled by insurance producers, who represent insurers as agents and insureds as brokers. Insurers rely on agents to solicit business, take applications, and sometimes issue policies. Agents can create contract liability for insurers even though the insurer may not have intended to be bound. Under the law of agency, insurance agents' commitments can be binding on insurers. An insurance policy, like any other contract, must contain the four necessary elements of a contract. See the exhibit "Elements of a Contract."

Elements of a Contract

A contract must have each of these elements to be legally enforceable:

- Agreement
- Capacity to contract
- Consideration
- Legal purpose

[DA06178]

Offer and Acceptance

When a producer contacts a prospective insured to sell an insurance policy, is the producer making an offer to contract or merely soliciting offers? Generally, the producer's selling efforts are merely a solicitation of offers that the insurer might not accept and are not offers themselves. The insurance application, signed by the applicant and sent to the insurer through the producer, is the offer. The insurance policy issued later is the acceptance. If the policy issued does not conform to the application—the initial offer—the policy is a counteroffer requiring the applicant's specific acceptance.

Often the insurance applicant does not make an offer but merely invites the insurer to make an offer. For example, if an applicant has not decided to take the insurance but submits an application to determine whether the insurer will accept the risk, the application is not an offer. In that case, when the insurer issues the policy and the insured accepts it by paying the premium, they have concluded an offer and acceptance. Similarly, if the policy as issued does not comply with the coverage or rates the applicant requested, the policy is a new offer that the applicant can then accept or reject.

As with contracts in general, the communication of the offer to the offeree is essential in an insurance agreement. Only the person to whom an offer is addressed, or that person's agent, can accept an offer. For example, if a proposed insured has died before taking action to accept a policy, the widowed spouse cannot accept the offer.

The mailing of an acceptance binds an insurance contract at the time of mailing, whether or not the other party receives it. Thus, if the insurer's issuance of a policy is the offer, the insured's mailing the premium in response to that offer is the binding acceptance.

For property and casualty, oral insurance contracts are as binding as written ones. When the insurance producer has authority to enter into oral agreements to bind coverage, the parties' words and conduct govern the offer and acceptance just as with any other contract. Generally, acts or words of intent to offer and accept establish a binding insurance contract. For example, Mary calls her insurance agent asking to increase the limits on her policy, and the agent tells her, "Done! We'll send you the revised policy in the mail." Before Mary receives the policy, she suffers a loss that exceeds the previous limits of her policy. The agent's oral promise is binding and will hold the insurer responsible for the promised higher coverage limits. In property-casualty insurance, oral applications and contracts are common.

When an agreement between a producer and a prospective insured for a property-casualty insurance policy does not specify immediate coverage, examination of the parties' conversations, as well as the producer's authority, is necessary to determine when the policy became effective. Without the immediate coverage requirement, the application is an offer that the insurer can accept by issuing a policy conforming with the offer.

Effective Date

Determination of the exact moment when insurance contract coverage begins and ends can be crucial in some cases when a loss occurs. Unless a loss occurs within the policy coverage period, no benefits are payable.

The general rules of contract law concerning the time at which acceptance becomes effective also apply to the insurance contract. Frequently the policy itself specifies the effective date and time of the contract. Binders and conditional receipts have both aided and complicated the law with respect to the effective dates of insurance contracts. **Binders** frequently apply to property-casualty insurance, and conditional receipts apply to life insurance.

The binding slip, or binder receipt, although temporary in nature, provides evidence of insurance and interim coverage until the policy is issued. Binders are informal written contracts summarizing the basic coverages and terms of the insurance agreement. They frequently provide extension of coverage for thirty days, pending issuance of the policy.

Even though a binder is usually evidence of an insurance contract, the insurer can produce evidence to prove that the parties orally agreed that the insurance was not to take effect until a specific condition was met. For instance, the parties might have agreed that temporary coverage was not to be effective until another insurer assumed part of the risk.

Absent such conditions, all policy provisions are effective the moment the binder is created. The binder is effective until actual notice of cancellation or until a policy is issued. An insurer's cancellation of a binder must conform to the methods the policy prescribes.

In property-casualty insurance, binders provide immediate coverage when issued by authorized agents. Most insurers have written policies that control the binder's actual coverage. Although brief, the binder must contain the basic information needed for an agreement and must indicate types of coverage.

The binder should identify the insurer and the insured. If an object such as a car is insured, the binder should describe the car briefly and indicate the amounts of coverage clearly enough to establish policy limits. With agreement on these basic points, the more detailed policy provisions can be determined by referring to the policy the insurer will issue.

Silence or Delay

Contract law requires unequivocal manifestation of both parties' mutual assent, by either words or conduct. At common law, courts consider either a party's silence or a party's delay as equivocal and insufficient acceptance to form a contract.

This rule was subject to the qualification that if a prior course of dealings indicated that silence was acceptance, those prior dealings would determine

Binder

A temporary written or oral agreement to provide insurance coverage until a formal written policy is issued.

acceptance. For example, Gina, a producer, has for many years handled insurance on Mike's property under annual policies. At the expiration of a policy, and consistent with prior dealings, Gina sends Mike a renewal policy and a bill for the premium. This year, Mike holds the policy for two months, remaining silent, and then refuses to pay the premium on demand. Mike is liable for the premium that accrued before his rejection. The course of prior dealings between the parties gave Gina, the offeror producer, a reasonable basis for concluding that silence would constitute acceptance.

Assume instead that Gina directs a letter to Mike indicating that "Your home-owners insurance policy will be renewed for another three years unless I hear from you to the contrary." Mike does not reply. Because there was no prior course of dealings indicating that Gina could infer acceptance by silence, continued coverage does not result automatically. Mike's silence is not an unequivocal promise to accept Gina's promise to renew and is not sufficient to infer acceptance.

Another reason for the contract rule that mere silence is not an acceptance of an offer involves unsolicited offers. If silence were always acceptance of an offer, salespeople could flood consumer mail with offers that would bind recipients to buy unless they expressly rejected the offer. The law prohibits sellers from forcing prospective buyers to reject or return offered goods or services. The enterprising insurance agent who mails policies to everyone in the area advising, "Unless I hear from you in a week, I will assume that you accept this coverage" imposes no duty to respond on the recipients of the offers. If a merchant mails an unsolicited item to a person's home, the recipient has no duty to respond or to return the item.

Similarly, when an applicant submits an application for coverage to an insurer and the insurer fails to act within a reasonable time, the insurer's silence or delay is not acceptance. An insurer, however, can be liable under its contract if it delays action on an application beyond a reasonable time. Courts apply the rationale in this situation that insurance is a business affected with a public interest. Because insurers have generally solicited these offers, and because applicants frequently pay premiums in advance, the insurer must act promptly in accepting or rejecting the offer.

The nature of the insurance business imposes a duty to act on the insurer when considering applications for insurance. Some courts consider the obligation an implied contract, while others assert that after the lapse of a reasonable time, the insurance company should be estopped, or prevented, from claiming that the application was not accepted. Most courts, however, base recovery on the theory that the insurer has been negligent, having breached its duty to act on the application without unreasonable delay. If the applicant suffers a loss as a result, then the insurer can be held liable. The court bases recovery on the tort of negligence instead of on contract law. What constitutes unreasonable delay is a question of fact, not law. A court will consider some important facts:

- The distance of the insurer's office from the agent's office at which the applicant submitted the application
- Special difficulties in underwriting the risk
- The insurer's seasonal or other workload problems
- The type of coverage involved

Some state statutes prescribe the time limits within which an insurer must act on an application. The issue of unreasonable delay can arise despite the immediate coverage provided by property-casualty binders or life insurance conditional receipts. Property insurance binders often stipulate coverage for "thirty days only." Life insurance conditional receipts can be conditional and might not provide any interim coverage. In either case, an unreasonable delay in acting on the application could result in the insurer's liability for coverage.

Insurance Policy Content

The insurance contract is usually a result of negotiations. A frequent question concerns which papers and conversations form the ultimate contract. Once an insurer writes the policy, courts consider all prior negotiations or agreements, written or oral, as merged into the writing. Every contractual term in the policy at the time of delivery, as well as those written in afterwards as policy riders or endorsements with both parties' consent, are part of the written policy. The policy must refer to conditions, endorsements, applications, and other papers if they are to be part of the policy.

Insurers' advertising materials and circulars are not part of a policy unless the contract expressly states that they are. If these materials contain false representations, an insured can sue the insurer for fraud, but courts do not usually allow the wording of advertising materials to change actual policy terms.

Written Versus Oral and Informal Written Contracts

Even though oral insurance contracts are valid, written policies are preferable. Oral agreements often give rise to lawsuits, usually involving the insurer's word against the insured's, with a court making final judgment. An insured who does not have a written policy may be unable to recall an oral conversation with sufficient accuracy to persuade a jury of its content.

Oral contracts to write property-casualty insurance are common, particularly when the applicant completes the application process and binder by telephone. In all oral insurance contracts, as well as in the case of informal written contracts, such as preliminary binders and conditional receipts, the final contract is the policy form itself. The crucial question is what contract language is in force from the time of the original oral agreement or informal written contract until the insurer writes the insurance contract into a policy.

Necessary Terms in Insurance Contracts

To be effective, an agreement to insure, whether oral or written, must have these components:

- The types of coverage sought—The risks or events covered must be specific, such as fire, accident, liability, or life.

- The object or premises, if any, to be insured—If liability insurance in connection with ownership of property is involved, for example, the address of the premises must be clear. If the policy says only "my residence" and the proposed insured has several residences, the identification is ambiguous and can result in no coverage.

- The amount of insurance—This component establishes policy limits and the insurer's liability.

- The insured's name—While it is necessary to identify the insured, the establishment of the insurer's identity at the moment of the agreement is not necessary (as when a producer acts for an insurer).

- The duration of coverage—In some cases, duration of coverage might be implied from the parties' past dealings.

Implied Terms in Insurance Contracts

If the parties have agreed to the basic elements, then they and the courts can turn to several other sources, including previous dealings between the parties, customary usage of terms, and legal requirements, to establish the terms from the oral or informal written agreement.

Previous dealings between the parties provide the most accurate bases for determining implied terms of an insurance contract. If an insured has requested that a producer "renew my fire policy," the renewed policy implies all the terms of the previous policy, including the coverage and premium amounts. Provisions of renewal contracts by implication are the same as those of an existing policy. An insurer's customary usage of terms provides another important source for establishing terms the parties have not mentioned explicitly, such as the type of policy an insurer usually issues in a given situation or the type of policy most insurers usually issue.

The policy language and conditions set forth in the insurer's other policies are a good source for supplying implied terms. If the insurer does not usually provide a certain coverage, it is implied that the policy in question contains the provisions of policies the insurer customarily issues for the unclear coverage. When the parties have not specified the premium amount and the insurer and insured have had no previous dealings, a court will conclude that the contract implies the rate the insurer has filed with the insurance regulatory authorities or the rate the insurer usually charges others for the same type of risk.

Finally, courts consider the insured's coverage needs and practices by comparing them with those of others engaged in similar endeavors. Even so, while these needs and practices can bear on the implied terms, an insured's unique situation might not necessarily result in implied insurance provisions.

In many lines of coverage, statutory and administrative requirements have prescribed policy language. When an oral contract or a binding receipt for homeowners insurance is involved, statutory provisions usually contain all applicable language. State law prescribes many provisions, such as definitions of terms, the right to convert group life insurance to other types of coverage, and life insurance coverage in the event of suicide.

Insurance Company Designation

A producer representing two or more insurers can agree to provide coverage to an applicant without designating the insurer's identity at the outset. If a loss occurs before an insurer issues a policy, a question can arise as to which insurer the producer intended to bind coverage.

If a producer has placed previous business or oral renewals for an insured with a particular insurer, that producer's acceptance of another oral agreement usually binds the same insurer. The parties' previous dealings imply that insurer's liability. However, when the parties have had no previous dealings, or when the producer has changed insurers several times for renewals, more difficult problems arise.

If the producer has made a note or memorandum indicating that an insurer will write the coverage, the note is sufficient to bind that insurer. The producer must have made some outward indication of intent. For instance, a calendar notation might be a sufficient record. The producer's mere mental resolve to place business with "Insurer A tomorrow" is not sufficient to bind Insurer A if the loss occurs before the producer makes an actual notation.

The needs of modern business require and justify reliance on insurance producers' oral agreements formed while acting within their apparent authority. Courts reason that producers have considerable latitude in granting oral binders.

Delivery of Insurance Policies

Delivery is placing an insurance policy in the insured's control. Key legal issues concerning delivery involve whether the parties have intended a contract to become effective before delivery of the final contract. General contract law does not require delivery of a contract for it to be enforceable.

In most bilateral contracts involving the exchange of promises, delivery is not essential to contract formation. In unilateral contracts involving an offeree's performance of an act, delivery of goods or services may be necessary as acceptance.

In the case of insurance contracts, no common law or statutory enactment requires delivery of an insurance policy to complete its formation. Still, in cases in which no oral agreement, binder, or other written memorandum exists, the contract usually does not bind the insurer until delivery of the policy and the first premium payment. Delivery provides evidence of contract formation and communication of the insurer's acceptance of the insured's offer. The insurance policy is binding only upon delivery.

In property-casualty insurance, delivery is rarely in dispute. The wide use of preliminary oral agreements and written binders gives rise to effective dates of coverage that seldom involve the question of policy delivery.

A property-casualty insurance producer usually collects one of these at the time the applicant completes the application and the producer provides the binder:

- A down payment on the premium
- Complete payment of the premium
- A promise of payment by means of a payment plan or a premium financing arrangement

As in the case of policy delivery, the insurance contract parties can stipulate that the policy is not effective until the first premium payment is made. In the absence of a clear and express agreement, generally the first premium payment is not necessary to establish the validity of an oral preliminary contract, but payment will occur upon policy delivery.

Even in the absence of an express promise to pay a premium, an implied promise to pay a reasonable premium is sufficient consideration to support an insurance contract. However, if the parties clearly intend that no contract is to form until the first premium payment, then that intent is the determining factor. See the exhibit "Practice Exercise."

Practice Exercise

Case Facts

Yates has purchased all his property and liability policies from Alpha Insurance Company through Al's Agency, which represents Alpha, Beta, and Omega Insurance Companies. Al's Agency, having learned that Yates purchased a boat, mailed Yates a letter suggesting insuring the boat for $10,000 and quoting the premium for this coverage. Before receiving that letter and wanting to protect his new boat, Yates wrote to Al's Agency requesting $10,000 of boat insurance and offering to pay whatever the premium might be. Yates's boat sustained a fire loss before either party received either letter.

Is Yates's loss covered? Why or why not? Assuming that Al's Agency received Yates's letter before the fire and that it has not started to process his application, which, if any, of the three insurers is liable for the loss? Explain.

Case Analysis Steps and Answer

To be enforceable, an insurance contract must have four elements:

- Agreement
- Capacity to contract
- Consideration
- Legal purpose

Failure to conform to any one of these four elements renders the insurance contract unenforceable.

Yates's loss is not covered. Al's Agency's initial letter suggested that Yates obtain the $10,000 in coverage and quoted a premium. Yates wrote a letter that crossed in the mail with Al's Agency's letter. In effect, two offers were made, but no acceptances occurred, so no agreement resulted.

Assuming that Al's Agency received Yates's letter and had not started to process the application, no liability would arise unless either the insurer or the agent were negligent in delaying the application processing. No evidence indicates that any insurer is preferred for this policy, although past practices indicate that Alpha would be the assumed insurer in the absence of evidence to the contrary.

[DA06179]

INSURANCE AS THIRD-PARTY BENEFICIARY CONTRACT

Insurance contracts provide many examples of how third parties can benefit from agreements. In a life insurance policy, for example, the contract between the insured and the insurer is for the benefit of a third person, the beneficiary. Property insurance also can provide benefits to third parties in some circumstances, particularly when property interests are being transferred or when interests in real estate are limited or shared.

An insurance contract can benefit a third party, other than the insured under the policy, in two primary ways:

- Insurance contracts can protect third parties in cases of injury or damage.
- Insurance contracts can protect third parties in real estate sales and mortgages, as well as limited interests in realty, such as lease interests and life estates.

Third-Party Interests in Liability Insurance

Liability insurance protects against loss resulting from the insured's causing injury or damage, usually by negligence, to a third person. Although a named insured obtains the policy, the protection can extend to others, such as additional drivers of an insured's car.

Direct-action statute

A law that permits a negligence victim to sue an insurer directly or to sue both the insurer and wrongdoer jointly.

The victims of an insured's negligence also benefit from liability coverage. In recent years, some states have adopted **direct-action statutes**. In most jurisdictions, however, the purpose of liability insurance is to indemnify only insureds for their losses in paying damages to the victims. In these situations, the third-party victims cannot sue under the liability policies until courts have ordered judgments against the insureds. If an insurer denies claim payments after a judgment, then a third party can sue an insurer directly.

Real Estate Sellers and Buyers

Real estate buyers have loss exposures, even though they may be unaware of them. A real estate buyer obtains an equitable interest in the property as soon as both parties sign the agreement of sale. The real estate belongs to the buyer, subject to the payment of the purchase price, under the doctrine of equitable conversion. One result of this equitable ownership is that the buyer bears the risk of loss. If the property is destroyed before it is legally transferred, the buyer must still pay the full purchase price.

The buyer can avoid bearing the risk of loss by including in the contract a provision that places the burden of any loss on the seller until actual title transfer. After transfer, of course, the loss exposure goes to the buyer, and the seller's risk terminates.

The loss exposure can be on the buyer in three situations:

- Only the seller has property insurance—This arrangement is most common in residential sales. If fire damages or destroys the property, the sale still goes through. Which party receives the insurance proceeds depends on the sales contract terms.
- The seller and buyer each have property insurance to protect their respective interests—This arrangement is typical in commercial transactions and in some residential sales. It is good for the buyer, who then controls

the type and amount of coverage and the selection of insurer. Both seller and buyer can recover to the extent of their respective losses.

- The seller and buyer purchase a policy together—This arrangement is the most sophisticated. If the seller and buyer together have purchased homeowners insurance covering their respective interests in the property, insurance proceeds go to make each party whole. For example, the seller collects policy proceeds to the extent of the unpaid purchase price, and the buyer collects proceeds to the extent of the deposit.

Some states have adopted the Uniform Vendor and Purchaser Risk Act, under which innocent losses occurring during the contract period are allocated to the seller unless the buyer has taken possession before closing. The risk of loss is on the person in possession as the person in the best position to take care of the property.

Mortgagor's and Mortgagee's Interests

Both the mortgagor and mortgagee have separate and distinct insurable interests in mortgaged property. The mortgagor is the property buyer who provides a mortgage (claim against the property), and the mortgagee is the lender who receives the mortgage in return for providing the funds to purchase the property. It is customary for the parties to agree in the mortgage on who will obtain insurance on the property. If such a provision is not included on the mortgage, one of three situations can occur:

- The mortgagor can obtain separate insurance on the property, solely for the mortgagor's benefit.

- The mortgagee can obtain separate insurance on the property. If so, money the insurer pays in the event of loss does not accrue to the mortgagor's benefit and therefore is not payable to the mortgagor.

- The mortgagor can obtain insurance for the mortgagee's benefit by either assigning the policy to the mortgagee or including on the policy a standard mortgage clause making any proceeds under the policy payable to the mortgagee "as the mortgagee's interest may appear."

Mortgage, Mortgagor, and Mortgagee

What is a mortgage? Many people commonly use mortgage as a synonym for loan. A mortgage represents a financial claim against property such as real estate. The mortgagor/borrower signs a document providing a lien or title (claim) to the lender (mortgagee). Many people commonly (but inaccurately) say that the borrower "gets" the mortgage, but the borrower is the mortgagor, who is the pledger of the interest. The mortgagee "gets" the mortgage.

[DA06177]

Limited Interests in Realty

Legal issues often arise with respect to limited interests in real property. Limited interests are any interests in real property short of legal ownership, such as lease interests or life estates.

Lease Interests

Courts are divided with respect to the lessor's and the lessee's rights to recover under property insurance policies. The lessor is the owner of the leased property, and the lessee is the tenant or renter.

Until relatively recently, lessors' fire insurers did not make subrogation claims against lessees for the lessees' liability in causing fire damage to insured property. Protection can now take several forms:

- The insurer waives its subrogation rights against the lessee by endorsement to the lessor's fire policy.
- A lease provision placing "all-risks" loss on the lessor is included on the policy.
- The lessee is included as an additional insured on the lessor's policy.
- The lessee purchases an insurance policy protecting against liability for causing damage to the lessor's property.
- The lessee purchases a separate fire policy covering the leased premises.

Life Estates

A life estate is an interest in real property for the duration of a person's life. The person having that interest is a life tenant, and the person who has an interest in the property after the life tenant's death has a remainder interest.

The general rule is that, if a building has been insured before the creation of a life tenancy and is destroyed afterward, the interests in the property are converted to interests in personal property, and the life tenant has a life estate in the insurance contract proceeds. In other words, the life tenant's interest is no longer in the building or land, but only in its monetary worth. This arrangement is not satisfactory from the life tenant's or the remainder person's standpoint; it would be better if specific arrangements were made in advance for insurance coverage to apply toward repairs.

Assume a life tenant holds a policy in his own name and does not designate the remainder person as an additional insured. If the property is destroyed, the life tenant can recover the entire value of the property, even if it exceeds the cash value of the life estate. Insurers often choose to overlook this deviation from the principle of indemnity. Otherwise, they would be asserting a position inconsistent with having collected the premium that corresponds to the full value of the property.

Furthermore, the amount saved by resisting the life tenant's claim might not be worth the defense cost in expense and loss of goodwill. In addition, the life tenant could be the named insured on the policy, possessing a representative insurable interest on behalf of the remainder person. In this case, if a loss occurs, some of the proceeds would go to the remainder person.

Generally, in the absence of specific provisions to the contrary, the life tenant is not required to insure the premises for the remainder person's benefit and is not required to repair accidental damage to the property that does not result from his or her actions.

REPRESENTATIONS AND WARRANTIES IN INSURANCE

Statements on an insurance application are usually categorized as either representations or warranties.

Representations are oral or written statements made by an insurance applicant concerning a loss exposure that induce an insurer to enter into the insurance contract. In insurance contract law, warranties are statements or promises in a policy that, if untrue, would render the policy voidable, whether or not they are material. In the past, strict application of this common-law definition of a warranty frequently resulted in insurers attempting to escape liability for reasons not material to the person or property involved. In response, courts, whenever possible, have interpreted statements as representations rather than as warranties.

Representations

Representations precede and accompany an insurance contract and are not matters about which the parties contract. For example, to induce an insurer to issue an auto policy, a prospective insured might represent on an application that he or she has no history of traffic violations or accidents. The representation, however, is not the subject matter of the contract. False representation, or misrepresentation, makes an insurance contract voidable. An insurer's detriment is presumed in cases of false representation because the insurer has issued a policy in reliance on the false information. Misrepresentations are misstatements of past or present facts.

Elements Required to Establish False Representation

Three elements are required for a plaintiff insurer to establish false representation:

• A statement is made that is false or misleading.

• The statement relates to a material fact.

• The insurer relies on the false or misleading statement in issuing the policy.

The lack of intent to deceive or reckless disregard for the truth distinguishes misrepresentation from fraud. Even an innocent misrepresentation, if material and if relied upon by the insurer, makes the contract voidable. Statutory language sometimes specifies that the misrepresentation must be willful or intentional.

Representations and misrepresentations refer only to those conditions existing at the time the parties form the contract. Promises or statements about conditions that will exist after the contract completion do not involve representations. An applicant can withdraw representations found untrue at any time before the completion of the contract, but not afterwards.

The first element required to prove misrepresentation is that a false or misleading statement has been made. While an insurer might easily verify some facts, such as a type of building construction, the make of a car, or the location of property, other facts are not so easily verifiable and depend on the applicant's word.

Most of the confusion in law regarding misrepresentation has arisen in automobile insurance cases. For example, in completing an application for auto insurance, the applicant must indicate where the car is principally garaged and whether he or she has had an accident within the past five years. The applicant answers that the car is garaged in a suburb, when it is really in a large city that is a higher risk area. Because the insurer might not have issued the policy had it had the correct information, the representation is material. However, if the applicant has answered in good faith, mistakenly believing the car is in the suburbs, the insurer cannot avoid the policy.

Some expressions of opinion raise issues regarding misrepresentation. Statements of opinion and belief involve matters of judgment, possible inaccuracy, and personal viewpoint, rather than objective fact. Because an insurer should recognize subjectivity, courts frequently require evidence of fraudulent intent before they permit avoidance of the policy. In insurance law, therefore, it is important to determine whether the misrepresentation was of fact or of opinion.

Statements of opinion are false only if the person does not hold the opinion stated. Thus, the insured's intent is important, and the insurer must establish that the insured spoke fraudulently. For example, a person owns a building with an actual value of $150,000, carrying a mortgage of $75,000. In applying to insure the building, the owner represents that the building is worth $175,000, with an outstanding mortgage of $75,000. The representation of the building's value is an opinion and, although the amount estimated is far from accurate, that fact alone does not justify the insurer's avoidance of the policy. The insurer must show that the applicant actually did not hold this opinion but fraudulently misrepresented its value.

Mere silence on the insured's part is not a representation. A representation requires an active statement or conduct, such as shaking one's head. However, mere silence can give rise to the defense of concealment. A duty to speak exists in cases involving concealment, but no such duty applies to misrepresentation. Concealment requires fraudulent intent.

The second element required to prove misrepresentation is that the false statement relates to a material fact. The test for materiality is whether the insurer was influenced or induced to enter into the contract in reliance on the representation.

For example, a homeowners insurance application that represents a house to be brick when the house actually is wood has a misrepresentation of a material fact. The insurer assumes a much different loss exposure than the applicant represented. The insurer could avoid the policy, assuming that its reliance on the representation was reasonable. If, however, the applicant says the house is white when it is blue, the statement involves a false representation but does not relate to a material fact.

Depending on the jurisdiction, a court may determine materiality on two different bases:

- Using the objective reasonable insurer standard, the court asks, essentially, "What would a reasonable insurer have done with knowledge of the true facts?" The court examines what most insurers would have done in a similar situation.

- Using the subjective individual insurer standard, the court asks, essentially, "What should this insurer have done with knowledge of the facts misrepresented?"

Proof of misrepresentation also requires showing that the insurer relied on the statement. If an investigation reveals the insurer had the duty to conduct further inquiry, then it is difficult for the insurer to show reasonable reliance. An insurer that discovers the falsity of a representation before issuing a policy cannot then claim reliance on it.

Statutory Approaches to Misrepresentation

State statutes limiting an insurer's misrepresentation defense may require that the misrepresentation be intentional or material, or both. Many states have similar provisions for life insurance and set forth alternative requirements that the misrepresentation must either have been made with the "intent to deceive" or have affected or materially increased the likelihood of loss. Under such statutes, a statement of fact is material if it might have influenced the insurer's appraisal of the risk or influenced the premium rate.

Many states have enacted statutes to permit a materiality defense based on the effect of an alleged misrepresentation. These statutes fall into two groups, requiring proof of either an increase of the insurer's risk or of contribution to the insurer's loss, to prove materiality:

• Increase-of-risk statutes are more common and can set either an objective or a subjective standard for determining materiality. Under such a statute, an insured's representation that, contrary to fact, no driver under twenty-five years of age lives in his or her household would be misrepresentation of a material fact.

• The less common contribute-to-loss statutes modify the law more radically. The rule under most of these statutes is that, regardless of materiality, a misrepresentation does not allow an insurer to avoid the contract if, from its very nature, it could not contribute to the loss. Using this theory, a court could find, for example, that a contribute-to-loss statute prohibits an insurer from avoiding a homeowners insurance policy if the misrepresentation relates to a statement that the insured had never been refused other insurance or to the fact that an insured had other, concurrent, or additional insurance in violation of the policy.

Construction of Representations

Misrepresentation of facts, ideas, and circumstances can assume many forms. The problem of when a representation becomes a misrepresentation sufficient to justify avoidance of an insurance policy can be complex. Courts often interpret representations in favor of insureds. Even when a representation is not literally true, it is not a misrepresentation if it is substantially true, that is, more true than false.

Whether an inaccurate objective fact is substantially true depends on its materiality to the agreement. The test of materiality, in turn, is whether the contract would have formed had the applicant told the truth.

Warranties

Like representations, warranties also affect a contract's creation and voidability. Warranties are statements or promises that, if untrue, could render a policy voidable. For a promise to be a warranty, two requirements must be present:

• The parties must have clearly and unmistakably intended it to be a warranty.

• The statement must form a part of the contract itself.

In the absence of these requirements, the stated fact or promise is a representation, rather than a warranty. An insurer can require an applicant to agree to a policy provision that statements of fact or promises in the application are warranties. Therefore, if the facts the applicant stated are wrong in any respect, the insurer can avoid the policy. Examples of this are a warranty of seaworthiness or a jewelers block policy in which the application becomes part of the policy and the statements made in the application are warranties.

Warranties Distinguished From Representation

The different legal requirements and consequences of warranties and representations make it important to distinguish them clearly:

- Warranties are part of the final insurance contract. Representations are merely collateral, or indirect, inducements to the contract.

- The law presumes warranties to be material, and their breach makes the contract voidable. To constitute a valid defense, representations must be proven to be material.

- Insurers either write warranties in the policy or incorporate them by reference. Representations can be oral, written in the policy, or written on another paper and need not be incorporated by reference expressly.

- Warranties require strict compliance, but representations require substantial truth only.

Classification

A warranty is a written or an oral statement in a contract that certain facts are true. Warranties can take any one of three forms:

- Affirmative
- Continuing (promissory)
- Implied

An affirmative warranty states that specific facts exist at the time the contract forms. A continuing, or promissory, warranty states that the parties will do certain things or that certain conditions will continue to exist during the policy term.

Because they relate only to conditions that existed at the time of the contract, affirmative warranties are less strict than continuing warranties, and courts prefer to interpret warranties as affirmative. This approach is consistent with the general rule that if an insurance policy has two interpretations, a court will apply the interpretation favorable to the insured. If an insurer wants a continuing warranty, the policy language must state clearly that the warranty is to apply to future and continued use.

For example, a commercial property insurance application asks, "Who sleeps in the store?" The applicant writes, "A guard on premises at night." This statement is an affirmative warranty of conditions at the time of contract formation. If a guard slept on the premises at the application time, but not later, the insured has not breached the affirmative warranty. If the insurer wants a guard on the premises at night during the policy term, the policy language must clearly say so. Language referring to the future (continuing), such as "a guard will be on the premises at night," is necessary.

An implied warranty is an obligation that the courts impose on a seller to warrant certain facts about a product, even though they are not expressly stated by the seller. Implied warranties are considered to exist in order to render transactions reasonable and fair, particularly in sales of goods transactions. For example, safety is generally an implied warranty for all products. All warranties in insurance law, however, are generally expressed in the policies or incorporated by reference.

Lessening Warranty Effects

Insurers prefer that courts interpret the insured's statements as warranties rather than as representations because a representation must be material to be grounds for an insurer's avoidance of a policy. Insurers also prefer that warranties be continuing and that they therefore extend through the policy period.

State laws usually require that insureds' life insurance statements be considered representations. Although the principle that insureds' statements are usually warranties applies, courts have reduced the harsh effects this doctrine can cause by interpreting statements as factual representations and not as warranties, whenever possible. They also prefer to interpret warranties as affirmative rather than as continuing.

When possible, courts also interpret policies as severable. If one policy provision is invalid, it need not invalidate the entire policy but can be severed, or separated, from other provisions. Therefore, noncompliance with a warranty concerning one type of covered property will not defeat coverage for another type of property to which the warranty does not relate.

The parties' intention determines whether a policy statement is a warranty or a representation. A court interprets a policy as a whole, including the hazards insured, the language used, and the parties' situations. A court does not consider the use of the word "warranty" or "representation" as conclusive. For instance, a declaration that factual statements are warranties might have no effect if no other provisions or circumstances indicate this characterization as the parties' intention. A statement is a representation rather than a warranty unless the language unequivocally states that it is a warranty. When any doubt exists, the statement is not a warranty.

Some state statutes prevent insurers from specifying that representations have the same effect as warranties. Other statutes relate to the strict compliance aspect of warranties and specify that only substantial compliance is necessary. Still other statutes relate to the time at which the breach of warranty existed and prevent avoidance of the policy unless the warranty existed at the time of the loss.

WAIVER, ESTOPPEL, AND ELECTION

Insurance law uses the doctrines of waiver, estoppel, and election more frequently than any other field of the law. The three doctrines apply to almost every ground on which an insurer can successfully deny liability.

In insurance, the issues of waiver, estoppel, and election usually arise when an insured sues for payment of damages under the policy and the insurer asserts a defense, such as fraud, misrepresentation, concealment, mistake, or breach of a condition. In turn, the insured argues that the insurer has forfeited or is prevented from asserting the defense by any of these actions:

- Waiver of the defense
- Estoppel from asserting the defense
- Election not to take advantage of the defense

Waiver

A **waiver** can be express or implied, depending on the circumstances. In insurance, waiver means that an insurer's conduct has the legal effect of giving up a defense to a lawsuit. It applies to defenses based either on the insured's noncompliance with a condition or on misrepresentation.

Waiver
The intentional relinquishment of a known right.

For example, a homeowner makes a claim for water damage to the contents of his basement. The adjuster instructs the homeowner to make a list of the damaged items, then tells the homeowner to throw the items out. Under these circumstances, the adjuster's instructions result in a knowing waiver of the insurer's right to inspect the contents, which are no longer available. The insurer cannot later deny the claim on the basis that the insured failed to make the contents available for inspection.

Use of Waivers

A party can waive almost any contractual right or privilege. An insurer can waive any policy provision (providing it involves a right), standard policy language, and even a policy provision that specifically prohibits waivers. Producers, for example, can waive these rights and privileges:

- Notice of loss or proof of loss requirements
- Property inspection or medical examination requirements
- Policy suspension for premium nonpayment
- Occupancy requirements for insured property

For waiver to occur, an insurance policy must exist. A statement made before an insurance contract comes into existence is not a waiver of a known right, but an attempted waiver of a future right. For example, Carmen applies for an inland marine insurance policy that allows the insurer to declare the policy void if the insured fails to maintain the security system at the insured premises. In the application, Carmen expresses the intent to disconnect the system later, and the producer tells her that the insurer does not intend to enforce the security system clause. The producer is attempting to waive a future request in a policy that does not yet exist. The producer's attempted waiver of the clause is also ineffective because the parol evidence rule would exclude evidence of the conversation; therefore, the policy itself would represent the entire contract.

Insurers cannot waive some matters, including privileges that further public policy, such as the requirement that an insured have an insurable interest in the insured property or life. Insurers also cannot waive actual facts.

By definition, an exclusion of a cause of loss cannot be waived. Waiver applies only to the relinquishment of a right. An exclusion represents not the insurer's right not to cover a cause of loss, but a duty the insurer has chosen not to assume. For example, if an insurance policy excludes coverage for earthquake damage, the insurer has expressly chosen not to assume the duty of paying an earthquake loss under the policy. It cannot then waive the exclusion and assume the duty.

A producer's representation that a policy covers something it does not actually cover does not constitute a waiver. For example, a producer tells an insured that a policy applies when the insured is driving an employer's car. In reality, the policy contains a nonowned automobile clause excluding such coverage. The producer might be liable for the misrepresentation, but the insurer would not be liable.

Consideration

In general contract law, voluntary waivers are not binding, and a binding waiver requires consideration. In insurance law, some waivers are binding without consideration. For example, an insurer pays for a loss after the policy period for filing proof of loss has elapsed and without having received proof of loss. The insurer has waived its right to proof of loss and has received no consideration from the insured in exchange for the waiver.

Knowledge Requirement

An insurer must know of a breach of condition under the policy before it can waive that condition. Once it has knowledge of a breach, the insurer must act immediately to avoid a waiver. Whether the insurer has waived a right depends on the facts of each case.

Only pertinent knowledge can form the basis for a waiver. For example, a producer knows that an insured is constructing an addition to an insured building that has a sprinkler system to control the spread of fire. The producer, however, does not know that the building contractor will shut off the sprinkler system temporarily during construction. The producer's failure to act is not a waiver of the automatic sprinkler clause. But if the producer learns that the sprinkler system has been turned off and fails to inform the insured that coverage will be affected, the producer has waived the clause.

Policy Provisions

Courts generally do not enforce policy provisions requiring all waivers to be in writing, even though waiver is based on the contract principle that courts will enforce valid contractual provisions. Permitting insurers to negate the defense of waiver simply by inserting provisions in the policies would defeat the law of waivers entirely. Even if a nonwaiver clause is enforceable, however, it may contain loopholes. For example, if a producer who has the authority to make written and oral changes in a policy makes an oral change that results in a waiver, the producer's authority may negate the waiver provision.

Acts Constituting Waiver

Any words that express, or acts that imply, an insurer's intention to give up the right to assert a known defense can constitute a waiver. The insurer must know of the breach in a policy condition before it can waive it. With knowledge of the breach, the insurer has the option of declaring the policy void. If the insurer does not do so, a waiver occurs. Insurers' acts that can show an intent to continue a contract in force, therefore constituting waivers, include, but are not limited to, these:

- Receipt of a premium with knowledge of a breach of policy conditions.

- Demand for appointment of appraisers or submission of a dispute to arbitration according to policy provisions, or any other demand the insurer is entitled to only if the policy is in force.

- Request for proof of loss after knowledge of a breach in a contract without a nonwaiver agreement.

- Silence beyond a reasonable time after learning of a breach. For example, when a proof of loss is defective, the insurer's silence concerning the defect beyond a reasonable time constitutes a waiver.

Parol Evidence Rule

Waivers are subject to the parol evidence rule. The parol evidence rule prohibits the introduction into evidence at trial of any oral agreements made before, or contemporaneous with, the formation of a written contract. The law assumes that final written insurance policies contain all waiver agreements that have arisen from words or acts before or during the writing of the policy.

Thus, oral evidence of agreements preceding or accompanying a written insurance policy cannot be used to prove a waiver. An agent's oral promise to waive future breaches before or during the finalizing of a policy is ineffective as a waiver because of the parol evidence rule and is not admissible as evidence. On the other hand, parol evidence is admissible to prove waiver agreements made after the policy has been written and properly authorized.

Estoppel

Estoppel

A legal principle that prohibits a party from asserting a claim or right that is inconsistent with that party's past statement or conduct on which another party has detrimentally relied.

Estoppel is a legal principle that prohibits a party from asserting a claim or right that is inconsistent with that party's past statement or conduct on which another party has detrimentally relied. For example, Kim makes a statement to Carlos. Carlos relies on the statement and takes action as a result of the reliance. Kim refuses to abide by the statement, while Carlos suffers injury or detriment because of having relied on the statement. Carlos, in a lawsuit, might assert that Kim is estopped from acting in contradiction to the original statement. Parol evidence is admissible to prove estoppel, and it is immaterial whether the words or acts occurred before or after the making of the written contract.

Insurance Law and Estoppel

Estoppel arises in insurance law from this sequence of events:

1. False representation of a material fact
2. Reasonable reliance on the representation
3. Resulting injury or detriment to the insured

Distinguishing Estoppel From Waiver

In insurance law, the distinction between waiver and estoppel is often ambiguous. Although the legal effect of the two defenses is the same, they are different in these ways:

- Waiver is contractual in nature and rests upon agreement between parties. Estoppel is equitable in nature and arises from a false representation.
- Waiver gives effect to the waiving party's intention. Estoppel defeats the inequitable intent of the estopped party.
- The parol evidence rule applies to waiver and does not apply to estoppel.

Factors Establishing Estoppel

When an insurer knows that an insured has breached a policy condition, any of the insurer's words or acts that the insured can reasonably interpret as representations that the contract is still valid will prevent the insurer from avoiding the contract. The insured asserting estoppel, however, must come to court with "clean hands," that is, must not have committed fraud or have acted in bad faith.

The insured also must show that he or she acted in good faith and in reasonable reliance on the insurer's representation.

Practice Exercise

An insurer issues a fire insurance policy covering a building on leased land, a fact the insured disclosed on the application. The producer delivers the policy to the insured, saying, "Here is the policy, and it fully covers your building." The policy expressly provides that it is void if the building insured is located on leased land. The insured accepts the policy without reading it and puts it with other valuable papers. When the building later burns, the insurer denies the claim. Are the elements leading to estoppel present in this case?

Answer

All the elements leading to estoppel are present in this case. The insurer, through its producer, made a false representation by stating that the policy covered the building. The insured reasonably relied on the representation by accepting the policy and not purchasing other insurance. The insured's failure to read the policy does not mean reliance is unreasonable. For the insurer to defend its actions based on the policy would harm the insured, who would have no insurance coverage. The insurer is prevented, or estopped, from denying that coverage exists. The producer's statement was not a waiver, because the insurer did not intend to give up any right under the policy.

[DA06207]

Estoppel applies when an insurer's producer misinterprets questions or falsifies answers in an application and the insurer issues a policy based on the misleading information. Because the producer made the misrepresentation, the insurer cannot deny (is estopped from denying) the truth of the statements.

Similarly, if an insurer's producer states that agreed-on acts, such as including a certain policy endorsement, have occurred when they have not, that representation might be subject to estoppel. For example, if a producer states that an endorsement will be added to a policy to permit a building to be unoccupied for certain periods, and the policy issues without that endorsement, the insurer cannot deny the validity of the intended endorsement. That the insured failed to check the policy does not negate the element of reasonable reliance. Oral evidence is admissible in court to prove the facts. See the exhibit "Practice Exercise."

Election

Election is the voluntary act of choosing between two alternative rights or privileges. A choice of one available right can imply a relinquishment of the right not chosen. For example, an insurer that treats a contract as valid for the purpose of collecting premiums cannot treat it as invalid for the purpose of covering a loss. The essence of the election doctrine is that an insurer or insured cannot adopt a "heads I win, tails you lose" position.

Election
The voluntary act of choosing between two alternative rights or privileges.

Practice Exercise

One of an insured's duties is to report a loss promptly. This notice should include how, when, and where the loss happened and also should include any injured parties' and witnesses' names and addresses. The insured's failure to meet this obligation could result in a denial of coverage.

Facts

An insurer accepts a notification that the insured experienced a loss. This notice came from a party to the loss, not the insured. However, it is sufficient for the claim department to create a file and begin an investigation. Is there the potential for waiver and estoppel to apply here?

Answer

If the insurer begins an investigation without issuing a reservation of rights letter to the insured, the insurer has waived its right to deny coverage on the basis of the insured's failure to fulfill the obligation to report the loss fully.

In this case, estoppel also applies. The insurer has accepted whatever notice was given and begins an investigation without a reservation of rights letter. Relying on the belief that the insurer will fulfill its contractual obligation to indemnify and defend, the insured takes no further action, neither investigating the loss further or preserving the evidence. The insurer cannot use the defense of insufficient notice to deny its duty to indemnify and defend. Denial would put the insured in a detrimental position, and the insurer would be estopped from denying coverage.

[DA06208]

Application

Waiver, estoppel, and election are not interchangeable doctrines. Application of the doctrine of election limits a party's range of choices. Election requires proof of neither the waiver requirement of voluntary relinquishment of a known right nor the estoppel requirement of detrimental reliance.

An example of election involves choosing between alternative rights under a fire policy, which usually gives an insurer the option to repair or rebuild instead of paying monetary compensation for a loss. An insurer whose words or acts have led an insured to expect monetary compensation has elected that method of discharging its duty under the policy. The insurer has reserved the right to elect between two alternative duties and, having elected one (monetary compensation), has lost the right to choose the second alternative (repairing or rebuilding). Election applies even though the insurer has not voluntarily relinquished a known right, as would occur with a waiver, and no detrimental reliance applies that would lead to estoppel.

Insured's Election

The doctrine of election also applies to choices by the insured. In many instances, the insured must choose between two inconsistent legal remedies. Having elected one course of action, the insured cannot pursue the other. For example, an insurer cancels a life insurance policy including provisions for the payment of disability benefits. The insured elects to sue the insurer for fraudulent breach of the contract and receives damages, but not reinstatement of the policy. Later, the insured attempts to sue to recover disability benefits that would have accrued before the previous lawsuit had it not been for the insurer's cancellation of the policy.

In the first suit, the insured alleged a breach of contract and a right to damages. In the second suit, the insured demanded benefits that would have been payable absent a breach of contract. Election of the first remedy bars the insured's right to use the second remedy. The insured elected to treat the policy as canceled and demand damages in the first lawsuit. Therefore, the insured is barred from pursuing the second remedy, disability benefits, on the assumption that the policy had not been canceled. See the exhibit "Distinguishing Factors of Waiver, Estoppel, and Election."

Distinguishing Factors of Waiver, Estoppel, and Election

	Waiver	Estoppel	Election
Defined	Insurer's voluntary and intentional relinquishment or abandonment of a known right	Insurer's prohibition from enforcing certain conditions of a policy when insurer's representation, express or implied in words or conduct, caused insured to rely on the representation	Insurer's voluntary choice of an inconsistent alternative, which precludes subsequent selection of the other alternative
Relative advantages for insured	Requires no proof of insured's reliance and resulting detriment	Requires no proof of the insurer's voluntary relinquishment of a known right	Requires no proof of either voluntary relinquishment of a known right or detrimental reliance
Relative disadvantages for insured	Requires proof of the insurer's voluntary relinquishment of known right	Requires proof of detrimental reliance	Difficult to prove
Other distinguishing characteristics	Requires proof of insurer's act or conduct	Requires proof of act or conduct of both parties to the contract: • Insurer's representation of a fact • Insured's reliance on the representation and resulting detriment	Requires proof of insurer's act or conduct

[DA04622]

NONWAIVER AGREEMENTS AND RESERVATION OF RIGHTS LETTERS

Insurers use nonwaiver agreements and reservation of rights letters to preserve certain defenses against liability that they might have under policy terms. Claim personnel frequently use them when loss investigation reveals the possibility that the insurer might deny coverage under the policy.

The possibility of denying coverage poses a dilemma for the insurer. If the insurer continues to investigate a loss on its merits without determining whether it can legitimately deny coverage, its rights might be prejudiced. Such actions can raise issues of waiver, estoppel, or election that could negate the insurer's lack of coverage defense. However, if the insurer does not investigate, it might forfeit all defenses, and the loss can increase.

Both a **nonwaiver agreement** and a **reservation of rights letter** prevent subsequent claims of waiver, estoppel, election, and any other theories of rights that vary with policy provisions.

Use of Nonwaiver Agreements and Reservation of Rights Letters

Nonwaiver agreements and reservation of rights letters help solve the insurer's dilemma of whether or not to investigate a loss. They inform an insured that the insurer's activities regarding the loss are not the relinquishment of its right to stand on policy provisions. An insurer might be able to establish that it is not liable under the policy. The insurer can continue to investigate and evaluate the loss on its merits, an activity beneficial to both the insurer's and insured's interests. Simultaneously, the insurer can determine whether the insured has violated policy terms and whether the insurer will accept liability under the policy. When the insurer, knowing of grounds for forfeiture or noncoverage, manages the defense of a lawsuit against its insured without giving timely notice of its reservation of rights, it cannot refuse coverage on those grounds.

Nonwaiver Agreements

A nonwaiver agreement, which must be signed by both parties, protects the insurer from estoppel by reserving the right to deny coverage based on information developed during the investigation. It also alerts the insured to a potential coverage problem. The nonwaiver agreement is usually used when the claim representative is concerned about investigating a claim before the insured has substantially complied with the policy conditions or when there appears to be a specific coverage problem or defense. Such concerns can be identified from the initial claim report, during initial contact with the insured, or at any point during the claim investigation. For example, a claim representative may offer a nonwaiver agreement when the insured reports the theft of an auto but refuses to make a police report about the theft. If the insured refuses to sign the nonwaiver agreement, the claim representative can use a reservation of rights letter to protect the insurer's rights.

The insurer should attempt to enter into a nonwaiver agreement with the insured as soon as the potential coverage question surfaces. Occasionally,

Nonwaiver agreement
A signed agreement indicating that during the course of investigation, neither the insurer nor the insured waives rights under the policy.

Reservation of rights letter
An insurer's letter that specifies coverage issues and informs the insured that the insurer is handling a claim with the understanding that the insurer may later deny coverage should the facts warrant it.

practical difficulties arise in the attempt to secure the insured's consent and signature:

- The insured might refuse to sign a nonwaiver agreement, even after the claim representative has clearly explained its significance. This refusal can delay the investigation of the loss.

- The insured could challenge the nonwaiver agreement if the claim representative has not explained the importance of the agreement fully and fairly. The lack of adequate explanation can lead an insured to claim lack of contractual intent, misunderstanding, duress, or other defenses that can jeopardize the agreement's validity.

Reservation of Rights Letters

A reservation of rights letter serves the same purpose as a nonwaiver agreement but is in letter form, and it is a unilateral document, meaning it does not require the insured to sign or agree to the contents of the letter. It simply advises the insured of the potential coverage issue. Nevertheless, a reservation of rights letter can be as effective in protecting the insurer's rights to policy defenses as a nonwaiver agreement if the insurer has drafted the letter carefully and can show that the insured received it.

Requirements for Nonwaiver Agreements and Reservation of Rights Letters

Certain elements must be present for a nonwaiver agreement or reservation of rights letter to be effective. First, the insurer must communicate the nonwaiver agreement or reservation of rights notice to the insured, usually by letter. Oral notice is not advisable because it would be too difficult to prove oral notice. Second, the notice must be timely. A nonwaiver agreement or reservation of rights letter prevents estoppel because it gives the insured the option to hire a lawyer to take over the defense from the insurer. Because the notice must give the insured reasonable time to find alternative defense, the insurer's safest course is to give notice as soon as it obtains knowledge of the policy defense.

The notice must inform the insured fairly of the insurer's position, citing the policy provisions on which the insurer relies and the facts that, if proven, would result in a denial of liability.

If the insurer has acted in good faith and used every reasonable method to contact the insured, the insurer can assert its policy defense. For example, a liability insurer who questions coverage under an automobile policy writes six letters to the insured informing him or her that it will defend an action but with express reservations of its rights to contest the policy. The insured contends nonreceipt of the letters. Because the letters were addressed to the insured at both the insured's residence and workplace, a presumption arises that the letters were received.

Nonwaiver agreements and reservation of rights letters are usually sent by certified mail, with a return receipt requested, so the insurer has evidence of the insured's receipt. If the insured refuses to sign a nonwaiver agreement, the only way the insurer can protect itself against subsequent claims of variance is to resort to the reservation of rights letter. This unilateral declaration gives notice to the insured that the insurer intends to safeguard its rights to dispute liability under the policy terms and that its conduct in investigating the loss should not be interpreted contradictorily in this respect.

In most jurisdictions, nonwaiver agreements and reservation of rights letters are sent only to the insured and can be used on any type of first-party claim. Usually, they are not sent to third-party claimants because third parties have no obligation under the policy. However, there are some jurisdictions that require they be sent to third-party claimants. It is prudent to seek the advice of coverage counsel when contemplating the use of a nonwaiver agreement or a reservation of rights letter.

SUMMARY

Insurance contracts have special characteristics that distinguish them from other contracts. An insurance policy is a conditional contract; a contract involving fortuitous events and the exchange of unequal amounts; a contract of utmost good faith; a contract of adhesion; a contract of indemnity; and a nontransferable contract.

An insurance contract has unique characteristics with regard to these aspects: agreement, including issues concerning offer and acceptance, effective date, and silence or delay; content, which can be oral or informally written, must include necessary terms, can include implied terms, and must include insurer designation; and delivery.

An insurance contract can benefit a third party, other than the insured under the policy, in cases of injury or damage (primarily from negligence) and in real estate sales, mortgages, lease interests, and life estates.

Statements on an insurance application are usually either representations or warranties. Representations are oral or written statements made by an insurance applicant concerning loss exposures that induce an insurer to enter into the insurance contract. Warranties are statements or promises in an application that, if untrue, would render the policy voidable, whether or not they are material.

A waiver is the intentional relinquishment of a known right, requiring knowledge of the facts and relinquishment of a right based on knowledge of those facts. In insurance law, estoppel is one party's representation of fact that the other party relies upon, making it unfair to allow the first party to refuse to be bound by the representation. Election is voluntarily choosing between alternative rights or privileges. An insurer's or insured's choice between available rights can imply a relinquishment of the right not chosen.

Insurers use nonwaiver agreements and reservation of rights letters to protect certain defenses against liability that they might have under the policy terms from insureds' assertions of waiver, estoppel, or election. These notices and agreements allow insurers to advise insureds that the insurers' activities regarding losses do not waive their rights to stand on policy provisions. An insurer can continue to investigate and evaluate losses on their merits.

4

Commercial Law

Outline

Sales Contracts

Negotiable Instruments

Documents of Title

Secured Transactions

Consumer Protection Laws

Summary

Educational Objectives

After learning the content of this assignment, you should be able to:

▶ Summarize the significance of each of the following in relation to the creation and performance of a contract for the sale of goods:

- Uniform Commercial Code Article 2

- Types of sales contracts

- Formation of sales contracts

- Breach of sales contracts and remedies for the breach

▶ Summarize the significance of each of the following in the sale of goods that occurs at a distance or over time:

- Uniform Commercial Code Article 3

- Types of commercial paper

- Transfer and negotiation

- Holders in due course

▶ Describe the creation and uses of the following:

- Warehouse receipt

- Bill of lading

▶ Explain the following aspects of secured transactions in (or for) the sale of goods:

- Uses of security interests

- Forms of security interests

- Attachment of security interests

- Perfection of security interests

- Rights of perfected and unperfected security interests

- Default

4

▶ Explain how each of the following helps to ensure fair treatment of consumers in dealings with suppliers of goods and services:

- Fair trade laws

- Consumer credit laws

- Bankruptcy

Commercial Law

SALES CONTRACTS

Under the UCC, a sales contract is a legally enforceable agreement by which a seller and a buyer transfer, or agree to transfer, ownership of property for a fixed sum. Article 2 of the UCC governs the law of sales of goods. General contractual terms and concepts also apply to these sales.

A sales contract is an agreement between a seller and a buyer that involves the transfer of the ownership of goods for a price. Sales contracts are governed by the Uniform Commercial Code (UCC) Article 2, which defines "goods" as property that is tangible and movable, other than money.

Three specialized types of sales contracts are sale on approval, sale and return, and auction sales.

A valid sales contract requires agreement (offer and acceptance) and consideration and can be either oral or written. However, certain contracts that are not written and not properly signed are unenforceable under the UCC's Statute of Frauds. Performance as described in a sales contract is necessary for successful contract completion.

A sales contract is breached when one of the parties to the contract fails to carry out the performance it has promised under the contract. Both buyer and seller have remedies when a sales contract is breached.

UCC Article 2

The Uniform Commercial Code applies to commercial transactions such as the sale of goods, leases, contracts, and negotiable instruments. It is not a federal law but rather a model code to be considered for adoption as law by each state. Its purpose is to provide a consistent legal basis for business transactions throughout the United States and its territories. Because business is often conducted across state boundaries, it is important for all parties that relative uniformity exists among the laws regulating these business dealings, including sales.

The National Conference of Commissioners on Uniform State Laws and the American Law Institute collaborated over many years to create the UCC. In 1952, these two private nongovernmental organizations published the first edition of the UCC with the recommendation that the state governments adopt it. Since then, a number of updated UCC editions have been published. Today, all fifty states, the District of Columbia, and the U.S. territories have adopted the UCC in whole or in part; states and territories are free to modify the code to meet the needs of their citizens. For example, Louisiana adopted the code minus Articles 2 and 2A.

The UCC contains articles that relate to specific areas of commercial law. Article 2 governs the laws relating to the sale of goods. The UCC defines a sales contract as a legally enforceable agreement by which a seller and a buyer transfer, or agree to transfer, ownership of property for consideration. Article 2 defines "goods" as property that is tangible and movable, other than money. Growing crops and timber, for example, are goods, as are things that are part of or emanate from land, such as minerals, oil and gas, structures, or parts of structures—if a sales contract provides that they are to be severed from land.

The UCC provisions regarding sales contain many rules for merchants. A merchant is a person who deals in goods, or a professional, such as an agent, who purports to have special knowledge or skills concerning those goods.

Types of Sales Contracts

Sales contracts can be unilateral or bilateral:

- Under a unilateral contract, a promise is exchanged for an act. For example, Jack, the owner of the Old Saw Mill, offers to pay Bob $500 per thousand board feet for logs delivered to the mill. Jack has a unilateral contract with Bob. When (and if) Bob delivers the logs, his act will both form the contract and perform his duty under the contract.

- A bilateral contract is an exchange of promises of future action. A bilateral sales contract requires the agreement of both buyer and seller. For example, Billy promises to sell Jack five thousand board feet of oak logs at a price of $750 per thousand board feet, and Jack promises to pay that price for delivery of the logs by a specified date. A bilateral contract is formed under which both parties have a duty to perform in the future.

Sales contracts usually involve the exchange of specified goods at a specified price to be delivered at or within a specified time. There are, however, specialized categories of sales contracts:

- Sale on approval—Sale to a consumer who wants to try the goods before buying them. A buyer who is not satisfied with the goods can return them at the seller's risk. Title and risk of loss remain with the seller until acceptance. The seller will most likely obtain insurance coverage for the goods until their acceptance by the buyer.

- Sale or return—Sale to a person who intends to resell the goods but who has the right to return them if they do not sell. The buyer must pay for any goods not returned. The seller retains title until payment or resale. However, the buyer's creditors can attach the goods, that is, seize them under legal authority, if the creditors are not on notice of the seller's interest in the goods. For example, if a creditor knows that the buyer is in the business of selling other people's goods, the creditor cannot seize them. Return of the goods is at the buyer's risk.

- Auction sales—Public offering of goods for sale. At auctions "with reserve," the auctioneer's chant is the invitation to make an offer; the auctioneer reserves the right to reject offers. The bid is the offer, and the auctioneer's agreement to take the highest bid is the acceptance of an offer. Auction sales of goods without a set minimum bid must be advertised as "without reserve," and the highest bidder must get the article. Without reserve, the auctioneer's chant is a continuous offer, and the highest bid becomes acceptance. For some auction sales, the auctioneer sets a minimum bid for the goods, and if all bids are under the minimum, withdraws the goods from bidding. In any type of auction sale, the bidder can retract the bid at any time before the auctioneer announces completion of the sale. The bidder's retraction does not revive any prior bid. Instead, bidding begins again.

Formation of Sales Contracts

A contract requires an agreement, defined as an offer and an acceptance, and consideration. General contract principles apply to contracts for the sale of goods, unless superseded by a provision of the UCC. The general rules of fraud, mistake, duress, and undue influence also apply to contracts for the sale of goods.

Offer

An offer is the act of presenting to another the opportunity to purchase or acquire goods under certain conditions. The UCC requires that an offer must be definite enough that the parties understand their obligations. However, an offer may have one or more terms left open and still form a valid agreement to contract as long as the parties intended to form a contract and there is a reasonable basis on which a remedy for breach can be calculated.

Acceptance

An acceptance of an offer is the act of agreeing with or taking what is offered. The manner of acceptance may affect the validity of the contract. Under general contract law, if the offer says the offer may be accepted only by mail addressed to a specific person, the acceptance must comply with those terms. If the offer is silent as to how acceptance is to be communicated, the UCC allows the acceptance to be made in any manner that is reasonable under the circumstances.

If a definite expression of acceptance of an offer to buy or sell goods contains additional or different terms, it is still an acceptance of the original offer unless it is expressly conditioned on the seller's consent to the new terms. Whether the new terms become a part of the contract depends on two variables:

- If one of the parties is a nonmerchant, the new terms become part of the contract only if the nonmerchant party expressly agrees to them.
- If both parties are merchants, the new terms become part of the contract unless they would materially alter the contract or unless the other party objects within a reasonable time.

Consideration

Consideration is essential to sales contracts. If a contract leaves the price open or provides a method of determining the price, the price becomes the reasonable price at delivery time. However, contrary to general contract law, the parties' agreement to modify a contract for the sale of goods is binding even without new consideration.

Statute of Frauds

Statutes of fraud

A collection of laws that help prevent parties from becoming involved in fraudulently formed contracts.

The UCC contains **statute of fraud** provisions that deal with the unenforceability of certain contracts that are not written and not properly signed. The writing required as evidence of a contract can be in any form and can consist of several communications, so long as it provides evidence of the contract's existence. A written memorandum created by the parties sometime after the original negotiations can be sufficient to satisfy the statute's requirement, provided it reflects the essential elements of the contract.

The UCC Statute of Frauds[1] requires that the writing be signed by the party or parties to a contract against whom the other party or parties bring action to enforce the contract. Signing can consist of signatures, initials, typewritten names, electronic signatures, or any marks that appropriately identify the parties acknowledging the memorandum or communications as their writing.

Under the UCC, a contract for the sale of goods for $500 or more is not enforceable unless it is in writing. The $500 limit applies to the total price of all the goods the contract purports to sell. The written contract does not need to set forth all the material terms of the contract, only the term relating to the quantity of goods for sale. In addition, even if the quantity term is inaccurate, the contract is enforceable up to the quantity so stated. The plaintiff need not have signed the contract; only the defendant must have signed.

The UCC provides that oral contracts for the sale of goods for $500 or more are enforceable in two situations:

- The buyer accepts and receives part of the goods.
- The buyer makes partial or full payment for the goods.

Each of these conditions reflects the parties' acknowledgment that a contract does exist. Therefore, written evidence of a contract is not necessary.

Another situation in which an oral contract for the sale of goods for $500 or more can be enforceable involves goods manufactured specifically for the buyer. Under the UCC, such an oral contract is enforceable in these circumstances:

- The goods are not suitable for resale to others in the ordinary course of business.
- The seller either has made a substantial beginning in manufacturing the goods or has made commitments to procure them.

The seller must establish the contract's terms as part of the proof of claim that a contract exists.

Performance

Performance is the activity (or activities) necessary to successfully complete a contract. For example, in a sales contract, A agrees to sell B 500 items for $1,000, to be delivered in thirty days. A delivers the 500 items to B on the twenty-ninth day, and B pays A the $1,000 owed. The terms of the contract have been fulfilled; therefore, contract performance has occurred.

A and B could delegate their performance to someone else. Thus, rather than A manufacturing the items, A could have C manufacture them and arrange for D to deliver them to B as agreed. A would still have contract performance.

Title and Risk of Loss

As a practical matter, under the UCC, the **risk** transfers with the title to the goods except when the goods remain at the seller's residence or place of business and the buyer is to pick them up. If the seller is a merchant, risk of loss does not pass to the buyer until the buyer receives the goods. If the seller is not a merchant, risk of loss passes to the buyer when the seller tenders delivery.

Risk
The chance of financial loss.

When a buyer rejects delivered goods because they do not conform to the contract, the risk of loss remains with the seller until the seller remedies the deficiency or until the buyer accepts the goods.

The parties can agree that the risk of loss will pass at some other time than the UCC specifies, and the parties' prior practice, trade usage, or circumstances of the case also can change the time that the transfer of risk occurs.

Delivery Terms

Buyers and sellers have several options as to where goods will be delivered and which party bears the risk and expense of delivery. Common delivery and shipping terms in sales contracts, many of which are used in marine insurance, are these:

- FOB (free on board) place of shipment—The seller delivers goods to the carrier at the seller's risk and expense, and the ownership then shifts to the buyer.

- FOB (free on board) place of destination—Ownership passes from the seller to the buyer when the carrier delivers the goods to the buyer's premises.

- FAS (free alongside) vessel—Ownership passes from the seller to the buyer when the seller delivers the goods alongside a vessel for loading onto that vessel.

- FOB (free on board) vessel—Goods are loaded on board the vessel at the seller's risk and expense, and then ownership passes to the buyer.

- CIF (cost-insurance-freight)—The seller is obligated to pay for the insurance and freight charges for delivery to the buyer.

- CAF (cost and freight)—The seller is obligated to pay for the freight charges but not for the insurance for delivery to the buyer.

Inspection

Upon delivery, the buyer usually has the right to inspect the goods as a condition to acceptance and payment. The inspection can include reasonable testing at the buyer's expense. If a buyer rejects the goods for failure to conform, the buyer can recover the testing cost from the seller.

Buyers do not have a right to inspect in two situations:

COD (collect on delivery)

A shipping condition under which the buyer pays when the goods are delivered and has no right to inspect the goods as a condition to acceptance and payment.

- When the carrier delivers the goods **COD (collect on delivery)**
- When a contract requires the buyer to pay at the time of delivery of the document of title (unless the contract also requires payment only after the goods are available for inspection)

Time for Delivery

If the time for delivery is not set in or cannot be implied from the contract or the parties' past practices, delivery must occur within a reasonable time. Unless a seller assumes a greater obligation, such as by agreeing in the contract that time is of the essence, delay in delivery or nondelivery is not a breach of contract if performance becomes impracticable because of an occurrence unforeseen by both parties.

Conforming and Nonconforming Goods

Article 2 of the UCC defines conforming and nonconforming goods. To conform is to be in accordance with the obligations of the contract. Conforming goods are goods stipulated in the contract or those that fall within trade usage or the parties' prior course of dealing. Those goods that do not meet the contract obligations are considered nonconforming goods. Generally, the shipment of nonconforming goods is a breach of contract; however, Article 2 provides two exceptions to that rule:

- A shipment of nonconforming goods is neither an acceptance nor a breach of contract if the seller notifies the buyer that the shipment is only an accommodation to the buyer. An example would be the seller providing a product for the buyer's temporary use until delivery of the goods specified in the sales contract.
- If a buyer rejects goods as nonconforming, the seller can notify the buyer of its intention to "cure" the nonconformity of the shipment by delivering conforming goods. This notification must be made before the time for contractual performance has expired. If the performance time has expired, and if the seller has reasonable grounds to believe that the goods conformed to the contract, the seller still has a reasonable time to substitute conforming goods. An example of reasonable grounds would be the buyer's acceptance of the same kind or condition of goods as conforming in prior transactions.

Express and Implied Warranties

A warranty is a promise that something is true. Contracts for the sale of goods can contain statutory warranties, as well as the sellers' express or implied warranties. A seller's overt words or actions can create an express warranty. The law may infer the existence of an implied warranty because of the circumstances of the sale.

If a statement forms the basis of the sale, it is an express warranty. There are three kinds of express warranties:

- An affirmation of fact about the goods, such as the seller's promise that the goods conform to a certain standard, is a warranty. For example, a statement about a car's gas mileage is a warranty even without the words "warranty" or "guarantee."
- Any description of goods in a contract is a warranty that the goods conform to the description. For example, a contract to sell a new hay baler is an express warranty that the hay baler is new.
- A contract based on a sample or model is a warranty that the goods will conform to the sample or model.

Implied warranties in sales of goods fall into two categories:

- Implied warranty of merchantability
- Implied warranty of fitness for a particular purpose

Implied warranty of merchantability

An implied warranty that a product is fit for the ordinary purpose for which it is used.

An **implied warranty of merchantability** applies only to transactions in which the seller is a merchant. The goods sold must meet the following five qualifications:

- The goods must pass without objection in the trade under the contract description.
- Fungible goods, such as grain, must be indistinguishable and interchangeable and must be of average quality for the kind of goods sold.
- The goods must be fit for the ordinary purpose for which they will be used.
- All goods in a lot must be approximately like kind and quality.
- The goods must conform to the specifications, if any, on the container or label.

In addition, implied warranties can arise from the parties' course of dealings or from the usages of a particular trade.

Implied warranty of fitness for a particular purpose

An implied warranty that a product is fit for a particular purpose; applies if the seller knows about the buyer's purpose for the product.

An **implied warranty of fitness for a particular purpose** applies to both merchants and nonmerchants. For example, suppose that John has never been deep-sea fishing but wants to fish for marlin. He asks a sporting goods dealer to recommend suitable equipment, and he buys the equipment the dealer recommends. Without negligence on John's part, the equipment breaks while he is using it for marlin fishing because it was unsuited for that purpose. John relied on the dealer's expertise to select the appropriate equipment for deep-sea marlin fishing. The seller has apparently breached a warranty of fitness for a particular purpose.

Implied warranty of title

An implied promise in a contract for the sale of goods that the seller has legal ownership of goods and has no knowledge of any security interest or other lien on the goods other than those disclosed to the buyer.

A common type of implied warranty in contracts for the sale of goods is an **implied warranty of title**. A contract may exclude the warranty of title if the buyer has reason to know that the seller does not have full title. For example, agents sell goods as representatives of their owners, and the agent relationship alerts the buyer that the agent does not have title.

Another type of warranty extends to third parties. Article 2 of the UCC deals with sellers' contractual liability arising from express or implied warranties to third parties who are not the immediate buyers of goods. The UCC provides that a seller's warranty extends to any person in the buyer's family or household, or any guest in the buyer's home, who suffers injury resulting from breach of the warranty, if it is reasonable to believe that the person would either use or be affected by the goods. An express or implied warranty for an appliance, for example, would extend to the buyer's child or to a houseguest. See the exhibit "Exercise: Risk of Loss in a Sales Transaction."

Breach of Sales Contracts and Remedies

If goods do not conform to a contract, the buyer can accept or reject all or part of them. To sue for breach of contract, the buyer must first give reasonable notice of rejection to the seller, stating the particular defect. This notice gives the seller an opportunity to cure the defect. For contracts between

---

Exercise: Risk of Loss in a Sales Transaction

Wanda purchased certain bulky goods from Selma. The goods were identified and marked with Wanda's name. Wanda was to pick up the goods within a week and make the full payment at that time. During the week, a fire broke out in Selma's place of business. The fire was not a result of Selma's negligence, but the goods were destroyed.

Did title to the goods transfer to Wanda? If so, when? If not, why not?

Who bears the risk of loss, or, in other words, must Wanda pay Selma for the goods?

Wanda probably has title to the goods because the assumption is that Selma could transfer the title to her, the goods were marked with Wanda's name, and it appears that both parties intended title to the goods to pass to Wanda. The title transferred to Wanda at the time she made partial payment for the goods.

Wanda does not have to pay for the goods. The question of who has title does not affect the risk of loss in this case. Under the UCC, risk of loss passes with title except when the goods remain at the seller's place of business or residence where the buyer is to pick them up. In addition, if the seller is a merchant, risk of loss does not transfer to the buyer until the buyer receives the goods. In this case, Selma is a merchant because she has a place of business, and the goods were at her place of business when the loss occurred.

[DA06325]

---

merchants, the seller may also make a written request for a written statement of the defects claimed by the buyer.

If the seller has no agent or place of business in the buyer's market area, the buyer must follow the seller's instructions for what to do with the rejected goods. The buyer can demand indemnity for necessary expenses incurred in holding or shipping the goods. If the goods are perishable, the buyer can sell them on the seller's behalf. If the goods are not perishable, and the buyer does not receive instructions within a reasonable time, the buyer can sell them, store them, or ship them to the seller. In these cases, the buyer's acceptance of nonconforming goods does not waive or forfeit any right to sue for the breach. To sue for breach, however, the buyer must have notified the seller of the nonconformity within a reasonable time and must prove that the goods were nonconforming.

Revocation of Acceptance

A buyer can revoke an acceptance of goods under these circumstances:

- The buyer reasonably assumed that the seller would cure the defect but the seller did not do so.
- The buyer accepted the goods before discovering the nonconformity.
- The buyer accepted the goods in the first place because it would have been difficult to discover the defect and because the seller gave assurances about the quality of the goods.

In each of these situations, the buyer has reasonably relied on the seller's delivery of acceptable goods.

Excuses for Nonperformance

These circumstances provide excuses for nonperformance of a sales contract:

- Loss of identified goods—If specific and identified goods are destroyed before the risk of loss transfers to the buyer, and if neither party was at fault, the contract is void. If the loss is partial, the parties may void the contract or the buyer can accept damaged goods with an allowance in the price for the deficiency. In neither case, however, can the buyer sue the seller for breach of contract.

- Substituted performance—If the agreed-on carrier or berthing, loading, or unloading facilities become unavailable, no matter who was at fault, the buyer must accept any offer by the seller to use a commercially reasonable substitute. If the agreed means of payment fails because of government regulation, the seller may withhold or stop delivery unless the buyer provides a commercially equivalent means of payment.

- Failure of a presupposed condition—Subject to the section on substituted performance, delay in delivery or partial or complete non-delivery by the seller is not a breach of contract if performance is impracticable because of the occurrence of a contingency affecting a basic assumption in the contract. If it is feasible to do so, the seller may allocate production and delivery among customers. The seller must notify the buyer in a reasonable time of the delay or non-delivery, and the quota to be delivered if allocation is used.

Seller's Remedies

If a seller discovers before delivery that the buyer is insolvent, the seller can refuse to deliver the goods. If the goods are en route, the seller can stop delivery unless the buyer has already received a document of title for the goods or unless a carrier or warehouse operator has notified the buyer that it is holding the goods for the buyer. If the seller discovers that the buyer has received the goods on credit while insolvent, the seller can demand their return within a reasonable time period.

When a buyer wrongfully repudiates the contract, fails to make a payment due before delivery, or wrongfully rejects the goods, the seller can sue. If the lawsuit is successful, the seller can recover the difference between the contract and the market price at the time and place of delivery or, under certain circumstances, lost profits, if any.

If the goods are still being manufactured at the time of breach, the seller can complete their manufacture and sell them to another party or stop their manufacture and sell them as they are or for scrap value.

If the buyer fails to pay for goods after accepting them or after the liability passes to the buyer, the seller can sue for the goods' contract price even if the seller still possesses them, but only if the seller cannot sell them to another party at a reasonable price.

Buyer's Remedies

If the seller fails to deliver the goods or repudiates the contract, the buyer is entitled to the difference, if any, between the contract price at the time the buyer learned of the breach and the market price. Alternatively, if the undelivered goods are unique or if the buyer cannot obtain them from another source, the buyer is entitled to specific performance (delivery of goods). Specific performance is also the remedy if a buyer cannot obtain substitute goods to replace the undelivered goods.

Because buyers often need goods immediately, they may purchase substitute goods within a reasonable time after learning of a breach and then recover from the seller any difference between the cost and the contract price. A buyer who rightfully rejects delivery or revokes acceptance and who possesses the goods has all the rights that a seller has when the buyer breaches before delivery. The buyer can hold the goods for the seller's instructions or sell them.

A buyer who accepts nonconforming goods and informs the seller of the nonconformity is entitled to the difference, if any, between the value of the goods accepted and the value they would have had, at the time and place of acceptance, if they were as the seller warranted. In addition, the buyer can recover any loss resulting from the nonconformity that the seller had reason to know might follow from a breach that the buyer could not have prevented.

NEGOTIABLE INSTRUMENTS

Negotiable instruments are written documents that allow parties to pay at a distance or at a future time. They are also used as a convenient substitute for cash.

A basic requirement of commercial paper is that it be negotiable—readily salable—so that the seller does not have to wait for payment. To get immediate payment, the seller can sell the negotiable paper. If the paper is nonnegotiable, a buyer of the instrument would take these two steps before purchasing it:

1.   Check the credit rating of the payer
2.   Determine whether the payer has any defenses against a seller who sues, such as that full or partial payment was already made

A negotiable instrument avoids these time-consuming steps. The buyer of a negotiable instrument also buys the seller's personal liability and therefore needs to know only the seller's credit rating. In addition, the purchaser of the instrument can sometimes be free and clear of virtually all defenses that the drawer or maker might have against the payee, such as poor quality of delivered goods. These advantages can expedite the transaction. The instrument becomes freely transferable, almost like cash.

To be negotiable, an instrument must be in writing and must meet four requirements under Uniform Commercial Code (UCC) Article 3:

- It must be signed by the maker, or drawer.
- It must contain an unconditional promise or order to pay a certain sum of money and contain no other promise, order, obligation, or power on the part of the drawer or maker except as otherwise provided by Article 3.
- It must be payable on demand or at a definite time.
- It must be payable to order or to bearer.

UCC Article 3

Article 3 of the Uniform Commercial Code (UCC) governs negotiable instruments payable to order (to a designated payee) or to bearer (to the holder of the paper). The UCC Article 3 states that "order" means a written instruction to pay money signed by the person giving the instruction. The instruction may be addressed to any person, including the person giving the instruction, or to one or more persons jointly. An authorization to pay is not an order unless the person authorized to pay is also instructed to pay.

Article 3 does not apply to money, fund transfers, or securities. A negotiable instrument may be used instead of cash. Drafts and notes are the two categories of negotiable instruments. A draft instrument orders a payment to be made. A note instrument promises that a payment will be made.

Types of Commercial Paper

Commercial paper is any written or printed document or instrument, including a negotiable instrument, evidencing a debt. The two most common types of commercial paper are the draft (check) and the promissory note. See the exhibit "Promissory Note."

Promissory Note

$10,000	Anytown, June 1, 20X1

One year after this date I promise to pay to the order of Peter Finch Ten Thousand Dollars ($10,000).

Due June 1, 20X2	(Signed) Mary Chen

[DA04629]

Article 3 of the UCC covers four types of commercial paper:

- Draft (check)—A type of commercial paper containing an unconditional order by the drawer (person making out the draft), requiring the drawee to pay a certain sum to the payee or to the bearer. A check is a draft drawn on a bank.

- Certificate of deposit (CD)—A document issued by a financial institution acknowledging receipt of money and promising to repay it, with interest, at a specific time.

- Promissory note—A type of commercial paper containing a written promise to pay money on demand or at a definite future time.

- Trade acceptance—A two-party draft used when a seller wants cash immediately but when the buyer cannot provide it until the goods are resold. The seller (drawer) orders the buyer (drawee) to pay at some future time, with the seller named as the payee. The seller delivers the goods to the buyer and then sells the trade acceptance at a discount to get immediate cash. The buyer resells the goods and then pays the new holder of the trade acceptance.

Checks are the most familiar negotiable instruments. A bank depositor is a bank's creditor to the extent of the balance in the bank account. The bank is the depositor's agent in making disbursements from that account. See the exhibit "Draft (in the form of a check)."

Draft (in the form of a check)

(Date) June 1, 20XX

Pay to the
order of _____(Payee)_____ $10.00

Ten and ———————————————————— 00/100 Dollars

Bank/Drawee   _____(Drawer)_____

[DA04628]

Common check transactions include these:

- Failure to honor checks—A bank is liable for all damages caused by its failure to honor a check when the depositor's account contains sufficient funds.

- Overdrafts—A bank can honor a check not covered by the depositor's balance, thus creating an overdraft and making the depositor the bank's debtor.

- Altered checks—A bank can charge an altered check to the depositor's account only to the extent of the check's original terms. For example, if a wrongdoer changes $10 on a check to $100 by adding a zero, the bank can charge only $10 to the depositor's account.

- Stop-payment orders—An oral stop-payment order is effective for only fourteen days. A written stop-payment order is effective for only six months, unless renewed in writing.

Transfer

Transfer of a negotiable instrument gives the new holder the same right to enforce payment as the original holder had. For example, Brittany buys goods from Liam and gives Liam a promissory note as payment. Liam gives the promissory note to Kim in payment of a debt he owes her. Brittany fails to pay on the promissory note. Kim has the same right as Liam would have had, had he kept the promissory note, to sue Brittany for payment.

If the original payer has a defense against payment, the new holder is subject to that defense. In the example just given, assume Liam delivered defective goods and Brittany refused to accept them. If Kim, holding the promissory note, sues Brittany for payment, Brittany can use the same defense that would have been used against Liam: that the goods were defective.

Primary and Secondary Liability

Primary liability
The absolute obligation to pay a negotiable instrument according to its terms.

Secondary liability
The obligation to pay a negotiable instrument only if someone else refuses to pay or to accept the instrument.

The maker of a note has **primary liability**. For a draft, the acceptor is primarily liable; the drawer is not primarily liable because a drawer's liability arises only when the drawee refuses to accept or pay the draft. One who endorses a negotiable instrument assumes **secondary liability** only when the maker or drawee rejects (dishonors) the instrument.

Endorsements

An endorsement is a signature or the equivalent of a signature that legally transfers a negotiable instrument. An endorsement must appear in some form of writing, even a rubber stamp, on the instrument, usually on the back, and must transfer the entire sum. (The term "endorsement" here is not the same as an endorsement to an insurance policy.)

As long as a document contains a signature, other words do not affect the endorsement. For example, the words "I hereby assign my interest in this note to Lindsey," signed by Mark, are an effective endorsement. If the payee's or transferee's name is not correct, that person can take one of three actions:

- Endorse the instrument in the name in which it was made out
- Endorse it with the correct name
- Endorse it in both names

These are the major types of endorsements:

- Special endorsement—A signature or the equivalent of a signature that specifies the person to whom a negotiable instrument is payable. For example, the payee of a check can negotiate it to another person by writing "Pay to the order of Richard Roe," or "Pay to Richard Roe," above his or her signature on the back of the check.

- Blank endorsement (general endorsement)—A signature or the equivalent of a signature on a negotiable instrument that names no specific payee, making the instrument payable to the bearer. For example, a business owner might sign several blank checks for a trusted manager to endorse if cash is needed for business operations or to pay a vendor.

- Restrictive, or collection endorsement—A signature or the equivalent of a signature that includes language placing additional limits on further negotiation of a negotiable instrument. For example, "Pay Jill Doe only if she appears on June 23" or "For deposit only."

- Qualified endorsement—A signature or the equivalent of a signature that passes title to a negotiable instrument but limits the endorser's liability to later holders if the instrument is later dishonored. A qualified endorsement is usually made by writing "without recourse" over the signature.

- Unqualified endorsement—A signature or the equivalent of a signature that places no limits on the endorser's liability on the paper. These are more common than qualified endorsements.

Holders in Due Course

Although assignees of negotiable instruments are generally subject to any defenses the original payer may have, some holders can possess negotiable instruments free of all defenses. A holder in due course is the person to whom a negotiable instrument has been issued or endorsed and who possesses it for value, in good faith and without notice that it may not be valid, can be claimed by another, is overdue, or was previously dishonored. A party often must establish qualifications as a holder in due course to attain maximum rights on the instrument. Such proof is important only if the original holder has a legal defense to the instrument— for example, a defense for nonpayment.

One who obtains an instrument in one of these ways does not become a holder in due course:

- Purchasing the instrument at a judicial sale or taking it under legal process

- Acquiring it in taking over an estate

- Purchasing it as part of a bulk transaction (such as the purchase of all the assets of a business), not in the regular course of the transferor's business

Holder in due course status can be sold and transferred with a negotiable instrument. The status does not apply to a transferee who was a party to any fraud or illegality affecting the instrument or who, as a prior transferee, had notice of a defense against or claim to the instrument.

A holder in due course is free of **personal defenses**, such as lack or failure of consideration, misrepresentation, or fraud. **Real defenses** go to the very existence of the obligation. Examples of real defenses are the incapacity of the maker, drawee, or drawer; duress; illegality; and discharge in bankruptcy. For example, the maker's insanity might negate the existence of the obligation in the first place.

Personal defense

A claim to an instrument by any person and any defense that would be effective in a simple contract transaction.

Real defense

A defense of an obligor of a negotiable instrument that may be asserted even against a holder in due course.

DOCUMENTS OF TITLE

A commercial transaction dealing with the sale of goods may also involve the shipment and/or storage of the goods. Documents of title are important in the shipping and storing of commercial goods.

A document of title provides evidence of ownership rights to specific property, which include the elements of ownership, possession, and custody with the right to receive, hold, and dispose of both the document and the goods it covers. Article 7 of the Uniform Commercial Code (UCC) presents uniform standards for documents of title that provide efficiency for marketing and financial systems in the United States.

Specific documents of title relate to the shipment and storage of goods. An agreement for the storage of the goods is called the **warehouse receipt**. An agreement for the shipment of the goods is called a **bill of lading**.

Warehouse receipt

A legal document that provides title to the goods in storage and assures delivery to the holder of the receipt.

Bill of lading

A document acknowledging receipt of goods from the shipper, given by the carrier, which includes the terms of the contract of carriage for the goods.

Carrier

A person or organization in the business of transporting property of others.

UCC Article 7

The Uniform Commercial Code (UCC) Article 7—Warehouse Receipts, Bills of Lading and Other Documents of Title addresses the shipment, storage, and delivery procedures and requirements involved in the sale of goods.

During the sales transaction, the owner of goods may hire **carriers** to ship the goods to a buyer or to a warehouse for storage during the shipment process. The goods move out of the owner's control and possession and into the control and possession of the carrier or warehouse operator.

Bailment situations are thus created. The owner who puts the goods in the possession of the carrier to ship or the warehouse operator to store is the **bailor**. The carrier or the warehouse becomes the **bailee**.

Warehouse receipts and bills of lading, when formatted and completed in accordance with Article 7, become documents of title for the goods being shipped or stored. These documents are backed by the goods being shipped or stored and can become negotiable instruments. Therefore, Article 7 also deals with the laws of bailment and negotiable instruments.

Bailment
The temporary transfer of a property's custody.

Bailor
The owner of the personal property in a bailment.

Bailee
The party temporarily possessing the personal property in a bailment.

Documents of Title

A title is a document that meets certain legal standards and shows an entity's ownership rights to a specific property. A title indicates the elements of ownership, possession, and custody. The person who legally possesses the title has the right to control and to dispose of the property.

UCC 1-201 (b) (16) defines a document of title as a bill of lading, dock warrant, dock receipt, warehouse receipt, order for the delivery of goods, or any other document that, in the regular course of business or financing, adequately evidences that the possessor is entitled to receive, hold, and dispose of the document and the goods it covers. UCC Article 7 states that, to be valid, a document of title must be issued by or addressed to a bailee with the purpose of covering goods in the bailee's possession. Therefore, these elements are necessary for a document to be considered a title:

- It is created by the bailee (carrier or warehouse operator) as a receipt for goods received.
- It is a contract to ship or to store the goods.
- If it is negotiable, it contains a statement that: (1) the holder has the right to receive, hold, and dispose of both the goods and the document of title, and (2) the purchaser of the title does so free of claims and defenses of prior parties.

Article 7 of the UCC recognizes both electronic and tangible (such as traditional paper) formats for documents of title.

Warehouse Receipt

During the sale of goods, it may be necessary to store the goods for a time. This is particularly true in the agribusiness sector. For example, farmers harvest corn at one set time of year; therefore, all harvested corn enters the marketplace at about the same time. However, buyers purchase corn as needed throughout the year, so the corn must be stored until purchase. A farmer will store corn for a fee at an area grain elevator, which is considered an agricultural warehouse.

A warehouse operator stores goods for hire. The storage arrangement is a bailment; the warehouse operator is the bailee, and the person/entity storing goods is the bailor.

Warehouse operators provide the goods' owner with a receipt describing the amount, type, and condition of the goods, and the conditions of storage. This receipt can be considered a document of title to the goods, which, if properly worded, becomes a negotiable instrument that can be traded, sold, swapped, or used as collateral for borrowing.

A warehouse operator's negligence and degree of liability are determined according to the terms in its warehouse receipts. Although the UCC Article 7 does not prescribe the format of the receipt, it requires nine items of information:

- The location of the warehouse where goods are stored
- The date the receipt is issued to the bailor
- The receipt number showing a consecutive numbering of all receipts issued by the warehouse operator
- A statement indicating the individual or organization to whom the goods will be delivered at the end of the storage period
- The rate of storage and handling charges
- A description of the goods or their packages
- The warehouse operator's (or an authorized representative's) signature
- A statement of ownership if the warehouse operator is the owner or partial owner of the goods being stored
- A statement indicating the amount of any advances made or liabilities incurred for which the warehouse operator claims a security interest

A warehouse operator can be held legally liable for loss to customer property caused by its own negligence. UCC Article 7 allows a warehouse operator to limit liability through terms in the warehouse receipt or storage agreement. For example, the warehouse receipt may specify an amount per article or item or per unit of weight.

Bill of Lading

The term "bill of lading" is an old English marine term. Historically, the written document acknowledging receipt of goods on a ship for transport was known as a bill. Lading is the act of loading. To send one's goods to customers overseas, the goods were taken to the docks and loaded onto ships. The ship's master issued a document acknowledging that the goods had been loaded along with the type and quantity, the destination, and the party to whom the goods were to be delivered. The term is still used today for the transportation of goods by commercial carriers by rail, air, sea, and road.

The parties to a bill of lading include the **consignor**, the carrier, and the **consignee**. The bill of lading serves these purposes:

- As a contract for the transportation (carriage) of the goods
- As a receipt of the goods by the carrier for delivery
- Under certain circumstances, as title to the goods
- To identify the terms of the agreement, including goods by type and amount, the consignor, the carrier, provisions of the agreement for shipping, any special instructions, the consignee, date shipped, terms of delivery, and freight terms (prepaid, collect, or from third party).

Among the numerous types of bills of lading are two that are most frequently used:

- A straight bill of lading names a consignee and obligates the carrier to deliver the goods to that named consignee. The consignee cannot transfer the goods to another entity prior to delivery and then instruct the carrier to deliver the goods to that entity. Therefore, a straight bill of lading is nonnegotiable.
- An order bill of lading contains specific wording, such as "delivery to ABC Company or to order or assigns." This wording allows the consignee to transfer the goods to another entity prior to delivery and then, after the bill of lading has been signed, the goods are received, and shipping is underway, instructs the carrier to deliver the goods to that entity. An order bill of lading is negotiable.

UCC Article 7 as adopted by each state regulates bills of lading for goods shipped within the boundaries of the individual states. When shipments cross state boundaries, they also become subject to federal government regulation under the Interstate Commerce Act.

Delivery Order

An order of delivery can be included within or along with the warehouse receipt or bill of lading. UCC Article 7 defines a delivery order as a written order to deliver goods directed to a warehouse operator, a carrier, or another person who in the ordinary course of business issues warehouse receipts or bills of lading.

SECURED TRANSACTIONS

Buyers pay for goods with their own cash, with borrowed cash, or on open credit granted by the seller or a third party. The seller or a third-party lender can require the buyer to give the seller or lender a security interest in the goods sold, creating a secured transaction.

Consignor
The party who is shipping goods.

Consignee
The person or organization that receives property being transported by a carrier.

In a secured transaction, a buyer or borrower gives collateral to the seller or lender to guarantee payment of an obligation. Secured transactions have five elements:

Collateral

Cash, or near cash assets, that a principal pledges to secure credit, a loan, or other obligation.

Security interest

An interest in property (real or personal) that allows the property to be sold on default to satisfy the debt for which the security interest was given.

- Debtor—The person who is borrowing the money.
- Secured creditor—The person/entity that lends the money to the debtor.
- **Collateral**—The personal property of the debtor that is subject to the creditor's security interest; the debtor guarantees payment to the creditor by giving the creditor a legal interest in the property.
- Security agreement—The agreement between the debtor and creditor that establishes a security interest for the creditor.
- Security interest—The creditor's right to the debtor's personal property.

A **security interest** authorizes the seller or lender to take the goods that have been designated as collateral or otherwise prevent the buyer from disposing of them if the buyer defaults on payments. The seller or lender is the secured party. The security device affects only recovery of the goods. Even if a security device is ineffective, contract common law still provides relief in the form of damages.

UCC Article 9

UCC Article 9—Secured Transactions: Sales of Accounts and Chattel Paper provides a structure that unifies and simplifies the numerous types of secured-financing transactions in today's commerce environment. It sets out a comprehensive process for regulating security interests in personal property and fixtures, including how to perfect or validate a security interest.

Article 9 treats all security interests in personal property as secured transactions. When a buyer agrees to give a seller or lender a security interest in an article sold, the seller or lender can take the goods or otherwise prevent the buyer from disposing of them.

Forms of Secured Transactions

There are three main forms of secured transactions:

Pledge

A security device by which a borrower guarantees payment by delivering collateral to the lender to hold as security for the debt.

Chattel

Tangible, movable personal property.

- **Pledge**—The debtor delivers goods for the creditor to hold as security until payment has been made or the services performed. For example, Ina asks Jay for a loan of $50. Jay loans Ina the money, takes Ina's ring, and tells Ina that he will give the ring back when she repays him the $50.
- **Chattel** mortgage—The debtor is allowed to retain possession of the property while the creditor retains the right to take ownership of the property. For example, Miguel wants to borrow $1,000 from Chris. Chris agrees to loan Miguel the money but wants Miguel's car as security. Miguel needs his car to get to work; therefore, he has to retain possession of it. Chris is afraid if Miguel keeps his car, he might sell it, leaving no security for his

$1,000 loan. Therefore, Chris takes possession of the title to Miguel's car. Miguel has use of his car but cannot sell it. When Miguel repays Chris in full, Chris will return Miguel's car title.

- Conditional sale—A creditor lends money to a debtor, who uses the money to purchase a particular item. For example, Dameka's refrigerator stops working and needs to be replaced, but she is short of cash. James's Appliance store will sell Dameka a refrigerator on a twelve-month payment plan. In the sales agreement, James's Appliance has a lien on Dameka's refrigerator. If Dameka does not make payments, James can take the refrigerator from her.

Forms of Collateral

While any type of property can be accepted as security by a creditor, most collateral falls into one of five forms:

- Consumer goods—Items used primarily for personal, family, or household purposes.
- Equipment—Items used in business or government that have a value. For example, a computer is equipment, while a pencil is not.
- Farm products—Crops or livestock produced in a farm operation or supplies used in the process of farming.
- Inventory—Business goods held for sale or lease or under service contracts, raw materials for manufacture, goods while in the process of being manufactured, and items used or consumed in the business.
- Property on paper—Stocks, bonds, or chattel paper that serve as evidence of the debtor's rights in personal property. Chattel paper is a document showing that the possessor (holder) is owed money and has a secured interest in goods of value connected to the debt.

Attachment

Attachment is the creation of a security interest in property (collateral). The security interest is attached to the property, giving the creditor the right to the property. Attachment protects the creditor from the debtor's default by giving the creditor legal recourse against the debtor. However, attachment does not protect the creditor against claims that parties other than the debtor might also have on the property. Other creditors may have a security interest in the same property. Which creditor can take possession of the property depends on which one has the better claim.

There are three requirements for an attachment to occur:

- A consensual security agreement between the debtor and creditor—For pledges, oral agreements can be sufficient because the creditor possesses the collateral. Other types of security agreements must be written and include the signature of the debtor and a description of the goods. The creditor's signature is not required because the security agreement will be enforced against the debtor. The collateral may be goods acquired after the agreement is made, or items the creditor currently owns, such as inventory and fixed assets.

- The creditor must give value—Value may be either a new item of value, such as loan of money, or value from a preexisting debt, such as forgiveness of all or a portion of a loan.

- The debtor must have rights in the collateral—One cannot give up something that one has no right to. For example, Jane cannot use stolen jewelry as collateral for a loan to buy new bedroom furniture. Because the jewelry is stolen, Jane has no right to it. Normally the debtor must have possession of the property, or evidence of a right to the property, to create an attachment.

Perfecting a Security Interest

Perfection is the process of validating an attachment, which secures the creditor's rights against property of the debtor. Perfection is preferable to mere attachment, which does not protect the creditor against other creditors' nonperfected claims on the property. Perfection informs everyone else that the creditor has a security interest in the property. The creditor is protected from competing third-party claims against the collateral, including claims from those who buy the collateral from the debtor. Perfection also protects the creditor from other creditors.

Perfected security interest
A security agreement that has been filed with the appropriate court to provide the surety a priority interest over others who may also have security interests in the property.

Constructive notice
Knowledge that a person is assumed by law to have because that knowledge could be gained by reasonable observation or inspection.

Typically, a creditor obtains a **perfected security interest** by submitting a financing statement to the appropriate county office. The filing serves as a **constructive notice** to others that a security interest exists in the collateral. A valid financing statement has three elements:

- Names and addresses of the debtor and creditor
- The debtor's signature
- A general description of the collateral property

Financing statements are valid for five years and can be renewed for another five years. Renewals may be repeated indefinitely.

The security interest is perfected when two events have occurred: (1) the security interest has attached, that is, the goods have been sold and the security agreement has been executed, and (2) the financing statement has been filed. If the seller delays filing the financing statement until after the goods have been delivered to the buyer, the security interest is unperfected, and another security interest might attach to the property in the meantime.

When a debtor has met all obligations under the security agreement, a termination statement should be filed so that the secured party can no longer claim a security interest under the financing statement. If more than one perfected security interest applies to the same collateral, they rank in priority according to time of filing or perfection.

Another method of perfecting a security interest is for the creditor to obtain possession of the property. This can occur when the debtor transfers possession of the collateral to a secured party or when the creditor physically seizes the property. Any competing claim for the collateral must go through the creditor who has possession of the collateral. Physical attachment does not require filing a financing statement.

Transferring actual possession is the only way to perfect a security interest in a negotiable instrument, such as a bearer bond, because delivery transfers ownership.

Rights of Perfected and Unperfected Security Interests

A perfected security interest is superior to a later perfected security interest and to the interests of most subsequent lien creditors with limited exceptions, such as these:

- A **holder in due course** takes a negotiable instrument free of any perfected security interest in that instrument.
- An artisan's **lien** for services or materials with respect to the collateral takes priority over a perfected security interest in that collateral.

Even if a security interest is not perfected, it is a valid agreement between the parties and against a third party who buys the goods from a person who deals in them. However, the secured party's rights are subordinate to these parties' rights:

- One who obtains a perfected security interest
- A lien creditor, assignee, bankruptcy trustee, or receiver
- One who buys the property from a person who does not deal in that type of goods, if the buyer does not know about the unperfected security interest

Holder in due course
The person to whom a negotiable instrument has been issued or endorsed and who possesses it for value, in good faith and without notice that it may not be valid, can be claimed by another, is overdue, or was previously dishonored.

Lien
A creditor's legal right or interest in another's property, usually lasting until satisfaction of the specific debt or duty that the lien secures.

Satisfaction of a Secured Debt

Once a debtor has repaid the secured debt, full satisfaction has been obtained. The debtor can send a written request to the creditor for a termination statement and then file a termination statement with all offices that hold the financing statement. A termination statement is evidence that the debt has been paid in full.

Once the creditor receives the debtor's written request for the termination statement, the creditor has ten days to comply. If the debtor does not request the termination statement, the creditor or secured party must send the termination statement to the offices holding the financing statement within thirty days of the debt being paid in full.

Default

Nonpayment is the most obvious form of default. However, a security agreement may define other events as defaults, such as failure to insure the collateral, the debtor's bankruptcy, loss or destruction of the collateral, or removal of the collateral to another place.

If the debtor does not fulfill his/her obligations for a secured transaction, the secured creditor or secured party has the right to foreclose on the security interest. The creditor has the right to foreclose in several ways:

- Right to sue on the underlying debt—The secured party calculates the amount of the debt outstanding and sues the debtor for the amount owed but does not take possession of the secured property.

- Right to strict foreclosure—When the secured party has retained possession of the collateral, it can foreclose the debtor's interest in the collateral by retaining the collateral in full satisfaction of the debt. The secured party must send written notice to the debtor. When the collateral is other than consumer goods, notice must also be sent to any other parties having a security interest in the collateral. If anyone with a security interest objects to another secured party retaining possession, then the collateral must be sold or otherwise disposed of.

- Right to regain possession—The secured party has the right to regain possession of collateral through the courts or by other legal means, such as lawful repossession. The majority of states allow the secured party to regain possession without going to court if the collateral can be repossessed in a legal manner. For example, a bank cannot go into an auto loan debtor's personal garage to repossess the auto. This would be unlawful breaking and entering. However, if the auto is parked on the street or in a public garage, the bank can take the auto without a court order. Also, most states require that if the debtor has paid 60 percent or more on the debt, the creditor is required to go to court to sue for the remaining balance or return part of the money paid if the creditor takes possession of the collateral.

- Right to sell the collateral—The secured party elects to sell or lease the collateral and apply the proceeds to satisfy the claim. If the value received is not enough to satisfy the debt in full, the secured party can sue the debtor for the remainder. The secured party is allowed to charge the debtor for the expenses incurred in the sale or lease. Expenses must be reasonable. Expenses can include such items as attorneys' fees and court costs. If the value received exceeds the debt amount owed plus reasonable expenses, then the secured creditor is required to first distribute the additional amount to any other creditors who have an interest in the property and then give the remainder to the debtor.

- Right to dispose of the collateral as desired—The secured party may sell or lease the collateral at a public or private sale with notification to the debtor. The purchaser at such a sale takes the goods free of the security interest and any subordinate security interests or liens.

When the collateral is in the possession of the defaulting debtor, unless otherwise stated in the secured transaction, the debtor has the right to redeem the collateral prior to any action being taken. The debtor can pay the unpaid portion of the debt plus reasonable expenses incurred by the secured party. The debtor does not have to pay the entire remaining debt but only the amount that is in default, bringing the debt current. Some security agreements have an acceleration clause making all payments due immediately upon default. The debtor may request the court to determine that the acceleration clause is not enforceable if the debtor has brought it current.

The debtor or any other person subject to a security interest in the collateral can redeem the collateral at any time before its sale by tendering full performance of the contract.

CONSUMER PROTECTION LAWS

Consumer protection laws include federal and state legislation intended to ensure fair treatment of consumers in dealings with suppliers of goods and services.

In the commercial sale of goods, the most important transaction is the final sale of the goods to the consumer. Policymakers have deemed it important to protect the consumer in the purchase of goods in a number of ways.

Fair trade laws at both the federal and state levels protect the consumer by limiting restraints on trade to ensure a competitive marketplace. For example, these laws prohibit agreements among businesses within an industry that would limit competition by restricting the supply or cost of goods. Competition benefits the consumer by encouraging lower prices, higher product quality, and better distribution of products and by providing information and enforceable warranties. Fair trade laws include the Federal Trade Commission Act, state deceptive trade practices acts, and the Magnuson-Moss Act, which deals with consumer warranties.

State and federal laws seek to protect consumers by requiring full disclosure of information to consumers and fair treatment by credit providers. Consumer credit laws include the federal Truth in Lending Act, Fair Credit Reporting Act, Fair Debt Collections Practices Act, and Equal Credit Opportunity Act. The Bankruptcy Act allows debtors who are unable to pay their creditors to divide their assets among their creditors and discharge their debts in an orderly and legal process.

Fair Trade Laws

Both states and the federal government have enacted fair trade laws, including these:

- The Federal Trade Commission Act—Consumers benefit when there is free competition in the marketplace. When businesses in an industry have an agreement or understanding to control the supply of goods available to the consumer and/or to fix the price at a set amount, marketplace competition no longer exists. In the late 1800s, the United States marketplace was controlled by a few large businesses in major industries that restricted competition. In response, Congress enacted the Sherman Anti-Trust Act in 1890 and the Federal Trade Commission Act in 1914.

- State unfair trade practice acts—To protect their citizens from anti-competitive business practices within a state, state governments passed their own deceptive trade practices acts.

- State and federal consumer warranty laws—A warranty is the seller's assurance to the buyer that a product is fit for the purposes for which the product will be used. The buyer relies on the seller's assurances in deciding to purchase the goods. A seller's knowledge about a product is assumed to be greater than the buyer's. The Magnuson-Moss Warranty Act of 1975 was passed to protect consumers against deceptions and breaches of warranty by sellers. The law sets standards for warranties to make them more easily understood. States have passed similar warranty laws.

Federal Trade Commission Act

The Federal Trade Commission (FTC) Act of 1914 prohibits unfair methods of competition and unfair or deceptive acts or practices that affect interstate commerce. It is not strictly an antitrust act, although it overlaps with the Sherman Anti-Trust Act of 1890. The purpose of the Sherman Anti-Trust Act was to prevent companies from acting in ways that would hinder free competition by outlawing practices such as unlawful restraints of trade, price discrimination, price fixing, and unlawful monopolies.

The FTC Act is broader than the antitrust acts in that it prohibits unfair or deceptive acts that have no relationship to competition. For example, restraint of trade is a violation of the Sherman Act and also an unfair method of competition. However, misrepresentation is not usually a violation of the Sherman Act but is an unfair act affecting commerce within the meaning of the FTC Act.

The FTC Act does not apply to the insurance industry. Under the McCarran-Ferguson Act, the federal government generally does not regulate the business of insurance because it is subject to state regulation. States usually apply their own antitrust and trade laws to insurance. However, if a state does not have antitrust legislation applicable to insurance, federal antitrust laws apply. Even if states do regulate insurance antitrust matters, federal antitrust laws can apply in cases of insurance practices involving boycott, coercion, or intimidation.

The FTC Act established a five-member commission to oversee the enforcement of the act. The commission takes action against unfair or deceptive practices in three ways:

- Cease-and-desist orders are issued to violating parties after a hearing.
- Trade practice conferences deal with a subject, such as false and misleading advertising in a given industry, by devising a set of trade practice rules. The industry has the opportunity to help write its own regulatory rules.
- Informal settlements and consent orders are used to settle cases arising from violations of the act. Informal settlement is used in cases involving unintentional violations of the act. The accused party executes a stipulation agreeing to stop the challenged practice. Consent orders are similar to pretrial settlements in lawsuits; they are issued to settle a case after a complaint has been filed and a call for a formal hearing has been issued.

State Unfair Trade Practices Acts

In addition to federal laws, states have their own deceptive trade practices acts. State laws vary, but they generally prohibit one or more of these practices:

- Unfair acts (oppressive or bad-faith conduct)
- Deceptive acts (fraud, deceit, and misrepresentation)
- Unfair methods of competition (including antitrust violations such as price fixing and group boycotts)

State laws are designed to compensate for perceived inadequacies in the FTC Act. For example, some acts extend rights to sue that the FTC Act does not provide. Many of the state acts apply to insurance, unlike the FTC Act.

Many states also have unfair trade practices acts and unfair claim settlement practices acts specific to insurance. These generally follow the National Association of Insurance Commissioners (NAIC) model Insurance Fair Trade Practices Act. These are examples of unfair and deceptive insurance industry acts or practices:

- Misrepresentation and false advertising of policies
- Defamation of competitors
- Boycott, coercion, and intimidation
- Creation of false financial statements
- Unfair discrimination
- Use of rebates
- Issuing capital stock, certificates, or securities or using advisory board or similar contracts that promise returns or profits as an inducement to purchase insurance, a sophisticated form of rebate

Under the model act, a state insurance commissioner who believes an act is unfair or deceptive under the law can call a hearing and may order the person or organization to cease the act.

Magnuson-Moss Warranty Act

This act deals with consumer warranties. For many years, the Uniform Commercial Code (UCC) provisions relating to express and implied warranties governed consumer warranties. The UCC codified implied warranties of merchantability and fitness for a particular purpose and described the creation of express warranties. However, under the UCC, only consumers could enforce these warranties, and consumers could also unwittingly waive them. Inadequate controls led to increasing deception in product warranties and resulted in the 1975 passage of the Magnuson-Moss Warranty Act, which supplements the FTC Act and the antitrust laws. The FTC enforces Magnuson-Moss on the federal level. Many states have also passed their own warranty laws.

Under Magnuson-Moss, a producer of goods is not required to provide a warranty; however, if the producer does provide a written warranty, it must conform to certain standards. The law applies to consumer products, defined as tangible personal property for personal, family, or household use, including fixtures. The regulations require these disclosures in a written warranty:

- How to obtain redress under the warranty
- What it will and will not cover
- When it expires
- To whom it applies
- What the warrantor will do if a malfunction occurs
- What service and parts are free

When the product costs more than specified dollar limits, the warranty must be either "full" or "limited":

- A full warranty (also known as the "lemon provision") is a promise to remedy a product defect within a reasonable time and without charge and to refund the purchase price or replace the product if the repairs fail.
- A limited warranty contains the required disclosures with some limitations on the consumer's rights.

The term "lemon provision" is derived from slang describing a product that never seems to be right, no matter how often it is repaired. A lemon law applies to full warranties. If repeated efforts to repair the product fail, lemon provisions require that consumers of such products must have a choice of a full refund or a replacement without charge. To avoid this requirement, some manufacturers call their warranties limited, even though they could otherwise constitute full warranties. Many states have adopted their own lemon laws.

The UCC provides for implied warranties of merchantability and fitness for a particular purpose but permits sellers to disclaim them. Magnuson-Moss does not permit disclaimers of implied warranties but allows a limited warranty to apply the same time restriction to implied warranties as that specified in the express warranty. Under a full warranty, implied warranties cannot be limited in any way.

Consumer Credit Laws

Today's consumers use credit extensively in purchasing goods as varied as shelter, vehicles, food, clothing, travel, electronics, and entertainment. Credit is important to both individual consumers and the general economy. As a result, the protection of consumer credit is a significant area addressed and regulated by legislation. Such legislation endeavors to provide consumers these protections:

- Fair access to credit
- The right to know and understand the terms and interest of a loan prior to agreeing to take on the credit obligation
- Access to their credit reports and the means to correct and/or repair them
- Methods for resolving credit disputes and discrepancies

Consumer credit laws address truth in lending, credit reporting, debt collection practices, and equal credit opportunity.

Truth in Lending Act

In 1968, Congress passed the Consumer Credit Protection Act (the Truth in Lending Act). The purpose of this legislation was to ensure that consumers knew the terms and interest rates of their credit transactions. This act does not replace or preempt state credit disclosure laws unless they are clearly inconsistent with the act, and then only to the extent of the inconsistency.

The Truth in Lending Act applies to personal credit and to credit transactions for personal and real property purchased for personal, family, household, or agricultural purposes. It does not apply to transactions between commercial entities.

The act applies to individuals or organizations that regularly extend credit or make finance charges in connection with installment purchases. It also applies when the purchaser can pay for the item in more than four installments, whether or not there is a credit or a finance charge. It applies to any insurance premium financing plan in which the insured pays premium charges plus a finance charge and to any plan in which the premium is payable in more than four installments, regardless of charges.

Creditors must disclose finance charges. Costs incidental to real estate transactions are not finance charges. However, loan fees, finders' fees, charges for credit reports, and service or carrying charges are considered finance charges in connection with sales of personal property or consumer loans. These are examples of how the act applies to different types of credit transactions:

- Ordinary credit transaction for the sale of goods—The seller must disclose all the finance charges, the cash price, the down payment including trade-in, other charges not part of the finance charge, and the annual percentage rate (APR) of interest charged. The terms of the payment must be stated clearly, including any charge for delinquent payments, and must give a description of any security interest in the goods sold.

- Closed-end plan consumer loan—It has a definite amount and definite time payment. The creditor must provide the same information as in an ordinary credit transaction for the sale of goods.

- Open-end plan consumer loan—The seller must state the conditions of making a charge, the method of calculating the balance due, the method of determining the amount of the finance charge, and any different rates for different balances. The seller must disclose the conditions when other charges could be made and under which the creditor retains a security interest. The debtor can request the average effective annual rate or a projected rate of return.

Congress amended the Truth in Lending Act in 1970 to cover the issuance of credit cards and the liability of credit card holders. The amendment contains these provisions:

- Prohibits companies from issuing credit cards to people who do not request or apply for them

- Limits a cardholder's liability only for its authorized use

- Limits a cardholder's liability to $50 if the card is lost or stolen and used without permission

- Allows the cardholder to withhold payment without incurring a finance charge until the settlement of disputes over the price or quality of goods purchased

Under the Fair Credit Billing Act, an amendment to the Truth in Lending Act, a person who is dissatisfied with property or services purchased with a credit card has the right not to pay the remaining amount due if he or she first tries in good faith to return the property or give the merchant a chance to correct the problem. The credit cardholder's bank usually charges the bill back to the bank servicing the merchant, which in turn charges the merchant, who must make good or sue for the bill.

The Fair Debt Collection Practices Act, another amendment to the Truth in Lending Act, prohibits unfair and oppressive collection practices by agencies that collect debt for creditors. Collection practices prohibited include using violent or criminal acts, using profane language, publishing lists of debtors, calling debtors repeatedly or in the middle of the night, threatening legal action with no intent to follow through, and contacting a debtor at work or at any unusual time or place except with the debtor's consent.

The act also prohibits contacting the debtor's employer, neighbors, or friends, except for the limited purpose of locating the debtor, and even then, no information can be revealed concerning the agent's role in the collection process. The collection agency can send a written notice to the debtor. A debtor who wants to prevent further communications by the collection agency may indicate in writing the desire to stop all further contact, in which case the collector can choose to sue.

Electronic Fund Transfer Act

The Electronic Fund Transfer (EFT) Act was passed by Congress in 1978 and implemented by Regulation E of the Federal Reserve Board to define the rights and responsibilities of parties using electronic transfer of funds. An example of electronic transfer of funds is the use of a bank debit card to pay for a purchase. At the point of purchase, the seller instantly transfers the sales amount from the buyer's account to the seller's account. Buyers do not have the right to stop payment on an electronic fund transfer. However, liability in general is limited to $50 if the card is lost or stolen and the card owner reports the loss within two business days.

Fair Credit Reporting Act

The Fair Credit Reporting Act requires consumer-reporting agencies to exercise their responsibilities with fairness, impartiality, and respect for consumers' rights. It applies only to consumer reporting agencies that for money or on a cooperative non-profit basis regularly assemble or evaluate consumer credit information or other consumer information into reports furnished to third parties. Improper use of consumer credit reports can result in both criminal and civil liability.

A consumer report is a consumer-reporting agency's communication on the consumer's creditworthiness, credit standing, financial capacity, general reputation, personal character, or mode of living, used in whole or in part in establishing the consumer's eligibility for one or more of these:

- Credit or insurance primarily for personal, family, or household purposes
- Employment
- A business transaction involving the consumer, for personal, family, or household purposes

The agency can furnish a credit report only in three circumstances:

- In response to a court order
- Under written instructions of the subject of the report
- To a person who, it has reason to believe, intends to use the information in connection with a credit transaction, for employment purposes, in connection with insurance underwriting, to determine eligibility for a business license if the applicant's financial status is relevant, or for a

legitimate business need for information in connection with a business transaction

The law requires that the consumer receive notice of refusal of credit or insurance for personal, family, or household purposes or employment. The consumer also must receive notice of the consumer-reporting agency's name and address.

Equal Credit Opportunity Act

The Equal Credit Opportunity Act prohibits credit discrimination based on age, race, color, religion, national origin, or receipt of welfare benefits. It also prohibits treating married applicants more favorably than unmarried applicants, such as by failing to consider alimony payments as income.

A lender who rejects an application or withholds credit must either give the applicant specific reasons for the rejection or advise the applicant of the right to obtain those reasons. Married people can have separate credit histories so that they can develop credit histories and references under their own names, which is valuable if they become divorced, separated, or widowed.

Bankruptcy

Bankruptcy law

The body of federal law that allows debtors who are unable to pay their creditors to divide their assets among their creditors to discharge the debts.

Bankruptcy law provides two avenues for relief:

- Liquidation of the debtor's assets and distribution of the proceeds to the creditors
- Reorganization of the debtor's affairs, free of creditors' claims during that process, and partial or full repayment of the debts

The federal Bankruptcy Act and federal bankruptcy courts control bankruptcy in the U.S. States do not govern bankruptcy matters. Insurance companies, however, are unique in that they are not subject to federal bankruptcy law and are governed by state laws when they become insolvent.

Federal Bankruptcy Act

The Bankruptcy Act has several chapters. The two chapters that typically apply to consumers are Chapter 7 and Chapter 13.

- Chapter 7 is the last resort chapter. Under a successful Chapter 7 bankruptcy, the bankrupt entity's nonexempt assets are distributed to its various creditors, and the balance of the debtor's obligations are forgiven or discharged. This chapter applies to consumers (individuals and married couples) in addition to corporations and partnerships.
- Chapter 13 gives small business operators or wage earners the same reorganization opportunities available to corporations, partnerships, and certain individuals with large amounts of debt under Chapter 11. This chapter permits the consumer to set up a plan for paying a portion,

or possibly all, of the creditors without the threat of creditors' lawsuits. (Chapter 12 provides similar relief to small farm operations.)

Any person or entity can apply voluntarily for Bankruptcy Act relief. Any creditor who believes that a bankrupt person or entity favors other creditors or who continues to dispute the remaining assets of a bankrupt estate, can petition the federal bankruptcy court for involuntary bankruptcy. The alleged bankrupt party can contest the proceeding. The bankruptcy court, after a hearing, determines whether the bankruptcy action will proceed or be dismissed. If dismissed in the debtor's favor, the debtor is entitled to costs and expenses arising out of the court proceedings.

These are the parties to a federal bankruptcy proceeding:

- The debtor
- The creditors (both secured and unsecured)
- A trustee
- A bankruptcy judge
- Attorneys for any or all of the parties

Creditors can be represented by creditors' committees and can have more than one committee for each class of creditor. Usually, secured creditors have priority interests in secured property up to the value of the security interest in that property.

The trustee must inventory the bankrupt person's assets and either conserve them or dispose of them economically. The bankruptcy judge will sort out the various creditor and trustee claims and suggest the equitable payments under the law. All parties have a right to legal representation.

Federal law exempts a limited number of the debtor's assets from the bankruptcy estate. Exempt assets are the debtor's property that cannot be sold or dissipated in the bankruptcy proceedings. Examples are tools of the bankrupt person's trade, a limited homestead exemption for the bankrupt person's home, and life insurance.

Liquidation Proceedings

In a Chapter 7 liquidation proceeding, the bankrupt entity usually does not have enough assets to pay all creditors. Therefore, those creditors are prioritized by the six types of claims they have:

- Administrative expenses of the bankruptcy proceeding
- Unsecured business debts
- A limited amount of wage claims
- Contributions to employee benefits plans
- Claims of unsecured individuals
- Unsecured claims of governmental units

The goal is to eventually discharge the debtor from all debts prior to the court's order for relief and to give the individual (or married couple) debtor a fresh start. A corporation or a partnership is not eligible for discharge in liquidation because the organization will not continue in business and thus has no need for a fresh start. In reorganization, full performance of the plan discharges the debtor. Bankruptcy does not discharge some debts, including these:

- Certain tax claims
- Money, property, or services obtained by fraud
- Claims for willful and malicious injury to people or property
- Alimony or support
- Most education loans
- Debts incurred in court actions arising from drunk driving

Discharge is not automatic. The act sets penalties for debtors who intentionally hinder, defraud, or delay creditors; who unjustifiably conceal, destroy, mutilate, falsify, or fail to keep or preserve records; or who knowingly and fraudulently make false oaths. Prior bankruptcy within the past six years will usually result in the denial of a discharge.

SUMMARY

A sales contract is an agreement with consideration between a buyer and a seller to transfer goods. The Uniform Commercial Code (UCC), Article 2 applies to sales contracts. There are three specialized types of sales contracts— sale on approval, sale and return, and auction sales.

Formation of a sales contract requires an agreement, consisting of an offer and acceptance, and consideration. The Statute of Frauds in the UCC specifies the conditions for the enforceability of written and unwritten sales contracts.

Performance of a sales contract may require the fulfillment of terms and conditions regarding delivery of goods, transfer of title, conforming and nonconforming goods, and express or implied warranties.

A breach of sales contract occurs when one of the parties (seller or buyer) to the contract fails to perform the obligations specified in the contract. The remedies for breach of contract depend on whether the breach occurs before or after delivery of the goods.

UCC Article 3 governs negotiable instruments considered commercial paper. Types of commercial paper include drafts (checks), certificates of deposit, promissory notes, and trade acceptance.

When a negotiable instrument is transferred, the new holder has the same right to enforce payment as the original holder. An endorsement is a signature, or the equivalent of a signature, that legally transfers a negotiable instrument. It must appear in some form of writing, even a rubber stamp, on the instrument, usually on the back, and must transfer the entire sum.

A holder in due course is one to whom a negotiable instrument has been issued or endorsed and who possesses it free of personal, but not real, defenses to the obligation.

Article 7 of the UCC addresses the shipment, storage, and delivery procedures and requirements during the sale of commercial goods. Article 7 also deals with documents of title used in this process, including warehouse receipts and bills of lading. Under certain circumstances, such documents may be negotiable instruments.

A security interest authorizes the seller or lender to take the goods or otherwise prevent the buyer from disposing of them if the buyer defaults on payments. A secured transaction has five elements: debtor, secured creditor, collateral, security agreement, and security interest.

Attachment is the creation of a security interest in the property. Attachment gives the creditor legal recourse against the debtor if the debtor defaults. Perfection secures a creditor's rights against the property of the debtor by validating the attachment. Perfection can be achieved by the public filing of a financing statement, the transfer of collateral, or the seizure of collateral.

Nonpayment is the most obvious form of default of a security agreement. However, a security agreement may define other events as defaults, such as failure to insure the collateral, the debtor's bankruptcy, loss or destruction of the collateral, or removal of the collateral to another place. If the debtor defaults, the secured creditor or party has the right to foreclose on the security interest.

Consumer protection laws include fair trade laws, consumer credit laws, and bankruptcy laws. Fair trade laws include the Federal Trade Commission (FTC) Act that supplemented the antitrust acts, the states' own deceptive trade practices acts, and the Magnuson-Moss Warranty Act in 1975 that supplements the FTC Act and antitrust laws by addressing consumer warranties. Consumer credit laws include the Truth in Lending Act, Fair Credit Reporting Act, Fair Debt Collections Practices Act, and the Equal Credit Opportunity Act. The federal Bankruptcy Act governs most bankruptcies, although it does not apply to insurance companies, whose insolvencies are subject to state regulation.

ASSIGNMENT NOTE

1. Uniform Commercial Code, §2-201.

Property Law

Educational Objectives

After learning the content of this assignment, you should be able to:

▷ Explain how a person can acquire ownership of personal property in each of these ways:

- Creation

- Accession

- Confusion

- Gifts

- Bailments

▷ Describe the respective rights and duties of a bailee and a bailor.

▷ Describe these types of real property ownership:

- Fee simple estate

- Life estate

- Joint tenancy

- Tenancy by the entirety

- Tenancy in common

- Community property

- Cooperative ownership

- Condominium ownership

▷ Describe real property sales in terms of the following:

- The required elements of a contract of sale

- The types of deeds and the characteristics of each

- The requirements that deeds must meet

- How and why deeds are recorded

Outline

Ownership and Possession of Personal Property

Bailee's and Bailor's Rights and Duties

Real Property Ownership

Real Property Sales

Real Property Security Interests and Liens

Incidental Real Property Rights

Land Use Restrictions

The Landlord and Tenant Relationship

Summary

5

▶ Describe the purpose and operation of each of the following:

- Mortgages
- Trust deeds
- Land contracts
- Mechanic's liens

▶ Describe each of the following incidental real property rights:

- Adverse possession
- Rights to whatever is under, above, or on the land's surface
- Rights to lateral and subjacent support
- Water rights
- Ownership of fixtures

▶ Describe the following types of land use restrictions:

- Incorporeal interests
- Licenses
- Government controls

▶ Describe the landlord-tenant relationship in terms of the following:

- The three types of landlord-tenant estates
- Landlord's rights and duties
- Landlord's remedies
- Tenant's rights and duties

Property Law

OWNERSHIP AND POSSESSION OF PERSONAL PROPERTY

Personal property is all property that is not real property; it includes both tangible and intangible property. Owners and possessors of personal property have legally protected rights, which vary by the circumstances of the property's creation and the type of ownership.

In addition to buying personal property, a person can acquire ownership of personal property by creating intellectual property or through accession, confusion, gifts, or bailments.

Basic Concepts of Property Law

Property is the real estate, buildings, objects or articles, intangible assets, or rights with exchangeable value of which someone may claim legal ownership. Ownership is the unrestricted and exclusive right to something. In the United States, the law views property as a bundle of legal rights (interests), which are generally insurable, and protects them. In some societies, the concept of private property ownership is either nonexistent or more limited than in the U.S.

Property falls into two categories.

Real property, or realty, is land, including structures or rights attached to the land. Real property includes rights to water, minerals, and things attached to land, such as buildings, trees, and fixtures that have become part of the realty. It also includes rights closely related to land, such as the right to pass over another person's land. Personal property is all property that is not real property. Some personal property, such as goods one possesses physically, is tangible. Other property, such as patents and insurance policies, is intangible.

Ownership is a relationship between the owner and the rest of society that includes three features:

- The right to exclude all others from use and enjoyment of the property owned
- The right to pass valid ("good") title to the property
- The obligations of ownership, such as the obligation to pay taxes and to use property so as not to interfere with others' rights

Another term for legal ownership of property is title. Title is the highest right to property that a person can acquire.

Possession is the exercise of custody or control over property and is not, of itself, ownership. A person can possess property without owning it. When a person possesses property, the law generally protects that possession against everyone except the owner. When the owner grants possession, the possessor's rights to custody and control can be superior in some situations to the owner's, at least during the period for which possession is granted.

Creation of Intellectual Property

One can create intellectual property from one's own endeavors, such as writing a book or a song, inventing a device, or developing a process. In relation to intellectual property, the creative process leads to two results:

Intellectual property rights

The legal entitlement attached to the expressed form of an idea or of other intangible subject matter.

- The intellectual property itself, that is, the expressed form of an idea or intangible subject matter
- **Intellectual property rights**, which include copyrights, trademarks, trade secrets, and patents

Intellectual property rights are insurable rights that protect the creations of a person's mind and talents. For most purposes, federal, not state, law governs all intellectual property rights, although the states have limited jurisdiction over common-law intellectual property rights.

Copyrights

Copyright

The legal right granted by the United States government to a person or organization for a period of years to exclusively own and control an original written document, piece of music, software, or other form of expression.

A **copyright** grants the exclusive right to copy or otherwise reproduce the copyrighted material and to create additional, or derivative, works from the original. The federal Copyright Act of 1978[1] permits the "fair use" (that is, for purposes such as teaching, research, criticism, or comment) of copyrighted material without the owner's consent. Thus, people other than the copyright owner can use portions of copyrighted material. What constitutes fair use is not always easy to determine. Courts consider the following in determining fair use:

- Purpose of the use
- Nature of the work
- Amount and substantiality of the portion used
- Effect of the use on the work's value
- Extent to which the use might deprive the copyright owner of economic advantage

For works created on or after January 1, 1978, the copyright extends for 70 years after the author's death. For anonymous and pseudonymous works for which the author's identity is not revealed in the Copyright Office records, and for works created for hire, the copyright extends for 95 years from publication or 120 years from creation, whichever is shorter. For works originally created before January 1, 1978, but not published or registered until after that date, the duration of copyright is determined in the same manner.

For works created and published or registered before January 1, 1978, the duration of copyright protection has changed over the years. Initially, the copyright extended for twenty-eight years from the date of publication, or registration of an unpublished work, with an option to renew in the twenty-eighth year. Changes to the law now allow for a renewal term of sixty-seven years for a total copyright protection of ninety-six years.[2]

Patents

The federal government grants a **patent** to a person who has given physical expression to an idea. For example, Michael conceives of an invention and then physically creates it. He obtains a patent giving him the exclusive right to make, use, and sell the invention for seventeen years.

A patent is not renewable, and, once the period has elapsed, others can use the idea. To be patentable, an invention can be a new and useful device or machine or a combination of known elements that would perform an additional or different purpose. Over-the-counter and prescription drugs are examples of patentable items.

Patent

The right granted by the United States government to an inventor or applicant for a limited time period to exclusively own and control a new, useful, and nonobvious invention.

Accession

Accession can be by natural accretion, as when an animal produces offspring. It can result from a union of one thing with another, as a coat of paint applied to a house; or it can result from transformation of raw materials into a finished product, such as wood into barrels. The owner of an animal that gives birth also owns the offspring; for example, the owner of a cow owns each calf born to the cow.

Questions of ownership arise when one person adds value to another's personal property, knowingly without the owner's consent. The owner is not required to pay for the added value. Similarly, a person who wrongly takes another's property and then improves it does not acquire title to the finished product and is not entitled to payment for the improvements.

However, if the property is taken innocently, as when one mistakenly cuts trees on another's land and transforms them into lumber, a relative value test may be applied. Under this test, if the value of the finished products were greatly disproportionate to the value of the original goods, the innocent trespasser would retain title to the finished goods after reimbursing the owner for the reasonable value of the goods before improvement. The relative value test is applied to restore innocent parties to a status as close to their original status as possible.

Accession

An increase or addition to property.

Confusion

Confusion

In property law, the intermingling of goods belonging to different owners.

Fungible goods are goods that are commercially interchangeable with other property of the same kind. **Confusion** usually arises when fungible goods, such as wheat, belonging to different owners, are mixed so that identification and separation of the goods are impossible.

In such cases, courts consider whether the confusion resulted from willful misconduct or from an innocent act. If the intermixture of goods was willful or fraudulent, the wrongdoer loses title to the goods, and the other original owner obtains title to the wrongdoer's portion of the goods. When the confusion is innocent or accidental, the parties jointly own the entire mass in proportion to their respective interests.

If the parties can determine the original numbers or amounts they own, they will each own a proportionate interest in the mass. If determination of the original amounts contributed is impossible, the loss falls on the party who caused the intermixture. See the exhibit "Confusion of Goods Example."

Confusion of Goods Example

Bill and George own sheep in adjoining pastures. A storm breaks down a fence between the pastures, and the sheep intermingle. They are unidentifiable. Although Bill and George each know the number of sheep they had, they now jointly own the sheep. Each has an interest in the mass of sheep in proportion to the original number owned.

[DA06265]

Gifts

Gift

The voluntary and gratuitous transfer of property without consideration.

A **gift** requires three elements:

- Donative intent—The donor must intend to make a gift in the present. A promise to make a future gift is not enforceable. Although the donor's subjective intent determines donative intent, objective manifestations, such as the donor's comments and statements, can help prove intent. Subjective intent is what the donor believes is being done, and objective manifestations are what others might interpret as the donor's intent.

- Delivery—Delivery of a gift can be by actual physical transfer or by constructive delivery, which is delivery implied by law. In either case, the donor must give up all control over and possession of (dominion over) the property, and the **donee** must assume dominion over the article. If the donee already has the property, the donor need not repossess it and then return it to the donee. A donor handing car keys to a donee, for example, can establish constructive delivery of a car. When the tangible property is so extensive as to be incapable of physical delivery, a symbolic act is

Donee

The recipient of a gift.

sufficient to accomplish delivery. A written document can prove delivery of an intangible item, such as a bank account.

- Acceptance—Parties rarely dispute acceptance. However, when a donee does not want the burdens of ownership, such as having to pay taxes, acceptance becomes important. One cannot force a gift on a donee. The donee must agree to accept the goods.

Bailments

A person who takes clothes to a cleaner or a car to a garage for repair, or who lends a lawnmower to a neighbor, is a bailor. One who borrows a car or undertakes to care for someone else's personal property becomes a bailee.

A **bailment** has these three elements:

- The transfer of possession of personal property without transfer of title— The transfer of possession is more than the transfer of mere custody. In other words, when a shopkeeper hands an article to a customer to examine, the customer has custody, not possession, and therefore is not a bailee. Similarly, an employee such as a milk-delivery person is not a bailee of the company's milk; the employee merely has custody of the milk for delivery.

- The bailee's acceptance of the bailed property—For example, a restaurant customer who hangs her coat in an unattended cloakroom in the restaurant does not create a bailment, because no delivery to the restaurant owner has occurred. A bailment does arise, however, if the customer leaves the coat with a cloakroom attendant.

- The bailee's express or implied agreement to redeliver the property to the bailor or to a designated third person—If the person receiving the goods has the option to return other property in exchange for the goods or to pay for the goods, no bailment exists.

Bailment

The temporary possession by one party (the bailee) of personal property owned by another party (the bailor) for a specific purpose, such as cleaning or repair.

BAILEE'S AND BAILOR'S RIGHTS AND DUTIES

Everyone is a bailor or bailee at some time. Bailors and bailees have rights and duties related to the property in bailment, which vary depending on the nature of the bailment. The principal consideration in determining these rights and duties is whom the bailment is intended to benefit.

A bailment can benefit the bailee, the bailor, or both. A bailee has a duty to take reasonable care of bailed property, and the extent to which a bailee may use that property depends on the type of bailment. Also, the bailee's right to compensation depends on the type of bailment. The bailor has the right to have bailed property returned and can sue the bailee if property is not returned or is damaged. In some cases, the bailor must provide the bailee with goods that are fit for the purpose of the bailment.

Bailee's Rights

The extent of the bailee's right to use bailed property varies depending on whom the bailment is intended to benefit: the bailee, the bailor, or both.

In a bailment for the bailee's sole benefit, as when a bailee borrows a bailor's car for personal use, the right to use the property is limited to the bailor's contemplated use when lending the car. If the purpose is to travel between two points, any deviation from the route reasonably contemplated by the bailor can make the bailee liable for any loss that occurs during the deviation.

In a bailment for the bailor's sole benefit, the bailee may use or handle the property only to the extent necessary to preserve and protect it. For example, a bailee who accepts a fur coat for safekeeping should not wear it.

In bailments for mutual benefit, the bailee can use the property as specified within the agreement or contract. A person who leases a car can use it only according to the lease agreement's terms. On the other hand, if a person bails a car for the purpose of storage or parking, the bailee can only store or park the vehicle and cannot use it for other purposes.

Possessory lien

A bailee's right to retain possession of a bailor's property as security for the payment of a debt or performance of some other act.

Some bailment contracts require compensation. For those that do not, courts assume that the bailor intended to pay a reasonable value for the bailee's services if a reasonable person would have realized the services require payment. A bailment for the bailee's sole benefit does not imply a charge for services because it is not reasonable to assume charges. When expressed or implied compensation is not paid, the bailee can assert a lien or even a **possessory lien**. For example, an auto repair shop can keep a car until the owner pays the repair bill.

The lienholder is entitled to exclusive possession of the property until receipt of money owed. The lienholder, as a bailee, must take reasonable care of the property, including making repairs and expenditures reasonably necessary to protect and preserve the property.

Bailee's Duties

A bailee must take reasonable care of the bailed goods. If the bailee exercises due care, any loss or damage to the bailed property falls on the bailor because the bailor has title to it. Each type of bailment requires a different degree of care:

- When the bailment is for the bailor's benefit, the bailee is gratuitously in charge of the goods and only slight care is required. For example, if a bailor asks the bailee to care for his car, the bailee is liable for damage to the vehicle only if damage was foreseeable and the bailee could have prevented it without substantial trouble or expense.

- When the bailment is for the bailee's sole benefit, the bailee must exercise an extraordinary degree of care. For example, a bailee who borrows the bailor's car must exercise great care.
- When the bailment is for the bailor's and bailee's mutual benefit, the bailee must exercise reasonable care under the circumstances. For example, a bailee who rents a tent for a lawn party must exercise reasonable care to ensure it is not damaged.

A bailee can extend or limit liability for the bailed goods in the bailment contract. For example, household goods movers and airlines restrict liability for goods and baggage, often to a certain amount of money per pound. The right to limit liability extends only to liability for ordinary negligence, not to willful or wanton misconduct.

Because of the bailee's legal duty to care for the goods and to return them to the bailor, the bailee has an insurable interest in the goods and can obtain insurance to protect that interest. In the absence of a statute or specific contract requirement, however, the bailee has no duty to obtain insurance on the bailed goods. The bailee must hold insurance proceeds paid for the bailed property's damage in trust for the bailor, except for that amount representing the bailee's interest under the bailment agreement.

A bailee has possession only and therefore cannot transfer title to a third party. If the bailee sells the bailed goods to a third party, the bailor can recover them from the third party unless the bailor has represented the bailee as the owner of the goods.

The bailee must surrender the goods to the bailor on request unless the bailment is for a term, such as a car rental, in which case the bailee can retain possession for that period. A bailment for a specified period entitles the bailee to possession only for that period. If the bailment has no set period, the bailor can terminate at any time and end the bailee's right to possession. The bailee must redeliver the goods within a reasonable time after the bailment period ends. A bailee's attempt to sell bailed goods, or to cause extensive damage to the goods, automatically terminates the bailment and entitles the bailor to immediately recover the goods, as well as any repair or replacement costs.

Bailor's Rights and Duties

In mutual benefit bailments and in bailments for the bailee's benefit, the bailor has a right to compensation according to the agreement. However, in bailments for the bailor's sole benefit, the bailor is not entitled to compensation.

A bailor can sue a bailee who does not return the bailed property at the end of the bailment term. If the goods have been damaged, either negligently or willfully, the bailor can sue either the bailee or a third person responsible for the damage.

In mutual benefit bailments, the bailor owes the bailee a duty to supply goods that are reasonably fit for the purpose the parties envision. The bailor must make a reasonable inspection of the goods to determine any defects. The bailment agreement implies a warranty that the goods are in proper condition, and the bailor is responsible for any damage the bailee suffers because of unknown defects. In a bailment for the bailee's sole benefit, as when the bailor lends the goods to the bailee, the bailor must notify the bailee of known defects.

A bailor is not usually liable for a bailee's negligent use of bailed property. However, a bailor who negligently entrusts property to an incompetent bailee can be held liable for resulting injuries to third persons. Negligent entrustment is leaving a dangerous article, such as a gun or car, with a person who the lender knows, or should know, is likely to use it in an unreasonably risky manner. For example, a car owner who permits an unlicensed minor to operate the car on the highway can be liable to a third party who is injured in an accident caused by the minor.

A bailor who knows that the bailed property is in a dangerous condition can be liable for injury to a third party if the bailee is not aware of the danger.

In some cases, a bailor has a duty to reimburse the bailee. The cost of repairs ordinary and incidental to the use of bailed goods under a rental contract is usually the bailee's responsibility. However, the bailor must pay the cost of extensive repairs to the property. For example, if a bailee makes repairs that the bailor should have made, such as installation of a new transmission in a car, the bailor must reimburse the bailee.

REAL PROPERTY OWNERSHIP

There are various types of ownership interest in real property. Understanding the rights and constraints associated with each can help insurance professionals meet the needs of their clients.

Real property includes the surface of land and everything that is in, on, or above it, including oil, water, minerals, and gravel under the surface, as well as trees, shrubs, and plants on the surface. Real property also includes buildings and other structures permanently affixed to the land.

There are two types of estate, or ownership interest, in real property:

- Fee simple estate
- Life estate

When more than one person owns property, that ownership can take different forms:

- Joint tenancy
- Tenancy by the entirety
- Tenancy in common
- Community property
- Cooperative ownership
- Condominium ownership

Estate in Fee Simple

The owner of a **fee simple estate** can leave the property to heirs and sell, lease, or use it. The typical owner of a single family home has a fee simple estate.

Fee simple estate
A full ownership interest in property with the unconditional right to dispose of it.

Life Estate

Property owners can carve out part of a total interest to create lesser interests either in terms of the quality of the ownership or for the length of time ownership exists. A **life estate** is one type of lesser property interest. A life estate lasts only until the death of a specified individual. For example, David grants land to Mary for the period of her life. Alternatively, David grants land to Mary for the period of Betty's life. In each case, Mary is the life tenant. On Mary's death, or Betty's, title to the property reverts to David or to David's estate.

If the life tenant sells the land, the buyer's interest lasts only as long as the life estate. Therefore, a prospective buyer must be concerned with the life expectancy of the person on whose life the estate is based.

Life estate
An interest in which a person, called a life tenant, is entitled to possession of real property and to all income the land produces for the duration of that person's or someone else's life; the interest terminates on the death of the life tenant (or of the other person during whose life the life tenant possesses the property) and does not pass to his or her estate.

Concurrent Estates

Two or more persons, particularly husband and wife, often own property concurrently. Concurrent ownership can be in any of these forms:

- Joint tenancy
- Tenancy by the entirety
- Tenancy in common
- Community property

In each of these situations, the property owners can have **tenancy** interests they can insure even though they share the property with at least one other person.

Tenancy
A right to possession or ownership, or both, of property.

Joint Tenancy

Joint tenancy

A concurrently owned and undivided interest in an estate that transfers to a surviving joint tenant upon the death of the other.

Joint tenancy is probably the oldest form of concurrent ownership and usually occurs today among members of the same family. The distinguishing feature of joint tenancy is that, on one joint tenant's death, the estate goes entirely to the other joint tenant. If David, Mary, and Betty are joint tenants and David dies, his interest goes equally to Mary and Betty. If Mary then dies, the whole estate goes to Betty. If David is married, his wife has no interest in the property through marriage.

The parties create joint tenancy at one time, from one grantor, in equal shares. With two joint tenants, each must hold a one-half share, and so on. One of the joint tenants cannot be subject to a condition that does not apply to the others. The same deed must name them all as owners.

Tenancy by the Entirety

Tenancy by the entirety

A joint tenancy between husband and wife.

The usual form of deed for **tenancy by entirety** is "to Husband and Wife, as tenants by the entirety." If the deed does not state "tenants by the entirety" explicitly, the law considers that phrase implied in joint tenancy between husbands and wives. Half an estate may be taken as tenants by the entirety, and the other half by another person, as "to Husband and Wife, and Third Person." For example, Doris and Rick own half of a farm as tenants by the entirety, and Cheryl owns the other half.

A tenancy by the entirety is similar to a joint tenancy because the survivor takes the entire property. It differs from a joint tenancy in several ways:

- A sale or contract to sell does not sever the tenancy.
- Individual creditors of either the husband or the wife cannot subject the property to a claim. Unless both spouses are found liable for the same tort, judgment creditors cannot execute on the marital property. This can prevent a family from losing its home after either the husband or the wife causes a serious accident.
- Neither party individually owns a portion that can be mortgaged.

Divorce ordinarily severs a tenancy by the entirety, and both spouses can terminate it by joining in a transfer of the property or by transferring one spouse's interest to the other.

Tenancy in Common

Tenancy in common

A concurrent ownership of property, in equal or unequal shares, by two or more joint tenants who lack survivorship rights.

Tenancy in common differs from joint tenancy and tenancy by the entirety in these ways:

- It involves no survivorship.
- The parties can own unequal shares.
- The parties need not derive their interests in the same deed from the same grantor.

A will or deed can create a tenancy in common expressly, as when a deed is "to David and Mary, as tenants in common." More commonly, operation of law creates a tenancy in common. For example, if David dies intestate (without a will) and has three heirs, they inherit David's real property as tenants in common.

Community Property

Some states follow the Spanish civil law concept of **community property**. Under this concept, two types of property can belong to a spouse—separate property and community property. The separate property of either spouse is that which the spouse owned at the time of marriage as well as any property that the spouse acquires individually after marriage by gift or inheritance. Separate property is the respective spouse's sole property because communal effort did not produce it, and it is free from the other spouse's interest or control.

Under the community property concept, a husband and wife share equally in all community property, and the amount of their individual contribution to the joint effort does not change the equal interest. A gift to both spouses becomes community property. On a spouse's death, unless a will states otherwise, the property is divided in half. One-half goes to the surviving spouse; the other half goes to the deceased spouse's heirs, if any. A spouse cannot, by will, dispose of more than one-half of community property.

Community property
Property owned or acquired by both spouses during a marriage by their communal efforts. Each spouse has an undivided one-half interest in the community property.

Cooperative Ownership

Cooperative ownership is similar to concurrent ownership. However, it does not involve unity of possession or an equal right to occupy the entire premises with all other tenants. Cooperative ownership is a common method of owning real property, usually apartments.

In **cooperative ownership**, a corporation holds title to the property. The cooperative owner purchases stock in the corporation and receives a long-term proprietary lease for a certain apartment. The lease sets forth the parties' rights and liabilities, including provisions for monthly payments. The number of shares in the corporation that each tenant owns can be equal or can vary according to the values of the apartments. For example, ten people form a cooperative venture to construct ten apartments at a cost of $1 million. The five apartments on the ground floor are each valued at $120,000; the five on the second floor at $80,000 each. The corporation issues 100 shares of $10,000 stock. Those desiring ground floor apartments purchase twelve shares, and those wanting the second floor purchase eight shares each.

Cooperative ownership
Ownership, usually of real property such as an apartment building, by a corporation, the stockholders of which receive long-term proprietary leases to a portion of the property and a proportional vote in its affairs based on the number of shares owned.

The corporation ordinarily obtains a mortgage, constructs the building, and then operates it. Each tenant, as a shareholder in the corporation, has a proportional vote in its affairs based on the number of shares owned. The corporation levies monthly assessments to pay mortgage principal and interest, taxes, cost of operations, insurance on the structure in the name of the corporation, and other items.

Cooperative ownership provides for operation and maintenance by someone other than the tenant, while guaranteeing a right of occupancy for as long as desired. A disadvantage is the owner's limited control over external conditions, which can lead to a deterioration of the investment. Finding a purchaser for the premises can be difficult, particularly if it is beginning to deteriorate. Additionally, if other tenants do not keep up their payments, and as a result the mortgage payments lapse, the mortgagee can foreclose on the property. In that case, all tenants can lose any equity they have built up in the property.

Condominium Ownership

Condominium

A real estate development consisting of a group of units, in which the air space within the boundaries of each unit is owned by the unit owner, and all remaining real and personal property is owned jointly by all the unit owners.

Condominium ownership, like a cooperative, is concurrent ownership. However, it is closer to a true concurrent ownership than the cooperative and has two legal elements:

* Individual ownership of a "unit," or separate, defined area
* An undivided interest in common or public areas (common elements) that serve all individual units

Unless both elements exist, no condominium interest exists, and the two elements cannot be separated. A unit owner cannot retain title to a unit and sell the undivided interest in the common element. Condominiums are usually multi-unit buildings, but sometimes groups of single-unit buildings qualify in this category.

The common element is essentially the land and the building, together with attached or outside areas, such as parking and storage areas, and heating and cooling systems. The unit an individual owns often is described as a "box of air."

A condominium is created by a written declaration that details the number of units and the percentage interest that each unit has in the common elements. Bylaws usually govern day-to-day operations of an association established to run the common elements. All unit owners have interests as tenants in common in the common elements that can be, but usually are not, equal.

In contrast to cooperative ownership, the condominium owner, as a tenant in common, has a direct property interest in the land and buildings, rather than a secondary interest as a shareholder of a corporation. The individual can sell, transfer, mortgage, or leave to heirs his or her condominium interest.

REAL PROPERTY SALES

In the sale of real property, the contract of sale is the agreement between the buyer and the seller that outlines the terms and conditions of the sale.

The document that actually transfers title to the property is the deed. Understanding the requirements in both contracts of sale and the transfer of title to real property helps protect the interests of both purchaser and seller.

To be legally binding, a real estate contract of sale must meet certain requirements. It must be in writing and must include a description of the premises to be sold and the price. After property has been sold, a deed transfers title to the purchaser. There are three principal types of **deeds**: warranty deeds, bargain-and-sale deeds, and quit-claim deeds. Deeds are typically recorded as official documentation that transfer of ownership has occurred.

Deed
A written instrument that transfers interest in real property.

Elements of a Contract of Sale

Execution of a contract of sale usually precedes a transfer of real property. The contract need not be complex or lengthy, but it must contain certain elements to be binding, and the parties must be competent to enter into a contract.

Vendor and **vendee** are the terms that apply, respectively, to the real property seller and purchaser. After they execute the deed, they become the **grantor** and **grantee**, respectively. Even if title is in the vendor's name only, if the vendor is married, the spouse should sign the contract of sale.

A contract of sale for real property requires these elements:

- Writing—Under the statute of frauds, any agreement to transfer an interest in real property must be in writing and signed by the persons to be bound. If the vendor attempts to enforce the contract against the vendee, the vendee must have signed it, and vice versa. The parties, however, can orally rescind a contract of sale because the rescission does not transfer an interest in real property. Any modification of the contract must be in writing.

- Essential terms—The contract must describe the premises to be sold and the price. The description need not be precise but must be sufficient to identify the property. Thus, a reference to "1000 Park Avenue, to be sold for $100,000" would be sufficient.

Vendee
The purchaser of real property.

Vendor
The seller of real property.

Grantor
One who conveys property to another.

Grantee
The buyer of real property after execution of the deed.

Certain additional, nonessential terms are usually covered in a complete contract of sale. For example, the time of closing, if not stated, is to be within a reasonable time, and payment usually occurs at closing.

Types of Deeds

There are three principal types of deeds:

- The warranty deed can be of two types: general warranty and special warranty. A general warranty deed, in addition to transferring whatever title the grantor has, contains the grantor's warranty that the title is free of all encumbrances (prior claims on the property), that the grantor has the title being transferred, and that no one else has a better title. A special warranty deed contains warranties against only those encumbrances and defects in title that might have been created since the grantor took title. A title insurance policy is particularly important for a special warranty deed because otherwise the grantee has no protection against earlier defects. In the event of breach of any of these warranties, also called covenants, the grantee can sue the grantor. The deed states whether an encumbrance, such as a mortgage on the property, exists.

- The bargain-and-sale deed transfers whatever interest a grantor has in real property to a buyer for valuable consideration but lacks any guarantee from the seller about the validity of the title, and it includes no warranties that the title is free from encumbrances.

- The quit-claim deed transfers only the title or interest (if any) the grantor has in the land at the time of transfer. It contains no warranties, and, if mortgages or liens encumber the land, or any other claimants assert rights to the land—for example, if the grantor does not actually own it—the grantee has no recourse against the grantor.

Requirements That Deeds Must Meet

A deed must be absolutely accurate—more so than the contract of sale because if the two conflict, the deed prevails. Deeds must meet basic requirements:

- Under the statute of frauds, a deed must be in writing.
- The grantor must be legally competent, the grantor's name must be in the deed, and the grantor must sign the deed.
- The deed must name the grantee.
- The deed must state the consideration.
- The deed must contain words that specifically state that a transfer of the property is occurring.
- The deed must contain a description of the property conveyed.
- The deed must be dated.
- The deed usually contains a paragraph reciting who transferred the property to the grantor, date of transfer, and the location of the recorded copy of the deed.
- Some states require the grantor's signature under seal.
- Several states require witnesses to the grantor's signature.
- The deed must be delivered in order to effect the transfer.
- Most states require an acknowledgment, which is a formal, written statement by a public official, usually a notary public, that the grantor has appeared before the official and has transferred the property voluntarily.

Recording Deeds

To record a deed, the buyer takes it to a local government office, usually known as the office of the recorder or registrar of deeds, and files it. The purpose of recording is to give notice to the world that the transfer of real property has occurred.

All states have recording acts under which any deed, mortgage, or other instrument affecting land is not valid against a subsequent purchaser for value who had no notice or knowledge of the previous sale unless the instrument has been recorded.

For example, if David sold land to Mary in 2005 and later sells the same land to Betty in 2010, Mary would prevail if she had recorded the deed, even though Betty knew nothing about the prior transaction. However, if Mary does not record the deed, and if Betty, unaware of the sale to Mary, purchases the land from David and records the deed, Betty's ownership takes priority over Mary's.

An unrecorded document affecting property rights is effective between the immediate parties and persons who are not purchasers (such as donees and heirs), but not against subsequent purchasers for value without notice or knowledge.

REAL PROPERTY SECURITY INTERESTS AND LIENS

Real property is commonly used as collateral for loans, often to secure the funds to purchase the same property. In this case, the lender is typically given an interest in the property by the borrower. In addition, contractors and material suppliers have statutorily created security interests (called liens) in specific property to ensure that they receive payment for their work or materials.

Mortgages, trust deeds, and land contracts are all security devices designed to protect the lender from default on the part of the borrower in a real estate purchase. With any of these three devices, the lender retains an interest in the property until the loan has been repaid. Similarly, tradespeople and materials suppliers use mechanics' liens to retain an interest in labor or materials used in improving, repairing, or maintaining real or personal property to help ensure that they receive payment.

Mortgages

The mortgage used in most states today is in the form of a deed or transfer of land by the borrower to the lender, with a statement of the debt and a provision that the mortgage will be void at full payment of the debt.

A real estate mortgage transfers an interest in real property; it must be in writing and signed in the same manner as a deed. If not properly executed, it may not be eligible to be recorded in the local government office that gives notice to the public of the transaction. Between the parties, a mortgage's validity does not depend on compliance with other formal requirements. Thus, if the parties intended the transaction as a loan and security type of transaction, it is a mortgage, regardless of the form of the contract. However, an unrecorded mortgage is not valid against good-faith purchasers, subsequent mortgagees without knowledge, or creditors with liens on the property.

Mortgagor

The person or organization that borrows money from a mortgagee to finance the purchase of real property.

Mortgagee

A lender in a mortgage arrangement, such as a bank or another financing institution.

The **mortgagor** has the specific rights to sell, lease, or even put another mortgage on property. The mortgagor is effectively the property owner as far as everyone else except the **mortgagee** is concerned. However, transactions after recording of a mortgage do not affect the mortgagee's rights.

For example, assume that David mortgages land to Mary to secure a loan of $70,000 and records the mortgage properly. David then conveys the land to Melissa. The sale is appropriate, but if David or Melissa does not pay the loan when it falls due, Mary has a right to foreclose the mortgage. Melissa can lose her interest because it is subject to Mary's mortgage rights. If the proceeds of the sale are insufficient to satisfy the debt to Mary, she has the right to obtain a deficiency judgment against David as the original mortgagor, and possibly against Melissa, the subsequent buyer, for the amount of the deficiency. If the sale yields excess money, it goes to David as mortgagor or to Melissa, the subsequent buyer.

A purchaser's rights and liabilities depend on the wording in the deed. A purchaser who takes property subject to an existing, properly recorded mortgage, on which the mortgagor later defaults, can be liable to the mortgagee for a deficiency in payments. However, if the deed states that the buyer takes the property "subject to" the mortgage, the buyer is not liable for any deficiency in mortgage payments.

If the deed states that the buyer "assumes and agrees to pay the mortgage debt," the buyer also becomes liable for any deficiency. The original mortgagor who sells a property remains liable on the original agreement to pay the debt and cannot be relieved of this liability without the mortgagee's consent. In most states, the original mortgagor is a surety, or guarantor, for a buyer who assumes the debt. Therefore, if that buyer defaults in paying the mortgage and a deficiency in payments occurs, the mortgagee can proceed against either the original mortgagor or the purchaser. However, an original mortgagor who pays when the buyer defaults can recover the amount paid from the buyer, if the buyer is solvent.

The mortgagee's interest in the property is assignable at any time, and the assignment must include the debt. If a note, or series of notes, evidences the debt, assignment is accomplished by negotiating the notes and making an outright assignment of the mortgage paper to the assignee. In most states, negotiation of the notes carries with it the right to the security, and their holder receives the benefits of the mortgage.

Mortgage **foreclosure** is the mortgagee's remedy when the mortgagor defaults on mortgage payments. Foreclosure through public sale is the most common method.

To foreclose, the mortgagee sues the mortgagor. Following trial, the court enters a judgment for the amount owed and orders the property's sale. The proceeds of the sale first pay the judgment to the mortgagee. The surplus, if any, goes to the mortgagor. Generally, the mortgagor, or any other party claiming an interest in the property that a foreclosure might cut off, can redeem the property after default and before expiration of a redemption period, usually six months or one year.

Foreclosure

A legal proceeding to terminate a mortgagor's interest in property; the mortgagee's remedy when the mortgagor defaults on payments.

Trust Deeds

A regular mortgage has only two parties, the borrower (mortgagor) and the lender (mortgagee). The **trust deed** (deed of trust or trust indenture) has three parties: (1) the borrower (trustor) who transfers the land; (2) the trustee, to whom the land is transferred; and (3) the beneficiaries, for whose benefit the transfer is made. In many respects, the trustee is a mortgagee, and the standard mortgage clause in an insurance policy usually refers not only to a mortgagee but also to a trustee.

Trust deed (deed of trust or trust indenture)

A secured interest in real property that is held by a trustee to protect the lender (beneficiary) until the loan is repaid by the borrower (trustor).

Trust deeds have three important advantages:

- In several states, the trust deed can be foreclosed by a trustee's sale without any court proceedings, although some states treat it exactly like a mortgage and require court foreclosure.

- The trust deed facilitates borrowing large amounts of money. For example, a company borrows a large sum from a bank and executes a trust deed on its property to the bank as trustee. The bank, in turn, sells a large number of notes or bonds authorized by the trust deed to investors who are secured by the trust deed, simplifying what might have been a very complicated mortgage procedure of separate notes and separate mortgages for each investor.

- The holder of a bond secured by a trust deed can sell the bond with minimum expense and effort. Sale of a note secured by a mortgage requires an assignment of the mortgage, a complex arrangement.

The principal disadvantage of trust deeds arises when the number of beneficiaries or bondholders is large. When the borrower pays off the trust deed, the trustee must be certain that all bondholders are paid. If not, the trustee is personally liable. Additionally, in a sale resulting from foreclosure, the trustee cannot purchase the property at a foreclosure sale in most states, and a committee of bondholders must consummate the purchase.

Land Contracts

Under a land contract, the parties enter into an agreement of sale of property with a stipulation that the seller will not transfer title to the property until payment of a certain percentage of the price, frequently 100 percent. The percentage can be less than 100 percent, with the option to enter into a standard mortgage arrangement for the balance.

Land contracts are frequently used when buyers have poor or inadequate credit ratings or do not have enough money for down payments. The buyer takes possession of the land, pays all the taxes and assessments, insures the property, repairs it, and assumes all the obligations of an owner. In fact, the law treats the buyer as the owner, and the seller has only the legal title. If the buyer defaults, the seller can declare the contract breached and repossess the property, treating the buyer as an ordinary tenant.

Mechanics' Liens on Real Property

Artisans and contractors (traditionally referred to as "mechanics") and material suppliers furnish labor and material for the construction of improvements on land. Because those improvements become part of the real property, mechanics and material suppliers have statutorily created security interests in the property, called liens to ensure that they receive payment.

Mechanic's lien

A lien, granted by law to anyone who repairs a specific piece of property, that secures payment for the repairs.

A **mechanic's lien** may cover labor or materials supplied in improving, repairing, or maintaining real or personal property, such as a building or a car. Usually, for real property, the work done or material used must become a permanent part of the property in order for a mechanic's lien to apply.

A general contractor who seeks to assert a lien usually must show certain facts:

- Substantial performance of the contract
- Improvement of a specific piece of property under the contract
- Specific mention in the contract of the property to be improved

State statutes usually require the filing of a notice of lien in the appropriate public office within a specified period after completion of the work. Generally, the notice must state this information:

- Amount claimed
- Claimant's name and address
- Type of improvement
- Description of the land
- Owner's name

A mechanic's lien is usually operative for a specified time, and the lienholder must take steps to enforce or foreclose the lien within that time. Foreclosing a mechanic's lien resembles foreclosing a mortgage. In some states, the lien attaches only to the building but not to the land, and in some places only to the additions or improvements themselves. Because removal of the materials furnished may often damage the property, courts frequently order the sale of the property and give the mechanic's lienholder a share of the proceeds.

Priorities for Mechanics' Liens

States use four rules to determine when a mechanic's lien attaches to property to create priority over other secured interests:

- In most states, mechanics' liens relate to the day the work started. A mortgage recorded on the following day is subordinate to the lien of a subcontractor who was not hired until later because that lien relates back to the start of the work. Lienholders have no priorities.

- In some states, the lien attaches when the mechanic starts work. The lien cannot have priority over a mortgage recorded earlier.

- The lien attaches on the date the mechanic makes the contract for improvement. Such a lien is called a "secret lien" because improvement contracts are usually not recorded, and even an inspection of the property would not disclose that work is starting in the future. Nevertheless, a mortgage recorded after the date of the improvement contract is subordinate to the mechanic's lien.

- The lien attaches on the notice filing. A previously recorded mortgage, therefore, has priority.

Waiver of Lien

Parties can waive the right to a mechanic's lien in a contract for improvements. In some states, such a provision is not valid unless the contract is filed. In some states, the waiver is valid against everyone, including subcontractors, but in other states, it is valid only against the general contractor.

Another method of waiver is to obtain a partial waiver from the mechanic as work progresses and when the mechanic receives partial payments. The waiver usually states that the mechanic waives all liens "for work and materials furnished" up to the date of the waiver. A property owner can pay off a lien and then clear the public records by filing a release of mechanic's lien form in the office where the lien is filed.

INCIDENTAL REAL PROPERTY RIGHTS

Ownership of real property need not necessarily result from the purchase of that property. It can also result from possession. And ownership includes more than a right to the real property itself. It comprises a number of other, incidental rights as well.

Five important incidental rights arise from either possession or ownership of land:

- Adverse possession
- Rights under, above, and on the land's surface
- Rights to lateral and subjacent support
- Water rights
- Ownership of fixtures

Adverse Possession

Adverse possession

The claim of ownership of land by possession that is exclusive, open, hostile, unpermitted, and continuous for a statutory period.

Conflict can arise when a person who possesses land claims ownership and another who does not possess it also claims ownership. For example, Elliott lives on a lot, for which Dianne has had legal title, for over thirty years. During that thirty-year period, Dianne knew of Elliott's residence and, although she regularly asserts to Elliott that she owns the land and wants him to leave, she does not pursue legal action to have him evicted. Dianne, the person who is not in possession but who claims legal ownership, can sue the person in possession, Elliott. Elliott may claim he owns the land by **adverse possession**, which has four elements:

- The adverse party must have exclusive possession of the property and occupy it in the usual way, such as living in a residence.
- Possession must be open and obvious.
- Possession must be adverse, or hostile, and without the owner's permission.
- Possession must be continuous for a statutory period, usually a lengthy period, such as twenty years or more.

Rights Under, Above, and on the Land's Surface

Ownership of land includes the incidental rights to whatever is under, above, and on the surface.

Ownership of land below the surface includes such things as minerals, clay, stone, gravel, and sand. A transfer of land also transfers these materials; however, a seller can reserve mineral rights in the deed. Oil and gas, on the other hand, flow freely under the surface, and no person owns them until he or she possesses the rights to seek them. These rights (which can vary by state) are divided up in different ways; by deeds, by leases, and by profits (similar to easements).

Ownership of land carries with it limited rights over the air space above the land. An owner can halt unauthorized intrusion into this air space, such as projections from an adjoining building or utility lines stretched across the air space. Generally, planes can fly over land as long as they do not interfere unreasonably with the owner's use and enjoyment of the land.

The property owner also has rights to products of the soil. Annual products, such as crops, are personal property. Perennial products, such as timber, can be real property.

Rights to Lateral and Subjacent Support

A landowner also has the right to lateral and subjacent support systems that might not be on the landowner's property.

The right of **lateral support** applies to land in its natural condition only. For example, David and Mary own adjoining vacant lots, and David excavates his land close to the property line, causing a part of Mary's land to fall into the excavation. David is liable to Mary for the damage to her land. However, if Mary's lot has a building on it, David is not liable for damage to the building because the duty to provide lateral support extends only to land in its natural state. The support of the land need not be natural; for example, David can avoid liability by building a retaining wall to support Mary's land.

If a building stands on Mary's land, David must give her reasonable notice of his intent to excavate so that she can take steps to support the building. David must also excavate with reasonable care. If David fails to give notice and fails to excavate with reasonable care, he might be liable to Mary for damages should Mary's building collapse.

Two parties can have rights in one piece of land: one party may own the land, and the other may own the rights to minerals under that land. For example, Bob sells mineral rights to Chang but retains a natural right of **subjacent support** from the underlying mineral area. If Chang removes minerals, withdrawing subjacent support for Bob's land, and the surface subsides, Bob can recover damages without proving any negligence on Chang's part.

As with lateral support, a subjacent owner can furnish artificial supports, such as columns or braces, to prevent damage to the surface land.

Lateral support
A property owner's right to have land supported by the land adjacent to it.

Subjacent support
A property owner's right to have land supported by the earth below it.

Water Rights

Another incidental land ownership right is water rights. Property owners have rights to both underground and surface waters.

An owner can remove underground waters that percolate through the soil and follow no defined course. The owner can remove any quantity of the water, even if it deprives adjacent owners of water, so long as the owner uses it on the land and does not sell it at a distance, to the adjoining landowners' detriment. When water is scarce, an owner can use only a reasonable amount.

Discharging surface water from one's land onto another's land is not a basis for a suit as long as the water is not collected by artificial means and discharged on the adjoining land in new or concentrated channels, causing damage.

Streams and rivers can be property boundaries or can pass through property. Owners of the property can use as much water from the waterway as needed for domestic purposes but must use only a reasonable amount for industrial purposes and must consider downstream owners' needs. Owners have a right to a pollution-free stream, and polluters may be liable to them for resulting damages. Water beneath the surface and flowing in a well-defined course, such as an underground river, is subject to the same rules as those applicable to surface streams.

Ownership of Fixtures

Fixtures are property installed on, attached to, or used with land or buildings in such a way as to become real property themselves. Thus, if a tenant installs fixtures that were originally personal property, they become part of the real property and at installation belong to the owner of the real property. For example, a tenant installs a cabinet purchased as personal property at a home improvement store. Installation can make the cabinet part of the real property.

A seller of land transfers personal property that has become a fixture, without specific reference, along with the sale of land. Three tests help determine whether an item is a fixture:

- An article that cannot be removed without substantial injury to the realty is a fixture, even though the damage can be repaired. For example, a fireplace insert is a fixture even though the fireplace from which it is removed can be repaired.

- An article that is specially constructed or fitted for use in a building, or that is installed in the building to enable people to use the building, is a fixture. A heater and a door in a house are examples.

- If the party who attached an item intended it to become part of the land or building, that item is a fixture. The relationship of the parties often controls what becomes a fixture. For instance, a landlord who hangs a mirror that cannot then be removed from the wall without substantial damage to the premises might intend it to stay there permanently. However, a tenant who attaches a similar mirror might intend to remove it at the end of the lease term.

Trade fixtures

Fixtures and equipment that may be attached to a building during a tenant's occupancy, with the intention that they be removed when the tenant leaves.

Improvements and betterments

Alterations or additions made to the building at the expense of an insured who does not own the building and who cannot legally remove them.

When a tenant rents a building for business, the test of intention regarding fixtures usually applies in the tenant's favor. Between a landlord and tenant, the law considers all **trade fixtures** as removable, including such articles as bakery ovens, cabinetry, and steam boilers. An article is a trade fixture if the tenant can remove it without permanent injury to the land or building and if the tenant installed it solely for trade purposes.

For insurance purposes, a tenant's **improvements and betterments** become part of the leased structure. For example, painting and wallpapering as a part of a general plan of altering the premises for a tenant's initial occupancy is an improvement, not a repair and not a fixture.

LAND USE RESTRICTIONS

Land ownership does not confer unlimited rights in terms of the use of the land. It can involve restrictions that benefit either private parties or the public.

Land use restrictions include incorporeal interests such as easements, profits à prendre, a seller's restrictions on the use of land, licenses, and government controls such as zoning, building codes, and the exercise of eminent domain.

Incorporeal Interests

The law recognizes four major **incorporeal interests**. This section discusses three of those interests. Lease situations, which include rentals, are the fourth.

Incorporeal interest
A nonmaterial interest in real property.

Easements

An **easement** can be created by express words, by implication, or by prescription. Parties can expressly create an easement by reserving it when the land that is subject to the easement is sold. The usual easement must benefit adjacent land.

Easement
A nonpossessory right to use another person's real property for a particular purpose.

For example, David owns a piece of land fronting on a road. He subdivides the property into two lots. Lot 1 is on the back of the property with no access to the road. Lot 2 is in front with all the road frontage, and it blocks access to Lot 1. David's house is on Lot 1. David sells Lot 2 but expressly reserves a right of access to the road across Lot 2 from his Lot 1.

Parties also can create an easement by implication. In the previous example, if David sells Lot 2 without expressly reserving an easement, the easement might be implied by law to give David access to the road.

Profits à Prendre

The rights to mine coal, remove sand and gravel, and cut down trees are examples of **profits à prendre** rights. The profits à prendre right includes the right to do anything reasonably necessary to obtain the materials, including entering the land and digging holes to get to the substances.

Profits à prendre
A right or privilege to enter another's land and take away something of value from its soil or from the products of its soil.

Seller's Restrictions on Land Use

In selling real property, an owner can restrict its use to preserve or enhance the value of any land retained by the seller or to benefit the public.

Examples of legally valid restrictions are contracts prescribing the minimum cost of homes to be built on land, the minimum size of buildings, and the types of construction. On the other hand, discriminatory agreements prohibiting sale to certain racial or ethnic groups are unenforceable.

Some states expressly limit restrictions on land use to a statutory period of, for example, thirty or forty years. Changed conditions, such as economic conditions in the area, can make restrictions unenforceable.

Licenses

License

The permission to use real property for a particular purpose.

A ticket for a theater seat and rental of a hotel room are typical **licenses**. A license grants no interest in the land. However, without the permission granted by a license, the licensee's use of the land would be a trespass (illegal entry) or another illegal act.

A license can be oral, written, or implied. For example, by implication, the public has a license to use the public halls in an office building.

Government Controls

Government has certain powers over the use of land on the public's behalf. The government cannot, under the guise of protecting the public, interfere arbitrarily with lawful land use or impose unreasonable and unnecessary restrictions on it. An example of the lawful exercise of government's power is the regulation of the number of oil and gas wells allowed on property and the flow of oil and gas from those wells. The government can protect the public as well as adjoining landowners against waste from wells. The most common methods governments use to restrict land use are zoning, building codes, and eminent domain.

Zoning

Zoning

A government's regulation of building construction and occupancy and of land use according to a comprehensive plan.

Exclusionary zoning

The act of restricting land use either by prohibiting additional building or by requiring high standards.

Spot zoning

A provision in a general zoning plan that assigns a different use for a small area of land than that of the surrounding area.

Special exception

A land use explicitly permitted by a zoning ordinance but subject to certain limitations.

A **zoning** ordinance must provide a comprehensive general plan for the entire community and must be uniform for each class or kind of occupancy or use of land within a given district. Requirements can vary by district. However, within limits, all property in like circumstances must be treated the same. Matters affected by zoning laws and **exclusionary zoning** include, for example, lot size, minimum building size, number of families that may reside in the buildings, maximum height of each building, and parking areas. A zoning ordinance cannot allow **spot zoning** when the result would benefit the owner of that area to the neighbors' detriment.

Two ways to relieve a property from compliance with a zoning ordinance are special exceptions and variances.

Special exceptions can apply to uses considered desirable for the general welfare, but only when controlled, such as the building of a school or a church in a residential zone. An ordinance can permit the use, but only if the governing body approves it.

There are two types of **variances**:

- The governing body can grant a **hardship variance** if strict application of the zoning requirements would result in peculiar and exceptional difficulties or undue hardship on the owner.

- In particular cases and for special reasons, the government can grant a **use variance** to allow for a use that would benefit the general welfare. In some cases, governing bodies allow **nonconforming uses**. To avoid the constitutional prohibition against taking property without due process, any nonconforming use existing at the time an ordinance passes can continue. The use cannot be enlarged and can be terminated by total destruction of the structure, by abandonment of the use, or by a change in use.

Building Codes

Many cities and states have adopted **building codes** that sometimes overlap zoning ordinances. However, they address the more technical construction details, such as electrical wiring and heating. An owner must submit building plans to a government regulator to determine whether construction conforms to the building code. If it does, a building permit is issued.

After the structure's completion, an inspector from the regulatory agency inspects the structure before anyone can occupy it and, if approved, issues a certificate of occupancy.

Eminent Domain

Governments can seize private property through **eminent domain**. This action usually requires a **condemnation proceeding**. The petition states the exact property desired and the public use involved and seeks a court's permission to seize property. There are two conditions for granting the petition:

- The land must be taken for public use or public benefit.
- The "Takings Clause" of the Fifth Amendment to the U.S. Constitution provides that the federal government cannot take private property for public use without paying just compensation to the property owner. The due process clause of the Fourteenth Amendment to the Constitution extends the principle to state governments. Just compensation is the fair market value at the time of the taking.

Variance

An exception to the strict application of a zoning ordinance to permit a use that is not permitted otherwise.

Hardship variance

An exception to the application of a zoning ordinance for lots that, because of size, topography, or other physical limitations, do not conform to the ordinance requirements for the zone.

Use variance

An exception to the application of a zoning ordinance to permit an otherwise prohibited use within the zone.

Nonconforming use

A land use that is impermissible under current zoning restrictions but that is allowed because the use was lawful before the restrictions took effect.

Building codes

Local ordinances or state statutes that regulate the construction of buildings within a municipality, county, or state.

Eminent domain

The right of a government to seize private property for public use.

Condemnation proceeding

A legal procedure by which a government body seeks a court's permission to seize private property by eminent domain.

THE LANDLORD AND TENANT RELATIONSHIP

Landlord (lessor) and tenant (lessee) law governs lease interests in real property. State and local laws vary significantly regarding the landlord-tenant relationship.

Landlord-tenant law focuses on four specific areas:

- The types of landlord-tenant estates, or relationships
- Landlords' rights and duties
- Landlords' remedies
- Tenants' rights and duties

Types of Landlord-Tenant Estates

Estate for years
A landlord-tenant estate created for a definite period.

Tenancy at will
A landlord-tenant estate in which the tenant has permission to occupy a premises as a landlord desires.

Periodic tenancy
A landlord-tenant estate with no fixed termination date and automatic renewal until one of the parties gives notice of intent to terminate.

Holdover tenant
A tenant who has a lease for a number of years and, at the expiration of the lease, continues to occupy the premises.

The three types of landlord-tenant estates are **tenancy at will**, an **estate for years**, and a **periodic tenancy**.

A landlord and tenant can create a periodic tenancy by an express agreement, usually called a "tenancy from year-to-year" or "from month-to-month." The parties also can create a periodic tenancy by implication. For example, a lease states no expiration date but states that the rental is $10,000 per year, payable one-twelfth each month. This implies a tenancy from year to year, based on the periodic rent payments.

A periodic tenancy also can arise by implication of law. This occurs when a tenant is a **holdover tenant**. If the landlord expressly approves the occupancy or accepts rent, then a periodic tenancy is implied. If the landlord does not agree to the occupancy, the tenant becomes a tenant at sufferance and can be ejected by the landlord.

The periodic tenancy can be from month to month or year to year, depending on the terms of the prior tenancy. By statute in some states, it is a month-to-month tenancy unless the parties have agreed otherwise. The other terms of the prior lease continue to apply. The notice of lease termination period is usually one entire lease period. However, if the period is one year or longer, most states require three to six months' notice.

Landlord's Rights and Duties

The landlord's primary duty is to deliver possession of the premises to the tenant on the lease's inception date. The landlord's primary rights are to receive the rent when due and recover the premises at the end of the lease in the same condition in which they were leased, except for reasonable wear and tear.

If the tenant defaults, the landlord has no duty to lessen the financial loss by trying to find another tenant. If a tenant abandons the property, the landlord can treat abandonment as an anticipatory breach and receive as damages the amount of the remaining rent payments. In these cases, the landlord must mitigate, or lessen, the loss. Many long-term leases provide that, in the event of default, the landlord can accelerate the payments, reenter the premises, act as the tenant's agent to sublet, and sue the tenant for any resulting losses.

Many landlords require tenants to pay a security deposit at the inception of leases. The lease usually provides that, in case of default or damage to the property, the security deposit represents damages that the landlord can retain. Some statutes provide that the security deposit is the tenant's property, that the landlord must keep it in a bank escrow account, and that the landlord must return it to the tenant after lease termination.

Landlord's Remedies

When a tenant remains in possession at lease termination, or if the tenant owes rent or has breached the lease, the landlord can evict the tenant with court assistance. Many states provide for summary eviction proceedings when the lease is terminated and the tenant refuses to move, or during the lease term if the tenant defaults on the rent. The landlord must send the tenant a written notice terminating the tenancy and demanding possession. After a period of time, the landlord serves a summons and complaint, and a hearing is held. If the landlord establishes a right to possession, the court enters an order of repossession followed by a warrant of removal. The tenant has only two defenses: that the tenant has paid the rent, or that the rent is not legally due.

Eviction can be either actual or constructive. Actual eviction from the whole or even a part of the premises ends the obligation to pay rent. Constructive eviction occurs when actions or inactions of a landlord prevent the tenant from enjoying a substantial or integral part of the premises. Examples include the landlord's allowing inadequate heat or hot water, leaky plumbing, serious disturbances by other tenants, and pest infestation. If a landlord seeks a court eviction for nonpayment of rent, the tenant may assert a defense of constructive eviction.

When the tenant defaults on rent, the landlord can seize possession of the tenant's property and hold it for the rent, a right called distraint. The landlord must seize the goods peacefully and sell them at a public sale.

Tenant's Rights and Duties

The tenant's rights and duties complement those of the landlord. For example, the tenant must pay rent and leave the premises in the same condition they were in at the lease inception, except for reasonable wear and tear. The tenant has a right to occupy the premises; and, on eviction, the obligation to pay rent can end.

When the property has a significant defect, the tenant need not pay rent if these three conditions have occurred sequentially:

1.   The tenant has demanded that the landlord correct the situation.
2.   The landlord has not corrected the situation within a reasonable time.
3.   The tenant has left the premises at the end of that reasonable time.

The tenant's remaining on the premises can constitute a waiver of the right to withhold rent. The tenant has a right to vacate the premises and escape liability for rent but does not have an action for damages. However, if an express agreement in the lease requires the landlord to make repairs, the tenant might have a right to sue for damages, if any, for breach of contract.

Generally, landlords are liable to third parties for injuries sustained on the leased premises to the same extent they are liable to tenants. Liability is restricted to a landlord's negligent acts or latent defects on the premises.

In many states, the landlord can escape liability to the tenant by including an exculpatory clause in the lease in which the tenant agrees to relieve, or excuse, the landlord of any liability to either the tenant, third parties, or both. However, such a clause usually does not affect the landlord's liability to third persons.

SUMMARY

Real property is land, including structures or rights attached to the land. Personal property is all property that is not real property. Personal property can be obtained through creation, accession, confusion, gifts, or bailments.

In bailments, a bailor leaves personal property with a bailee. Bailments can benefit the bailor, the bailee, or both. A bailee has possession only, and cannot transfer title to the property, but may have a right to use the property. A bailee has a duty to take reasonable care of bailed property and to return it to the bailor at the end of the bailment. Depending on whom the bailment is intended to benefit, the bailee may have a right to compensation and, if payment is not received, may assert a lien or a possessory lien on the property. In mutual benefit bailments, the bailor owes the bailee a duty to supply goods that are reasonably fit for the purpose the parties envision. A bailor who knows that the bailed property is in a dangerous condition can be liable for injury to a third party if the bailee is not aware of the danger.

There are eight common forms of ownership interest:

*   Fee simple estate
*   Life estate
*   Joint tenancy
*   Tenancy by the entirety
*   Tenancy in common

- Community property
- Cooperative ownership
- Condominium ownership

A real property sale involves a contract of sale and a deed, both of which, under the statute of frauds, must be in writing. To be valid, both documents must also meet other requirements. Recording of real estate transfer documents protects buyers against ownership claims made by subsequent purchasers.

Security interests in real property include mortgages, trust deeds, and land contracts. Liens give certain creditors rights to have their debts paid out of debtors' property, usually by sale. Mechanics' liens give those who repair property a right to retain the property to secure payment.

Incidental real property rights include adverse possession claims; rights under, above, and on the land's surface; the right to lateral and subjacent support; water rights; and the ownership of fixtures.

Land use restrictions include easements, profits à prendre, restrictions on land use, licenses, zoning, building codes, and eminent domain.

Landlord-tenant law governs lease interests in real property, which are limited interests of limited duration. A landlord's primary duty is to deliver possession of the premises to the tenant at the inception of the lease. The tenant must pay rent and leave the premises in the condition in which they were received, except for reasonable wear and tear. The landlord has the same liability to third parties for injuries sustained on the premises as does the tenant, and the tenant is liable to third parties for injuries caused by any of the tenant's acts.

ASSIGNMENT NOTES

1. 17 U.S.C., § 101.
2. United States Copyright Office, "Copyright Basics," www.copyright.gov/circs/circ1.pdf, p. 5 (accessed July 13, 2010).

Tort Law

Outline

Negligence

Defenses Against
Negligence Claims

Liability of
Landowners or
Occupiers of Land

Intentional Torts:
Part 1 of 2

Intentional Torts:
Part 2 of 2

Liability in
Extraordinary
Circumstances

Products Liability

Damages in Tort
Suits

Liability Concepts
Affecting Tort
Claims

Summary

Educational Objectives

After learning the content of this assignment, you should be able to:

▹ Describe negligence claims in terms of:

- The elements of negligence

- The required proof of negligence

▹ Describe these defenses against negligence claims: comparative negligence, releases and exculpatory clauses, immunity, statutes of limitations and repose, and tortfeasor's capacity.

▹ Explain how negligence applies to landowners or occupiers of land.

▹ Describe these intentional torts, the circumstances under which they can occur, and common defenses to them:

- Battery

- Assault

- False imprisonment and false arrest

- Intentional infliction of emotional distress

- Defamation (libel and slander)

- Invasion of the right of privacy

▹ Describe these intentional torts, the circumstances under which they can occur, and common defenses to them:

- Fraud

- Bad faith, or outrage

- Interference with relationships between others

- Misuse of legal process

- Trespass

- Nuisance

- Conversion

6

▶ Explain how liability attaches as a result of the unique circumstances presented by the following:

- Ultrahazardous activities

- Ownership and/or possession of animals

- Escape of toxic substances

▶ Describe these causes of action for products liability and the possible defenses to them:

- Misrepresentation

- Breach of warranty

- Strict liability and negligence

▶ Describe the types of damages a court can award a plaintiff for a tort claim.

▶ Explain how any of these concepts can affect a tort claim:

- Joint tortfeasor's liability

- Expanded liability concepts

- Vicarious liability

- Good Samaritan issues

- Class actions and mass tort litigation

Tort Law

NEGLIGENCE

Negligence is an important tort classification for insurance professionals to understand because it is the basis of many property-casualty insurance claims.

Torts are civil (or private) wrongs, as distinguished from crimes, which are public wrongs. Torts are either unintentional or intentional.

Negligence is the broad term used for unintentional torts. All other torts are intentional. A tort results from a **tortfeasor's** breach of duty that results in injury or loss. Describing negligence involves an understanding of two of its aspects:

- The elements of negligence
- The required proof of negligence

Elements of Negligence

A **plaintiff** in a negligence claim against a **defendant** must establish each of the four essential elements of negligence:

- The defendant owed a legal duty of care to the plaintiff.
- The defendant breached the duty of care owed to the plaintiff.
- The defendant's negligent act was the proximate cause of the plaintiff's injury or damage.
- The plaintiff suffered actual injury or damage.

Legal Duty

The first essential element of negligence is a **legal duty** of care owed by a defendant to a plaintiff. In establishing the existence of a legal duty, the courts ask whether the plaintiff's interests are entitled to legal protection against the defendant's conduct.

Legal duties of care are created by **statutes**, contracts, and the **common law**.

Consider that many automobile hit-and-run laws impose a duty on drivers involved in accidents to stop and assist injured persons. Failure to obey the statute generally constitutes negligence, and the violator is liable for any damages directly caused by failing to give assistance.

Tort

A wrongful act or an omission, other than a crime or a breach of contract, that invades a legally protected right.

Tortfeasor

A person or an organization that has committed a tort.

Defendant

The party in a lawsuit against whom a complaint is filed.

Plaintiff

The person or entity who files a lawsuit and is named as a party.

Legal duty

An obligation imposed by law for the preservation of the legally protected rights of others.

Statute

A written law passed by a legislative body at either the federal or state level.

Common law (case law)

Laws that develop out of court decisions in particular cases and establish precedents for future cases.

For example, a surgeon has a legal duty to perform surgery properly. If the duty is breached, the patient can sue for negligence.

Failure to perform a contract or performing a contract improperly can violate a legal duty. For example, the subcontractor did not use the concrete formula specified in the contract and the parking garage collapsed. Damage to the garage would be related to a breach of contract. If persons or third-party property were injured or damaged in the collapse, then the subcontractor could also be held liable because of negligence.

Most legal duties arise from the common law. Many such duties are well established; others are defined based on the facts of new cases that raise new legal issues. In response, courts may develop new rules that form compromises between the conflicting positions of plaintiffs demanding protection and defendants claiming they owe no legal duty of care.

For a negligence lawsuit to be successful, the defendant must have owed a duty to the plaintiff. However, the duty need not be owed to a specific person. That the defendant could foresee that harm would occur to someone because of the negligent act or omission is sufficient. Duty extends to all persons and property within the zone of hazard, or area of danger. For example, the duty might extend to an unforeseen plaintiff, such as a guest of the purchaser of a defective product.

A moral obligation to act is not the same as a legal duty. For example, a person who fails to attempt to rescue a drowning child may not be liable for the child's death because he owed her no legal duty, even though he might have had a moral duty to save her.

However, a person who voluntarily undertakes a moral duty has a legal duty to exercise reasonable care in carrying it out. When one volunteers to undertake an act or to perform a service necessary to another's safety, and that person suffers harm in reasonable reliance on the volunteer's performance, the volunteer is liable. Having undertaken a task, the volunteer must act as an ordinary, reasonable person would act in performing it.

Breach of Duty

The second essential element of negligence is the defendant's breach of the duty of care owed to the plaintiff; that is, the failure to conform to the standard of care required in the situation. The courts usually apply a **reasonable person test** to determine the standard of care. The question is whether the person's conduct would be the conduct of a reasonable person under the circumstances.

The reasonable person test is an external, objective test under which the defendant's individual or personal judgment, or that of other parties involved (subjective factors), is not considered. The test is not based on how jury members would have acted under like circumstances, but only on how the jury perceives that a reasonable person would have acted.

Reasonable person test
A standard for the degree of care exercised in a situation that is measured by what a reasonably cautious person would or would not do under similar circumstances.

Circumstances further qualify the reasonable person test. For example, if applied to a person with disabilities, the general legal rule would be to consider how a reasonable person with a disability would act under the circumstances. However, the rule varies according to mental incapacity. Courts hold people who are not sane to the same standards as reasonable, sane people and hold people who are intoxicated to the same standards as those who are sober.

The standard applied in cases of professional negligence is the skill and knowledge of reasonably competent members of that profession applied with reasonable care. Professionals are not liable for mere errors in judgment, provided that they have used reasonable care in reaching a judgment. This standard applies to practically all professions and skilled trades, such as lawyers, engineers, accountants, and airline pilots.

The legal standard applied to professionals is usually the standard of professionals in the local community. For example, a rural doctor may not be expected to know about diagnostic machines used only in metropolitan teaching hospitals. The duty is not based on the particular community in which the tort occurred, but on that general type of community in the same geographic area. Doctors coming to the aid of an injured person in a volunteer, or "Good Samaritan," situation are subjected to the standard of care for the doctors in their own community.

The standard or degree of care varies with the nature of the activity. Therefore, the care required of a reasonable person varies according to the possibility of harm involved. As the possibility of harm increases, the party must exercise greater caution, commensurate with the risk. Many courts have established different degrees of care, such as ordinary care or a high degree of care.

A high degree of care is legally necessary in two situations:

- **Common carriers**, those who operate buses, trains, and taxicabs, for example, must exercise the utmost caution characteristic of a very careful person, which is the highest possible care commensurate with the risk or nature of the undertaking.
- People who handle or store dangerous materials, such as explosives, must exercise care commensurate with the risk associated with the materials' dangerous character.

Common carriers
Airlines, railroads, or trucking companies that furnish transportation to any member of the public seeking their offered services.

Proximate Cause

The third essential element of negligence is **proximate cause**. Proof of a wrongful act and harm are not sufficient to prove negligence. The wrongful act must also have been the proximate, or direct, cause of the harm.

For example, a guest in a hotel is severely injured in a fire and sues the hotelkeeper. At the trial, the plaintiff proves that the hotel did not have legally required sprinklers. This violation of law is not enough to create liability on

Proximate cause
A cause that, in a natural and continuous sequence unbroken by any new and independent cause, produces an event and without which the event would not have happened.

the hotelkeeper's part. The plaintiff also must prove that the absence of the sprinklers was the proximate cause of the injuries. To illustrate further, the plaintiff might have been at the other end of the hotel with an easy escape route that the plaintiff failed to use.

In determining tort liability, courts have always attempted to place the burden of loss on the person responsible, at the same time recognizing that some limit of liability should exist when the act was so remote as not to be chargeable to the actor. An early case, *Scott v. Shepherd*,[1] known as the "lighted squib" case, illustrates this concept.

In the lighted squib case, the defendant, Shepherd, threw a lighted squib, a type of firecracker, into a crowd. It fell near Y, who picked it up and threw it near Z, who in turn threw it near Scott, where it exploded, injuring Scott. The issue was whether the injury was the result of Shepherd's original act of throwing the squib into the crowd or whether Y or Z, who actually threw the squib near Scott, caused the injury. The court held that Shepherd had set the cause of loss, the squib, in motion and was liable for the resulting injury.

The question in the case was whether, if the squib had been thrown successively by, say, five persons, or had landed in a powder keg rather than near a person in a crowd, Shepherd still would be liable. The controlling doctrine is that one who commits a wrongful act is responsible for the ordinary consequences that can foreseeably flow from the act. The person is not liable for results that could not have been reasonably foreseen, or if an independent intervening cause breaks the chain of causation. Some courts deem proximate cause as a substantial, direct cause, one that would have caused all or at least a substantial part of the injury on its own.

Distance between the act and the injury is not in itself sufficient to make the cause remote. Remoteness is a matter of degree, as the squib case indicates. Likewise, passage of time does not necessarily create remoteness. For example, when a fire damaged a building, and a wall of the building collapsed thirty-eight days later, the fire was still considered the proximate cause of the collapse.

In tort law, rules have evolved to determine proximate cause:

- **"But for" rule**—To illustrate the "but for" rule, if Al drove his car onto a sidewalk and injured Bob, it is readily apparent that, but for Al's action, Bob would not have been injured. The act is the proximate cause of Bob's injury.
- **Substantial factor rule**—Sometimes two parties' acts coincide to cause a loss, and the "but for" rule does not produce a satisfactory result. In these situations the substantial factor rule applies. Assume that cars driven by Al and Bob collide at an intersection, and Al's car then swerves onto a sidewalk, injuring Carol. Evidence shows that both Al and Bob are at fault in the collision. If the "but for" rule is applied, the loss would not have occurred "but for" both drivers' negligence; and neither could be

"But for" rule

A rule used to determine whether a defendant's act was the proximate cause of a plaintiff's harm based on the determination that the plaintiff's harm could not have occurred but for the defendant's act.

Substantial factor rule

A rule used to determine proximate cause of a loss by determining which of the acts are significant factors in causing the harm.

held liable. To avoid this unsatisfactory result, the courts have developed the substantial factor rule.

- Proof of defendant's responsibility—An injured person cannot succeed in a lawsuit merely by proving that harm resulted from another person's act. The plaintiff still must prove by a preponderance of the evidence that the defendant caused the harm. When the evidence is clear that it is at least as probable that the act was a third person's responsibility, the plaintiff has failed to win the case.

- **Foreseeability rule**—Under the foreseeability rule, the plaintiff's harm must be the natural and probable consequence of the defendant's wrongful act and such that an ordinarily reasonable person would have foreseen it. However, the defendant need not have foreseen the particular result that followed.

The defendant is not liable if the harm is caused by an independent, intervening agency, or **intervening act**. The intervening agency, rather than the original cause, then becomes the proximate cause. The intervening agency must be independent of the original act and not readily foreseeable as one that would arise from the original act.

For example, a speeding motorist's negligent driving knocks down a tree on the side of the road. An enterprising motorist the next day stops to cut branches for firewood and injures himself with a hand saw. The act of the enterprising motorist is not connected with the car accident, and it is unlikely that speeding motorist who knocked down the tree could foresee that an enterprising motorist would cut up the tree for firewood. A court might find differently if the local municipal worker tasked to remove the accident's debris was injured cutting up the same tree.

Concurrent causation arises when each of two or more defendants is liable for the entire harm, even though the act of either would not have produced the harm. For example, on a cold, icy day, Jane and Martha, each driving cars at excessive speeds, slide on the ice, collide, go up on the sidewalk, and injure a pedestrian, Kelly. In this case, both Jane and Martha are liable. Their individual acts combined to produce Kelly's injury.

Actual Injury or Damage

The fourth essential element of negligence is actual injury or damage to the plaintiff. For a person to sue successfully for negligence, the negligent act must result in actual injury or damage, or quantifiable harm for which the plaintiff seeks damages. The harm could be bodily injury or financial loss, such as property loss.

Required Proof of Negligence

In a negligence lawsuit, the plaintiff has the burden to prove all the elements of negligence, and the defendant has the burden of proving any defense. The

Foreseeability rule

A rule used to determine proximate cause when a plaintiff's harm is the natural and probable consequence of the defendant's wrongful act and when an ordinarily reasonable person would have foreseen the harm.

Intervening act

An act, independent of an original act and not readily foreseeable, that breaks the chain of causation and sets a new chain of events in motion that causes harm.

Concurrent causation (concurrent causation doctrine)

A legal doctrine stating that if a loss can be attributed to two or more independent concurrent causes—one or more excluded by the policy and one covered—then the policy covers the loss.

defendant is presumed at the outset of a lawsuit to have used due care until the plaintiff proves otherwise. In some kinds of cases, presumptions favor the plaintiff. For example, a bailee, such as a dry cleaner, who returns the plaintiff's property in a damaged condition is presumed to be negligent and has the burden of proving otherwise.

If the facts are undisputed and point to only one presumption, the court must decide whether, as a matter of law, negligence occurred. If the facts are in dispute or uncertain, or if they are undisputed but are such that fair-minded people might reasonably reach different conclusions, then the court must make findings of fact (supported by the evidence) and may also have to make findings of law (the applicability of a rule of law to the facts of the case) to determine whether negligence occurred.

Negligence Per Se

Negligence per se

An act that is considered inherently negligent because of a violation of a law or an ordinance.

The law treats certain actions as **negligence per se**, which a court can determine without submitting the question to the jury.

Although not all statutes create standards of care for negligence suits, often failure to comply with a statutory standard is negligence *per se*, and proof that the defendant violated the statute is sufficient to establish liability. For example, a victim is killed when his vehicle collides with a disabled truck parked in the fast lane of a divided interstate highway. The truck's location violates traffic regulations requiring that disabled vehicles move immediately from the traveled portion of the highway and provide adequate warning devices to other motorists. Proof that the truck driver neither moved the truck nor provided the warning devices might be sufficient to establish negligence *per se*.

Res Ipsa Loquitur

Res ipsa loquitur

A legal doctrine that provides that, in some circumstances, negligence is inferred simply by an accident occurring.

Res ipsa loquitur, Latin for "the thing speaks for itself," permits an inference of negligence if the action or event causing injury was under the defendant's exclusive control and the accident ordinarily would not have happened if the defendant had exercised appropriate care. The doctrine is based on the conclusion that, in the absence of proof to the contrary, such an accident would likely arise from lack of due care. Although negligence is not actually presumed, the circumstances provide evidence from which a jury might presume negligence.

The *res ipsa loquitur* doctrine involves two factors:

- The probability that, under the given circumstances, the defendant was negligent
- The defendant's duty to rebut the inference of negligence as the party who had **exclusive control** and superior knowledge of the causative circumstances

Exclusive control

The control of only one person or entity; in tort law the control by the defendant alone of an instrument that caused harm.

The exclusive control concept is a flexible one that the courts have adapted to modern manufacturing, packing, shipping, and marketing practices. For example, a plaintiff injured by an exploding carbonated beverage bottle can use the doctrine of *res ipsa loquitur* against the bottler even though the bottle was not in the bottler's physical possession. The bottler could challenge application of the doctrine with evidence that either the plaintiff had mishandled the bottle or that other parties did so after the bottle left the bottler's control. *Res ipsa loquitur* also can apply to airplane crashes because the airlines have control over the equipment and airplane operation.

Courts frequently apply *res ipsa loquitur* in lawsuits by passengers against common carriers. The doctrine also can apply in instances such as bricks that have fallen off buildings, poisonous drugs sold as harmless medicine, and sponges or surgical instruments left inside patients during surgery.

An unexplained injury alone does not mean that *res ipsa loquitur* can be applied. For example, the discovery of a dead person near railroad tracks does not imply in and of itself that the railroad was involved. Several explanations are conceivable other than the railroad's failure to act with due care. See the exhibit "Practice Exercise: Elements of Negligence."

Practice Exercise: Elements of Negligence

Coal Company conducts mountaintop mining operations in the mountains on both sides of a creek. Joseph's house is in the creek valley. Studies have shown that this kind of mountaintop mining can cause flooding in creek valleys if appropriate precautions are not taken, although this valley had a history of flooding caused by spring rains before Coal Company's operations began. In the spring, the valley flooded after unusually heavy rains, destroying Joseph's home in the valley. Joseph sues Coal Company, claiming that its negligence caused the destruction of his home. Describe how the elements of negligence might apply to Joseph's case.

Answer

Joseph must establish that Coal Company owed a legal duty of care to him, and its coal operation in that area probably involves a legal duty to all valley landowners to conduct mining operations so as not to damage their property. Joseph also must establish that Coal Company breached its duty of care by not taking appropriate precautions, and he would need to introduce evidence proving that element. Joseph should have no problem proving that he suffered damage because his home was destroyed. However, proximate cause might be the most difficult negligence element for Joseph to prove if the spring rains would have flooded the valley even without Coal Company's mountaintop mining.

[DA05828]

DEFENSES AGAINST NEGLIGENCE CLAIMS

A defendant has several available defenses against a negligence action. Some defenses can prevent recovery of damages, or reduce the amount, even when the defendant is found negligent.

The burden is on a defendant to prove any of these available defenses against a plaintiff's negligence action:

- Comparative negligence
- Releases and exculpatory clauses
- Immunity
- Statutes of limitations and repose
- Tortfeasor's capacity

Comparative Negligence

Contributory negligence

A common-law principle that prevents a person who has been harmed from recovering damages if that person's own negligence contributed in any way to the harm.

Comparative negligence

A common-law principle that requires both parties to a loss to share the financial burden of the bodily injury or property damage according to their respective degrees of fault.

Last clear chance doctrine

A defense to negligence that holds the party who has the last clear chance to avoid harm and fails to do so solely responsible for the harm.

Assumption-of-risk defense

A defense to negligence that bars a plaintiff's recovery for harm caused by the defendant's negligence if the plaintiff voluntarily incurred the risk of harm.

Pure comparative negligence rule

A comparative negligence rule that permits a plaintiff to recover damages discounted by his or her own percentage of negligence, as long as the plaintiff is not 100 percent at fault.

Comparative negligence evolved from the common-law principle of **contributory negligence**, which completely prevented a plaintiff who was also at fault in a situation from recovering damages even though the defendant's negligence caused the plaintiff's injury. The contributory negligence defense often caused extremely harsh results for plaintiffs, and today almost all jurisdictions have abandoned contributory negligence in favor of a comparative negligence approach.

The concept of **last clear chance** was an attempt by courts to alleviate the harsh results of contributory negligence on plaintiffs by placing responsibility for harm on the party who had the "last clear chance" to avoid harm but failed to do so. Similarly, the **assumption-of-risk defense** meant that a plaintiff could not recover for harm caused by the defendant's negligence if the plaintiff voluntarily assumed the risk of harm even though the defendant was negligent. The assumption-of-risk defense is generally used for hazardous activities. For example, a spectator at a hockey game assumes the risk of being hit by a puck. Use of these two concepts is jurisdiction-specific, so checking statutes is essential to determining the use and applicability of both the last-clear-chance and assumption-of-risk defenses.

The specific rules for the application of comparative negligence vary by jurisdiction but have four variations:

- The pure comparative negligence rule
- The 50 percent rule
- The 49 percent rule
- The slight versus gross rule

The **pure comparative negligence rule** is the maximum departure from the contributory negligence rule. Under this rule, a plaintiff who is 99 percent at fault can still recover 1 percent of the claimed damages.

A principal objection to the pure rule is that it does not base recovery on apportionment of fault, but on the relative amount of loss. It allows a party whose negligence was a major factor in the incident to recover damages from a party who was less at fault. No matter how great the degree of the claimant's own negligence, as long as it is not 100 percent, a claimant may still recover for an amount discounted by his or her own negligence. Under pure comparative negligence, a claimant who is 90 percent at fault for an accident still collects 10 percent of his or her damages from the defendant.

The **50 percent comparative negligence rule** permits a plaintiff to recover reduced damages up to and including the point at which the plaintiff's negligence constitutes not more than 50 percent of the total in a case involving two parties.

A plaintiff whose negligence is 51 percent or more than the other party's negligence can recover no damages. Accordingly, if the plaintiff is 30 percent at fault and the damages are $100,000, a court would reduce damages to $70,000. If the plaintiff is 49 percent at fault, a court would reduce the damages in the example to $51,000. If the plaintiff is 50 percent at fault, a court would reduce the damages to $50,000. A plaintiff 51 percent at fault could not recover.

The **49 percent comparative negligence rule** is a slight variation of the 50 percent rule, but the proportion of the total negligence at which the plaintiff can collect no damages is one percentage point lower, 50 percent rather than 51 percent. See the exhibit "Example: Multiple-Parties' Degrees of Fault."

50 percent comparative negligence rule

A comparative negligence rule that permits a plaintiff to recover reduced damages so long as the plaintiff's negligence is not greater than 50 percent of the total negligence leading to harm.

49 percent comparative negligence rule

A comparative negligence rule that permits a plaintiff to recover reduced damages so long as the plaintiff's negligence is less than the other party's negligence.

Example: Multiple-Parties' Degrees of Fault

Al, Barry, and Connie were all negligent in causing an accident, but not equally so. They contributed to the accident in the following degrees:

Party	Degree of Fault
Al (plaintiff)	30 percent
Barry	30 percent
Connie	40 percent

If Al is the plaintiff, and if the court follows the 50 percent rule, Al would recover against both Barry and Connie because his negligence is not greater than that of either Barry or Connie. Under the 49 percent rule, Al would not recover against Barry because his negligence is not less than Barry's. However, he could recover against Connie, who would have to pay 70 percent of the total.

Party	Degree of Fault
Al	30 percent
Barry	30 percent
Connie (plaintiff)	40 percent

Assume that Connie is the plaintiff in this case. Under the straight application of either modified rule, Connie could recover nothing, although her negligence is less than half the total. To deal with this situation, many states have modified the rule to provide that the comparison of negligence must be against the combined fault of those against whom recovery is sought.

Slight versus gross rule

A rule of comparative negligence that permits the plaintiff to recover only when the plaintiff's negligence is slight in comparison with the gross negligence of the other party.

Release

A legally binding contract between the parties to a dispute that embodies their agreement, obligates each to fulfill the agreement, and releases both parties from further obligation to one another that relates to the dispute.

Under the **slight versus gross rule** of negligence, a court reduces the plaintiff's damages by an amount proportional to his or her contribution. Unlike the percentage rules, which provide strict guidelines, the slight versus gross rule leaves the decision on assigning proportional damage with the court.

Releases and Exculpatory Clauses

A written general **release** of liability, agreed to by both parties, can be a defense to a tort lawsuit if a court recognizes the release as a valid release in settlement of a claim.

Releases can be voided by mutual mistake, a misunderstanding shared by all parties to the release. To void a release, the mutual mistake must relate to a past or present fact and not to an opinion about a future condition based on a present fact. A misconception of the extent of the injuries the plaintiff suffered is not a mutual mistake that voids a release.

Parties to contracts also frequently use exculpatory clauses, or exculpatory agreements, in their contracts to avoid liability for negligence. For example, under an exculpatory clause, Lyle agrees not to sue Tim for any injuries that Lyle might sustain as a result of Tim's negligence.

Courts tend to view exculpatory agreements unfavorably. To make such agreements more legally acceptable, parties sometimes set them up as liquidated damages provisions. If liquidated damages in a contract are so low as to be considered nominal, a court will probably find that the liquidated damages clause is actually an exculpatory clause. However, a court will uphold an exculpatory clause under certain circumstances:

- If the exculpatory clause is not adverse to a public interest and is not against public policy
- If the party excused from liability is not under a duty to perform, as is a public utility or common carrier, for example
- If the contract does not arise from the parties' unequal bargaining power or is not otherwise unconscionable

Gross negligence

An act or omission that completely disregards the safety or rights of others and is exaggerated or aggravated in nature.

Exculpatory agreements can excuse or limit liability expressly for negligent contract performance, including **gross negligence**, but they are void if they exclude willful or wanton misconduct. Some jurisdictions have enacted laws that limit or prohibit the use of exculpatory clauses in a variety of situations.

Immunity

A defense that, in certain instances, shields organizations or persons from liability.

Immunity

Primarily for reasons of public policy, the common law granted **immunity** from liability for torts to certain classes of people under certain conditions. Court decisions and legislatures have followed a steady trend towards restricting or eliminating these immunities. The trend varies by jurisdiction and also by the type of immunity involved.

Four possible major classes of immunities may be available as defenses:

- Sovereign, or governmental, immunity
- Public official immunity
- Charitable immunity
- Intrafamilial immunity

Sovereign, or Governmental, Immunity

The doctrine of **sovereign immunity (governmental immunity)** derived its name from the English system in which the sovereign rulers exercised all powers of government and theoretically could do no wrong.

Courts created the doctrine of governmental immunity, and some jurisdictions have held that they have the power to change or eliminate it. Several courts, in fact, have eliminated state governments' immunity from tort liability. Other courts have held that the immunity is so firmly embedded in the law that only legislation can change it. In fact, some jurisdictions virtually remove tort immunity, and others impose liability on cities for governmental functions such as controlling riots or other violence, street and sidewalk repair, and removal of ice and snow.

The Federal Tort Claims Act (FTCA) of 1946[2] provides a limited waiver of governmental immunity for claims against the federal government. This law provides the only means for suing for damages and collecting them from the United States government in any cause in which the government, if it were a private person, would be liable. Many local jurisdictions have enacted similar tort claim acts.

Municipal corporations have an unusual status with regard to governmental immunity. As political subdivisions they should have the same immunity as the state. Conversely, they perform many functions performed by private enterprise. From this situation came the common-law application of governmental immunity to municipal bodies only when functioning in a governmental capacity—that is, performing a function that only government can perform.

Today, governments frequently engage in ordinary business pursuits that any private enterprise could perform. A city might supply gas or electricity or maintain a swimming pool or a theater. These functions, when performed by a local government, are termed **proprietary functions**, in contrast with **governmental functions**. A political body performing proprietary functions is subject to suit just as any private entity is. The legislature, however, can by statute confer immunity on certain of these proprietary activities, such as those performed by a municipal transit authority.

Sovereign immunity (governmental immunity)

A defense to negligence that protects the government against lawsuits for tort without its consent.

Proprietary function

A local government's act that is not considered part of the business of government and that could be performed by a private enterprise.

Governmental function

An act that can be performed only by government.

Public Official Immunity

Public official immunity also extends to local governmental officials. Judges and legislators have absolute immunity for acts performed in their official capacity. Other officials have only a qualified immunity in limited situations, such as civil rights cases.

Administrative act (discretionary act)

An act, a decision, a recommendation, or an omission made by a government official or agency within the authority of that office or agency.

Ministerial act

An act that is directed by law or other authority and that requires no individual judgment or discretion about whether or how to perform it.

The extent of the immunity depends on whether the acts are **administrative, or discretionary, acts** or **ministerial acts**. For example, a district attorney has discretion to decide whether to prosecute an alleged criminal. Public officials generally have full immunity in carrying out discretionary acts, as long as those acts are within the scope of their authority and performed with no malice or bad faith.

An official is liable for damages for ministerial acts performed improperly, even if performed in good faith and without malice. Most tort claim acts grant immunity to public officials while they are acting within the scope of their duties, to the same extent as they would grant immunity to a governmental body. However, these laws frequently do not grant immunity for certain acts, such as operation of cars, assault and battery, and malicious or fraudulent acts.

Charitable Immunity

Charitable immunity

A defense that shields charitable organizations from liability.

Under common law, all charitable organizations enjoyed immunity from suit in tort. A majority of states have rejected the doctrine of **charitable immunity**, particularly as applied to hospitals, and treat such cases under the general rules of negligence, specifically vicarious liability.

Intrafamilial Immunity

Under common law, one family member cannot sue another in tort. The reasons for intrafamilial immunity vary, including the belief that such suits would disrupt family peace and harmony, deplete family financial resources, and lead to collusion and fraud, particularly when insurance is involved. These immunities can be divided into two principal categories:

*   Interspousal immunity
*   Other family relationship immunities

Interspousal immunity

A defense to negligence that grants immunity to one spouse from the other spouse's lawsuit for torts committed before, during, and after the marriage.

Parent-child immunity

A defense to negligence that grants immunity to parents from their children's lawsuits for torts.

All jurisdictions have abolished, in whole or in part, **interspousal immunity**. Although most jurisdictions have also abolished **parent-child immunity** wholly or in part, those that still recognize it in some form do not apply the immunity if a child has been released from parental control (emancipated), or if a child is injured in a parent's business activity. The parent-child immunity rule has never extended to other family relationships. For example, siblings cannot claim immunity against each other.

Where parent-child immunity has been abolished, many insurers now insert an intrafamilial exclusion in liability policies. Courts vary as to whether such an exclusion is void because it violates public policy.

Statutes of Limitations and Repose

Statutes of limitations and **statutes of repose** both limit the time periods within which plaintiffs can file suits. A statute of repose is designed to bar action after a specific period of time has run from an event, such as the sale of a product. Thus, the time limit of a statute of repose may expire before a cause of action such as an accident with injuries has even accrued.

For example, a jurisdiction has a two-year statute of limitations that begins to run when the cause of action accrues. The jurisdiction also has a six-year statute of repose that begins to run when a merchant first sells a product. Carla purchases a product seven years after the initial sale to the original owner and sustains an injury from using the product six months after purchase. The statute of limitations has not run because the cause of action accrued within two years (six months after purchase), but the statute of repose has expired and bars her from suing because she was injured seven and a half years after the original sale—a year and a half beyond the statute of repose period.

Today, courts are more liberal so as not to deny plaintiffs their day in court. Statutory time periods vary by jurisdiction and also within the same jurisdiction for different torts. In most jurisdictions, the statute begins to run from the time the cause of action accrues. A major problem is establishing when all elements of the cause of action exist, or when material facts have been discovered, in order to determine when the statutory period begins.

In many cases, such as in an automobile accident, fixing the time of the accident and the time the cause of action accrued is simple. In some torts, the right to sue is complete upon the commission of the wrongful act, regardless of consequences, such as injury or damage. For example, the right to sue for trespass begins when the trespass occurs; damages are implied, and a plaintiff need not prove them. In such a case, the cause of action accrues and the statute begins to run when the wrongful act is committed.

In other torts, the right to sue is not complete unless harm results. In these cases, the cause of action accrues and the statute begins to run from the date the plaintiff sustains injury or damage. For example, the defendant negligently installs lightning rods on the plaintiff's house. Six years later, lightning strikes the house and destroys it. Did the cause of action accrue when the defendant negligently installed the lightning rods or when the house burned? Some courts would say it accrued at the time of installation, but others at the time the house burned.

Statutes of limitations for torts, unless otherwise indicated, also apply to products liability and medical malpractice suits. Because of the unique problems these suits present, most jurisdictions have enacted special statutes of limitations for medical malpractice, usually ranging from one to three years. Many jurisdictions also have a statute of repose for medical malpractice, usually ranging from three to ten years.

Statute of limitations

A statute that requires a plaintiff to file a lawsuit within a specific time period after the cause of action has accrued, which is often when the injury occurred or was discovered.

Statute of repose

A statute that requires a plaintiff to file a lawsuit within a specific time period after a wrongful act by a defendant, such as improper construction of a building, regardless of when the injury occurred or was discovered.

The statutes of limitations for damage to real or personal property are usually longer and can run up to ten years. Suits for breach of warranty usually fall under the state statute applying to contracts, and the applicable statutes of limitations can range from four to six years. For example, an injured party could lose the right to file a suit in tort by the running of the statute and still be able to recover under a breach of warranty suit (although the types of damages recoverable may differ according to whether suit is filed in contract or in tort). Many states have statutes of repose for architects and builders, limiting suits to four to fifteen years after a building's completion, with the average length of time being about eight years.

The law does not penalize a minor or an incompetent for failing to file suit. For example, a child injured as a result of a tort should not suffer from the parents' failure to file suit within the statute of limitations period.For minors and incompetents, the time period of the statute of limitations begins to run from the date they come of age or the date the incompetence is removed (such as by court order). This rule applies only if the incompetence existed before the statute began to run. Once the statutory period begins to run, it is not tolled (stopped) by the occurrence of a subsequent disability or another event.

When a plaintiff dies before the expiration of the time within which a suit must be filed, the plaintiff's personal representative usually has one year after the plaintiff's death within which to sue.

If a defendant is not in the jurisdiction and a plaintiff cannot, therefore, serve a complaint on the defendant, the running of the statute is tolled until service of the complaint is possible.

Tortfeasor's Capacity

All people are liable for their tortious acts regardless of mental capacity. This rule applies to acts of minors and of insane or intoxicated persons. However, if the tort requires intent, the defendant can establish lack of capacity to form intent as a defense. Under common law, minors were generally liable for torts if they were over the age of seven. See the exhibit "Practice Exercise: Defenses Against Negligence Claims."

> ### Practice Exercise: Defenses Against Negligence Claims
>
> Ashley was talking on her cell phone after stopping at a four-way stop sign and failed to see Kelsey, who was driving over the speed limit and who had failed to stop at one of the other stop signs. Because Ashley was distracted, her car drifted toward the middle of the road and hit Kelsey's car. Kelsey was injured and sued Ashley for $10,000 in damages for negligence. Ashley suffered no injury, and her very old car was only minimally damaged. How might a court decide this case with regard to Kelsey's recovery under comparative negligence principles?
>
> **Answer**
>
> If the court finds Ashley 60 percent at fault for being distracted and failing to see Kelsey and finds Kelsey 40 percent at fault because she was speeding and disregarded the stop sign, under comparative negligence principles, Kelsey would receive $6,000. The amount of her damages is reduced according to her degree of fault (40 percent).
>
> If Kelsey were found to be 50 percent at fault, and Ashley also 50 percent at fault, some comparative negligence states would still allow Kelsey to recover $5,000 (50 percent rule), while other states would not allow her any recovery because she and Ashley would be equally at fault (49 percent rule).

[DA06000]

LIABILITY OF LANDOWNERS OR OCCUPIERS OF LAND

A landowner or occupier of land owes certain duties to the public and to adjoining landowners. A breach of these duties can result in a tort lawsuit for damages.

In a lawsuit for damages involving injury suffered on land, a plaintiff usually sues the party in possession of the land. However, sometimes ownership, rather than possession, determines liability; therefore, the owner of land that has tenants can be the defendant in a lawsuit.

A plaintiff can sue for harm caused by either natural or artificial conditions on the land. The nature of a landowner's or occupier's duty can vary, depending on the injured party's status. For example, the plaintiff may be a trespasser or may have an express or implied license to be on the land as either a public or business invitee.

Natural Conditions

In general, a landowner is not liable for natural conditions on the land that cause injury either on or off the land. For example, if a rock falls down a hillside and injures someone on a highway below, the landowner of the hillside is not liable. However, some courts have rejected the traditional rule and have adopted a reasonableness standard. For example, if a defendant's sloping land is known to have frequent landslides, and a landslide pushes debris onto neighboring property, the landowner can be liable for negligent failure to correct or control the landslide condition.

Trespasser

A person who intentionally enters onto the property of another without permission or any legal right to do so.

The possessor of land is under no duty to correct natural conditions on the land even though they can create a danger to a **trespasser**. For example, if a trespasser sleds on a hillside, the owner of the hillside has no duty to warn the trespasser of dangerous rocks on the hillside hidden by the snow.

The natural conditions rule is modified for trees. When a tree falls and causes damage on an adjacent premises or a highway, the landowner might be liable for negligence if he or she knew that the tree might fall and failed to take reasonable steps to remove it. In rural areas, the rule usually is that the landowner or occupier has no affirmative duty to inspect trees to discover whether they are prone to collapse or dropping branches. However, the owner or occupier of land with trees in urban areas has a duty to use reasonable care to inspect the trees.

Artificial Conditions

Nuisance

Anything interfering with another person's use or enjoyment of property.

An owner who alters land in any manner can be liable either for negligence or for creating a **nuisance** because of those alterations. Examples of such alterations include these:

- Concentrating the flow of water discharges on adjoining land
- Permitting artificial devices, such as downspouts, to discharge over public ways
- Creating any other artificial condition that discharges water or snow on adjoining premises or roads

A landowner who creates an artificial condition on land that could cause severe injury or death has a duty to warn of the hazard if a trespasser probably would not discover it without warning. Posting signs, for instance, could constitute adequate warning. Therefore, an owner who had strung a potentially dangerous wire one or two feet off the ground across a hill where sledding occurred would have a duty to warn others.

Attractive nuisance doctrine

A doctrine treating a child as a licensee, or guest, rather than a trespasser on land containing an artificial and harmful condition that is certain to attract children.

While in general the same rules apply to children as to adults, an exception is the **attractive nuisance doctrine**, which states that when an implied invitation exists for a child to enter on land, the possessor must keep the premises in a suitable and safe condition and use ordinary care to protect trespassing children from harm.

An occupier of land abutting a sidewalk or street has a duty to avoid placing an unguarded excavation or ditch on the land that might endanger a traveler using the premises. The distance from the sidewalk or street to the excavation is not crucial, but is relevant to whether the owner could foresee that a traveler might be injured. This duty extends only to travelers and is not applicable to trespassers.

In most jurisdictions, landowners are not liable for defects in adjoining side-walks or streets. However, some jurisdictions impose a duty on landlords and tenants of commercial properties to keep adjoining sidewalks and streets in repair because they benefit from these thoroughfares.

Duties to Those Who Enter the Land or Premises

The permission to use or enter another's land is called a license. The party who receives the permission is either a licensee or an invitee. The owner or occupier owes different duties to **licensees** than to **invitees**. In contrast, a landowner or occupier owes trespassers a very minimal duty of care not to cause intentional harm to the trespasser.

A license to use or enter another's land may be either an **express license** or an **implied license**. The person granted a license must conform to the conditions on which it was granted or risk becoming a trespasser. For example, entering a store and then going into a stockroom not open to the public without permission is a trespass.

An express or implied license is revocable at any time, even if the licensee has paid for it. For example, a person who causes a disturbance in a theater can be ejected even though he paid for his admission ticket (license). An act of the landowner showing an intention to revoke the license may terminate it.

Licensees

The person granted a license is generally a licensee. A social guest, even though on the premises at the landowner's express invitation, is usually considered a licensee. A volunteer helper is also a licensee, as is a lodge member visiting another's house on lodge business. Firefighters and police officers are licensees when they enter property to perform their duties.

A licensee takes the property in the condition in which it exists. A landowner owes an affirmative duty to a licensee to refrain from willfully or wantonly injuring the person or acting in a way that would increase that person's peril. The landowner has a duty to warn of hidden defects. Usually, the occupier is not liable for the acts of third persons on the premises.

Invitees

An invitee is a special type of licensee. An invitee may be either a **public invitee** or a **business invitee**. Attendees at public meetings, visitors to national parks, and people entering amusement parks on free passes are all public invitees. A business benefit necessary to convert a licensee to a business invitee is ordinarily economic. A shopper, a restaurant guest, and a theater patron are examples of business invitees.

Invitee
Person who enters a premises for the financial benefit of the owner or occupant.

Licensee
A person who has permission to enter onto another's property for his or her own purposes.

Express license
The oral or written permission to enter onto another's land to do a certain act, but not the granting of any interest in the land itself.

Implied license
The permission to enter onto another's land arising out of a relationship between the party who enters the land and the owner.

Public invitee
A person invited to enter onto premises as a member of the general public for a purpose for which the land is open to the public.

Business invitee
An individual who has express or implied permission to be on the premises of another for the purpose of doing business.

For invitees, the land occupier owes a duty to exercise reasonable care to keep the premises reasonably safe and to warn of concealed dangerous conditions. The occupier need not warn of dangers of which the invitee is aware.

Trespassers

A landowner or occupier owes a trespasser a very minimal duty of care not to cause intentional harm to the trespasser. For example, a landowner who sets a trap for animals that injures a trespasser would not be liable for that harm. However, a landowner or occupier could not escape liability for intentional harm to a trespasser, except in situations where appropriate force might be necessary to remove a trespasser. For example, rigging a shotgun to go off when the door is opened by a trespasser would probably be considered excessive force.

Hotel Guests and Tenants

Under common law, a landlord or hotel operator was under no duty to protect tenants from intruders. However, this area of the law is changing. Many courts now impose a duty on landlords, hotel operators, and public entities to take reasonable precautions to secure their premises against foreseeable risks of harm by intruders. Failure to do so can result in liability.

What is reasonable involves an analysis of several factors, including prevailing practices in the type of occupancy, such as motels, the extent of crime in the area, and the kinds of security that are reasonable to provide under the circumstances. For example, a hotel that fails to provide proper security measures can be liable to a guest who is a victim of an intruder's actions. Likewise, a landlord can be liable to a tenant for injuries received during an attack in an unlighted parking lot. This concept also applies to public parking garages, college campuses, condominium common areas, and automated teller machine (ATM) premises.

Under common law, hotel operators or innkeepers had to furnish lodgings to anyone who could pay for them, provided prospective guests were not objectionable for a valid reason, such as intoxication. If the innkeeper improperly refused lodgings, the person could sue the innkeeper. This common-law rule did not apply to those furnishing services at other public places, such as restaurants and theaters, although later anti-discrimination laws developed that applied similar statutory rules.

A property owner who leased the property to another was not liable under common law for injuries resulting from the disrepair of the property or from other dangerous conditions, whether the condition resulted in injury to the tenant or to a third person. Today an owner or landlord is liable when injury results from negligently made repairs or from a concealed danger on the premises that the owner knows about but that the tenant cannot know or easily discover by the use of ordinary care. See the exhibit "Practice Exercise: Liability of Landowners or Land Occupiers."

Practice Exercise: Liability of Landowners or Land Occupiers

James owns a small, two-acre orchard that is situated about 300 yards behind his house. He operates a produce stand by the road in front of his house to sell the fruit his orchard produces. The orchard is fenced off from the public, except for an opening in the fence that he and his family use to access the orchard. Donna and her six-year-old daughter, Wendy, stop at James's stand to buy some peaches. While Donna is talking with James, Wendy runs behind James's house, then through the opening in the fence into the orchard, where James has hung a swing for his own children from one of the trees. The public cannot see the swing from either the road or the produce stand. Wendy subsequently falls out of the swing and breaks her arm. Is James responsible for Wendy's injury?

Answer

Donna and Wendy are business invitees at James's produce stand. James has not invited them into the orchard and actually has a fence to dissuade anyone but his family from entering the orchard. Because the swing is not visible to the public, and because James has the orchard fenced off, the swing probably would not be considered an attractive nuisance for children. James is probably not responsible for Wendy's injury.

[DA06002]

INTENTIONAL TORTS: PART 1 OF 2

Torts are civil (or private) wrongs, as distinguished from crimes, which are either unintentional or intentional public wrongs. Negligence is the term used for unintentional torts, and all other torts are intentional.

An **intentional tort** requires the tortfeasor's intent to harm or to act to cause harm, and intent differs from motive. For example, one person could shoot at another with the intent to kill but with the motive of self-defense, jealousy, or rage. Generally, intent and motive have no relationship, but motive can influence damages. An act done in self-defense might justify lower damages than an act done in rage, while tortfeasor's malice might warrant higher damages.

These torts are among the most common types of intentional torts:

- Battery
- Assault
- False imprisonment and false arrest
- Intentional infliction of emotional distress
- Defamation (libel and slander)
- Invasion of the right of privacy

Intentional torts, as distinguished from unintentional torts (collectively termed negligence) include a variety of civil wrongs.

Intentional tort

A tort committed by a person who foresees (or should be able to foresee) that his or her act will harm another person.

Battery

Battery
Intentional harmful or offensive physical contact with another person without legal justification.

Battery involves bodily contact, no matter how slight. Throwing a stone that hits another person, snatching a paper from another person's hand, or brushing against another person's clothing, for example, may all constitute battery. For such an act to constitute battery, the person need not be in fear of bodily harm or even be aware of the contact. For example, a doctor can commit a battery on a patient who is under anesthesia by performing an act the patient has not consented to beforehand.

A battery can be a crime as well as a tort.

To be classified as a tort, an act must be intentional and hostile or offensive. Merely blocking passage by standing in front of a person or lightly touching a person to gain attention is not battery. Similarly, the naturally occurring and inevitable touching of people in a crowd is not battery.

A person sued for battery may have one of several defenses:

- The plaintiff consented to the act—To consent to an act is to permit it. Consent can be actual or implied. For example, participation in a contact sport, such as football, can constitute implied consent to be touched.

- The act was in self-defense or defense of others—One can use reasonable force to repel an attack on one's own self or on another person. What constitutes reasonable force depends on the circumstances.

- The act was one of physical discipline—Physical discipline as a defense involves the parent-child relationship or contact with persons who have the legal authority to discipline others. The defense is successful only if the force used is reasonable, and the use of force must be in good faith.

Assault

Assault
The threat of force against another person that creates a well-founded fear of imminent harmful or offensive contact.

In contrast to battery, **assault** does not involve physical contact, but the other person must anticipate, or expect, contact and fear harm. Pointing a knife at another or swinging a fist close to another person's face are examples of assault.

False Imprisonment and False Arrest

False imprisonment
The restraint or confinement of a person without consent or legal authority.

False arrest
The seizure or forcible restraint of a person without legal authority.

False imprisonment and **false arrest** are similar torts. False imprisonment entails unlawful nonphysical restraint, such as blocking a door out of a room. False arrest involves unlawful physical restraint or threats of physical restraint.

Defenses to false imprisonment and false arrest relate to whether the acts occurred in connection with a crime, the nature of the crime, and the capacity of the individual involved. For situations involving felonies (serious crimes), a police officer has almost complete immunity from charges of false imprisonment or false arrest when making an arrest under a warrant issued by a competent judicial authority. Police officers can make arrests without warrants for felonies committed in their presence and for felonies committed outside their presence if they have reasonable grounds to believe that those arrested have committed felonies. Under these conditions, police officers are not liable even if no felonies were committed and even if those arrested did not commit them.

Citizens who make arrests without warrants to prevent commission of felonies in their presence usually can defend successfully against charges of false imprisonment or false arrest. Like police officers, citizens can make arrests for felonies committed out of their presence, provided they have reasonable grounds to believe that those arrested did commit felonies. However, private citizens can be liable if the particular felonies were not, in fact, committed, or if they had no reasonable grounds to believe that those arrested committed the felonies.

When false imprisonment or false arrests are made in connection with a misdemeanor (minor crime), different rules apply. A police officer can make an arrest for a misdemeanor under a valid warrant and can make an arrest without a warrant for such misdemeanors as forcible breaches of the peace, like riots or civil commotions, and also for peace-disturbing activities such as vagrancy and public drunkenness. However, mere impudence or argument does not constitute a breach of the peace that would justify arrest.

Warrantless arrest is justifiable only when the misdemeanor is committed in the presence of the officer who makes the arrest. An officer cannot arrest a person for a misdemeanor committed elsewhere, or for a past misdemeanor, without a warrant. As a general rule, private citizens cannot make arrests for misdemeanors except when they constitute breaches of the peace.

People detained by store personnel on suspicion of shoplifting have sued for false imprisonment. Many state laws now permit detention for a reasonable time so that stores can investigate suspected shoplifting without facing unreasonable litigation. A reasonable time usually is relatively short, such as an hour or less.

Intentional Infliction of Emotional Distress

An essential element of the tort of **intentional infliction of emotional distress** (or, in Canada, the intentional infliction of mental suffering) is its effect on the plaintiff—mental distress that may result in physical symptoms. An example would be an intentionally false report that a person's spouse is having an affair, resulting in that person's feelings of distress and a physical reaction, such as vomiting. A defense for intentional infliction of emotional distress is that the act was not intentional.

Plaintiffs can also allege **negligent infliction of emotional distress**, a similar, but unintentional, tort. The defense for negligent infliction of emotional distress is that the act was not negligent.

Intentional infliction of emotional distress

An intentional act causing mental anguish that results in physical injury.

Negligent infliction of emotional distress

An unintentional act causing mental anguish that results in physical injury.

Common law required proof of physical injury resulting from emotional distress. A plaintiff could not recover for emotional distress alone, such as fear, anxiety, or sorrow. For example, a mother who witnessed a car hit her child and who suffered only emotional distress had no right to sue the driver for infliction of emotional distress unless she also suffered physical injury or harm. This rule is no longer prevalent.

Some courts now interpret the term "physical injury" (also called "physical manifestation") to mean any condition or illness capable of objective determination. A few courts have eliminated the physical injury requirement and permit a suit for pure emotional injury on the grounds that emotional injury alone can be as severe as physical harm.

A defense for intentional infliction of emotional distress is that no intent was involved. For negligent infliction of emotional distress, the defense would be that negligence was lacking. Additionally, a defendant might defend on the basis that no actual physical injury or manifestation occurred, except in states where pure emotional injury is sufficient ground for a plaintiff's recovery.

Defamation (Slander and Libel)

Libel

A defamatory statement expressed in writing.

Slander

A defamatory statement expressed by speech.

Defamation

A false written or oral statement that harms another's reputation.

Defamation includes **slander** and **libel**. The law recognizes a difference between written and spoken defamatory words and treats them differently. Spoken defamatory words are slander, and written defamatory words are libel. Courts differ as to whether defamation occurring through broadcast media or on the Internet constitutes slander or liable.

To be defamatory, a statement must concern the complaining party personally. For example, Joe publicly calls Fred a liar or a tax cheat in a town meeting hall filled to capacity.

Slander

Because defamatory statements constituting slander are oral, they usually are heard only once. Unless spoken statements are repeated, the chance that a large audience will hear them is remote. Therefore, the law requires substantial proof of injury to a plaintiff's reputation.

Publication

In tort law, the communication of a defamatory statement to another person.

For a statement to be slanderous, a **publication** to a third person other than the party slandered must occur. Publication, for slander, is only oral—neither written nor recorded in any other way. For example, If Al accuses Sarah of committing murder when the two are alone, no publication and no harm to Sarah's reputation have occurred. However, if Al tells Carol that Sarah committed murder, Al's communication to Carol constitutes publication.

Libel

Because libel is written or printed, it has wider circulation and is more permanent than slander; therefore the potential for damage to a person's reputation by libel is much greater than that associated with slander.

As with slander, publication of the libelous statement to a third person or persons is necessary for a successful lawsuit. If a person receives a letter containing false statements about him or her and destroys it, the letter is not libelous.

News media have a special status in defamation law. Until 1964, the same common-law principles that apply to all other persons applied to the media. However, in the landmark case *Sullivan v. New York Times*,[3] the United States Supreme Court held that public officials suing news media for libel must prove that the statement was false and, further, that the defendant made it with knowledge of its falsity or with reckless disregard for its truth or falsity.

Reckless disregard means a high degree of certainty of a statement's probable falsity, approaching the level of a knowing, calculated falsehood. The *Sullivan* decision balanced the importance of public, open debate, as embodied in the First Amendment, against the individual's right of privacy. Later, the rule expanded to include statements made about public figures, that is, people who have voluntarily assumed positions that place them in the public eye, such as politicians, entertainers, and sports figures.

Many articles about public figures, if written about ordinary people, would be libelous. However, the law holds that accepting this form of communication is part of the price public figures pay for being famous. Therefore, a public figure must prove actual malice to recover damages in a libel suit, and malice can be very difficult to prove.

The defenses for slander and libel are essentially the same:

- The statement was the truth.
- The defendant made or printed a retraction—not a complete defense, but it can reduce damages.
- The statement had absolute privilege—applies to statements made in judicial and legislative proceedings, executive officers' communications, and spousal communications, and when consent was given by the injured party.
- The statement had conditional or qualified privilege—applies to statements made without malice as a matter of public interest, in petitions concerning appointments, in common interest communications, as fair comment on matters of public concern, and by credit reporting agencies.

Commercial Speech

Commercial speech, which can involve libel, has much less protection than speech concerning public issues. Commercial speech is solely in the speaker's individual interest and concerns the speaker's specific business activity. These statements have much less constitutional protection than speech concerning public issues. Such speech might involve injurious falsehoods that are not personally defamatory. The major types of commercial speech that might be defamatory are comparative advertising and product disparagement.

Comparative advertising is advertising in which a party marketing Product A makes a direct comparison with Product B by name. Advertisers used to avoid direct comparison, but they now use it frequently. If the comparison is truthful and fair, advertisers are not liable for defamation.

Generally, the usual defamation rules apply to comparative advertising. To be grounds for a lawsuit, the claims of Product A's superiority over Product B must be specific and not just general "puffing" that the product is better or superior. The defendant must have made specific claims about product performance or must have described objective tests. Comparisons that are false, misleading, or incomplete can be libelous.

**Product disparagement,
or trade libel**

An intentional false and misleading statement about a characteristic of a plaintiff's product, resulting in financial damage to the plaintiff.

Product disparagement, or trade libel, involves intentionally false or misleading statements about the quality of the plaintiff's product, resulting in financial damage to the plaintiff. Examples are false statements denying the plaintiff's title to property and false statements regarding the quality of the plaintiff's property or the plaintiff's conduct of business.

The plaintiff must prove that the publication played a material part in loss of customers or prospective customers. The statement can be either intentional or negligent, and truth is a complete defense.

Invasion of the Right of Privacy

Invasion of privacy

An encroachment on another person's right to be left alone.

Invasion of privacy includes several different common-law torts, as well as the statutory offense of invasion of rights.

The common-law tort invasion of privacy is based on an individual's right to be left alone and to be protected from unauthorized publicity in essentially private matters. Acts that constitute invasion of privacy include intrusion on solitude or seclusion; physical invasion; and torts that involve use or disclosure of information. The information used or disclosed must be by printed matter, writing, pictures, or other permanent records, not merely word of mouth.

Intrusion on Solitude or Seclusion

Intrusion on physical or mental solitude or seclusion is an invasion of something personal, secluded, or private pertaining to the plaintiff. This intrusion is not confined to a physical invasion of the person or premises. Placing a hidden microphone, eavesdropping, tapping of telephone lines, using telephoto lenses, and using similar types of surveillance can constitute unlawful invasion if the intrusion would be highly offensive to a reasonable person.

Physical Invasion

Physical invasion is a separate version of the tort of invasion of privacy. For example, searching a shopping bag in a store or the unauthorized taking of a blood sample can constitute a physical invasion. Ordinarily, a defendant has no liability for taking photographs in a public place. However, photographs of a person in a compromising or embarrassing position can give rise to suit.

Torts Involving Use or Disclosure of Information

Several torts involving invasion of privacy relate to the use or disclosure of information. Unlike the similar torts of libel and slander, which are based on the falsity of the information, these torts are based on interference with privacy:

- Public disclosure of private facts—This tort usually involves gossip columns or similar disseminations of stories about a plaintiff's private life. To a certain extent, a right to sue depends on the plaintiff's public prominence. An entertainer or politician, for example, is not entitled to privacy to the same degree as an ordinary citizen.

- Publicity placing plaintiff in a false light—This tort usually involves using a statement that has been taken out of context or is based on information that is not true. The defendant has presented the publicity in such a way that the plaintiff has good cause to be offended, even if the plaintiff's reputation is not damaged.

- Unauthorized release of confidential information—Sometimes courts treat unauthorized release of confidential information as a tort separate from invasion of the right of privacy, although it contains many of the same elements.

- Appropriation of plaintiff's name or likeness—The tort is based on one's rights to one's own name and likeness. Anyone who makes unauthorized use of another's name or likeness for publicity or commercial gain may be liable, but most courts base the tort on the defendant's commercial benefit.

Defenses to Invasion of Privacy

In an action for any form of invasion of the right of privacy, one or several of these defenses may apply:

- The plaintiff previously published the information.
- The plaintiff consented to publication.
- The plaintiff is a public figure, or the information is public knowledge.
- The information was part of a news event.
- The publication would not offend an individual of ordinary sensibility.
- Matters were disclosed in judicial proceedings.
- The information is of public interest, such as the public's right to know.

INTENTIONAL TORTS: PART 2 OF 2

Torts are civil (or private) wrongs, as distinguished from crimes, which are either unintentional or intentional public wrongs. Negligence is the term used for unintentional torts, and all other torts are intentional.

An intentional tort requires the tortfeasor's intent to harm or to act to cause harm, and intent differs from motive. For example, one person could shoot at another with the intent to kill but with the motive of self-defense, jealousy, or rage. Generally, intent and motive have no relationship, but motive can influence damages. An act done in self-defense might justify lower damages than an act done in rage, while a tortfeasor's malice might warrant higher damages.

Among common forms of intentional torts are these:

- Fraud
- Bad faith, or outrage
- Interference with relationships between others
- Misuse of legal process
- Trespass
- Nuisance
- Conversion

Fraud

The terms fraud, deceit, and misrepresentation are often interchangeable, but fraud is the generic term. Proof of fraud requires proof of six elements:

- A false representation has been made.
- The misrepresentation is material (important) and concerns a past or an existing fact.
- The misrepresentation was knowingly made, that is, made with the knowledge of its falsity, in reckless disregard of the truth or without knowledge or concern as to whether it was true or false.
- The misrepresentation was made with intent to influence or deceive.
- The party to which the misrepresentation was made places reasonable reliance on its truth. The misrepresentation must be a reasonable inducement to the other party to act. If the party would act regardless of the representation, no fraud occurs. The reliance must be justified. Relying on a layperson for a medical opinion, for example, would not be justified.
- The complaining party must suffer a detriment, or actual damage.

Defenses to fraud focus on disproving one or more of the elements of fraud:

- The statement was not false.
- The statement did not relate to a material fact.
- The defendant did not know the statement was false.

- The defendant did not intend to deceive.
- The plaintiff did not rely on the statement.
- The plaintiff suffered no harm or loss because of relying on the statement.

Bad Faith, or Outrage

Bad faith, or outrage, is a tort of intentionally or recklessly causing another person severe emotional distress through one's extreme or outrageous acts.

Bad faith is similar to intentional infliction of emotional distress but has been a separate cause of action, principally in suits for breach of insurance contracts. It is based on the theory that, in certain cases, the plaintiff is entitled to damages above those typically awarded for breach of contract. These cases involve alleged outrageous or extreme conduct or the defendant's breach of an implied duty of good faith and fair dealings. Bad faith applies to several situations, including breach of employment contracts involving wrongful discharge or discrimination.

Bad faith (outrage)
A breach of the duty of good faith and fair dealing.

Damages

Traditionally, courts award only contractual damages for breach of contract. Contractual damages include compensatory damages and foreseeable consequential damages, but do not include damages for mental anguish or punitive damages.

A plaintiff can seek to recover additional, punitive damages in a breach of contract action by alleging that the defendant has acted in bad faith, resulting in an additional injury. Many jurisdictions recognize the independent tort of bad faith or outrage to provide the injured party with an additional recovery in breach of contract actions.

Insurance Cases

In insurance cases, the tort of bad faith is based on an insurer's implied duty to act fairly and in good faith in discharging its duties under an insurance contract. Usually, insureds allege negligent or intentional denial of a claim or failure to process or to pay a claim without reasonable cause. Such allegations might include failure or delay in pursuing claim investigation and settlement or the delay of claim payment to coerce insureds into settling for less than the full amount due. Most jurisdictions hold that, if the defendant has a reasonable cause to delay payment, no bad faith has occurred.

In addition to claim practices, courts also have recognized causes of action for retaliatory cancellation of policies and unfair increases in premiums after the filing of claims.

An insurer's duty to an insured in a case in which a third party has sued the insured for damages is well established. The insurer must act in good faith and without negligence in defending the case because the insured has relinquished the valuable right to settle or defend the action. Some courts hold that failure to protect the insured's rights makes the insurer liable for the full amount of the loss, even if the loss exceeds the policy limit.

Not all courts recognize the tort of bad faith or outrage in connection with breach of contract suits. Further, many states now have laws imposing various penalties for failure to settle insurance claims properly. Many states and provinces also have adopted unfair claim settlement practice acts or unfair and deceptive acts and practice laws or regulations, which can preempt any private lawsuits for bad faith.

Defenses

Several defenses are possible in suits alleging bad faith:

- No intent or recklessness was involved.
- No outrageous or extreme conduct occurred.
- The defendant did not breach any implied duty of good faith and fair dealings.
- If contract damages are involved, the defendant owned no contractual duty to the plaintiff.
- In an insurance case, no valid insurance contract existed; therefore, the defendant owed the plaintiff no duty to act fairly and in good faith.

Interference With Relationships Between Others

Another category of intentional tort relates to interference with relationships between others. Many torts involve interference with either personal or business relationships of other parties. These torts are not mutually exclusive in that one court might recognize an act as a violation of one right, and another might recognize the same act as a violation of another right.

Interference with relationships between others includes these torts:

- Injurious falsehood
- Malicious interference with prospective economic advantage
- Unfair competition
- Interference with employment
- Interference with copyright, patent, or trademark
- Interference with right to use one's own name in business
- Interference with family relationships

Injurious falsehood

A group of torts involving disparagement that causes harm to any kind of legally protected intangible property right.

Injurious Falsehood

Legally protected property rights grouped under torts constituting **injurious falsehood** include almost any intangible property right, such as an interest in a title, lease, or trademark.

Injurious falsehood can include disparaging statements referring to the quality of merchandise or the validity of a person's title to property. The tort is similar to defamation, and both torts apply in some cases. Injurious falsehood differs from defamation primarily in that the plaintiff must prove both the falsity of the statement and the actual damage or loss, while defamation might not result in actual damages.

The essence of the tort of injurious falsehood is interference with an economically advantageous relationship resulting in monetary loss. Therefore, it primarily concerns damage to a property right, while defamation usually involves damage to a person's reputation. Examples of injurious falsehood are allegations of improper business conduct or poor quality of goods.

The defenses for this tort are essentially the same as those for defamation (slander and libel):

- The statement was the truth.
- The defendant made or printed a retraction—not a complete defense, but it can reduce damages.
- The statement had absolute privilege—applies to statements made in judicial and legislative proceedings, executive officers' communications, and spousal communications, and when consent was given by the injured party.
- The statement had conditional or qualified privilege—applies to statements made without malice as a matter of public interest, in petitions concerning appointments, in common interest communications, as fair comment on matters of public concern, and by credit reporting agencies.

Malicious Interference With Prospective Economic Advantage

Malicious interference with prospective economic advantage involves interference with commercial dealings, such as interfering with one's obtaining a job or purchasing property. However, the concept has expanded to cases involving interference with an expected gift or legacy under a will and expectations of economic advantage other than those arising out of business.

The usual defense in a suit for malicious interference with prospective economic advantage is that the defendant was making a lawful effort, without **malice**, to promote his or her own welfare and not to injure the plaintiff.

Unfair Competition

Unfair competition is a counterpart of malicious interference with prospective economic advantage. The essence of unfair competition is deception, and it starts when one party deceives the public into buying its product in the mistaken belief that it is another party's product.

Malicious interference with prospective economic advantage

A tort involving intentional interference with another's business, or with another's expected economic advantage.

Malice

The intent to do a wrongful act without justification or excuse.

Unfair competition

Use of wrongful or fraudulent practices by a business to gain an unfair advantage over competitors.

The common law prohibited people or organizations from pretending that their goods were competitors' goods by using similar trademarks, labels, or wrappers. If such an action deprived the competitor of the value of the goodwill in the business, the competitor could sue for unfair competition.

No unfair competition exists without competition. Conversely, no injury results unless the two parties are competing directly with the same product or service. However, one party cannot legally make or label goods in any manner that leads the public to believe those goods are the product of a manufacturer in another field, thereby obtaining the benefit of the other party's goodwill and reputation. It does not matter that the two parties are not in direct competition.

Unfair competition applies to literary and artistic properties as well as to merchandise. To illustrate, reproducing photographs or copying paintings and passing them off as the works of another photographer or artist creates a right to sue.

A defense to a lawsuit for unfair competition might include the assertion that the defendant did not perform one or more of these acts:

- Compete
- Compete directly
- Harm the plaintiff
- Mislead the public
- Deceive anyone

Interference With Employment

Interference with employment

An unjustified intentional act that interferes with another's valid or expected business relationship.

The tort of **interference with employment** can take many forms and in certain instances overlaps with other torts involving interference with relationships. An example of this tort is spreading negative information about a person applying for a job. The same act also can be defamation, either libel or slander, depending on the means of publication, if the information is false.

A defense to a lawsuit for interference with employment might include the defendant's allegations that he or she did not do any of these things:

- Interfere with or prevent employment
- Induce a breach of contract
- Harm the plaintiff
- Act in furtherance of an unlawful object
- Use unlawful means to procure discharge
- Blacklist

Interference With Copyright, Patent, or Trademark

Copyright, patent, and trademark rights are property rights, and interference with any of these rights has historically been a tort. Today, federal legislation preempts the common law and governs most matters concerning these rights. As defenses to a lawsuit for interference with copyright, patent, or trademark, the defendant might assert that he or she did not interfere with the copyright, patent, or trademark or that the plaintiff did not own the intellectual property in question.

Interference With Right to Use One's Own Name in Business

A person has a right to use his or her own name in business even though a similar business is conducted under the same or a similar name. This right applies both to individuals and to corporations. In the case of corporations, businesses must register names, and most states will not grant a charter if a name is too similar to a name already registered.

Courts give the original user of a personal name some protection, and they require a notice that no connection exists with the original. For example, John Doe Co. might be required to put a notice on its products reading "Not connected with the Mary Doe Co." to distinguish its products from Mary Doe's.

Interference With Family Relationships

The family has no collective legal rights. However, individuals have rights as members of a family. Under common law, neither spouse could sue a third party for personal injury against the other spouse. Most jurisdictions have abandoned this rule. Additionally, in most jurisdictions, a spouse can now sue for assault and battery or false imprisonment. Many spousal rights were only for the husband's benefit at common law. Today, laws favoring husbands over wives either have been eliminated totally or apply equally to wives. Spouses' rights against third persons fall into three general categories:

- Alienation of affection—A third party's interference with the husband-wife relationship is commonly called alienation of affection. A spouse has a right to sue a person who persuades the other spouse to leave the marriage. Some states, either by statute or court decision, have eliminated alienation of affection actions.

- Personal injury—A spouse, or both spouses together, can sue a third person for causing personal physical injury to one spouse. In addition, the spouse of an injured person can also sue for loss of consortium.

- Loss of consortium—Loss of the husband-wife relationship is commonly called loss of consortium and involves loss of services, companionship, and comfort. The amount of damages is based on the spouses' existing relationship.

Parents also have family relationship rights. Under common law, parents could sue third persons for injury to children based on loss of services because children helped families economically. On farms, for example, children performed essential duties. Under modern law, it is not necessary to show an actual loss of services, even though that loss remains the underlying theory of the suit. Enticing a child away or kidnapping, negligently injuring, or seducing a child can give rise to a right to sue regardless of economic deprivation.

Under common law, children had no right to sue their parents for injuries or failure to provide support. Children also had no right of action against third persons who injured their parents, thus depriving them of their source of support. Today, a child can recover for injuries that third persons cause to parents. Also, although under common law a child had no right to sue parents for cruel or abusive treatment, children now can allege that the force used was unreasonable or was used in bad faith.

Other torts relating to family relationships—wrongful life and wrongful pregnancy—are of recent origin and are not frequent bases for lawsuits.

Wrongful-life action

A lawsuit by or on behalf of a child with birth defects, alleging that, but for the doctor-defendant's negligent advice, the parents would not have conceived the child or would have terminated the pregnancy so as to avoid the pain and suffering resulting from the child's defects.

Most jurisdictions have rejected **wrongful-life actions**. A child born with a physical disability can be the plaintiff in a suit for wrongful life, based on an allegation that the defendant, usually a doctor, negligently failed to diagnose a disability or warn the parents of the probability that the child would be born with the disability. As a result, the parents were deprived of the ability to make an informed judgment about whether to carry the child to term. Recovery in such cases is limited to special damages and does not include pain and suffering or other general damages.

Wrongful-pregnancy action (wrongful-conception action)

A lawsuit by a parent for damages resulting from a pregnancy following a failed sterilization.

The companion tort to wrongful life is a **wrongful-pregnancy action**, also called a wrongful conception action in some jurisdictions. This claim is frequently alleged by the parents in wrongful life cases and can arise in two situations:

- When an unplanned birth of a healthy baby follows a failed sterilization
- When parents give birth to a child with disabilities after a doctor misdiagnosed or failed to detect a condition ("wrongful birth")

In these cases, the parents can recover the extraordinary expenses involved in taking care of the child. Some courts limit recovery to the period before the child reaches majority; others impose no such limit. Many jurisdictions recognize the wrongful death cause of action, including those in several states that have rejected the wrongful life cause of action.

Misuse of Legal Process

Misuse of legal process takes two forms: malicious prosecution and malicious abuse of process. Courts discourage lawsuits alleging these torts because of public policy, which favors use of the courts to resolve disputes. However, misuse of legal process can sometimes be appropriate grounds for suit.

Malicious Prosecution

Historically, **malicious prosecution** related only to criminal cases. For example, Al files a groundless criminal complaint against Bob to harass him. Bob is acquitted as defendant in the criminal action. Bob, as plaintiff in a civil action, can sue Al for malicious prosecution. Today some jurisdictions apply malicious prosecution to certain civil proceedings, such as bankruptcy and actions to have a person declared incompetent.

Malicious prosecution
The improper institution of legal proceedings against another.

The plaintiff's inability to prove any of the elements of the tort is a defense. In addition, these acts can also bar a lawsuit for malicious prosecution:

- Defendant's action on advice of counsel—Lack of **probable cause** is an essential element of this tort. Showing that the defendant fully disclosed all facts to an impartial attorney and, with a genuine belief in the plaintiff's guilt, acted on the attorney's advice, strongly indicates the presence of probable cause.

Probable cause
The grounds that would lead a reasonable person to believe that the plaintiff committed the act for which the defendant is suing.

- Plaintiff's guilt of the crime—If the defendant proves the plaintiff was guilty, and the plaintiff is convicted, no cause of action remains. The plaintiff's acquittal, however, is not conclusive evidence of lack of probable cause. Acquittal does not prove conclusively that a person is innocent but merely indicates that a jury was not convinced beyond a reasonable doubt of the defendant's guilt (in a criminal case).

- Probable cause—Proof of probable cause for an arrest completely prevents a malicious prosecution action.

Malicious Abuse of Process

Malicious abuse of process is distinguished from malicious prosecution, or maliciously causing process to issue. Abuse of process relates to improper use of process after it has issued. An example of malicious abuse of process is bringing a person into a jurisdiction, supposedly as a party or witness in one action, but in reality to serve process in the form of a complaint in connection with another action.

Malicious abuse of process
The use of civil or criminal procedures for a purpose for which they were not designed.

The plaintiff's inability to prove an ulterior motive is the usual defense to a claim of malicious abuse of process. Therefore, if the defendant can show that the use of the process was regular and legitimate, even though the process was initiated with a bad intention, it is not a malicious abuse of process.

Trespass

A **trespass** can be against either real property or **personal property**, and the elements are essentially the same for both. Trespass is an act against possession and not against ownership. That is, the plaintiff must be in possession of the property. An owner not in possession has no right to sue. A tenant in possession can sue only for injury to his or her interest. Entry upon another's land is justified if the owner or occupant either expressly or impliedly permits it.

Trespass
Unauthorized entry to another person's real property or forcible interference with another person's personal property.

Personal property
All tangible or intangible property that is not real property.

The law presumes at least nominal damages merely because an unauthorized entry onto another's land has occurred. The defendant is liable even if the entry is accidental. The magnitude of the entry is not important. Merely walking on the property is sufficient to constitute trespass. In fact, actual entry is not required. For example, throwing debris onto a neighbor's land or cutting a tree that falls on another's land are both trespasses.

Trespass to personal property is the forcible interference with another's possession of the property. Any type of property, including animals, can be the subject of a trespass. For example, if a person unjustifiably kills another person's dog, the killing would be a trespass to personal property.

Defenses to the claim of trespass to real or personal property are these:

- The plaintiff did not own or possess the property.
- The plaintiff consented to the defendant's entry.
- The defendant did not enter onto or take control of the property.

Nuisance

A court will decide what constitutes a nuisance by considering the discomfort the act would inflict on a normal person under normal conditions and not its effect on persons who are too sensitive or who are ill, either physically or mentally.

Private nuisance

An unreasonable and unlawful interference with another's use or enjoyment of his or her real property.

A nuisance can be either private or public. To constitute a **private nuisance**, the interference must be substantial enough to be unreasonable and can take almost any form, such as producing undue noise, causing dust to fall on adjoining property, blasting, or interfering in any other material way with the enjoyment of property.

Public nuisance

An act, occupation, or structure that affects the public at large or a substantial segment of the public, interfering with public enjoyment or rights regarding property.

A **public nuisance**, as contrasted with a private nuisance, affects the public. For example, a person who operates a plant that pollutes a river with poisonous waste commits a public nuisance. Only a person who has suffered personal damage can recover damages for injury resulting from a public nuisance. The injury must be particular to the individual plaintiff. The remedies for public nuisance include a civil tort suit for damages and criminal charges and usually include a court order demanding curtailment of the nuisance.

Intentional nuisance

Purposeful interference with another party's enjoyment of his or her property.

The invasion of others' rights can be either intentional or unintentional. Examples of **intentional nuisance** (sometimes called an absolute nuisance) are erection of a fence whose height interferes with an adjoining landowner's enjoyment of property and spraying of chemicals with the knowledge that they are damaging a neighbor's land. Defendants are liable for unintentional nuisances when their conduct is negligent, reckless, or ultrahazardous.

Nuisance per se

An act, occupation, or structure that is a nuisance at all times and under any conditions, regardless of location or surroundings.

Nuisance per se is a nuisance at all times, and a lawfully built structure generally cannot be a nuisance *per se*. However, a leaky hazardous-waste storage facility is a nuisance *per se*.

A common defense to a nuisance lawsuit is that the act complained of was a reasonable and legal use of the property by the defendant. Historically, people have been entitled to use their property in any way as long as the uses do not interfere unreasonably with others' enjoyment of their own property.

Conversion

Conversion applies to chattel and does not apply to land. The party must be deprived of possession of chattel by a wrongful taking, wrongful disposal, wrongful detention, or severe damage or destruction. The interference with possession must be major and not just temporary or fleeting. Conversion is founded on the legal wrong of deprivation of one's right to property. Any person with a legal right to possession, including a finder or bailee, can sue for conversion.

These defenses are valid against conversion:

- A plaintiff's failure to establish the right to possession of the property
- A plaintiff's refusal to demand return, followed by the defendant's consequent refusal to deliver

A bailee can defend by showing that the property is not in his or her possession because it was lost or destroyed without the bailee's fault, such as by an act of nature.

Conversion
The unlawful exercise of control over another person's personal property to the detriment of the owner.

LIABILITY IN EXTRAORDINARY CIRCUMSTANCES

In addition to liability based on intention or on negligence, sometimes liability is imposed even when a defendant has acted reasonably and would ordinarily not be at fault. A person who commits certain acts is liable for injury to another regardless of whether the act was willful or negligent.

An activity that exposes others or their property to the risk of substantial damage may cause the person who conducts the activity to be held liable for any harm that results even though he or she is not negligent. This liability may attach as a result of **strict liability (absolute liability)** or liability imposed by a statute when the liable party is performing an **ultrahazardous activity (abnormally dangerous activity)**, owns and/or possesses an animal, or allows escape of a toxic substance.

Strict liability (absolute liability)
Liability imposed by a court or by a statute in the absence of fault when harm results from activities or conditions that are extremely dangerous, unnatural, ultrahazardous, extraordinary, abnormal, or inappropriate.

Ultrahazardous activity (abnormally dangerous activity)
An activity that is inherently dangerous; if harm results, the performer may be held strictly liable.

Ultrahazardous Activities

Generally, people can use their property in any way they see fit as long as the use does not harm others. Some uses are considered ultrahazardous. A use or an activity is ultrahazardous or abnormally dangerous under these circumstances:

- It has a high degree of risk of serious harm.
- It cannot be performed without the high degree of risk.
- It does not normally occur in the area in which it is conducted.

In the landmark English tort case of *Rylands v. Fletcher*,[4] which dealt with the escape of water onto neighboring land, the court extended the doctrine of strict liability to certain activities on real property. The court held that people who bring anything onto their land that, if it escapes, is likely to result in injury, are strictly liable for all damages that are the natural consequence of the escape. The decision applies only to things artificially brought onto the land and not to natural things such as trees and weeds. It also does not apply when the cause is natural, such as an unprecedented rainfall that causes a reservoir to overflow.

The justification for imposing strict liability on those who carry on ultrahazardous activities is that they have, for their own purposes, created an unusual risk in the community. If the activity causes an injury or damage, then another person's or animal's unexpected action, or a force of nature, is immaterial to the defendant's liability.

The storage and transportation of explosive substances is an ultrahazardous activity. Aviation is also an ultrahazardous activity, although many states take the position that it is now so commonplace as to present no unusual danger.

The occupiers of adjacent property are not required to refrain from using their property as they please merely because of an ultrahazardous activity taking place nearby. For example, owners of property adjacent to a blasting operation are under no obligation to vacate their premises, construct explosion-proof shelters, or take other protective steps to mitigate any damage that occurs.

Ownership and/or Possession of Animals

For liability for animals, the law differentiates between domestic and wild animals, based on local custom. At common law, an owner was strictly liable for damages caused by the trespass of any domestic animal. If, for example, a cow broke out of a fenced field onto a neighbor's land and caused damage, strict liability applied, and proof of negligence was not necessary.

In most cases, the rule of strict liability does not apply to dogs and cats, because they are domestic animals that seldom cause serious damage. However, the rule may apply to a dog or a cat if the owner knows the animal has a vicious propensity to cause injury. In most jurisdictions, an owner who knows of a dog's propensity to be vicious is liable.

Owners of wild animals are absolutely liable for all acts of and damage caused by the animals. Wild animals are animals that, by local custom, are not devoted to people's use.

Escape of Toxic Substances

The related concepts of **toxic torts** and **environmental law** represent a rapidly expanding and changing area of the law. Toxic torts suits are similar in many respects to products liability suits. The name "toxic tort" does not refer to a specific tort, but to several types of tort suits that can arise from the use of toxic substances.

The additional factor present in toxic torts is that, in many instances, liability is established by statute rather than by common law. Further, in many of these lawsuits, a governmental agency is a party and a private-party plaintiff may be involved.

Toxic tort lawsuits seek compensation for damages to individuals caused by toxic substances. As in all tort cases, a plaintiff in a toxic tort case must prove that the defendant breached a duty, that the breach caused injury or loss to the plaintiff, and that the loss resulted in actual damages.

Environmental law includes measures to prevent environmental damage, such as requirements for environmental-impact statements, and measures to assign liability and provide cleanup for incidents resulting in environmental damage. Because most environmental suits involve governmental agencies as enforcers, environmental law is intertwined with administrative law.

Environmental suits arise from laws to protect the general public, for example, a suit brought to clean up a waste site. In these suits, an administrative agency first determines whether a party is liable for damages, such as cleanup costs under a statutory regulation. Findings in those lawsuits relate more to whether the defendant violated a law than to whether the defendant actually has caused damage to someone. Both administrative agencies and courts may at times equate violation of regulatory statutes with proof of failure to discharge a duty of care that is the basis of tort liability.

Environmental law
The body of law that deals with the environment's maintenance and protection.

Toxic tort
A civil wrong arising from exposure to a toxic substance.

PRODUCTS LIABILITY

Under common law, contractors, manufacturers, and sellers of products were not liable for negligence to third parties with whom they had no contractual relationships. Today, products liability is a rapidly expanding area of tort law.

Most **products liability** suits are based on one or more of these legal principles:

- Misrepresentation
- Breach of warranty
- Strict liability and negligence

Although negligence and strict liability are dissimilar in many respects, considering them together provides comparisons of how each applies in products liability cases.

Products liability
A manufacturer's or seller's liability for harm suffered by a buyer, user, or bystander as a result of a product that has a dangerous manufacturing defect or design defect or that is not accompanied by a warning of an inherent hidden danger.

Misrepresentation

Manufacturers make representations to the public through advertisements, brochures, labels on goods, and instructions for use. These representations extend beyond mere sales promotion by providing safety information on which consumers rely. For example, an automobile manufacturer's brochure described the windshield glass as shatterproof. The owner, injured when a pebble struck and shattered the glass, sued the manufacturer and recovered damages. Many lawsuits for misrepresentation in relation to products or services are based on the assertion that the misrepresentation constitutes an **express warranty**. However, in the windshield case, the court determined the liability on the basis of innocent misrepresentation, a form of deceit.

Breach of Warranty

A breach of warranty lawsuit can involve either an express warranty or an **implied warranty**. In a significant United States case, *Henningsen v. Bloomfield Motors, Inc.*,[5] the wife of a new car buyer was injured while driving the allegedly defective car. In the contract of sale, the manufacturer had attempted to disclaim any liability relating to the quality or condition of the car. The court held that the car was subject to a nonwaivable implied warranty of merchantability, that no privity (contractual relationship) was required, and that the warranty ran to any person who might reasonably be expected to use the car.

Examples of cases based on the concept of implied warranty include an employee's lawsuit for injury caused by a defective machine sold to the employer and to a tenant's lawsuit against a faucet manufacturer for burns to the tenant's child caused by excessively hot water from a bathroom faucet with no mixer valve.

In the U.S., the Uniform Commercial Code (UCC)[6] applies the implied warranty of merchantability to a merchant-seller's sales of goods. Generally, the merchant-seller warrants that the goods meet the standards of the trade, are fit for the ordinary purposes for which such goods are used, and conform to representations made on the container or label, if any. The seller concept now includes suppliers, or those who supply products for value (consideration).

Strict Liability and Negligence

Products liability cases can be based on negligence, on strict liability, or on both. Products liability lawsuits may involve both liability for harm caused by a product and liability for harm resulting from a service or process. Generally, if only a service or process is involved, the suit must be based on negligence. If the suit concerns a product, or a combination of product and service or process, then the suit can be based on either negligence or strict liability. Courts define products to include advertising materials, labels, computer software, instruction manuals, and aircraft instrument landing charts.

Express warranty

An explicit statement about a product by the seller that the buyer or other user may rely on and that provides a remedy in the event the product does not perform as claimed.

Implied warranty

An obligation that the courts impose on a seller to warrant certain facts about a product even though not expressly stated by the seller.

In a general negligence case involving products liability, the plaintiff must prove that the manufacturer failed to use reasonable care in designing or manufacturing the product that caused the injury. Negligence focuses on the reasonableness of the manufacturer's conduct.

In contrast, strict liability constitutes the breach of an absolute duty of safety, and it applies most often to products or ultrahazardous activities (such as transportation, storage and use of explosives or radioactive substances, and keeping wild animals or dangerous dogs). Proof of either negligence or an intent to harm is not required. The manufacturer's conduct is irrelevant, and the focus is on the product itself. In a products liability lawsuit based on strict liability, the plaintiff must prove five elements:

- The seller was in the business of selling products.
- The product had a defect that made it unreasonably dangerous, meaning dangerous to an extent beyond that which would be contemplated by the ordinary user who has common knowledge about the product. (Not all courts require this element.)
- The product was dangerously defective when it left the manufacturer's or seller's custody or control.
- The defect was the proximate cause of the plaintiff's injury.
- The product was expected to and did reach the consumer without substantial change in condition.

In such cases, a manufacturer may have used the utmost care in making the product. However, if, in fact, the product is unsafe, the manufacturer may nevertheless be liable under the doctrine of strict liability.

As in negligence cases, proximate cause is a necessary element of a products liability suit based on strict liability. A plaintiff must establish not only that the defective product caused the injury, but also that it was the specific defect that caused the injury. A manufacturer is not liable for injury caused by defect that occurred after the product has left the manufacturer's possession.

Types of Product Defects

Generally speaking, three major types of product defects can lead to liability suits:

- Defect in manufacture or assembly—The product does not correspond to the original design.
- Defect in design—The product corresponds to the design, and the manufacturer built the product exactly as intended, but the design itself is faulty, and the injury has resulted from the design defect. The defendant

is liable because of a design flaw that affects all products of the same kind and not because of a defect in the single item that injured the plaintiff.

- Failure to warn—The product is defective in neither design nor manufacture, but it poses some inherent danger about which the manufacturer has failed to provide adequate warning.

Defects in manufacture include the use of poor-quality materials or shoddy assembly work. Examples include the use of grades of steel that quickly corrode during assembly and failure to install key engine bolts.

Defect in manufacture is the simplest type of strict liability to prove because improper manufacture or assembly of the product, in itself, is a defect. Whether the product is unreasonably dangerous is not an issue because its having caused injury demonstrates that it was dangerous or defective.

Courts vary considerably in decisions about defective design cases. Generally, a seller is liable for injuries caused by a product if, at the time of sale, it is not fit and safe for its intended or reasonably foreseeable use and is unreasonably dangerous. If the defect is not open and obvious, some courts do not consider the product unreasonably dangerous, and strict liability does not apply.

Several jurisdictions have eliminated the unreasonably dangerous requirement and replaced it with one of these rules:

- A product is defective if it does not meet the consumer's reasonable expectations.
- A product is defective if it lacks any element that would make it safe.

A manufacturer must consider a product's safety within the constraints of cost, efficiency, weight, and style. For example, a lawnmower could incorporate so many safety features that it could not cut grass adequately, or a fully crash-resistant auto could end up being extremely heavy. Many courts now compare the practicality of selling a product with a certain level of safety features against the magnitude of the risk associated with that level of safety features.

Many design defect cases arise out of defective safety devices or failure to install safety devices. The manufacturer is strictly liable only if the defects or failure made the product unreasonably dangerous in normal use. Common defects include lack of guards or defective guards on machines such as punch presses, metal shears, or pizza dough rollers.

Even if a product has no assembly or design defects, it can still be the basis for liability if the manufacturer has failed to warn of the product's dangers. A manufacturer has a duty to warn when it would be unreasonably dangerous to market a product without a warning. A manufacturer should consider three factors in this regard:

- Degree of the danger
- Knowledge of the danger
- Foreseeability of dangerous use

The degree of danger varies with products. A gun, for example, has a higher degree of danger than an automobile.

In failure-to-warn cases, the standard for manufacturers' liability is the same under both negligence and strict liability. The manufacturer must provide warnings about all dangers associated with the product about which the manufacturer knows, or should know; that is, all foreseeable dangers.

Potentially Liable Parties

Strict liability generally applies to entities that engage in the business of selling products. In addition to manufacturers, most courts also include distributors, wholesalers, and retailers. Those who make an occasional sale of a product outside the regular course of business are not usually subject to strict liability. Many courts have expanded the application of strict liability in sales to include bailors and lessors.

One significant extension of strict liability in many jurisdictions has been to builders and contractors. For example, courts have held contractors strictly liable for installing a faulty hot water heater that caused a fire; for installing a defective heating system that required replacement; and even for failing to compact dirt in a filled lot on which a builder constructed a house, which later caused building damage.

Parties Protected

Strict liability for products protects certain classes of people. Protection can extend to the ultimate user or consumer, which can include the ultimate buyer; however, the ultimate buyer may be different from the ultimate user or consumer. For example, the ultimate user or consumer may have received the product as a gift or may be a buyer's family member, for example. Most courts also hold that any nonuser, such as a bystander, may assert a strict liability claim. For example, a person injured by the explosion of a companion's defective shotgun can assert strict liability.

In determining who has legal standing to sue, either in negligence or in strict liability, most courts use the traditional foreseeability test. Anyone who could foreseeably have been injured by the product has standing to sue. Because a plaintiff must allege specific injuries, courts generally do not permit class action suits in products liability cases.

The public policy supporting strict liability is to protect the individual consumer and to allocate the loss to the party best able to bear the loss.

Defenses

Several defenses are available in products liability lawsuits, for both negligence and strict liability for products. Some are complete defenses that, if successful, totally defeat plaintiffs' claims, while others merely reduce damages:

- State-of-the-art defense—The defendant claims that its product was safe according to the state of the art at the time the product was made. State of the art is the highest level of pertinent product scientific knowability, development, and technical knowledge existing at the time of a product's manufacture. This standard is more concise than the standard of a product's conformity with traditional industry customs and practices. Scientific knowability means the technological feasibility of producing a safer product based on existing scientific knowledge. If no indication of danger or no technique for obtaining knowledge of such danger exists, the manufacturer has no reason to prevent manufacture of the product. The state-of-the-art defense is not a complete defense. Additional evidence must be introduced to justify placing the product on the market.

- Compliance with statutes and regulations defense—The defendant's compliance with statutes and regulations (such as industrial safety codes) is not a conclusive defense against negligence or product defect. A plaintiff may introduce evidence to show that a reasonable manufacturer could have taken additional precautions.

- Compliance with product specifications defense—Manufacturers frequently make products to conform to specifications established by buyers or others. In negligence suits, a manufacturer is generally not liable for products built to someone else's specifications unless the defect is sufficiently obvious to alert the manufacturer to the potential for harm. Third parties in such cases should sue the one who prepared the specifications.

- Open and obvious danger defense—A manufacturer has no duty to warn or take other precautions regarding a common, open, and obvious propensity of the product. Hazards connected with knives, guns, and gasoline, for example, are well known, so warnings would be superfluous.

- Plaintiff's knowledge defense—If the person who uses the product has knowledge of the product that is equal to the manufacturer's knowledge, the manufacturer has no duty to warn.

- Comparative negligence versus the assumption-of-risk defense—Most states and provinces allow a comparative negligence defense in strict liability suits, and the assumption-of-risk defense no longer applies in those jurisdictions. However, for some other jurisdictions, **active negligence**, or **assumption of risk**, is a defense to a strict liability suit. The defendant asserts that the product's user took on the risk of loss, injury, or damage. In considering this defense, most courts distinguish between active negligence and **passive negligence** and hold that passive negligence does not bar recovery. Assumption of risk applies when a person knows of the potential danger resulting from a product defect but voluntarily and

---

Active negligence

A plaintiff's voluntary use of a defective product with knowledge of the potential danger resulting from the defect.

Assumption of risk

A defense to negligence that bars a plaintiff's recovery for harm caused by the defendant's negligence if the plaintiff voluntarily incurred the risk of harm.

Passive negligence

A plaintiff's failure to discover a product defect or to guard against a possible defect.

unreasonably proceeds to use the product. For example, a worker who knows that a substance can burn skin but does not use protective gloves may not prevail in a lawsuit because of the defense of assumption of risk. The defendant has the burden of proving that the plaintiff knew of the defect or danger.

- Misuse of product defense—Closely akin to active negligence is product misuse or abnormal use. For example, failing to follow directions on a container or attempting to open a glass container by tapping it against a sink may constitute sufficient misuse or abnormal use sufficient to bar recovery for any resulting injury. Because the defendant's liability in such cases is based on the assertion that the product is defective, the plaintiff must prove that the product was used in an appropriate and foreseeable manner in order to establish the defect.

- Alteration of product defense—The manufacturer is usually not liable for modifications made to a product after it is sold. Liability is based on conditions as of the time of sale. Any post-sale modifications can be considered independent, intervening acts that break the chain of causation. Therefore, most courts hold that third-party alterations, no matter how foreseeable, do not create liability.

Damages

A plaintiff can recover damages for bodily injury in lawsuits based on strict liability. Several jurisdictions apply strict liability in wrongful death suits. Plaintiffs may also recover punitive damages in strict liability suits.

Most jurisdictions also permit recovery for property damage in cases of strict liability for physical damage from such causes as fires or explosions arising out of product defects. An example is recovery for fire damage to a dwelling caused by a defective television set.

In some jurisdictions, plaintiffs may recover consequential damages for commercial loss in strict liability lawsuits; that is damages for loss of the product's use for business purposes or loss of profits. However, most jurisdictions deny recovery for pure consequential economic loss in strict liability suits. For example, if Martha buys a truck but cannot use it in her business because of a defect, she cannot sue for economic loss under strict liability.

DAMAGES IN TORT SUITS

One of the elements a plaintiff in a tort suit must prove is a resulting injury or loss sufficient for a court to impose damages. The purpose of awarding damages is to recompense the injured party and not to punish the tortfeasor, although a court may decide that punitive damages are appropriate.

When a plaintiff proves damages in a tort suit, a court can award various kinds of damages, which are usually monetary. Courts determine the amount of damages based on the facts of cases. A plaintiff is usually entitled to tort damages that the injury proximately caused, whether or not the defendant could reasonably have foreseen the damage, unlike contract damages, which are limited to damages the parties could reasonably foresee.

In tort suits, courts typically award two broad categories of damages:

- Compensatory damages
- Punitive damages (exemplary damages)

Courts also award damages for wrongful death.

Compensatory Damages

In the usual tort suit, the award is for compensatory damages. Compensatory damages include both special and general damages.

Special damages (also called particular damages, or out-of-pocket losses) can include the amount expended to restore lost property. For bodily injury, they include hospital and doctor bills and related expenses. **Loss of wages and earnings** is another form of special damages.

General damages (also called direct damages or necessary damages) are often presumed when special damages are proven and may include compensation for **pain and suffering**; disfigurement; and loss of a limb, sight, or hearing; as well as **emotional distress** or other noneconomic intangible loss. Many physical injuries leave some permanent effect such as scar tissue, torn muscles, and limited use of limbs. The injured person is entitled to have any future effect of permanent injuries considered in evaluating damages.

Jury awards for general damages have grown so large that legislatures have made a concentrated effort to limit them, usually by placing a dollar limit, or cap, on some types of general damages. Many state statutes limiting damages apply only to medical malpractice, but several now apply more broadly.

Courts originally awarded damages for bad faith in suits for other, underlying torts. Damages for bad faith can arise in connection with the independent tort of outrage, and bad faith can result in punitive damages.

Punitive Damages

In certain cases, courts may assess punitive, or exemplary damages. These damages punish and make an example of the defendant, thereby deterring the defendant and others from committing similar acts. Even though a court can award punitive damages to a plaintiff, the law does not intend or categorize these damages as compensation.

Special damages

A form of compensatory damages that awards a sum of money for specific, identifiable expenses associated with the injured person's loss, such as medical expenses or lost wages.

Loss of wages and earnings

The compensatory damages to compensate a plaintiff for any loss of income directly related to a tort.

General damages

A monetary award to compensate a victim for losses, such as pain and suffering, that does not involve specific, measurable expenses.

Pain and suffering

Compensable injuries that are difficult to measure, such as physical and mental distress and inconvenience associated with a physical injury.

Emotional distress

A highly unpleasant mental reaction resulting from another person's conduct, for which a court can award damages.

Ordinary negligence does not support a claim for punitive damages. A court can award punitive damages only in certain situations:

- The defendant actually intended to cause harm.
- The defendant acted oppressively, maliciously, or fraudulently.

These situations collectively fall under the term "outrageous conduct," which can consist of fraud, malice, gross negligence, or oppression. A court can find it when a defendant commits a wrongful act with a motive to harm or so recklessly as to imply a disregard for social obligations; or if the defendant shows such willful misconduct or lack of care as to raise a presumption of the defendant's conscious indifference to the consequences.

To assess punitive damages, courts usually consider three factors:

- Nature of the defendant's actions
- Size of the defendant's assets
- Purpose of punitive damages

Generally, the wealthier the defendant, the larger the punitive damage award. Also generally, employers, or principals, are liable for punitive damages if they directed or ratified acts of employees or agents with knowledge of malice, fraud or oppression.

Damages for Wrongful Death

A **wrongful death action** is in a different category from the ordinary claim for bodily injury. Damages can vary depending on the relationship of the deceased to the claimant. Damages can compensate for lost earnings or for mental anguish, or they can be punitive. Under common law, when an injured person died, any right to sue ended upon the person's death. For example, a person might live for several months after sustaining an injury, incurring large expenses and suffering much pain from the injury; but, upon death, the right to sue ends. Likewise, if the tortfeasor died, the right to sue also ended. This inequity led to the enactment of **survival statutes**, under which a cause of action for an injury can survive after an injured person's death.

A typical survival statute might read: "All causes of action or proceedings, real or personal, except suits for slander or libel, shall survive the death of one or more joint plaintiffs or defendants."

Survival statutes preserve the right of a person's estate to recover damages that person sustained between the time of injury and death. They permit recovery of compensatory damages, including general damages. They do not include any damages for shortening the person's life. If death is instantaneous, then a court will not award survival damages. However, if the person lives even a second or a minute after an injury, the estate can allege sufficient pain and suffering to support the suit. Any damages recovered pass onto the person's estate.

Wrongful death action

A legal cause of action that exists for the survivor of the deceased.

Survival statute

A statute that preserves the right of a person's estate to recover damages that person sustained between the time of injury and death.

LIABILITY CONCEPTS AFFECTING TORT CLAIMS

To obtain relief from a court, an injured person not only must be ready to prove damage suffered, but also must, among other tasks, choose whom to sue and develop a theory of liability to present to the court.

Liability concepts affecting tort claims focus primarily on the parties who can sue and those parties who are potentially liable in lawsuits:

- Joint tortfeasors
- Expanded liability concepts
- Vicarious liability
- Good Samaritan issues
- Class actions and mass tort litigation

Joint Tortfeasors

When an act of negligence involves more than one person, issues of joint liability arise. Generally, all people participating in the act of committing a tort are jointly (together) and severally (individually) liable. An individual participates by being an active contributor, either in person or through an agent or employee; by acting; by ratifying or permitting the act; or by advising about the act.

When two or more persons owe a common duty to a third party and, by a common act of neglect of this duty, cause injury to the third party, a joint tort has occurred. Additionally, when the separate negligent acts of two or more people come together to produce a single indivisible injury, a joint tort has occurred. For example, if the drivers of two cars racing on a highway collide and injure a third person, the result is a joint tort.

Tortious acts that are sequential or that involve some aspect of vicarious liability can complicate determination of liability. Also, certain relationships can create a joint tort. For example, employers are liable for the torts of their employees committed while in the scope of their employment; the employees are also liable. Similarly, each partner is jointly liable for the torts of all other partners.

Joint tortfeasors
Two or more parties who act together to commit a tort or who commit separate torts that combine to cause an injury or loss.

Under common law, **joint tortfeasors** were jointly and severally liable for the full amount of the damages. Therefore, the plaintiff could proceed against all tortfeasors jointly or against any number of them. If a plaintiff sued only one tortfeasor, that defendant could not use as a defense the fact that the plaintiff did not include the others in the suit. Each tortfeasor was responsible for the whole tort regardless of degree of participation in the tort. About half the jurisdictions have abolished this rule and today do not hold a joint tortfeasor automatically liable for all of a plaintiff's damages. This change came in response to increased litigation against "deep-pocket" defendants who often had little role in causing plaintiffs' injuries but had to pay entire damage awards.

Under common law, a release of one joint tortfeasor released all joint tortfeasors, even if the release specifically prohibited release of the other tortfeasors. Although this rule still applies in several jurisdictions, it has fallen into disfavor. Most jurisdictions, either by court decision or legislation, have provided that, when a plaintiff settles with one joint tortfeasor, a pro rata credit goes to the other joint tortfeasor if the intent of the agreement was to release only one tortfeasor and not to operate as a full release.

Many jurisdictions have adopted the Uniform Contribution Among Joint Tortfeasors Act (UCAJTFA). UCAJTFA provides that, when two or more persons become jointly or severally liable in tort for the same injury or damage, or for the same wrongful death, they have a right of **contribution** among them even though the plaintiff has not recovered judgment against all or any of them. The act creates rights in favor of tortfeasors who have paid more than their pro rata share of their joint liability for the amount of the excess. It provides that, in assessing pro rata liability, the relative degree of fault is not a consideration.

Contribution

The right of a tortfeasor who has paid more than his or her proportionate share of the damages to collect from other tortfeasors responsible for the same tort.

Under the UCAJTFA, the plaintiff can release one or more defendants without releasing the others if it is a good-faith release that indicates intent only to release part, not all, of the liability and if the payment is full compensation. What constitutes good faith, particularly if the released defendant's payment appears nominal, is a matter of frequent dispute in these cases. The harshness of the UCAJTFA has led to legal maneuvers to mitigate its effects.

Several jurisdictions have abolished the concept of joint liability entirely and have adopted several liability only. Other jurisdictions have adopted modifications, such as applying that joint liability only when the plaintiff's fault is less than the respective defendant's, or only when the defendant is at least a certain percent at fault, for example, 25 or 50 percent at fault. Several of these laws still retain the concept of joint liability for certain areas, such as product liability, toxic torts, or auto liability.

Expanded Liability Concepts

A basic tort law principle is that the plaintiff must prove not only injury but also that a specific defendant caused the injury. For example, a person hit by an unidentifiable object from the sky cannot sue all the airlines that have flown in the area because one of them probably caused the injury. The injured person must prove which airline dropped the object. Because of mass production, many goods are not traceable to specific producers, and the problem is even more acute because it is usually impossible to identify which manufacturer produced the product that harmed an individual. To help injured parties sue successfully, some courts have adopted expanded liability concepts. While these concepts have generally applied to products liability situations, they also

Enterprise liability (industry-wide liability)

An expanded liability concept requiring each member of an industry responsible for manufacturing a harmful or defective product to share liability, when a manufacturer at fault cannot be identified.

Alternative liability

An expanded liability concept that shifts the burden of proof to each of several defendants in a tort case when there is uncertainty regarding which defendant's action was the proximate cause of the harm.

Market share liability

An expanded liability concept that applies when a product that has harmed a consumer cannot be traced to a single manufacturer; all manufacturers responsible for a substantial share of the market are named in the lawsuit and are liable for their proportional share of the judgment.

Concert of action

An expanded liability concept that applies when all defendants acted together or cooperatively.

Conspiracy

An expanded liability concept that applies when two or more parties worked together to commit an unlawful act.

can apply to other situations. Types of expanded liability concepts include these:

- In **enterprise liability (industry-wide liability)**, probably the first expanded liability concept, a limited number of businesses engage in similar business, following industry-wide standards. If those standards result in a defective product causing harm, a court can treat these businesses as a single enterprise to prove causation, with an entire industry liable for harm to a plaintiff. For example, if several producers manufacture a defective product under industry standards, resulting in injuries, each producer can be held liable based on its market share.

- **Alternative liability** involves shifting the burden of proof to each of several defendants when it is uncertain which one caused the injury. Each defendant has the burden of proof of causation and must prove either that he or she did not cause the harm or that someone else did. Under this concept, a plaintiff can sue one or more defendants, but not necessarily all of them.

- **Market share liability** resembles the alternative liability concept in that it can create a situation in which one defendant is liable for the damages of an entire industry. The plaintiff must sue all manufacturers responsible for a substantial share of the market. Defendants are not liable individually for the entire amount, but only for their pro rata share of the judgment based on their respective shares of the market unless they can prove that they could not have made the product involved.

- Under **concert of action**, probably the most commonly recognized expanded liability concept, a plaintiff must prove either (1) that the defendants consciously parallel each other, as the result of an actual agreement or an implied understanding to do or not to do a given act, or that (2) even though the defendants acted independently, the effect of their acts was to encourage or assist others' wrongful conduct. A plaintiff need not sue all potential defendants. For example, tire manufacturers, following industry standards, might have manufactured defective tires independently; but their close connections in the automotive industry might have encouraged each to manufacture defective tires.

- **Conspiracy** requires a plaintiff to establish the responsibility of defendants involved by proving an agreement existed among all defendants either to commit a wrongful act or to carry out a legal act by illegal means, resulting in the plaintiff's harm.

- A **joint venture** is a group of people or entities working together toward a common goal. To establish a joint venture to prove causation, a plaintiff' must prove four facts: (1) an agreement by the parties to associate for a business activity, (2) profits and losses shared by each party, (3) joint control of the venture by the parties, and (4) contribution to the venture's assets by each party.

Vicarious Liability

A person can become liable for others' tortious acts under the concept of **vicarious liability**. This liability can result from contractual relationships and from partnerships. Vicarious liability also can arise out of three types of relationships:

- Principal and agent—The term "agency" describes the relationship in which the principal, authorizes another, the agent, to act on the principal's behalf. Principals are vicariously liable for the torts their agents commit in the course of the agents' employment and within the scope of their actual or apparent authority. This liability applies even though the act directly contravened the principal's orders. The agent is also individually liable for the same act.

- Employer and employee—Employers are vicariously liable for torts their employees commit while acting within the scope of their employment. Courts use several methods to determine the scope of employment, and determination of liability must meet certain criteria.

- Parent and child—Generally, a parent is not liable for a minor child's torts merely because of the family relationship. However, several well-established exceptions exist. For example, if the child is acting as the parent's agent or employee at the time the tort occurs, the parent is liable just as any other principal or employer would be liable. The parent is also liable for a child's torts when the tort involves a dangerous instrumentality, such as a gun or even a vehicle that the parent has given to the child under such circumstances that the parent should expect the child to cause harm. Parents may also be liable for a child's torts resulting from the parents' **negligent entrustment** or **negligent supervision**. Some jurisdictions have also adopted the **family purpose doctrine**, which applies only to torts caused by a family-owned automobile. Finally, several jurisdictions make parents liable for certain torts of their children under statutes, which apply to theft or vandalism. Jurisdictions adopted them to control and reduce acts children commit on certain properties such as schools. Under parental responsibility statutes, a parent can be liable without proof of negligence.

Good Samaritan Issues

Historically, helping a person one has no duty to help has been called a Good Samaritan situation. If a person owes no duty to another person, the refusal to act does not create grounds for a suit. For example, Luke becomes ill in Bob's presence. If Bob owes no duty to Luke, Bob can let Luke become worse, or even die, and incur no liability. However, if Bob voluntarily undertakes to save Luke by some act and performs the act negligently, Bob can incur liability.

Joint venture

A business association formed by an express or implied agreement of two or more persons (including corporations) to accomplish a particular project, such as the construction of a building.

Vicarious liability

A legal responsibility that occurs when one party is held liable for the actions of a subordinate or an associate because of the relationship between the two parties.

Negligent entrustment

The act of leaving a dangerous article with a person who the lender knows, or should know, is likely to use it in an unreasonably risky manner.

Negligent supervision

A parent's failure to exercise reasonable control and supervision over his or her child to prevent harm to others.

Family purpose doctrine

A liability concept that holds the owner of an automobile kept for the family's use vicariously liable for damages incurred by a family member while using the automobile.

A common example of a Good Samaritan is a physician who stops to give first aid to an accident victim. If the victim later claims the physician was negligent, the victim may be able to sue the physician successfully.

The result of the example demonstrates an inequity: A person who does not volunteer to help another has no liability, even if the other dies; but a person who does help can be liable for negligence. In response to this inequity, all jurisdictions have adopted some form of **Good Samaritan laws**, which protect any person who gives emergency assistance. However, some jurisdictions protect only medical personnel. Generally, Good Samaritan laws apply to gratuitous emergency services performed at the scene of an emergency and exempt one who provides such services from liability for ordinary negligence but not gross negligence.

Good Samaritan law

A statute providing that a person will not be liable for damages as a result of rendering aid to an injured person, without compensation, at the scene of an accident.

Class Actions and Mass Tort Litigation

When a single tort has many victims, a **class action (class action lawsuit)** permits one person, or a small group of people, to file suit on behalf of all of the harmed members of the group. Courts allow class actions when individual cases present common questions and the amount of damages in each claim is too small to warrant individual suits.

Class action (class action lawsuit)

A lawsuit in which one person or a small group of people represent the interests of an entire class of people in litigation.

Traditionally, class actions seldom involved torts because each person harmed had different liability issues. However, courts began accepting dissimilar tort victims in **mass tort litigation** for claims involving such products as tobacco, asbestos, birth control pills and devices, prescription drugs, and pollutants; in suits against insurers for their use of aftermarket auto parts in auto repairs; and the misuse of medical managed-care techniques.

Mass tort litigation

A class-action suit based on tort law rather than on contract law.

Class action suits provide access to the courts for a large group of people interested in a single issue, and one or more of them can sue or be sued as a representative of the class. To illustrate, fumes that escape a malfunctioning chemical plant cause lung injuries throughout the local community. A single member of the community who suffered an injury to her lungs can bring a class action suit.

A trial court must consider four features to certify a suit as a class action:

- Numerosity—The plaintiffs are so numerous that it would be impractical to bring all of them separately into court.
- Commonality—An ascertainable class with a well-defined common interest in the questions of law and fact affecting the parties is necessary for class-action certification.
- Typicality—The representative parties' claims or defenses must be typical of all the class members.
- Adequacy of representation—The named parties must fairly and adequately protect the interests of unnamed class members.

Courts also consider the extent to which individual class members would have interests in controlling the prosecution of their claims in a separate suit, the extent and nature of any litigation already started, the desirability of concentrating the litigation in one forum, and the difficulties of managing a class proceeding. See the exhibit "Practice Exercise: Liability Concepts Affecting Tort Claims."

Practice Exercise: Liability Concepts Affecting Tort Claims

Three drivers were all speeding during the evening rush hour, between fifty and sixty miles per hour. They were on a two-lane road with a thirty-five-mile per hour speed limit, in sleet that was causing icing on the road. The first driver in front of the line of drivers, Annie, slammed on her brakes when she saw a runner in front of her on the edge of the road. She could have missed hitting the runner, but the second driver in line, Burt, slid into Annie's car; and the third car, driven by Charlie, slid into Burt's car, so that Annie hit the runner, pushed by the impact of the other cars behind her. The runner suffered serious injuries, totaling $100,000 in damages, and sued all three drivers. The court determined that each driver was one-third at fault (for $33,333) for this accident and further determined that, had the three drivers not been speeding, they could have avoided this accident because the runner was not at fault. How might the concept of joint and several liability affect the outcome of the runner's lawsuit?

Answer

First, the court has determined that all three drivers were equally at fault and apparently found no fault on the runner's part. Additionally, the runner sued all three drivers and has not excused any one of them from fault. If joint and several liability exists in the state where the accident happened, then one driver could theoretically be liable for the full amount of damages, or $100,000, and not just for a proportionate share of $33,333. This possible outcome would be the same for all three drivers, each of whom would be responsible for the full award of $100,000. However, the runner has sued all three drivers, the court has determined equal fault on the part of each driver, and the runner would collect one-third of the $100,000 from each driver. If Annie proves to be insolvent and uninsured, and Charlie and Burt have sufficient assets or insurance, the runner could collect $50,000 each from Charlie and Burt.

[DA05996]

SUMMARY

Negligence is a broad term used for unintentional torts. Describing negligence involves an understanding of two of its aspects: the elements of negligence (including duty, breach of duty, proximate cause, and actual injury or damage) and the required proof of negligence.

A defendant in a negligence lawsuit has the burden to prove any defenses, including comparative negligence, releases and exculpatory clauses, immunity, statutes of limitations and repose, and tortfeasor's capacity.

A plaintiff can sue for harm caused by either natural or artificial conditions on land and can have had an express or implied license to be on the land as either a public or business invitee. Landlords occupying land have legally determined responsibilities with regard to others on the premises.

These torts are among the most common forms of intentional torts: battery, assault, false imprisonment and false arrest, intentional infliction of emotional distress, defamation (libel and slander), and invasion of the right of privacy.

These torts are among the most common forms of intentional torts: fraud, bad faith or outrage, interference with relationships between others, misuse of legal process, trespass, nuisance, and conversion.

Strict liability or liability imposed by a statute can attach, regardless of intent or negligence, if the liable party is engaged in an ultrahazardous activity, owns or possesses animals, or allows escape of a toxic substance.

Most products liability suits are based on one or more of these principles of law: misrepresentation, breach of warranty, and strict liability and negligence.

Courts award nominal damages only to establish a right. However, when a plaintiff proves tort damages, courts award two broad categories of monetary damages: compensatory and punitive damages. Courts also award damages for wrongful death.

These liability concepts affecting tort claims focus on the parties who can sue and those parties who are potentially liable in lawsuits: joint tortfeasors, expanded liability concepts, vicarious liability, Good Samaritan issues, and class actions and mass tort litigation.

ASSIGNMENT NOTES

1. *Scott v. Shepherd*, 96 Eng. Rep. 525 (1773).
2. 28 U.S.C., §§ 2671–2680.
3. Sullivan v. New York Times, 376 U.S. 254 (1964).
4. *Rylands v. Fletcher*, 1 Eng. Rul. Case 235 (1868).
5. *Henningsen v. Bloomfield Motors Inc.*, 32 N.J. 358 (1960).
6. UCC, § 2-314.

Direct Your Learning ▶▶

Agency Law

Educational Objectives

After learning the content of this assignment, you should be able to:

▸ Explain how an agency relationship can be created by each of the following:

- Appointment
- Estoppel
- Ratification

▸ Describe an agent's authority in terms of the following:

- The scope of authority granted (actual or apparent)
- The third party's duty to ascertain scope of authority

▸ Describe the principal-agent relationship in terms of the following:

- Duties an agent owes to the principal
- Remedies a principal has for an agent's breach of duties
- Duties a principal owes to an agent
- Remedies an agent has for a principal's breach of duties

▸ Describe the various means by which parties can terminate agency relationships.

▸ Describe the potential contractual rights and liabilities of a principal and its agent in terms of the following:

- A third party's rights against a principal
- A principal's rights against a third party
- An agent's liability to a third party
- An agent's rights against a third party

Outline

Agency Creation

Agent's Authority

Agent's Duties and Remedies

Agency Termination

Contractual Rights and Liabilities

Tort Liability of Principal and Agent

Summary

▶▶

7

▶ Describe the potential tort liability of a principal and its agent in terms of the following:

- Respondeat superior liability of the principal for the agent's torts
- Direct liability of the principal for the agent's torts
- Principal's liability for torts of independent contractors
- Principal's liability for agent's misrepresentations
- Agent's liability for agent's own torts

Agency Law

AGENCY CREATION

An agency is a fiduciary relationship—that is, the agent holds a position of trust, manages the principal's affairs or funds, and has a duty to the principal to act in a trustworthy manner. In insurance, producers may act as the agents of either insurers or insureds. Understanding how the agency relationship is created is essential to knowing whether a purported agent actually has the authority to make legally binding agreements on behalf of the principal.

The parties to an **agency** are the **agent** and the **principal**. Although many agency relationships involve contracts, a contract is not essential to form an agency. The agency relationship is consensual rather than contractual, and that consent can be written or oral, express or implied.

An agency relationship can be established in three ways:

- By appointment
- By estoppel
- By ratification

Principal

The party in an agency relationship that authorizes the agent to act on that party's behalf.

Agent

In the agency relationship, the party that is authorized by the principal to act on the principal's behalf.

Agency

A legal, consensual relationship that exists when one party, the agent, acts on behalf of another party, the principal.

Appointment

The usual method of creating an agency is by express appointment. That is, Anita authorizes Brian to act in her behalf, and Brian assents to the appointment. The agent must consent to the relationship because agency law requires the agent to assume fiduciary duties (those involving trust).

As in contract formation, the principal's proposal can make a communicated acceptance unnecessary. If the principal asks another to act and indicates that no further communication is necessary, and the other person acts, the agency relationship arises. For example, Margaret writes to Joe, a real estate broker, and asks him to purchase a particular piece of real property for her in his name. Joe purchases the property in his own name and then refuses to convey it to Margaret. The circumstances indicate an implied agreement to form an agency relationship. Joe purchased the property on Margaret's behalf and must transfer it to her.

A principal can extend additional power to an agent through **power of attorney**. If an agent contracts to sell a principal's real estate, the principal must sign the deed. Otherwise, unless the agent has a power of attorney, the agent's signature on a deed has no effect. A power of attorney can be specific, such as

Power of attorney

A written document that authorizes one person to act as another person's agent or attorney-in-fact.

a power to sell real estate, or it can be general, giving the agent power over all of the principal's property.

Estoppel

Agency by estoppel

An agency relationship created by a principal's words or conduct that cause a third party to reasonably believe that an agency exists.

If a principal's words or conduct cause a third person to reasonably believe that an agency exists and to rely on that representation in dealing with the supposed agent, the principal is estopped (prevented) from denying the agency, resulting in **agency by estoppel**. For example, if an insurer's owner allows a customer service representative to find insurance coverage for applicants, the owner has created an agency by estoppel and cannot deny coverage placed by the employee. The reason for agency by estoppel is that one should be bound by one's words and conduct if another person materially relies on them.

Because the principal has given the agent no actual authorization, an agency by estoppel is not a genuine agency in the sense that agency by appointment is. The practical legal effects, however, are the same to the third party as if the principal had appointed the agent. The acts of the apparent agent bind the principal.

No agency by estoppel is formed if the person for whom the act is performed (who would be the principal if an agency relationship existed) is unaware of the supposed agent's action. For example, Bob has created the appearance that he is Paul's agent by printing stationery that falsely implies an agency relationship. As long as Paul neither knows nor should know of Bob's deception, Paul can deny the agency. Anyone relying on the deceptive stationery relies on appearances that Bob, not Paul, created. Therefore, Paul would not be liable for Bob's actions as an alleged agent.

However, a person who knowingly permits another person to represent that an agency exists can be estopped from denying the agency. For instance, Paul owns a jewelry store and permits his friend, Anne, to display and sell her handcrafted jewelry in his store. Their businesses are separate, but customers could reasonably believe that Anne works for Paul. Although Paul and Anne are not principal and agent, any customer who deals with Anne and believes her to be Paul's agent can hold Paul liable as principal if the customer has suffered loss in reasonable reliance on that belief.

What if Anne has falsely represented that Paul is her principal? Must Paul disavow the relationship? Can his silence create agency by estoppel? The answer is not certain. A court would consider Paul's silence in relation to what a reasonable person would do to disavow the relationship. Clearly, if Paul were to come face-to-face with a person who believes that Ann is Paul's agent, he must disavow the agency relationship. Suppose, however, that Anne advertises the purported agency in newspapers in a distant city where Paul does no business? Although the legal question concerns what a reasonable person would do, it is doubtful that a court would submit this question to a jury in the absence of unusual circumstances.

Ratification

If a person acts as agent for one who has given no actual consent or authority, the purported principal has two options:

- Ratify or confirm the transaction
- Refuse to approve the purported agent's unauthorized acts

When an agency relationship is created by **ratification**, the agent's authority comes into existence, and a contract arises between the principal and the third party.

A ratification must meet four conditions to be effective:

- The agent must have purported to act for the principal. If the agent failed to disclose a principal's existence, then ratification by the undisclosed person will not create an agency relationship. The purported agent need not identify the principal but must purport to act for someone.
- The principal must ratify the entire transaction, not just the favorable parts.
- The principal must ratify the agreement before the third party elects to withdraw from the agreement. If the third party has withdrawn, died, or become incompetent to contract before the principal ratifies the agreement, the ratification is ineffective.
- The principal must have all material facts available before the ratification is binding.

Ratification establishes the agency relationship. In contrast, an estoppel does not create an agency relationship but only protects the third person from a loss that would result if the agency were denied. In both agency by estoppel and agency by ratification, the legal effect to the third party is the same. The third party has an enforceable contract with the principal.

Rather than ratification, a purported principal may refuse to approve the acts of a person who has claimed to be an agent. See the exhibit "Ratification or Refusal."

Ratification

Creation of an agency relationship resulting when a principal adopts the act of another who has purported to act for the principal and has neither power nor authority to perform the act for the principal.

Ratification or Refusal

Steve is an agent for Movers Insurance Company, which has given him authority to bind coverage for up to $200,000 for cargo policies. Steve issues a transit certificate to Planes Inc. for $500,000 for the transportation of a shipment from Florida to California. The tractor-trailer hauling the cargo overturns, destroying the cargo.

Planes Inc. files a claim for the $500,000. Movers Insurance has a problem: Steve had authority to write a policy up to only $200,000, and he violated his agency authority in writing the $500,000 transit certificate. Movers can ratify Steve's actions by accepting the loss and paying the $500,000, or it can refuse to approve Steve's actions and deny the claim.

AGENT'S AUTHORITY

Agents must generally act within the scope and limitations of the authority specifically granted them by the principal. However, in some situations, even if the agent acts outside of that authority, the principal may still be bound to a third party by the agent's actions.

From the perspective of a third party, an agent's authority can be either actual authority or apparent authority. Actual authority can be either express or implied. The scope of an agent's authority depends on which type of authority the agent has.

Scope of Authority

A court analyzing a question about an agent's authority first determines whether the agent was acting under actual authority. If no actual authority exists, the court should determine whether the agent had apparent authority.

Actual Authority

Actual authority

Authority (express or implied) conferred by the principal on an agent under an agency contract.

Express authority

The authority that the principal specifically grants to the agent.

Implied authority

The authority implicitly conferred on an agent by custom, usage, or a principal's conduct indicating intention to confer such authority.

Actual authority can be express or implied.

Express authority applies not just to carrying out the principal's specific instructions, but also to performing acts incidental to carrying out those instructions. To determine the scope of express authority, courts examine the goals of the agency in light of all surrounding circumstances. For example, the power to sell generally includes authority to collect payment and to make customary warranties. However, a sales agent who has no possession or indication of ownership has no authority to collect the purchase price. In most commercial situations, the agent has authority only to solicit orders or to produce a buyer with whom the principal can deal.

Custom is the most common source of **implied authority**. Agents can reasonably infer that they have authority to act according to prevailing custom unless the principal gives different instructions. Without different instructions, an agent's authority extends to, and is limited to, what a person in this agent's position usually does.

Implied authority can also apply when an agent acts beyond the usual scope of authority in an emergency. If the agent needs to act to protect or preserve the principal's property or rights but is unable to contact the principal, and if the agent reasonably believes that an emergency exists, he or she has authority to act beyond, or even contrary to, the principal's instructions.

An agent who acts reasonably in an emergency has authority to act even if the agent is mistaken about the necessity for the actions or is at fault in creating the emergency. The agent, however, can be liable to the principal for any expenses resulting from the agent's wrongful conduct.

Apparent Authority

Unlike actual authority, a principal neither confers **apparent authority** on an agent nor creates it. Apparent authority is based on appearances and includes all the authority that a reasonable person, acquainted with the customs and nature of the business, could reasonably assume the agent has. It generally arises in one of two overlapping circumstances:

Apparent authority
A third party's reasonable belief that an agent has authority to act on the principal's behalf.

- A principal grants less authority than agents in the same position in that business usually have.
- The method of operation of the principal's business differs from that of other businesses of the same kind in the principal's area.

For example, principal Paul instructed agent Ann not to sell goods on credit if the total credit to a customer exceeds $200, an unusual restriction in Paul's business. Ann sold goods on credit to Lee for $250 with no actual authority to do so. Lee, however, neither knew nor had reason to know of the restriction. A third party could have reasonably believed that Ann had the usual authority in that situation. The authority was apparent, and Paul cannot deny it.

As a second example, Paul puts Ann in charge of a jewelry store and instructs her not to stock or sell watch batteries. All other jewelry stores in that area do stock and sell watch batteries. Ann contracts with Larry to purchase a supply of watch batteries. Ann has apparent authority to do this as long as Larry is unaware of the restriction on Ann's authority.

Duty to Ascertain Scope of Authority

A principal's representation to a third party—that is, the appearance the principal has created—determines the existence and the scope of an agent's apparent authority. A third person is not entitled to rely on an agent's statements about the scope of the agent's authority. Only the actual authority the principal has given, or the apparent authority the principal has manifested to the third party, controls the extent of the agent's authority. If an agent acts in a way adverse to the principal's best interests, the third party has notice that the agent might be exceeding his or her authority. The third party must ascertain the scope of the agent's authority by a direct inquiry to the principal. If the third party fails to inquire, and the agent does not have authority, the transaction in question does not bind the principal.

AGENT'S DUTIES AND REMEDIES

In an agency relationship, the principal and agent have specific obligations to each other. If either party fails to fulfill these obligations and thereby harms the other party, legal remedies are available to allow the injured party to recover.

An agent's duties to a principal include loyalty, obedience, reasonable care, accounting, and information. If the agent fails to fulfill these duties, the principal can sue the agent to recover any resulting loss or damage.

The principal's duties to the agent include an agreed-on period of employment, compensation, reimbursement for expenses, and indemnity for losses. If the principal breaches these duties, the agent can sue or can retain the principal's property until the principal has paid the amounts due.

Agent's Duties to Principal

An agent's implied fiduciary duties to a principal include these:

* Loyalty
* Obedience
* Reasonable care
* Accounting
* Information

Violation of any of these duties subjects the agent to discharge and to liability for any damages to the principal even if the agency contract does not expressly state these duties.

A subagent, who is the agent of an agent, owes the same duties to the principal that the original agent owes. An original agent is responsible to the principal for any subagent's violation of duty, even if the agent has exercised good faith in selecting the subagent. Further, a subagent owes the agent who did the hiring substantially the same duties.

If a subagent is employed without a principal's authority, no agency relationship arises between the principal and the subagent. The principal is not liable to third parties for an unauthorized subagent's acts. At the same time, the unauthorized subagent owes no duties to the principal.

Loyalty

One of the agent's most important duties is loyalty to the principal's interests. The agent must not undertake any business venture that competes with or interferes with the principal's business.

The principal can claim any profits the agent realizes in dealing with the principal's property. For example, any gift the agent receives from a third party while transacting the principal's business belongs to the principal. The duty of loyalty, however, does not obligate the agent to shield a principal who is acting illegally or dishonestly. To illustrate, Jo learns that her principal, Pete, cheated Tom on various contracts that Jo had arranged between Pete and Tom. Jo can disclose Pete's actions to Tom. If Tom obtains a judgment against Pete for his improper dealings, Pete cannot recover from Jo for breach of the duty of loyalty. Jo's duty does not extend to concealing Pete's dishonest acts from persons those actions affect.

Obedience

An agent owes a duty to obey a principal's lawful instructions. If the agent disobeys a reasonable instruction, the principal can sue for any resulting damages and can also terminate the relationship. Generally, the agent cannot challenge the instruction, unless it calls for illegal or immoral acts.

The agent owes a duty to perform according to the principal's instructions. If the principal has given ambiguous instructions, the agent owes the duty to exercise his or her best judgment in carrying them out. However, if harm to the agent is possible, or if an emergency arises, the agent might be justified in disobeying the principal's instructions.

An agent cannot delegate the authority granted by a principal to another person. The principal selects the agent because of personal qualifications. However, three exceptions apply to the nondelegation rule:

- **Ministerial duties**—If certain tasks do not require judgment or discretion, an agent can delegate their performance.

- Customary appointments—If custom and usage of a particular business involve the delegation of authority, the agent can delegate.

- Emergency appointments—In an emergency that requires the appointment of another to protect the principal's interests, the agent can make an emergency appointment.

Ministerial duties
The routine or mechanical tasks performed by agents.

Reasonable Care

An agent must exercise the degree of care and skill that a reasonable person would exercise under the same or similar circumstances. An agent with special skills or training is held to the standard of care of a reasonable person possessing those skills. Thus, a real estate broker employed to sell property must exercise the reasonable care of any real estate broker dealing with similar property.

An agent's failure to act when action is reasonably required also constitutes a breach of this duty. An agency contract carries an implied promise that the agent will carry out the duties of the agency with reasonable care to avoid injury to the principal. To illustrate, Charles asks Marcie, an insurance broker, to obtain an automobile insurance policy with collision coverage for his car. Marcy obtains a policy and delivers it to Charles, but the policy does not include collision coverage. After Charles has an accident, he learns that no collision coverage is in force. Charles may have a cause of action against Marcie for breach of the duty of reasonable care.

Reasonable care is required whether or not the agent is paid for the services. Unpaid agents cannot be compelled to perform duties, but once they begin performance, they are held to the standard of reasonable care. For example, real estate broker Betty gratuitously promises to act as Clark's agent in the sale of his real estate. Clark cannot sue Betty for her failure to try to sell the property. However, suppose Betty convinced Tony to purchase Clark's property and failed to have Tony sign a binding sales agreement. If Tony later declined to proceed with the purchase, Clark could sue Betty for negligence for her failure to exercise the degree of reasonable care.

An agent and a principal can agree that the agent is not to be liable to the principal for ordinary negligence. An agent, however, cannot evade liability for gross negligence. To limit the agent's liability for gross negligence would be against public policy.

Accounting

An agent must account to the principal for all the principal's property and money that come into the agent's possession. As part of this duty, the agent must keep the principal's property, including money, separate from the agent's. If the agent commingles the property or money, then the law assumes that it all belongs to the principal unless the agent clearly proves otherwise.

Money held by the agent should be deposited in a separate bank account in the principal's name. If the agent deposits it in his or her own name and the bank then fails, the agent is liable for any loss the principal sustains. The agent should account promptly for any of the principal's money held. Failure to do so makes the agent liable for interest payments to the principal.

Information

An agent owes a duty to keep the principal informed of all facts relating to the agency. Therefore, if a principal authorizes an agent to sell property for a specified amount and the agent later learns that the property's value has materially changed, then the agent must give the principal that information. Generally, the agent owes a duty to make reasonable efforts to provide the principal with information relevant to the affairs entrusted to the agent. Failure to perform this duty makes the agent liable to the principal for any resulting loss.

The law imputes the knowledge an agent obtains during the course of performing a principal's business to the principal and therefore imposes on the agent the duty to give the information to the principal. Most courts do not impose a duty to communicate information that the agent obtains outside the scope of the agent's employment. Additionally, if an agent acts adversely to the principal's interest, by colluding with a third party to defraud the principal, for example, that knowledge will not be imputed to the principal.

Principal's Remedies

Depending on the offense, a principal can sue an agent for breach of the agency contract or in tort for harm done. Remedies include requiring the agent to transfer improperly held property, pay the value of the benefit the agent received, or pay damages for negligence or tort.

If the agent is insolvent, the principal's best remedy is a suit to transfer the property. If the agent has personally profited from the transaction, then a suit for the value of the benefit the agent received represents the principal's best alternative. In other cases, a suit for breach of agency contract may be preferable to a suit in tort because the statute of limitations is generally longer for contract suits than for tort suits.

In still other cases, the principal can sue for an injunction prohibiting the agent from revealing trade secrets obtained during the course of employment or from competing with the principal in violation of a noncompetition agreement after termination of employment.

Principal's Duties to Agent

The principal owes these duties to the agent:

- Agreed-on period of employment
- Compensation
- Reimbursement for expenses
- Indemnity for losses

Agreed-On Period of Employment

Either party can terminate an employment contract at will unless the contract specifies a fixed period of employment. A contract to pay a salary by the month or year does not necessarily indicate that employment is guaranteed for the stated period.

A contract with a fixed period of employment makes the parties liable for any breach of their contract within that period. Because the agency relationship is consensual, the parties can refuse to continue the relationship during the contractual period, but they are subject to damages for breach of the contract.

When an employment contract provides for a specified period of employment and the principal's business terminates during the period, the agency also terminates because of changed conditions.

Compensation

The principal must pay the agent the agreed-on compensation for the services performed. If no compensation agreement exists, the agent is entitled to the reasonable value of the services rendered. If the contract does not mention compensation but an agent under similar circumstances would receive compensation for services, compensation is required for the reasonable value of the services. However, an agent who breaches agency duties is not entitled to compensation.

A principal is not responsible for a subagent's compensation if the agent was given no authority to hire subagents. Likewise, if the agent has the authority merely to delegate duties to a subagent, the agent, not the principal, is responsible for compensation.

Reimbursement for Expenses

A principal must reimburse an agent for any expenses necessarily incurred for the discharge of agency duties. For example, if the agent must incur travel and advertising expenses to accomplish agency purposes, the principal must reimburse these expenses. The agent must spend the money reasonably. If the agent's negligent conduct results in unnecessary expense, the agent bears the expense rather than the principal.

Indemnity for Losses

The principal owes a duty of indemnity, or reimbursement, for any losses or damages the agent has suffered because of the agency and incurred through no fault of the agent. If a principal directs an agent to commit a wrong against a third party, and the agent does not know that the act is wrongful, the agent is entitled to indemnity for the amount paid as a result of a lawsuit arising from the act. To illustrate, a principal directs an agent to cut down and sell trees on land that the principal incorrectly believes he owns. The landowner sues the agent to recover damages for loss of the trees. The agent is entitled to indemnity by the principal.

A principal must indemnify an agent for the expenses incurred in defending any lawsuits resulting from the agent's authorized acts. If the expense resulted from the agent's own intentional or negligent conduct, even though the principal directed the act, the agent is usually not entitled to indemnification. To illustrate, Paul promises to reimburse his sales representative, Anne, for money she pays out in illegal gratuities to purchasing agents to whom she sells goods. Anne is not entitled to indemnification from Paul for money she pays illegally.

An agent who makes payments or becomes subject to liability to third persons because of a subagent's authorized conduct has the same right to indemnity from the principal as if the conduct were the agent's. Because a subagent is both the agent's and the principal's agent, the subagent is entitled to indemnity from either of them.

Agent's Remedies

An agent can sue for compensation, indemnity, or reimbursement and can also obtain a court order requiring an accounting from the principal. An agent discharged by a principal during a specified employment period can sue for compensation for the remainder of the period.

An agent can also exercise a lien, or right to retain possession of the principal's goods, until the principal has paid the amounts due. Some agents, such as attorneys, bankers, and stockbrokers, can enforce a general lien against the principal; that is, they can hold the principal's goods and papers until all accounts are settled. The general lien is not limited to the immediate transaction between the parties but to all transactions between the agent and principal. Many other kinds of agents can assert only a special lien, which allows retention of the principal's property until the account for the immediate transaction between the principal and agent is settled.

AGENCY TERMINATION

Parties often find it more difficult to terminate an agency relationship than to enter into one. Wrongful termination is a breach of contract, and the terminating party can be liable. Understanding the ways an agency can legally be terminated protects both parties from liability.

If an agency is "at will," either the principal or the agent can terminate the agency at any time without legal liability. If, however, the agency is to continue for a certain period or until accomplishment of a specific purpose, then both the principal and the agent have the power, but not the right, to terminate the agency. Termination can be accomplished in one of several ways:

- Just cause
- Lapse of time
- Accomplishment of purpose
- Revocation
- Renunciation
- Death or incapacity
- Changed circumstances

Just Cause

An agency can be terminated for just cause. Examples of just cause include fraud, criminal activity, and flagrant violations of agency contracts. If an agency is at will, it can be terminated without cause.

Lapse of Time

Lapse of time can also terminate an agency. Authority granted to an agent for a specified period terminates at the expiration of that period. If the parties forming the agency specify no time, lapse occurs after a reasonable period, depending on the circumstances. For example, if Margaret authorized Joe to sell her property five years ago and they have not communicated since, the agency has probably terminated through lapse of time. If, however, Joe made occasional reports to Margaret about prospective buyers and Margaret gave no indication that the agency was terminated, Joe would continue to have authority to sell.

Accomplishment of Purpose

Many agencies are terminated when their purpose has been accomplished. If the agent has the authority to accomplish a particular purpose, that authority terminates upon its accomplishment. This is the case even if the purpose is accomplished by another agent or by the principal. The agency usually continues until the agent has received notice that the agency's purpose has been accomplished. To illustrate, Paul has given authority to two separate agents, Anne and Betty, to lease or sell Paul's house. With Anne's knowledge, Betty leases the house to Terry. Anne's authority to lease or sell the house ends, as does Betty's.

Revocation

A principal may terminate an agency through revocation. To revoke an agency, the principal notifies the agent, by word or act, that the agent no longer has authority. A contract provision requiring revocation in a specific manner does not always prevent agency termination in another manner. The principal always has the power to terminate the agency, although the agent can sue for damages if the termination violates the agency contract.

If the principal appoints another agent to accomplish the authorized purpose, and if the new appointment conflicts with the first, the original agent's authority is terminated. For example, if a client engages a new attorney to try a case with the knowledge of the original attorney, the original attorney's agency ends because the two agency relationships conflict.

However, appointment of a second agent does not always terminate the first agency. For example, the mere fact that a second agent is given authority to sell the same property as a first agent is not sufficient to terminate the original agency. Unless the first agent has an exclusive right to sell property, the principal reserves the right to sell or to authorize another agent to sell. The appointments are consistent and the first agent who sells gets the benefit.

Renunciation

An agent's termination of the agency relationship is a "renunciation of authority." The renunciation is effective even if it breaches the contract that binds the agent to perform. For example, Lyle, an actor, hired Rachel to represent him as his agent for two years. After one year, Rachel resigned. Although Rachel may be liable under contract to Lyle for the cost of finding a replacement, Rachel's renunciation has terminated her authority as his agent and ended the agency relationship.

Death or Incapacity

Death or incapacity can terminate an agency in three ways:

- The death of either principal or agent terminates the agency.
- The incapacity of the principal terminates the agency.
- The principal has the right to terminate the agency upon learning of the agent's incapacity.

Agency termination occurs upon a principal's death even though the agent or third party has no actual notice of death. Death is a matter of public record, so the law assumes that the public has notice of death. However, courts have found that the necessities of modern banking and commerce require relaxation of this rule. For example, until a bank receives actual notice of a depositor's death, the bank has authority to pay checks drawn on the depositor's account.

A principal can also become incapacitated. Courts generally treat a principal's incapacity in the same manner as they treat a principal's death. Because the agent acts in the principal's place and the principal cannot act, agency authority ends during incapacity. Incapacity that terminates agents' authority can occur when principals are declared legally incompetent. This can occur, for example, when a principal is declared mentally incompetent because of the inability to understand the consequences of his or her actions.

An agent does not need capacity to contract to be an agent. The principal's capacity is the determining factor, not the agent's. A mentally incompetent agent may represent a principal, and the agent's contract binds the principal unless a party involved in the contract knows of the incompetency.

To illustrate, Paul authorizes Anne to sell his property. Anne contracts to sell the property to a buyer, who does not know that Anne is under the influence of drugs. Anne's contract binds Paul to sell the property to the buyer. Paul can terminate the agency upon learning of Anne's incompetency.

Changed Circumstances

Changed circumstances can terminate an agency. If, because of a substantial change in circumstances, the agent should reasonably infer that the principal would not want the agency to continue, authority to act terminates.

For example, if Paul has authorized Anne to sell his land for $100,000 and Anne learns that the discovery of oil on the land has increased its value to $5 million, Anne's authority to sell the land for $100,000 terminates. An agent can exercise authority only with a reasonable belief that the principal still wants that authority exercised.

The principal's bankruptcy is a changed circumstance that usually terminates the agent's authority with respect to all assets under a bankruptcy court's control. In bankruptcy, the principal's assets and the power to deal with those assets pass to a trustee in bankruptcy, even without notice to the agent. Ordinarily, the principal's mere inability to pay bills is not sufficient to terminate the agent's authority.

If an agent's bankruptcy affects the agent's ability to perform the agency's purpose, or the principal's business standing, the agency terminates.

CONTRACTUAL RIGHTS AND LIABILITIES

Agency contract liability deals with situations in which parties to a contract fail to fulfill their obligations. When this occurs, the party that suffers a resulting loss has a right of recovery against the party in breach. Agency contract liability focuses on these respective rights:

- A third party's rights against a principal
- A principal's rights against a third party
- An agent's liability to a third party
- An agent's rights against a third party

A contract establishes rights and duties of the various parties to it. For example, in a sales contract, the seller agrees to supply goods and the purchaser agrees to pay a specified amount for those goods. If either party breaches the contract, the other party has the right to seek damages or to seek to have the contract enforced. In addition, some transactions can create implied warranties, breach of which can also create a right of recovery. In contracts arranged by agents, third parties may have rights of recovery against both the principal and the agent, and both the principal and the agent may have rights of recovery against third parties. In determining these rights, courts examine both the agent's authority to act and the status of the principal.

Third Party's Rights Against a Principal

The rights a third party has against a principal for an agent's properly authorized and executed contracts depend on the principal's status. There are three types of principals: **disclosed principals**, **partially disclosed principals**, and undisclosed principals.

In contracts involving partially disclosed principals and undisclosed principals, third parties enter into the agreements largely on the strength of the agent's credibility. The agent is liable for agreements made until the third party elects to hold the principal liable. The third party, on learning of the principal's existence or identity, can elect to enforce the contract against the principal rather than against the agent.

An undisclosed principal is responsible for all contracts the agent enters into within the scope of the agent's actual authority, and the third party can sue the principal when the principal's existence becomes apparent. Being unknown to the third party, the principal could not have created any apparent authority. Therefore, liability is limited to the agent's actual authority.

The right to sue an undisclosed principal on a contract is subject to these exceptions:

- A third party cannot sue the principal for nonpayment under a contract if the principal has made a good-faith settlement of the account with the agent. For example, when an undisclosed principal has supplied an agent with money to purchase goods, but the agent purchases the goods on credit and keeps the money, a settlement has occurred. The principal is not liable to the creditor for a second payment. The settlement can occur before or after the formation of the contract with the third party, but it must occur before disclosure of the principal to the third party.

- A third party cannot sue the principal if, having learned of both the principal's existence and the principal's identity, the third party expresses the intention to hold the agent liable for the contract. Election of the agent discharges the principal. However, this does not apply if the principal is only partially disclosed. The third party can obtain a judgment against either the agent or the partially disclosed principal without discharging the right against the other.

Principal's Rights Against a Third Party

If a contract binds a principal to a third party, it also binds the third party to the principal. It is immaterial whether the third party knew nothing of the principal's existence and thought the contract was formed with the agent alone. In transactions between a third party and an agent of a disclosed principal or a partially disclosed principal, the principal has rights against the third party to the same extent as if the principal had conducted the transaction.

Disclosed principal

A principal whose existence and identity are known to the third party dealing with the agent.

Partially disclosed principal

A principal whose existence is known, but whose identity is not known, to the third party dealing with the agent.

When undisclosed principals are involved, their rights against third parties can be limited in four situations:

- If an agent has fraudulently represented to a third party that the contract is on the agent's behalf alone or that the agent represents someone other than the real principal, the third party has the right to rescind the contract. If the agent or principal knows or should know that the third party is unwilling to deal with the principal, the principal's identity becomes a material fact. Misrepresentation of a material fact by the agent allows the third party to void the contract. If the agent does not actively misrepresent the principal's identity, but knows that the third party would not agree to contract with the principal, the agent has a duty to disclose the principal's identity to the third party.

- An undisclosed principal cannot enforce a contract against a third party if enforcement would impose a substantial additional burden on the third party. For example, Sophie, an agent, contracts to purchase from Kate "all of the oil that Sophie requires." Kate is unaware that Sophie represents Will, whose oil requirements are substantially greater than Kate knows or is able to meet. Under the circumstances, Will cannot enforce the contract against Kate.

- If a contract specifies the agent's personal performance, the principal cannot substitute his or her own performance in fulfillment of the contract. For example, Peter is an undisclosed principal and Daniel is his agent. Daniel contracts to personally paint Kyle's house. Peter cannot do the painting; it must be done by Daniel. Once Daniel completes the painting, Peter can demand payment from Kyle under the contract.

- When a third party sues an agent for breach of a contract with an undisclosed principal, a judgment against the agent destroys the principal's right of recovery against the third party. However, a judgment either for or against the agent obtained by the third party after the principal's identity becomes known does not necessarily diminish the rights of a principal who took no part in the suit.

Agent's Liability to a Third Party

Generally, an agent is not liable to a third party under a contract made on a disclosed principal's behalf. The principal alone is liable. Six situations represent exceptions to that rule:

- When an agent acts on a principal's behalf, the agent warrants by implication that he or she has actual authority to do so. If the agent is not authorized to act on the principal's behalf or exceeds the authority granted by the principal, the agent breaches that implied warranty of authority. The agent is liable to the third party for that breach. The agent may also be liable for fraud if he or she intentionally misrepresents the existence or extent of authority. However, if the third party knows or has reason to suspect that the agent lacks authority, the agent is not liable for breach of warranty. Full disclosure to the third party of all facts relating to the agent's authority protects the agent against suits for breach of warranty. Also, the agent's liability for breach of warranty terminates if the principal ratifies the contract before the third party withdraws from it. However, ratification that occurs after the third party withdraws due to the agent's lack of authority or sues the agent for breach of warranty is ineffective in discharging the agent's liability to the third party.

- If an agent acts on behalf of a minor or a mentally incompetent person, the agent is personally liable for breach of the warranty of authority if the third party was not aware of the principal's incapacity. Part of the agent's implied warranty of authority is that the principal can be legally bound under the contract.

- If a third party has intended to contract with the agent and the agent purported to act personally and not for a principal, to avoid personal liability on a contract with the third party the agent must disclose both the existence and identity of the principal. It is not sufficient that the third party knows facts that could disclose the principal's identity.

- The third party can ask the agent to agree to personally guarantee the contract. An agent who voluntarily assumes responsibility for performing the agreement is liable for the principal's nonperformance. The principal is liable on the contract, and the agent is liable on the guaranty.

- If a third party pays money to an agent who has no authority to collect it and the agent does not turn the money over to the principal, the third party can sue the agent for the money. The agent cannot avoid liability by subsequently paying wrongfully collected funds to a principal. In addition, a third party can recover payments made to an agent resulting from the agent's mistake or misconduct even though the agent has turned the funds over to the principal.

- An agent is liable for fraudulent or malicious acts that harm a third party. That the agent was acting in good faith under the principal's direction is not a defense against personal tort or criminal liability. An agent who wrongfully injures a third party or is guilty of theft is personally liable.

Agent's Rights Against a Third Party

A third party is usually not liable to an agent for breach of contract between the agent and the third party on behalf of a disclosed principal. However, the third party can be liable to the agent if the agent intended to be bound or if the principal is undisclosed or partially disclosed.

- An agent can sue a third party for breach of contract if both the agent and the third party have agreed that the contract obligates the agent. For example, if the principal's credit standing is unacceptable to the third party, the agent can become an actual party to the contract. In this case, the agent is potentially liable but also has the right to sue the third party for breach of contract.

- An agent can sue a third party for breach of contract entered into without the third party's knowledge of the principal's existence and identity.

However the principal can also sue, and the principal's right to sue the third party is superior to that of the agent.

- An agent who falsely represents authority to act on a principal's behalf and who, therefore, fails to bind the principal to the contract cannot later sue under the contract. The agent cannot prove the existence of the alleged contract.

- In a suit by a third party against an agent concerning a contract entered into on a principal's behalf, the agent can set up personal defenses as though the agent were the sole contracting party. These defenses include that the principal or agent performed the contract; that the third party failed to perform the contract; or that the statute of frauds or statute of limitations precludes recovery.

- With the disclosed or partially disclosed principal's consent, the agent can assert the principal's defenses or counterclaims against the third party. The third party cannot, therefore, be in a better position by suing the agent than by suing the principal because defenses that are purely personal to the principal become available to the agent.

TORT LIABILITY OF PRINCIPAL AND AGENT

Generally, principals and agents are liable to third parties for their own torts. However, in several situations, a principal may be held liable for torts committed by an agent.

Employee
A person hired to perform services for another under the direction and control of the other party, called the employer.

Independent contractor
A person (or organization) hired to perform services without being subject to the hirer's direction and control regarding work details.

Agents can be **employees** of the principal or they can be **independent contractors**. The distinction between employees and independent contractors is important in agency relationships, because the extent to which the principal is liable for an agent's torts depends on the relationship between the agent and the principal. Although it can sometimes be difficult to determine whether an individual is an employee or an independent contractor, the most important distinguishing factor is the extent to which the principal controls the details of the work being done.

Principal's Liability for Agent's Torts

As a principal's authorized representative, an agent can bind the principal to contracts and complete transactions on the principal's behalf. If, in the course of the agency, an agent commits a tort against a third party, to what extent, if any, is the principal liable for that tort? Although individuals are generally liable for their own torts, in several circumstances, a principal becomes liable for an agent's torts.

Respondeat superior
The legal principle under which an employer is vicariously liable for the torts of an employee acting within the course and scope of employment.

Respondeat Superior Liability

If an agent commits a tort, the principal may be held liable for that tort under the doctrine of **respondeat superior**. *Respondeat superior* means "let the master answer," and it attributes vicarious liability to a principal for the torts of an agent when two conditions are met:

- The agent must be an employee of the principal.
- The tort must be committed while the agent is acting within the scope of his or her employment.

Employers often grant their employees authority to act as their agents. For example, a manufacturer's management might authorize an employee in the purchasing department to contract with raw materials suppliers on the company's behalf.

In most cases, determining whether an agent is an employee or an independent contractor is relatively easy. Determining whether an employee was acting within the scope of his or her employment when a tort was committed can be more challenging. Generally, agents are considered to be acting in the scope of employment if they are performing work assigned by the employer or undertaking activities subject to the employer's control. The critical element is that the employer controls or has the right to control how the agent performs the assigned work. If an agent undertakes activities independently with no intention of serving the employer's interests, the agent is not considered to be acting in the scope of employment.[1]

If an agent is an employee, the principal and agent may have **joint and several liability** for any tort committed, and an injured third party may elect to sue the principal, the agent, or both to recover damages.

Direct Liability

A principal who commits a tort against a third party is directly liable to that party for any resulting harm.

A principal may be directly liable to a third party for an agent's tort that is committed at the specific direction of the principal. For example, a landlord (principal) who directs a property manager (agent) to unlawfully evict a tenant is liable for any harm or damage to the tenant.

A principal may also be directly liable to a third party for an agent's tort if the principal has been negligent in hiring, training, or supervising the agent. The principal is responsible for selecting appropriate individuals as agents; giving them clear instructions; providing them with appropriate tools, equipment, or materials; monitoring their performance; and discharging those that do not perform appropriately.

Liability for Independent Contractor's Torts

Generally, a principal is not liable for the torts of agents that are independent contractors. This is because the principal does not have authority to specify

Joint and several liability
The liability of multiple defendants either collectively or individually for the entire amount of damages sought by the plaintiff regardless of their relative degree of responsibility.

the way in which the agency is to be performed. However, this general rule has three exceptions:

- A principal who negligently enters into an agency with an independent contractor that is unsuitable or incompetent can be held liable for resulting harm to third parties. For example, if a mall owner contracts a security firm, knowing that the firm's employees all have several previous convictions for assault and battery, and a security guard attacks and injures a mall patron while on duty, the mall owner may be held liable to the injured party.

- Certain duties are considered so important that responsibility for them cannot be delegated to another party. For example, a municipality has a duty to keep public roads in good repair. While the municipality can delegate the repair work to an independent contractor, it cannot delegate responsibility for ensuring that the work is done, and done in an acceptable manner. If a principal hires an independent contractor to perform one of these important duties and the contractor fails to perform or performs inadequately, the principal may be liable for any resulting harm or damage to third parties.

- A principal who hires an independent contractor to perform highly dangerous activities, for example building demolition, must ensure that the contractor takes appropriate safety precautions. If the independent contractor negligently fails to do so, the principal may be held liable to third parties for any resulting harm or damage.

Liability for Agent's Misrepresentations

When an agent makes a material misrepresentation to a third party in a transaction, the third party can rescind (avoid) that transaction. Alternatively, the third party may elect to recover in tort for any harm resulting from the misrepresentation. A principal may be liable to a third party for misrepresentations by an agent in two situations:

- If a principal intended that an agent make a misrepresentation during a transaction, the principal is directly liable for that misrepresentation. In some states, a principal may also be directly liable for negligently allowing a misrepresentation by an agent.

- When an agent has actual or apparent authority to make true statements about a particular subject, the principal is vicariously liable for any misrepresentations made by the agent even if the principal did not direct or condone the misrepresentation. For example, a real estate agent could have actual or apparent authority to make true statements about a property for sale. If the real estate agent misrepresents details about the property to a third party, the principal could be held liable.

In an attempt to relieve themselves of liability for agents' misrepresentations, principals may include an exculpatory clause in the contracts agents make with third parties. An exculpatory clause limits the principal's liability for statements made to only statements that are specifically included in the contract. Such a clause may protect a principal against tort liability resulting from misrepresentation by an agent, but a third party injured by the misrepresentation can still choose to rescind the transaction.

Agent's Liability for Own Torts

Even when they are acting on behalf of a principal, agents are generally liable for their own torts. For example, an agent who slanders or libels a third party while performing acts related to the agency is liable for his or her actions. However, this rule has four exceptions:

- If a principal has been granted permission to do something, the principal's agent is considered to have the same permission. For example, if a neighboring business allows a construction company to park its heavy equipment in the neighbor's parking lot overnight, the construction company's agent may also park the company's equipment there without committing a trespass. The scope of the agent's permission is strictly limited to that granted to the principal.

- If a principal is legally entitled to take action to defend his or her person or property, the principal's agent may take similar action in protection of the principal. For example, a principal who is attacked can use physical force to defend against the attacker; the principal's agent can also use physical force against the attacker to protect the principal.

- An agent who makes misrepresentations in a transaction is not liable if the agent did not know, and had no reason to know, that the statement was a misrepresentation. For example, if the principal misrepresented information to the agent and the agent, in good faith, relayed that misinformation to a third party, the agent is not liable to the third party for any resulting harm or damage.

- If a principal supplies defective tools or instruments to the agent and a third party is injured because of the defect, the agent is not liable if he or she did not know or have reason to know that the tool or instrument was defective.

SUMMARY

The usual method of creating an agency is by express appointment. A principal can extend additional power to an appointed agent through power of attorney.

In agency by estoppel, if the principal's words or actions lead a third person to believe that an agency exists, the principal cannot subsequently deny the agent's authority to act on the principal's behalf. Although agency by estoppel is not a genuine agency, it protects third parties from potential loss that could result if the agency were denied.

In agency by ratification, if a person acts as an agent without the principal's consent or authority, the principal can chose to ratify the transaction, and an agency is created. Alternatively, the principal could choose to refuse to approve the purported agent's unauthorized actions.

An agent's authority can be either actual authority or apparent authority. An agent's actual authority can be express or implied. Apparent authority generally occurs when a principal grants less authority than agents usually have, or when the principals business operates differently from similar businesses in the area.

A third party cannot rely on an agent's statements about the scope of the agent's authority, but must ascertain it by direct inquiry to the principal.

Principals and agents owe different obligations to each other. An agent's duties to a principal include loyalty, obedience, reasonable care, accounting, and information. The principal has four remedies for an agent's default or wrongdoing. The principal can sue to require the agent to transfer improperly held property to the principal; sue for the value of the benefit the agent received; sue for breach of agency contract; or sue in tort for harm done.

A principal has the duty to provide the agent with an agreed-on period of employment, compensation, reimbursement for expenses, and indemnity for losses. If the principal breaches any of these duties, the agent can sue for compensation, indemnity, or reimbursement; alternatively, the agent can retain possession of the principal's goods until the principal has paid any amounts due.

Agency can terminate for just cause, lapse of time, accomplishment of purpose, revocation by the principal, renunciation by the agent, death or incapacity, and changed circumstances.

To determine the rights and liabilities of principals, agents, and third parties in breach of contract cases, courts must answer questions about the existence of the agency, the extent of the agent's authority, and the extent to which the principal's existence and identity were disclosed.

A principal can be held vicariously liable for the torts of an agent under the doctrine of *respondeat superior*. A principal can also be directly liable for an agent's torts if they were committed at the principal's direction or if the principal has been negligent in selecting or managing the agent. Although principals are not generally liable for the torts of independent contractors, they can be under certain circumstances. A principal can also be liable for an agent's misrepresentations. In addition, although agents are generally liable for their own torts, in some situations they can be relieved of that liability.

ASSIGNMENT NOTE

1.   Restatement (Third) of Agency § 707 (2006).

Agency Law: Insurance Applications

Educational Objectives

After learning the content of this assignment, you should be able to:

▶ Describe the agency relationship that exists between insurers and each classification of producers:

- Agents

- Brokers

▶ Distinguish a producer's actual authority, both express and implied, from apparent authority.

▶ Explain how the extent of a producer's authority is affected by these factors:

- Producers' status as general agents, special agents, or brokers

- Producers' notice and knowledge

- Producers' authority to bind coverage

- Appointment of subagents

▶ Explain how producers' authority can be terminated.

▶ Describe producers' duties and liabilities to insurance customers, third parties, and insurers.

Outline

Insurance Producer Classifications

Producers' Authority

Extent of Producers' Authority

Termination of Producer Authority

Producers' Duties and Liabilities

Summary

Agency Law: Insurance Applications

INSURANCE PRODUCER CLASSIFICATIONS

Like other businesses, insurers act through various representatives to accomplish their goals. Some of these representatives are employees of the insurer, and others are independent contractors who perform certain functions for the insurer. The acts of these representatives on behalf of the insurer may legally bind the insurer.

The insurance business uses the generic term **insurance producer** to denote the broad category of persons involved in arranging the placement of insurance business with insurers. The term producer encompasses agents and brokers, because the person or group acting as intermediary between the insurer and insured "produces" the business.

An understanding of how the roles of agents and brokers interrelate is necessary to understand the respective duties of producers. The producer classifications have distinct legal significance, as the authority and potential liability of each type of producer differs significantly.

Agents

The term **insurance agent**, or agent, refers to an intermediary who arranges contracts of insurance between a specific insurer with which they have an ongoing relationship and prospective insureds. The prospective insured is the customer. Insurance agents can fall into three categories based on the degree of discretion they have in carrying out their functions: (1) **general agent**, (2) **special agent**, and (3) **soliciting agent**. See the exhibit "Categories of Insurance Agents."

Brokers

While an insurance agent represents the insurer, the insurance **broker** usually represents the insurance customer. An insurance broker is independent, does not work for a particular insurer, and typically assists large insureds to obtain coverage from competing insurers.

Some insurance brokers have expanded their roles beyond finding available insurance coverage and coordinating the placement of their clients' insurance business. Some brokers have become risk consultants, who advise clients how to handle their loss exposures. This includes using both alternative risk

Insurance producer
Any of several kinds of insurance personnel who place insurance business with insurers and who represent either insurers or insureds, or both.

Insurance agent
A legal representative of one or more insurers for which the representative has a contractual agreement to sell insurance.

General agent
An agent that transacts all of a principal's business of a particular kind or in a particular place.

Special agent
A person or an entity that is employed to act for the principal in a specific transaction or only for a particular purpose or class of work.

Soliciting agent
An insurance producer whose authority is limited by contract with an insurer to soliciting applications for insurance and performing other acts directly incident to those activities.

Broker
An independent producer who represents insurance customers.

Categories of Insurance Agents

General Agent	Special Agent	Soliciting Agent
Broad powers within underwriting guidelines	Authority restricted by express agreement with insurer	Narrow authority derived directly from the agency contract
• Solicits applications for insurance	• Induces third parties to apply for insurance	• Solicits applications for insurance
• Receives premiums	• Forwards applications to the insurer	• Forwards applications to the insurer
• Issues and renews policies	• Delivers policies to the insureds on receipt of premium	
• Appoints subagents		
• Adjusts losses, in some cases	• Possible additional duties, such as inspecting property, quoting rates, collecting premium payments, and assisting with changes in coverage	

[DA06284]

financing techniques and traditional insurance. Brokers may also offer risk control or claim services, or assist insurers in obtaining reinsurance coverage.

PRODUCERS' AUTHORITY

Arising from different circumstances, the different forms of a producer's authority differ in legal significance for insurers.

There are two types of producer authority:

- Actual authority
- Apparent authority

The insurer can bind itself to the unauthorized acts of a producer through subsequent conduct ratifying the producer's acts. If an insurer ratifies a producer's unauthorized actions with full knowledge of the acts, then the insurer accepts the benefits or consequences of those actions.

However, an insurer must be careful in ratifying such producer actions. If the insurer develops a pattern or practice of ratifying this producer's actions, an agency relationship can arise by implication. The insurer must evaluate whether it should enter into a formal relationship through an agency contract or deny the relationship and refuse to ratify the producer's submissions.

Actual Authority

Actual authority is that which the principal (insurer) intentionally confers upon the producer or allows the producer to believe he or she possesses. See the exhibit "Example: Agent's Authority."

Example: Agent's Authority

Jane is an insurance agent associated exclusively with MutualCo, a regional insurer. When MutualCo appointed Jane as an agent, they entered into a standard written agency contract that MutualCo uses for all agents. This agreement sets out, among other things, the following terms:

- The agent's commission arrangement with the insurer, financial assistance, and other support that MutualCo will provide to Jane's agency
- Jane's authority and methods allowed for binding coverage
- Types of insurance Jane can write
- Duration of the agency contract
- Termination methods for the agency contract

Jane has express authority to act within those terms.

[DA04653]

Typically, the insurance producer and the insurer establish the terms of the principal/agent relationship through a formal written contract that grants the producer express authority. This agency contract states the producer's powers and authority and specifies any restrictions on that authority. If the contract does not state an authority, the producer does not have that express authority. An insurance producer who is an exclusive agent of one insurer might have one contract. A producer who is an independent agent representing multiple insurers might have several contracts.

The application for insurance and the insurance policy itself also can limit the extent of the producer's express authority. For example, a clear statement on the insurance application that the producer has no authority to bind coverage eliminates the producer's express power to do so. A producer has no express or implied authority to act contrary to those limitations. Unless the producer has some other basis for the authority, such an action does not bind the insurer.

Actual authority can also be implied. Although express agreements create most insurance principal and agent relationships, the parties can agree to the relationship by less formal means. For example, an agent's submission of an insurance application can create an agency relationship if the producer has solicited and forwarded insurance applications to the insurer previously, and if the insurer has accepted them. The agent has the implied authority to bind the insurer in this manner. The insurer must voluntarily accept the applications from the agent and then voluntarily issue policies. Merely forwarding applications for insurance under an automobile assigned risk or other residual market automobile insurance plan does not create an implied authority for the agent. See the exhibit "Exercise: Determine Producer's Authority."

Exercise: Determine Producer's Authority

Alice is an independent insurance agent who places her insurance customers' business with a variety of insurers with whom she has agency contracts. Alice does not have a contract with CoverageCo, a large national insurer.

In a local professional meeting, Alice hears that CoverageCo is soliciting independent agents to send business to them. Alice sends business to CoverageCo on several occasions, and CoverageCo issues a policy and forwards its standard commission to Alice.

CoverageCo then forwards to Alice its application forms for use in soliciting more insurance applicants along with rating material and manuals describing CoverageCo's products and procedures.

Does Alice have authority as a producer for CoverageCo?

Alice is CoverageCo's agent by implication, not by express authority. The parties did not create an agency contract, nor did CoverageCo give Alice any direct expression of authority to act on its behalf. CoverageCo's conduct in accepting applications submitted by Alice and forwarding to her applications and manuals, however, gives her implied authority in the agency relationship.

[DA06282]

Apparent Authority

Even without actual authority, an agent can have apparent authority. An insurer does not give apparent authority to the producer (nor does the producer create this authority), but appearances may lead a third party to believe that a producer has authority. Apparent authority usually arises in one of two overlapping circumstances:

- An insurer grants less actual authority to the producer than producers in the same position in that business usually have.

- The method of operation of the principal's business differs from the method of operation of other businesses of the same kind in the principal's area.

If a third party's assumptions regarding an agent's authority are unreasonable and do not have a factual basis, the insurer can legally deny the existence of the agency relationship. Likewise, the purported agent's statements or actions are insufficient to create an agency by estoppel. The insurer's acts alone create the apparent authority. For example, if an insurance agent created the

---

Example: Producer's Apparent Authority

Beta Agency advertises that it is an agent for Jumbo Insurance Company. The other insurance agency in town, Alpha Agency, is also an agent for Jumbo. Alpha is a general agent for Jumbo with express authority to issue auto insurance policies for Jumbo. Beta is a special agent for Jumbo with authority only to submit applications for auto insurance policies.

After receiving a quote from Alpha for an auto insurance policy with Jumbo, Henry goes to Beta Agency to compare prices. Beta quotes Henry a price that is $50 lower for a Jumbo auto policy. Henry pays the premium to Beta, and Beta tells Henry that the policy is in effect. There is no statement on Jumbo's application form regarding authority of the agent to bind coverage.

Jumbo's price for the policy is actually the amount that was quoted by Alpha. However, Beta had apparent authority to Henry to quote a price for the policy. Jumbo may need to issue Henry a policy, although Jumbo may seek to recover the additional $50 from Beta.

[DA06283]

appearance of an agency relationship with an insurer by stating falsely that he or she is its agent, by misappropriating its company logo, or by copying its applications without authorization, the insurer could deny the agency relationship because it did nothing to create this misunderstanding. However, if the insurer becomes aware of this situation and fails to act in a timely fashion to prevent the agent from improperly using its logo, an agency by estoppel can arise.

EXTENT OF PRODUCERS' AUTHORITY

A producer's authority is defined by whether the producer represents an insurer or an insurance customer and is limited to the authority conferred by the insurer or the customer.

Once an agency relationship is established between a producer and an insurer, the producer can act on the insurer's behalf. The producer's actions must be consistent with the authority granted within the agency relationship. An insurer, like any other principal, is liable for the acts performed or contracts made by one of its agents within the scope of that agent's actual or apparent authority.

Producers' Status as General Agents, Special Agents, or Brokers

The extent of a producer's authority varies depending on whether the producer is a general agent, special agent, or broker. The general agent has the broadest authority of all insurance agents and fully represents an insurer, meaning any action the producer takes according to the agreed-on authority binds the insurer. General agents can accept loss exposures, agree on and settle the terms of insurance, waive policy provisions, issue and renew policies, collect premiums, and adjust claims. Even if the contract does not confer the broad powers discussed, the producer may have those powers by apparent authority.

If a contract between producer and insurer expressly limits the producer's power to soliciting business, as is the case with many special agents, any action the agent takes beyond soliciting and forwarding prospective business to the insurer usually will not bind the insurer unless an insured can establish apparent authority. See the exhibit "Examples: Producer's Authority."

Examples: Producer's Authority

- Paul has an agency contract with InsurCo that calls him a general agent and that specifically grants him several powers, among them the power to renew policies. One of Paul's insurance customers' policies comes up for renewal. Without consulting InsurCo, Paul tells the customer that the policy is renewed and collects the renewal premium. Paul is acting pursuant to express authority, and his action binds InsurCo, whether or not InsurCo wanted to renew the policy.

- JoAnne has an agency contract with InsurCo that does not attach any description to the relationship created. The contract gives JoAnne several powers, among them the powers to bind the insurer to new business, to collect premiums, to issue policies, and to adjust small claims. JoAnne does not have the power to renew policies. Her office displays the company logo prominently in several places, and all of InsurCo's forms that JoAnne uses have her name on them and label her as InsurCo's agent. JoAnne places a substantial amount of insurance with InsurCo. One day, JoAnne decides to renew one of her best customers' insurance on her own, without consulting InsurCo, and collects the appropriate renewal premium. A covered loss occurs the next day. Despite JoAnne's lack of actual authority to renew the policy, she has bound InsurCo to cover the loss. JoAnne acted with apparent authority. Under these circumstances, JoAnne's customer reasonably believed that she had the authority to renew the policy on InsurCo's behalf. InsurCo has acted as though JoAnne is its general agent and is estopped from denying this relationship.

[DA04654]

The extent of producer authority for brokers is different from that for general and special agents. Brokers represent insureds. Thus, the broker's principal is the insurance customer, not the insurer. Accordingly, an insurance broker usually has no actual or apparent authority to bind the insurer. Instead, the broker typically has the power to bind the insurance customer.

A broker's typical duties include these:

- To procure insurance for the insurance customer-principal
- To select the insurer to provide the desired coverage

- To arrange for the payment of premiums
- To cancel and receive unearned premiums on a policy the broker has obtained
- To obtain a new policy upon cancellation of one previously obtained

A broker can be both an agent and an insured's representative in two instances. First, through apparent authority, the broker is legally the insurer's agent if the insurer allows the broker to act in a manner leading a reasonable third party to believe that the broker is the insurer's agent. Apparent authority does not arise merely by the insurer's furnishing a broker with application forms that the broker routinely submits to the insurer. However, a broker who has a particular insurer's application forms, receives premiums ostensibly on that insurer's behalf, and issues material identifying the customer as presently covered by that insurer can be the insurer's agent.

Second, some state statutes provide that, for some specific purposes, a broker is the insurer's agent. Once a policy is issued, the broker acting on the insured's behalf is the insurer's agent regarding premium payments, and the broker's receipt of the payments is effectively the insurer's receipt. The reasoning behind such statutes is that, once a policy is issued, the broker who facilitated the placement of the customer's business with the insurer is indistinguishable from an insurance agent in the eyes of many customers; therefore, the laws provide some extra protection to insurance customers.

Producers' Notice and Knowledge

In agency law, any knowledge possessed by an agent, general or special, is considered to be possessed by that agent's principal as well. In an insurance context, the authorized agent's knowledge is imputed to the insurer—whether the insurer actually receives the information from the agent is irrelevant.

Questions of imputed knowledge often arise when agents possess knowledge that would have caused the insurer to decline coverage, had the insurer been aware of the information. In these circumstances, a court will hold that the insurer knew what the agent knew, and the court typically finds that coverage exists. See the exhibit "Example: Imputed Knowledge."

Example: Imputed Knowledge

John, the insurer's authorized agent, assisted a customer, Mary, in arranging automobile insurance for a car owned by Mary's son. John told Mary that the insurer's policy provided the coverage. Later, a loss occurs. The insurer denies coverage based on policy language conferring coverage only for a named insured's vehicles, and not for the insured's son's vehicle. The insurer cannot deny coverage, because it is held to know what its agent knew at the time the policy was issued.

[DA04655]

Imputed knowledge also applies to a physical location to be insured. For example, a court may hold that a binder conferring coverage on an insured's business is effective over an insurer's objection that it would not have provided coverage if it had known the location of the insured. In such a case, the insurer's authorized agent might have been aware of the location of the property to be insured and that the binder issued was broad enough to cover the location. The insurer's lack of actual knowledge would be irrelevant.

A court might not bind an insurer by a producer's knowledge in these circumstances:

* When no actual agency relationship exists between the producer and insurer
* When the agent has supplied false information

An agent's knowledge is not imputed to an insurer if no agency relationship exists between them. Therefore, a general agent's knowledge is imputed to the insurer, but under most circumstances, an insurance broker's knowledge is not imputed. The broker's agency relationship is with the insured, not the insurer.

Cases involving soliciting agents are less clear. Some courts hold that the limited nature of the soliciting agent's authority is such that the insurer is not chargeable with that agent's knowledge. Because the soliciting agent cannot bind coverage, these courts reason that the connection between principal and agent is too tenuous to bind the insurer by the producer's knowledge.

Other courts hold that a soliciting agent is a general agent under their state laws; therefore, the soliciting agent's knowledge can be imputed to the insurer. Still other courts impute some of the soliciting agent's knowledge to the insurer if it is consistent with that agent's more limited authority to obtain and forward insurance applications.

In cases that involve an agent being aware that information provided by an insured was false, many courts refuse to bind the insurer by that agent's knowledge. The agent's decision to act adversely to the insurer's interests breaks the agency relationship, which is the basis of the imputed knowledge rule. No hardship results to the insured as an innocent third party because the insured was involved in the dishonest behavior. If an agent is unaware that information provided by an insurance customer is false, no knowledge is imputed to the insurer. The insurer can avoid liability under the policy if it can prove fraud, misrepresentation, or some other defense. See the exhibit "Exercise to Determine Imputed Authority."

Producers' Authority to Bind Coverage

The need for immediate insurance coverage arises frequently. In many cases, people or organizations acquire property or assume duties with little or no advance notice. Before issuing a policy on a given loss exposure, however, insurers usually must undertake an underwriting process that can take several

> ### Exercise to Determine Imputed Authority
>
> James visits Steve, a general insurance agent for InsurCo, to insure all his family cars through Steve's agency. James tells Steve that a member of his household has been convicted of driving while intoxicated. Steve knows this information would disqualify James from coverage with InsurCo. Eager to receive the commission from the sale, Steve falsely enters on the application that no driving offenses have occurred in James's household. James does not read the application before signing it, and InsurCo issues a policy to him. Later James has a loss, and InsurCo discovers the conviction during the claim investigation.
>
> **Will InsurCo be required to cover the loss?**
>
> InsurCo must cover the loss. The knowledge of its agent, Steve, is imputed to InsurCo. Steve, and thus InsurCo, knew of the conviction, but a policy was issued. Steve's knowledge stops InsurCo from denying coverage under the policy.
>
> **If James did not tell Steve about the driving while intoxicated conviction, is InsurCo required to cover the loss?**
>
> If neither Steve nor InsurCo had knowledge of the conviction and James falsified the insurance application, InsurCo can deny coverage for the loss based on fraud and misrepresentation.
>
> **If James and Steve colluded to conceal information about the conviction, is InsurCo required to cover the loss?**
>
> If James colluded in providing false information, InsurCo does not have a duty to provide coverage for the loss.

[DA04656]

weeks or longer to complete. Because this delay leaves applicants unprotected, many insurers authorize producers to issue temporary oral or written policies pending acceptance of the application.

In many cases, a producer can form an oral insurance contract with a customer. For example, an applicant can call an insurance producer from a car dealership, provide the details of the car to be purchased, and request immediate insurance on the car. By consenting to provide the coverage, the producer has created a valid insurance contract binding the insurer.

Courts generally have upheld the propriety of oral insurance contracts, although they are not valid in a few states. These contracts must contain sufficient agreement on essential terms, such as these:

- Subject matter of the insurance
- Loss exposures insured
- Premium
- Insurance contract duration
- Coverage amount
- Identity of parties

The contract need not mention these terms specifically, but the parties must agree to them, even if implicitly. In many situations a party can prove essential contractual elements by evidence showing an understanding, express or implied, that the insurer's customary policy terms are to apply.

Sometimes, a writing, such as a binder (binder receipt, or binding receipt), can provide a temporary insurance contract. A binder receipt contains a written temporary contract of insurance, sets out its essential terms and conditions, and proves the main elements of the temporary insurance contract. The contract remains in effect until cancellation occurs, the time period elapses, or the final insurance policy issues. The issuance of the insurance policy usually supersedes and replaces the temporary insurance contract.

These are the two most common legal issues regarding oral and temporary insurance contracts:

- A producer's lack of authority to form the contract
- A producer's failure to designate which insurer was to be bound by the oral or temporary contract

If the producer has actual authority, the oral or temporary insurance contract is valid and binding on the insurer. In those cases, the focus shifts to whether the producer had apparent authority. A third party could reasonably believe that a general agent had the power to bind coverage orally or in writing. If the producer is not a general agent and no apparent authority exists, the producer's oral or temporary contract would not bind the insurer.

If a producer representing multiple insurers contracts with a customer and then fails to designate the insurer providing coverage before a loss occurs, the legal issue is which, if any, insurer is liable for the loss. Courts look for reliable evidence that the producer intended to bind a particular insurer to the contract, as in these examples:

- The producer represents only one insurer that issues the coverage on the terms sought.
- In previous dealings, the producer has placed all the insured's business with one insurer.
- The producer issued a note or memorandum before the loss showing an intention to form the contract with a particular insurer. A mere mental note or a subsequent writing does not bind an insurer.

If the evidence does not reveal that the producer selected an insurer before the loss, the contract does not bind any insurer. The insured has no coverage but can sue the agent for errors and omissions and seek damages equivalent to the loss.

Appointment of Subagents

In many instances, insurance producers employ people to assist them in various aspects of their duties. These persons are subagents because they are the producer's agents. Insurance producers also may have clerical employees who assist in administration of their agencies, and they may retain the services of others who assist in the sales or marketing of their insurance products. The general rule is that an insurance producer cannot delegate duties that involve the producer's individual care, skill, and judgment. See the exhibit "Example: Subagent's Apparent Authority."

Example: Subagent's Apparent Authority

Martha is an agent representing multiple insurers. Alice, Martha's office administrator, has varied job duties, including taking new applications for personal insurance and making changes to existing accounts at customers' requests. Paula insures her cars, home, and business through Martha's agency. Paula has changed her car and homeowners insurance by telephoning Alice. Paula visits the agency to add business interruption coverage to her commercial coverage. Alice tells Paula she can handle this addition, obtains the necessary information, and issues a thirty-day binder. In fact, Alice has no authority to issue the binder, and Martha would not have approved adding this coverage for Paula. A court would have to determine whether Alice's action has bound Martha's agency to provide Paula the additional coverage. Paula probably reasonably believed that Alice had the authority she purported to have. Alice assumed a large number of duties for Martha, and a customer probably would not distinguish between Alice's other duties and the issuance of a binder.

[DA04657]

The appointment of subagents is permissible because of these three exceptions to a general rule against delegation to subagents:

- Producers can appoint subagents to discharge their mechanical, clerical, and ministerial (nondiscretionary) duties, including tasks relating to the placement or renewal of insurance with the producer's principal insurance agency. These acts include soliciting insurance applications, countersigning insurance policies when discretion is not involved (if state law allows), delivering policies, and collecting premiums. An insurance producer retained to use skill and judgment can delegate any duties that do not involve this skill and judgment.

- A subagent can discharge even discretionary duties and those involving skill and judgment when those acts are ratified by the insurance producer. For example, a producer could authorize a subagent to bind coverage for an insurer or could ratify the subagent's act. As long as the producer accepts full responsibility for the subagent's actions, a court will view those actions as the producer's actions.

- Appointing subagents is authorized when discharging the producer's duties to the insurance principal would not be otherwise possible. To illustrate, a producer may need to appoint a subagent to conduct business in another state. If the insurer has authorized the producer to market its products in the state and state law allows such marketing only by residents of that state, the producer may appoint a resident subagent.

The doctrine of apparent authority also can apply to subagents. To the public, an insurance producer's subagents appear to have authorization to act for the insurer, even when they do not have such authority. In many such circumstances, these subagents' acts bind the insurer under the doctrine of apparent authority. One frequent example involves commitments by producers' office employees to extend coverage in various situations. Generally, the insurer is bound by these commitments even if the employee acted without actual authority.

TERMINATION OF PRODUCER AUTHORITY

As with other agency relationships, if one party no longer wants the relationship to continue, that party has the power to terminate the relationship. Thus, an insurer can revoke a producer's authority to act on the insurer's behalf even if a valid agency contract that would not support the termination exists between the parties.

Usually the circumstances for termination of a producer/insurer relationship are specified in a contract. For example, a contract might identify a period after which the relationship will terminate, or it might set out circumstances that warrant termination of the relationship, such as failure to meet production standards or producer misconduct.

The producer/insurer agency relationship is terminated by any act of one of the parties that the other party might reasonably construe to show the intent to terminate. Typically, termination occurs through a written or an oral communication, which severs the producer's actual authority to bind the insurance principal. The principal must take appropriate action to inform third parties that the relationship has terminated to avoid the potential for apparent authority. After notification to third parties, the producer cannot bind the insurer in any way regarding that party. If a third party who has dealt with the producer does not receive notification, however, the producer's acts, purportedly on the insurer's behalf, might bind that insurer.

The producer can bind the insurer regarding third parties whom he or she has not dealt previously if these parties had prior knowledge of the existence of the former agency relationship, but no notice of the termination. The safest way to avoid the possible adverse consequences of apparent authority is for the insurer to take these actions:

- Notify all third parties known to have dealt with the producer
- Repossess from the producer any evidence of the agency relationship, such as application forms and insurer stationery

Although termination by the parties' contract or expression is most common, the agency relationship can terminate by other means, including operation of law, the producer's death or insanity, or the insurer's insolvency. See the exhibit "Example: Agency Termination."

Example: Agency Termination

John is an independent insurance agent. One of the insurers with which John has an agency contract for ten years, MutualCo, decides to terminate its arrangement with him and instructs him to stop writing business. John still has MutualCo application forms, manuals, and rating information in his office and displays a MutualCo plaque on the wall. MutualCo remains listed in the local telephone directory as one of the insurers with which John is associated.

One month after John's agency termination with MutualCo, a new customer, Alex, consults with John about his personal insurance needs. John issues a thirty-day binder to Alex through MutualCo covering all of Alex's cars, then forwards Alex's application for a one-year car insurance policy to MutualCo.

John's actions in issuing the binder bind MutualCo to coverage for Alex. John's actual authority has ended, but the various indications that John is still a MutualCo agent (manuals, office plaque, application forms, telephone listing) have created apparent authority on John's part.

A second example assumes the same facts, except that at the time John's association with MutualCo terminates, MutualCo representatives repossess from John all application forms, rating materials, manuals, and other material displaying the MutualCo company logo. At the time Alex visits John, John possesses no indication that he ever represented MutualCo. John's only connection to MutualCo is his unsupported assertions that he represents the insurer.

Because John has never represented Alex as a MutualCo agent, John's attempt to bind coverage probably would not bind MutualCo. John, of course, has no actual authority because MutualCo expressly terminated it. John also probably has no apparent authority because he possesses nothing that would support a reasonable conclusion that he represents MutualCo. Unless other facts emerge that provide Alex with a reasonable basis to conclude that John represents MutualCo, John's issuance of the binder is not authorized and thus is not binding on MutualCo.

[DA04659]

PRODUCERS' DUTIES AND LIABILITIES

Insurance producers often act on behalf of persons who have little or no knowledge of insurance matters. Insurance purchasers expect their producers to assist them capably in obtaining appropriate insurance. Insurers also rely on producers, with expectations of certain standards of conduct, in various relationships and transactions. The law recognizes the reasonableness of these expectations and imposes various duties and responsibilities on insurance producers.

It is important for insurance professionals to understand the legal principles that govern producers' roles and responsibilities in four key areas:

- Producers' duties and liability to insurance customers
- Producers' defenses to liability
- Producers' duties and liability to third parties
- Producers' duties to insurers

Producers' Duties and Liability to Insurance Customers

Insurance producers have a duty to exercise reasonable care and skill in performing their duties, to deal with their customers in good faith, and to exercise reasonable diligence on their customers' behalf. They also have a duty to have reasonable knowledge about the insurance policies they sell, the policy terms, and the coverages available in the areas for which their customers seek insurance protection. Insurance producers also have a duty to follow their customers' instructions. Producers who accept requests to insure must not exceed their authority or depart from the customers' instructions. The standard of care imposed on producers generally reflects the public's expectations that the producers be competent, diligent, loyal, and professional.

The general standard of care governing insurance producers applies to a variety of specific factual situations. There are five duties that producers owe their customers:

- Duty to follow instructions
- Duty to procure insurance
- Duty to maintain coverage
- Duty to place insurance with a solvent insurer
- Duty to advise

There is liability associated with failing to perform each duty.

Producer's Duty to Follow Instructions

The duty to follow instructions is clear and fundamental to the insurance producer and customer relationship. A producer must strictly follow the customer's instructions and is liable to the customer for any damages that result from not doing so. Therefore, a producer who fails to add an available coverage requested by an insured is liable for a subsequent loss that the policy would have covered had the producer followed instructions. Additionally, a producer who fails to add newly acquired property to the list of the insured's covered properties at the insured's request would be liable for the financial consequences resulting from any uninsured loss involving the property.

The insurance customer, however, also has duties. The customer has the duty to provide clear instructions to the producer. If instructions are ambiguous, the producer is justified in acting in good faith on any reasonable interpretation of the instructions. See the exhibit "Example: Producer's Duty to Follow Instructions."

Producer's Duty to Procure Insurance

The duty to procure insurance is similar to the duty to follow instructions. Although the latter duty might involve nondiscretionary acts, the duty to procure insurance involves care, skill, effort, and diligence on the insurance producer's part.

The producer cannot guarantee to the customer that the insurance can be obtained, because coverage might not be available for the customer's loss exposures, or at the price or limits the customer wants. However, the producer must make a good faith effort to procure the desired insurance and promptly inform the customer if this is not possible.

Issues about this duty arise when the customer solicits an insurance producer's services to locate an insurer who will accept the customer's business on favorable terms. The producer has the duty to exercise reasonable skill, care, and diligence in assisting the customer in obtaining insurance. A producer who undertakes to procure insurance and through neglect or fault fails to do so is liable to the customer for any resultant damages. See the exhibit "Producer's Liability for Failure to Procure Insurance."

Producer's Duty to Maintain Coverage

Producers also owe customers the duty to maintain coverage. A producer's status as an insurance agent or broker does not, by itself, impose a duty to secure renewal of a customer's insurance or to advise the customer of an insurer's impending cancellation or nonrenewal. However, these duties can arise by agreement between the parties or by their past course of dealings.

A producer who simply arranged insurance on a customer's behalf has no duty to advise the customer of cancellation or nonrenewal. Usually, the insurer handles such notifications, and the producer can reasonably rely on this practice. If by agreement, however, the producer assumed the obligation to advise the customer of any impending lapse in coverage, the producer must discharge this obligation or be liable to the customer for loss resulting from cancellation or nonrenewal.

Additionally, a producer who has previously advised a customer of any coverage cancellation or nonrenewal might be liable for damages resulting from the failure to give notice at a later time. To succeed in such a suit, the customer must show that the producer assumed this duty and that a course of conduct sufficiently lengthy and consistent warranted the customer's reasonable reliance on the producer for notification. The producer's occasional reminder

Example: Producer's Duty to Follow Instructions

Example 1

Paul is Jane's insurance producer for her personal and business insurance needs. Jane purchases two cars, a new Ford and an older Toyota. She instructs Paul to, effective immediately, place liability coverage and physical damage coverage on the Ford and only liability coverage on the Toyota, because of its age. Paul erroneously reverses the coverages on the cars and places only liability coverage on the Ford and liability and physical damage coverages on the Toyota. The Ford then sustains physical damage.

Has Paul breached the producer's duty to follow the insured's instructions?

Paul has breached the producer's duty to follow the insured's instructions. Jane's instructions were clear and not subject to reasonable disagreement or interpretation. Paul would likely be found liable for the physical damage to Jane's Ford.

Example 2

Alice is Joe's business insurance producer. Joe insures ten trucks through Alice's agency, all under separate business vehicle policies. Eight of the ten trucks are covered for liability and physical damage. The liability coverage limit is $500,000 per vehicle, aggregate. The physical damage coverages have $500 deductibles under each policy. The other two trucks in Joe's business are insured only for liability, with aggregate limits of $300,000 on each vehicle.

Joe contacts Alice just before he purchases two additional trucks and asks to insure them. Joe then says, "Because these are new trucks, I'll need more than just the liability coverage. Go ahead and write them with the full coverage." Alice places the same coverages on the new vehicles as the coverage on Joe's eight trucks—$500,000 aggregate liability limits and physical damage coverage with $500 deductibles.

The next day, one of the new vehicles is involved in a serious accident resulting in substantial damage to the vehicle and serious injury to the driver of the other vehicle. When Joe learns of the coverage on his truck, he asserts that what he meant by "the full coverage" was the maximum liability limits written by his insurer on commercial vehicles, $5 million aggregate, and the lowest physical damage deductible offered, $100 per vehicle.

Did Alice breach the producer's duty to follow the insured's instructions?

Alice's interpretation of Joe's instruction regarding the new trucks, "to write them with the full coverage," was one of several reasonable interpretations of an insured's instruction that was not clear. It was a reasonable interpretation on her part that by "full coverage" Joe meant her to provide the same coverage for the new trucks as the liability and property damage coverage in effect for his eight trucks. Although it would have been prudent for Alice to ask Joe to clarify exactly what he meant by "full coverage," Joe had a duty as an insured to provide additional instructions if he wanted something different than the type of coverage he had for eight of his trucks. It is unlikely that Alice would be found liable in this situation for any damages that exceeded the coverage limits, although a jurisdiction that applies comparative negligence principles in professional liability situations may hold her partially responsible for such damages.

[DA04661]

Producer's Liability for Failure to Procure Insurance

To sue the producer, the customer must prove that the producer agreed or undertook to obtain insurance coverage:

- If, for example, the producer promised to contact only one insurer on the customer's behalf, did so, and then advised the customer of the insurer's decision, no ongoing agreement to procure insurance existed. The producer would have no liability in that case. On the other hand, a producer who assumes the obligation to procure insurance could be liable for not doing so.

- If, for example, a producer agreed to locate an insurer and then waited several months before making any contacts on the customer's behalf, eventually making only one unsuccessful contact and failing to report to the customer, that producer would be liable. In this set of circumstances, an insurance customer would reasonably believe that the producer placed the insurance business promptly.

The duty to procure insurance also includes the duty to procure the appropriate coverage:

- A producer who succeeds in arranging the coverage the customer requests but who fails to advise the customer of exclusions for certain persons, property, or causes of loss for which the customer requested coverage, is liable for a subsequent uninsured loss falling within the exclusions.

- For example, a broker who promises to locate snowmobile coverage for all persons using a snowmobile, but who procures coverage only for the named insured and his family, would be liable to the customer for not obtaining the requested coverage.

These questions are important in cases of alleged failure to procure insurance:

- Was there an agreement to procure insurance?
- Did the producer fail to discharge the duties under the agreement?
- Did the insurance customer reasonably believe that the producer would secure the requested coverage under the facts presented?

The customer who can answer these questions affirmatively can sue the producer for failure to procure insurance. The producer would be liable for any damages resulting from the failure to obtain coverage.

[DA06333]

that a premium is due probably would be insufficient to prove the assumption of such a duty. See the exhibit "Example: Producer's Duty to Maintain Coverage."

Producer's Duty to Place Insurance With a Solvent Insurer

The insurer's solvency should be one of the most important criteria for placing insurance business. Both the producer and the customer should seriously consider factors bearing on solvency in reaching the decision about where to place the customer's business. The producer should make reasonable attempts to inquire into prospective insurers' solvency and to disclose to the customer any information revealing a weak financial condition.

> ### Example: Producer's Duty to Maintain Coverage
>
> #### Example 1
>
> Dave purchases his personal insurance through Martha, an InsurCo agent. Dave has met Martha only once, three years ago, to arrange his insurance through her agency, and there is no written agreement between Dave and Martha. Dave has always made coverage changes over the telephone, usually through Martha's assistant. Dave's car insurance lapses when he forgets to make a premium payment billed by InsurCo. He suffers a loss and claims he should have coverage because Martha failed to remind him when the premium payment was due.
>
> #### Did Martha breach a duty to maintain coverage for Dave?
>
> Martha is unlikely to be found liable for breach of a duty to maintain coverage. There was no agreement between Martha and Dave. The prior dealings between Dave and Martha also do not support the allegation that she had a duty to maintain coverage for Dave. There were no previous reminders from Martha, or anyone in her office, to Dave regarding premium due, and nothing in Martha's conduct would reasonably have led Dave to rely on her to keep his coverage in force.
>
> #### Example 2
>
> John has been insured through Martha's agency for ten years. Martha has John's payment dates on her office calendar so she can have her assistant call John to remind him to pay his premiums. Martha has told John on several occasions, "I don't usually do this, but yours is a very good account and I understand that you travel frequently on business, so I'll make sure your coverage won't lapse." Three times in the last ten years Martha has actually paid John's premium for him when he was traveling to prevent a lapse in his coverage. John reimbursed Martha after he returned from his business travel.
>
> Martha leaves for two months to assist with the opening of a new agency branch, and her assistant forgets to remind John about his premium payments. John is out of the country on business, and his coverage lapses. While he is driving home from the airport after returning from his travels, he is in an accident, and he finds he does not have coverage for his Mercedes.
>
> #### Did Martha breach a duty to maintain coverage for John?
>
> Martha would likely be found liable for breach of duty to maintain coverage in this situation. Martha's explicit statement to John and her conduct over the course of ten years indicate that she had an agreement with John to maintain his insurance coverage and that she owed him this duty.

[DA04663]

The producer is not usually liable for any loss to the insurance customer resulting from an insurer's insolvency. The producer is not the guarantor of the insurer's financial condition or solvency. However, a producer might be liable for negligently placing business with an insurer when the producer either knew or should have known of the insurer's insolvency. A reasonable effort, not a perfect one, to remain informed of the insurer's financial condition is required. The producer does not need to request a financial audit or examination of each insurer when contemplating placement of business. The producer can rely on public information, financial rating services, and any information available through a state department of insurance. At a minimum, a producer should disclose any information relevant to the solvency of an insurer to the insurance customer and make an appropriate record of this disclosure.

A producer also should be careful in placing business with an insurer not legally admitted to do business in a state. All states have enacted excess and surplus lines (E&S) statutes that establish requirements for procuring policies from nonadmitted insurers. Examples of such requirements include these:

- Only licensed producers can sell E&S insurance.
- E&S insurers must comply with minimum capital/surplus requirements.
- Producers must place E&S insurance only with an E&S insurer approved by the state as a nonadmitted insurer.
- Producers must appropriately notify the insured of the nonadmitted insurer's status.

In some states, if an insurer does not meet the requirements of the surplus lines statute, the agent or broker might be liable to the insured for any unpaid claims if the unauthorized insurer becomes insolvent.

Producer's Duty to Advise

Producers have the duty to advise their customers. Customers generally do not regard insurance producers as mere order-takers but seek out producers who are professional and knowledgeable about the insurance products they market. Many insureds rely extensively on their insurance producers' professional advice in selecting personal and commercial insurance coverages.

Occasionally, an insured has either inadequate or no insurance coverage for an unanticipated event or an event the insured incorrectly believed was covered. In these situations, the insured might sue the producer, claiming that the absence of or shortfall in coverage resulted from the producer's failure to advise the customer correctly about insurance needs. Traditionally, courts have rejected claims based on a producer's failure to function as an expert adviser because the producer has no duty to advise, guide, or direct a customer after procuring the insurance for the customer. In most jurisdictions, status as an insurance producer alone does not require the producer to undertake the duty to counsel and to advise insurance customers about their loss exposures, available coverages, or the adequacy of insurance coverage limits.

Applied strictly, this rule appears inconsistent with the concept of producer professionalism and customers' expectations. Accordingly, many jurisdictions have qualified this general rule, imposing liability on insurance producers for failure to advise their customers adequately if the facts show a special or expanded relationship between the producer and the customer. This relationship exists when a producer purports to be an insurance specialist, consultant, or counselor and has advised a particular customer about the customer's insurance needs on a long-standing basis.

Such a relationship would be, for example, a long-term producer-customer relationship in which producer and customer have discussed issues of coverage and the customer has come to rely on the producer's expertise. Evidence of the producer's acceptance of compensation for services (apart from a commission received from an insurer) is not essential to establish the special or expanded relationship, but it supports the producer's duty to advise. A court might consider a number of factors in determining whether a special or expanded producer-customer relationship gives rise to an affirmative duty to advise the customer completely about insurance needs.

Several important conclusions derive from case law dealing with the producer's duty to advise the insurance customer:

- The greater the producer's involvement in the customer's insurance matters and other matters bearing on insurance, such as the customer's business, the greater the chance that the courts will find a special or expanded producer and customer relationship.

- The more the producer leaves the arena of insurance order-taker or application conduit and begins to act as insurance adviser or counselor, the greater the chance that a court will find a special or expanded relationship.

- The more a customer relies on the producer's expertise and knowledge, the more likely that a court will find a special or expanded relationship.

- The greater the complexity of the insurance coverage sought, and the greater the level of specialized producer knowledge required, the greater the chance that a court would find the duty to advise on the producer's part.

Many producers are expanding their roles and offering more services, such as full insurance reviews, to their customers. As they do so, they approach the line separating the standard producer and customer relationship from the special or expanded relationship. Accordingly, insurance producers face a greater risk of liability for breach of the duty to advise. Producers need to be aware that they must advise their customers carefully on insurance matters to make sure the information provided is complete and accurate. As with the discharge of other producer duties, producers should keep written documentation of their advice to all insurance customers. See the exhibit "Exercise: Producer's Duty to Advise."

Producers' Defenses to Liability

The producer may have a defense to an allegation of breach of a duty owed to the customer. The producer can avoid liability by showing that his or her conduct was reasonable and appropriate or that factors not within the producer's

Exercise: Producer's Duty to Advise

Example 1

Allen obtains his homeowners coverage through Maria, a producer recommended by a friend of his. He wants to save money on his insurance premiums. The homeowners policy Maria obtains for Allen excludes watercraft liability. Maria was aware through casual conversation at the time of Allen's visit to her agency that Allen did not own any watercraft at that time and they did not specifically discuss watercraft coverage in the homeowners policy.

Allen does not read the insurance policy when he receives it. He later purchases a watercraft. Because Allen knows that his friend's homeowners policy, obtained through Maria, covers watercraft, he assumes that his policy also provides this coverage. Allen meets with Maria again at the time of policy renewal, but he does not mention his purchase of the watercraft. She does not ask about watercraft, nor does the topic come up during their casual conversation on this occasion. Shortly after the policy renewal, Allen sustains a loss to his watercraft and then discovers that it is excluded from coverage in his policy.

Did Maria breach a duty to advise Allen about coverage for his watercraft?

Maria did not breach a duty to advise Allen about coverage for his watercraft. Allen did not request from Maria, nor did she provide, expert advice on loss exposures and coverage options. At the time Allen first met with Maria to obtain a homeowners policy, Maria had knowledge that Allen did not own any watercraft and also that he wanted to save money on his insurance premiums. Allen did not advise Maria at the time of purchase or at the time of policy renewal that he had acquired a watercraft. Maria did not owe Allen a duty to inquire about additional loss exposures.

Example 2

A maritime construction company has a long association with a producer, a large commercial insurance brokerage that has expertise in maritime insurance. The company consults with the brokerage about buying a specific type of maritime insurance policy. The broker gathers extensive information about the customer's business to find the appropriate coverage. The customer leaves policy details to the broker to negotiate with the insurer.

The broker negotiates a maritime construction insurance contract that omits key language that would have provided the customer with coverage for "stand-down time," which includes costs for mobilized workers and equipment that must remain idle when a loss occurs. The insured sustains a covered loss but receives no compensation for "stand-down time."

Did the broker breach the duty to advise this customer?

The broker did breach the duty to advise the maritime construction company. Because of their special relationship and the broker's expertise, the broker owed the customer the duty to advise. The brokerage is not merely an order-taker and order-placer because of these criteria:

- Specialized line of insurance requiring unique knowledge
- Producer's specific knowledge about the customer's business and insurance needs
- Customer's clear reliance on the producer's expertise in a highly specialized field
- Customer's ceding of responsibility to the producer to negotiate an insurance contract
- Long-standing relationship between the customer and producer

responsibility caused the damage to the customer. These are the five defenses available to the producer:

- The producer assumed no duty to the customer.
- The producer did not breach a duty to the customer.
- The insurance customer was partly at fault.
- The insurance customer failed to read the policy.
- Insurance was not available to the customer.

Producer Assumed No Duty to Customer

An insurance customer cannot force a producer to act on the customer's behalf. An agreement forms the basis of the producer-customer relationship, and the producer generally owes only duties that have been expressly or implicitly assumed. Therefore, a producer who has not agreed to obtain insurance for the client is not liable for breach of any duty to the client. When a customer alleges breach of the duty to maintain coverage, the producer who said or implied that the customer's insurance would be kept in force may have a valid defense if there was no agreement regarding the producer's responsibility. In cases alleging a breach of the duty to advise, the producer can defend the allegations on the basis that no special or expanded relationship ever existed between the producer and the customer and, therefore, the producer did not expressly or implicitly assume an obligation to advise the customer on insurance coverage matters.

Frequently, the outcome of cases against producers turns on what, if anything, the producer promised to do for the insurance customer. Any conversations between the parties and any supporting documents are important in establishing this defense. It is necessary for producers to retain good written documentation of transactions with their insurance customers.

Producer Did Not Breach Duty to Customer

If a customer can show that a producer agreed to do something, the next question is whether the producer carried out the agreement. If so, the producer has discharged the duty to the customer, has not breached the assumed duty, and is not liable to the customer.

The producer who has followed clear instructions fully and completely or followed ambiguous instructions according to a reasonable interpretation of their meaning is not liable to the insurance customer. When allegations of failure to procure insurance arise, the producer has a valid defense if he or she acted reasonably and promptly on the customer's behalf and kept the customer informed about the progress toward obtaining the requested insurance coverage.

In a claim for failure to advise the insurance customer appropriately, the producer's defense would be to show that the advice provided was reasonable and appropriate, even if not perfect. The producer need not anticipate all possible contingencies or give perfect advice on insurance matters. Producers comply with the duty to advise their customers when they provide the advice that a reasonable producer would give under the circumstances.

Insurance Customer Was Partly at Fault

Although insurance customers can generally rely on the producer's knowledge, care, and skill, they must also act reasonably regarding the insurance transaction. If the injury or loss to the customer occurred through the customer's fault in whole or in part, the producer can offer this conduct in defense to the customer's claim.

Depending on the degree of the customer's fault, a court might reduce the claim against the producer either wholly or proportionately. For example, in a claim for an alleged breach of duty to procure insurance, the producer might offer the defense that the customer failed to cooperate in furnishing information that prospective insurers required.

In a claim for failure to advise an insurance customer appropriately, the producer might show that the customer did not present all of the facts necessary to allow the producer to give full and appropriate advice. For example, if a customer omitted essential details concerning a business operation in applying for broad, multi-peril coverage, the producer might not have had sufficient information to assess the various risks the exposure presented. If an uninsured loss occurs later and the customer sues, the producer can defend the lawsuit by showing that the customer's failure to provide essential information resulted in the lack of coverage.

In a claim for breach of duty to follow instructions, the insurance customer could be at fault because of vague, misleading, or erroneous instructions. A customer's inadequate instructions can defeat a claim or can result in reduced damages in proportion to the customer's own fault.

Insurance Customer Failed to Read Policy

Historically, a producer could defend a lawsuit successfully because an insured failed to read the policy. The insured's behavior was measured against what a reasonable insured would do, and courts considered the insured's reasonable conduct to be, at minimum, to read the insurance policy and verify the coverages requested. The rule was that an insurance customer's claim against a producer would fail if an examination of the insurance policy would have revealed the absence of coverage or a term or condition that defeated coverage.

The strict application of this rule has eroded. Some states do not recognize the rule at all, reasoning that the insurance customer has the right to rely on the producer's expertise in insurance matters. These courts also recognize that many insureds do not read their insurance policies and that policy language is often difficult for customers to understand. In these states, the producer cannot use the defense that the customer could have discovered the lack of coverage by examining the policy and then could have taken steps to secure coverage.

Courts that recognize the traditional rule have developed exceptions. A producer who has intentionally misrepresented policy provisions or coverage cannot use the defense because the producer's fault is greater than the simple negligent conduct of the insurance customer. Additionally, some courts, either implicitly or explicitly, recognize this defense only when an examination of the policy reveals that exclusions, limitations, or conditions are clear without extensive analysis or interpretation. This line of reasoning requires only a reasonable examination of the policy, not an expert examination.

Insurance Was Not Available to the Customer

In most states, if a producer wrongfully fails to obtain insurance that actually is unavailable, the defense of "insurance not available" has been successful. The underlying concept is causation: if the producer cannot obtain insurance, the producer's alleged failure to act appropriately is not the true cause of the loss.

That the insurance was difficult to locate or would have required a great deal of effort to obtain is not a defense. That the insurance desired was more expensive than anticipated or was otherwise available on less favorable terms would also not likely constitute an adequate defense of unavailability. In these circumstances, the producer must locate the insurance and advise the customer of its terms and price. Unavailability would be a defense, however, if the customer clearly specified that certain terms or a price limit were necessary in the desired policy, and no insurance was available within these limits.

Some jurisdictions have declined to recognize the defense of unavailability of insurance. They reason that the producer still has a duty to act appropriately and diligently on a customer's behalf and must advise the customer promptly that coverage is not available. The customer then can assess options and plan to manage loss exposures through other means.

Producers' Duties and Liabilities to Third Parties

Under general contract law principles, the parties to an agreement owe duties and obligations to each other, but not to third parties who might come in contact with either of them.

The principal and agent relationship is based on consent, whether express or implied. The producer-insurance customer relationship is one of principal and agent. Accordingly, third parties generally acquire no rights under this relationship. The breach of any duty a producer owes to a customer does not create any rights in third parties. A third party who intends to sue an insurance customer (typically in tort) cannot sue a producer who wrongfully failed to assist the customer in obtaining insurance coverage for the event that is the subject of the suit. See the exhibit "Example: Third-Party Suit Against Producer."

Example: Third-Party Suit Against Producer

Joe, owner of a moving company, obtains his business and personal insurance through Insurance Agency. Recently, he met with Darla, an Insurance Agency broker, to review his business insurance. Joe advised Darla that he will soon acquire two new trucks, and as of July 30 of this year he will need full liability coverage on these trucks. Additionally, Joe said that he needs coverage for any damage to his customers' property while in the custody of his company, regardless of whether any member of his company is at fault. Darla said that she will obtain this coverage.

Darla does not obtain the liability coverage that Joe requested. Later, one of Joe's new trucks is involved in a serious accident, destroying the household property of his customer, Pete. Pete had no insurance for this property. He relied on Joe's insurance during the move.

As the insurance customer, Joe would have an action against Darla for failure to follow instructions and for failure to procure insurance. However, any lawsuit Pete files against Darla probably would not be successful. Pete was not a party to Joe's and Darla's producer-customer relationship and therefore acquired no rights under their contract.

[DA04668]

Many courts have held that the producer owes a duty to act competently and appropriately only to the producer's principal and not to any third party. That a third party could have collected from the customer had the producer discharged all duties appropriately and arranged for insurance coverage, but now cannot collect, usually does not give the third party any rights against the producer.

Some courts, however, have recognized a third-party right to sue an insurance customer's producer under certain circumstances. Generally, these cases concern automobile or workers compensation insurance and are based on the contractual principle of third-party beneficiary rights. In some cases, the importance of drivers' liability insurance as a source of compensation for other drivers has resulted in conferring third-party beneficiary status on any driver who suffers loss from another driver's conduct. In other cases, injured drivers can sue negligent drivers' insurance producers if the negligent driver lacked liability insurance because of the producer's breach of a duty.

In workers compensation or employer's liability cases, some courts have allowed third parties, such as injured workers or their families, to sue the producers who provided the employer's insurance for failure to discharge a duty regarding insurance coverage. Courts have recognized this third-party right to sue because of the importance of injured workers receiving compensation and because workers are the intended beneficiaries of workers compensation or employer's liability insurance.

Producers' Duties and Liability to Insurer

In addition to the duties owed to the insurance customer, producers authorized to act on behalf of insurer principals must abide by a certain standard of conduct toward them. In many insurance transactions, a producer must represent both the insurer and the customer. Producers must, therefore, deal with insurers with care, skill, diligence, and loyalty. Breaches of duty to the insurer may make the producer liable for any resulting consequences.

The producer has four duties to the insurer:

* Duty to disclose risks
* Duty to follow instructions
* Duties of loyalty and accounting
* Duty to transmit information properly

Duty to Disclose Risks

The producer's first duty to the insurer is the duty to disclose risks. In most cases, producers are the "eyes and ears" of the insurers they represent. They have the first contact with prospective insureds and at times know them personally. Frequently, the producer is directly involved in the underwriting process and might, in some cases, be responsible for obtaining all of the information upon which the underwriting decisions are based.

Accordingly, producers owe a duty to their insurer principals to fully disclose any information material to the underwriting decision. Material information is that which would affect the decision about whether to issue an insurance policy covering the risk or that would affect the coverage, terms, or premium.

An insurance producer who fails to fully disclose all matters concerning the risks and hazards of a prospective insured is liable to the insurer for damages resulting from the lack of full disclosure. If the insurer establishes that it would not have issued the policy had it received the appropriate information, the producer is liable to the insurer for the amount of the loss the insurer must pay to the insured. For example, having noticed conditions on premises to be insured that place the property below the insurer's underwriting standards, the producer must advise the insurer of this or bear the consequences of any loss that the insurer would not have covered had it known the facts. Similarly, a binder would not be appropriate if the producer knew that a building was below the applicable underwriting standards. The producer owes a continuing duty to protect the insurer and cannot let coverage take effect if it is based on false or inaccurate information.

If the insurer would have issued the policy but with a higher premium, the producer would be liable to the insurer for the difference in the premium. The producer is not strictly responsible for information not known. For example, producers in some lines of insurance assist in obtaining completed applications and do not become further involved in the underwriting process. These producers must truthfully and accurately note the information they receive from the insurance customer.

However, absent specific agreements with their insurer principals, producers need not investigate the accuracy of the information they receive. If, by agreement, the producer assumes certain duties in the underwriting process, such as inspection of premises or examination of books and records, the producer must discharge these duties and must disclose any information material to the underwriting decision. The failure to disclose immaterial information probably would not subject the insurance producer to liability.

Duty to Follow Instructions

The producer owes the insurer the duty to follow instructions, which essentially mirrors the duty to follow the insurance customer's instructions. Producers must follow insurers' general statements of authority or specific directions. A producer who exceeds the authority given or who fails to comply with specific directions is liable to the insurer for resulting damages. For example, a producer who fails to disclose factors that could preclude underwriting a policy could be liable to the insurer for losses resulting from the nondisclosed information. See the exhibit "Example: Producer's Liability to Insurer."

Example: Producer's Liability to Insurer

Martha is an insurance agent associated with InsurCo. Formerly, InsurCo gave Martha express binding authority regarding certain specified types of small commercial exposures. InsurCo has provided Martha with appropriate binder and application forms, as well as rating manuals and policy forms. For the last five years, she has issued binders for these types of exposures.

Recently, InsurCo underwriters have noted increasing losses in Martha's commercial book of business. InsurCo's underwriting manager decides that a full review of Martha's accounts is necessary and withdraws Martha's binding authority for commercial business pending the outcome of the review.

After Martha receives notice of the withdrawal of her authority from InsurCo, she meets with Paul to discuss insurance for his small business. This exposure falls within the category of those for which Martha could formerly bind coverage. Martha believes that InsurCo would accept this risk. Despite the absence of actual authority, she binds coverage for Paul. Three days later, during the binder term, Paul sustains a loss.

Would InsurCo be required to cover this loss?

InsurCo must cover the loss. Although Martha did not have actual authority to issue the binder, she had apparent authority to do so.

Would Martha be liable to InsurCo for the cost of Paul's loss?

Martha would be liable to InsurCo for breach of the express direction not to bind any commercial insurance coverage.

[DA04670]

Cases involving breach of the duty to follow instructions arise in two areas. The first is in the improper use of binding authority. By agreement between the parties, insurers frequently grant producers the authority to bind coverage on the insurer's behalf, typically under a detailed statement outlining the circumstances under which the insurer can be bound. The doctrine of apparent authority can sometimes result in a producer binding an insurer to cover certain risks beyond those authorized. If a producer binds coverage contrary to explicit insurer instructions, the insurer must provide coverage but can sue the producer for the amount of the loss.

A second common situation involving breach of duty to follow instructions relates to an insurer's specific instructions to cancel, reduce, or otherwise limit coverage. A producer who has been instructed to cancel a certain policy and fails to do so is liable for the full amount of a loss that the insurer must cover. A producer who has failed to limit coverage as instructed is responsible for the difference between the coverage the insurer had to provide and the amount it would have paid had the producer followed its instructions.

A producer may have a defense against a lawsuit for failure to follow instructions if not given reasonable time to comply with the instructions, or if insurers' instructions were not clear. If the instructions were not clear, a producer who has acted according to a reasonable interpretation of the instructions would not be liable.

Duties of Loyalty and Accounting

The producer also owes the insurer loyalty and accounting. In many cases, insureds forward their premium checks to their insurance producer rather than directly to the insurer.

Under the law, payment to a producer, with actual or apparent authority, constitutes payment to the insurer. For example, an insured who brings a premium check for the amount due to the producer's office one hour before coverage is to lapse is covered for a subsequent loss, whether or not the premium check ever reaches the insurer.

The producer must receive and process premium payments on the insurer's behalf and transmit them to the insurer promptly. The producer also must keep accurate records of premiums received and verify receipt of correct compensation for coverage in force. A producer who causes any loss to an insurer because of failure to account appropriately is liable to the insurer for the financial consequences of the loss.

Duty to Transmit Information Properly

The producer has the duty to transmit information properly to the insurer. As discussed previously, producers must provide insurers with material information. One type of material information is a report of the facts surrounding a loss involving an insured. When an insurance agent receives notice of a covered loss, typically in a report completed by the insured, it must be forwarded promptly to the insurer. A producer is liable to the insurer only if failure to forward such records results in adverse consequences or harm to the insurer. For example, a producer receives a report of an insured's loss shortly after it occurs but waits six months before advising the insurer of the loss. If the six months' delay has not prejudiced the insurer's ability to investigate and resolve any claims resulting from the loss, the insurer has no cause of action against the producer.

In some instances, the producer's failure to transmit important information promptly does cause loss to the insurer. For example, an insured who is being sued sends notice of the suit to the insurance producer for forwarding to the claims department of the insurer. Typically, an insured's answer to a complaint is due at the court within a specified period. If the insurer fails to appear in court or to answer a pleading on behalf of the insured, the result is a default judgment against the insured. That is, the insured automatically loses the lawsuit, and the insurer is liable to the insured for the consequences of this judgment. In this case, the insurer can sue the producer for failure to transmit notice of a lawsuit promptly.

The producer is liable to the insurer for any money the insurer had to pay in resolving the liability claim over the amount it would have had to pay had it received prompt notification of the loss. The producer might be liable for the entire loss if the insurer had a valid defense to the insured's liability that was not asserted because of lack of notice.

SUMMARY

Insurance producers place business with insurers. Producers include agents, who typically represent insurers, and brokers, who typically represent insureds. Agents can be general, special, or soliciting agents. Brokers may provide consulting services in addition to assisting clients in obtaining insurance coverage.

Producers may have actual authority, express or implied, that an insurer intentionally confers or allows the producer to believe has been conferred. Producers may also have apparent authority when there is the appearance to a third party that an insurer has granted authority to a producer.

The extent of a producer's authority depends on four major factors. The first factor is the producer's status. General agents have the broadest authority of all insurance agents. Special and soliciting agents have more limited authority. Brokers represent insureds and usually have neither actual nor apparent authority to bind insurers. The second factor is the producer's knowledge and notice. The third factor is the producer's authority to bind coverage. The fourth factor concerns the producer's appointment of subagent.

Usually the contract specifies the circumstances for termination of the producer/insurer relationship. The agency relationship can also terminate by express communication from one of the parties or, occasionally, by other means. It is important for insurers to take steps to avoid a producer operating with apparent authority after the termination of an agency relationship.

Insurance producers have duties to their customers; to insurers; and, in certain circumstances, to third parties. Breach of these duties can result in liability. However, the law, in addition to requiring producers to meet certain requirements and standards, also provides defenses to producers against allegations of breach of duty.

Direct Your Learning ▶▶

Employment Law and Business Entities

Educational Objectives

After learning the content of this assignment, you should be able to:

▷ Describe the employment-at-will doctrine and its exceptions.

▷ Summarize the laws prohibiting discrimination on the basis of each of the following:

- Age
- Sex, race, color, religion, or national origin
- Disability
- Other factors

▷ Summarize the laws governing labor-management relations in terms of the following:

- Collective-bargaining relationships
- Collective-bargaining process
- Economic pressures

▷ Summarize the laws that protect employees' rights in the following areas:

- Employee safety and health
- Employee wages and hours
- Family medical leave
- Employee benefits
- Employee privacy

▷ When contemplating incorporation, explain how each of the following would factor into the decision:

- Advantages of incorporation
- Federal and state regulation of corporations

Outline

Employment at Will

Antidiscrimination Laws

Labor-Management Relations

Employee Welfare Laws

Corporations: Formation

Corporations: Duties and Obligations

Corporations: Mergers, Dissolution, and Reorganization

Partnerships

Unincorporated Associations

Summary

9

- Foreign corporations
- Incorporation process
- Corporate ownership

▸ Explain the rights, duties, powers, obligations, and liabilities of a corporation and the corporation's directors, officers, and stockholders.

▸ Describe the procedures by which corporate existence can terminate through merger, dissolution, and reorganization.

▸ Describe the characteristics, purposes, and functions of the following:

- Partnerships
- Limited partnerships
- Limited liability partnerships
- Limited liability companies

▸ Describe the characteristics, purpose, and functions of unincorporated associations.

Employment Law and Business Entities

EMPLOYMENT AT WILL

A basic understanding of employment law is important for any insurance professional. An insured's compliance with employment laws and regulations may be a consideration for underwriters, claim adjusters, producers, risk control representatives, and premium auditors.

Laws involving employer-employee relations are complex and vary by state. The employer-employee relationship in every state is rooted in a legal doctrine known as employment at will. However, statutory changes, at both the state and federal levels, and court decisions have created a web of exceptions to the doctrine. There are four types of exceptions to the employment-at-will doctrine:

- Public policy exception
- Implied-contract exception
- Covenant-of-good-faith exception
- Statutory exception

Employment-at-Will Doctrine

Under the traditional common law doctrine of employment at will, in the absence of an express contract or union collective bargaining agreement stating otherwise, an employer is free to terminate any employee at any time, for any reason or for no reason at all.

The employment-at-will doctrine stems from the philosophy that employees and employers are on equal footing and should be free to enter into and terminate employment relationships as they choose. Beginning with the industrial revolution, however, this philosophy began to change, and a number of exceptions to the employment-at-will doctrine arose through court decisions or statutory change. The employment-at-will doctrine continues to form the basis of employment law in every state and the District of Columbia except Montana, where it was substantially modified by statute. Today every state recognizes statutory exceptions to the employment-at-will doctrine, and nearly every state recognizes one or more of the other exceptions.

Public Policy Exception

Wrongful discharge

A cause of action an employee may have against an employer for illegal termination of employment.

Under the public policy exception, an employee may not be fired for reasons that violate established public policy of the state. For example, an employee may claim **wrongful discharge** if the employee is fired because of refusal to participate in an illegal act at the request of the employer. Violation of a law is clearly contrary to public policy. When an employee is fired contrary to established public policy, the employee may bring suit based on wrongful discharge, a cause of action for illegal termination of employment.

However, whether an action violates public policy may not always be clear and is a matter for the court to decide. The employee also bears the burden of proving that the termination was in retaliation for refusal to perform an action deemed contrary to public policy. The public policy exception to the employment-at-will doctrine is the most widely accepted exception, recognized by nearly every state. See the exhibit "Examples of Public Policy Exceptions."

Examples of Public Policy Exceptions

In a state that recognizes public policy exceptions to the employment-at-will doctrine, an employee may have a cause of action for wrongful discharge if the employee can prove that he or she was fired for a reason contrary to public policy. These are examples of grounds for firing that fall under the public policy exception:

- Refusing to commit perjury at the request of the employer
- Filing a workers compensation claim after being injured on the job
- Applying for medical leave specifically provided under state or federal law
- Refusing to participate in illegal price-fixing
- Refusing to violate another employee's or a customer's privacy without permission

---

[DA06180]

Implied-Contract Exception

Breach of contract claims may arise when a party to a contract alleges that another party has failed to fulfill a contractual promise. Under an express contract, the terms and intentions of the employment relationship are explicitly stated, resulting in a relatively clear determination as to whether a breach of contract has occurred. Breach of contract claims may also involve implied contracts.

An implied contract may exist if the terms and intentions of employment are indicated by the actions of the parties to the contract and the surrounding circumstances, rather than expressly written. For example, an employee handbook or supervisor's statement that an employee could be fired only for "just cause" might be interpreted as an implied contract that prohibits termination without cause. The majority of states recognize the implied-contract exception.

Covenant-of-Good-Faith Exception

Some courts have recognized the covenant-of-good-faith exception, also called the implied-in-law contract exception, to mean that an obligation exists due to the conduct of the parties or some special relationship between them. Even in the absence of an actual contract, an employer could be found to have acted in bad faith for firing an employee without just cause. For example, an employer might be found to have acted in bad faith for firing a long-term employee, without just cause, just before that employee becomes eligible for retirement benefits.

The covenant-of-good-faith exception creates a very broad exception to the employment-at-will doctrine, essentially interpreting a requirement of good faith as part of the employee-employer relationship. This type of exception is not as widely recognized by the states as the other types of exceptions.

Statutory Exception

Beginning in the mid-twentieth century, Congress and the states began to enact laws and adopt regulations specifically intended to protect employees and to define and prohibit certain discriminatory practices. Such statutes and regulations, which prohibit firing employees due to stated reasons, provide specific and generally clear exceptions to the employment-at-will doctrine.

An employee who believes he or she has been fired contrary to the applicable state's law or recognized exceptions to the employment-at-will doctrine may have a cause of action against an employer.

Various court cases in the **common-law system** expand or add exceptions to employment at will. Unless specific administrative procedures are established by a statutory exception, the remedy for employees who believe they have been wrongfully discharged is by legal action through the courts. Employees may also claim damages for other issues stemming from termination of employment, such as defamation.

Common-law system
A legal system in which the body of law is derived more from court decisions as opposed to statutes or constitutions.

ANTIDISCRIMINATION LAWS

Laws prohibiting discrimination in employment affect all aspects of the employee-employer relationship, from the application process through termination. By expressly prohibiting termination of employees on specific grounds, these laws define major exceptions to the employment-at-will doctrine.

Employment at will

A legal doctrine under which an employer may terminate any employee at any time for any reason or for no reason.

Antidiscrimination laws represent exceptions to the doctrine of **employment at will**. Congress has enacted laws that prohibit an employer from intentionally treating individuals differently solely because of several characteristics:

- Age
- Sex, race, color, religion, or national origin
- Disability
- Other factors (military service, jury duty, wage garnishment)

Every individual legally employed in the United States today falls under the protection of one or more federal antidiscrimination laws.

Discrimination Based on Age

Two federal laws protect workers from age discrimination: The Age Discrimination in Employment Act (ADEA) of 1967[1] and the Older Workers Benefit Protection Act (OWBPA) of 1990.[2]

Age Discrimination in Employment Act (ADEA)

The ADEA prohibits discrimination, on the basis of age, against persons age forty or older. This prohibition extends to all aspects of employment, including hiring; pay; terms, conditions, and privileges of employment; and termination. The Act applies to employers with twenty or more employees in an industry affecting interstate commerce, as well as to labor organizations, employment agencies, and governmental agencies.

ADEA addresses three legal employment practices regarding age:

Bona fide occupational qualification (BFOQ)

The minimum qualification, under federal antidiscrimination laws, that an employee needs in order to be able to perform the duties of a particular job.

- An employer may establish an age limit on employment if age is a **bona fide occupational qualification (BFOQ)**. An example of a BFOQ is a mandatory retirement age for commercial airline pilots established for safety reasons.

- An employer may use preference in hiring, promoting, and paying employees if it is based on "reasonable factors other than age." For example, an employer might determine that a particularly strenuous job requires a high degree of fitness; however, the employer may not assume that everyone over a certain age is physically unfit to handle the job.

- An employer may hire, promote, pay, or dismiss employees according to a bona fide seniority system as long as the employer does not require retirement based on age.

The ADEA prohibits mandatory retirement based on age with the exception of two types of employees:

- Executives in high policy-making positions who are over age sixty-five and entitled to a pension exceeding a minimum amount per year

- Employees over age seventy who are serving under contracts of unlimited tenure at institutions of higher learning

The ADEA is administered by the Equal Employment Opportunity Commission (EEOC). A person alleging age discrimination must file a complaint with the EEOC, or the appropriate state agency, and exhaust an administrative process that usually takes at least six months (unless a compromise is reached) before filing suit. The complainant may be eligible for remedies including back pay, reinstatement of employment, and legal damages.

Older Workers Benefit Protection Act (OWBPA)

The OWBPA, enacted in 1990, amended the ADEA. Congress specifically intended this act to prohibit age discrimination in the offering of benefits, but to allow employers to reduce benefits to older workers when such "age-based reductions in employee benefit plans are justified by significant cost considerations." For the most part, benefits offered must be the same for employees of all ages. However, where the cost of the benefit is much higher for older employees (for example, for life insurance), the employer may meet the requirements of the OWBPA by spending the same amount for the benefit among all groups, even though the older employees may receive lesser benefits than younger employees. In some cases, employers may also offer lesser benefits to older workers if additional benefits, including those offered by the government, make up the shortfall.

The OWBPA also allows waivers of rights under the ADEA if done knowingly and voluntarily. Employers may choose to provide severance payments to discharged employees only if the employee agrees to a general release of all claims against the employer. The employee must be given at least twenty-one days to consider such an agreement (or forty-five days in the case of an exit incentive program), advised to consult with an attorney prior to signing, and given at least seven days after signing in which to revoke the agreement.

Discrimination Based on Sex, Race, Color, Religion, or National Origin

Congress has passed several laws prohibiting discrimination based on sex, race, color, religion, or national origin. Because the laws differ in protection provided and remedies available, an individual alleging discrimination may choose to bring suit under the law that is most favorable to his or her case.

Civil Rights Acts of 1866 and 1871

The first law prohibiting discriminatory practices in employment was the Civil Rights Act of 1866,[3] more commonly called Section 1981. Congress passed this act shortly after the Civil War for the purpose of giving "all people within United States jurisdiction the same rights as white citizens" (in the wording of the act). While the law originally addressed only the right to make contracts, the courts interpreted the law to apply to all aspects of employment. The Supreme Court later interpreted Section 1981 to protect not only African-Americans, but all identifiable classes of persons who might be subject to intentional discrimination solely due to ancestry or ethnic characteristics. Section 1981 does not apply to discrimination based on sex or religion. The Civil Rights Act of 1866 allows for recovery of compensatory and punitive damages in a potentially unlimited amount.

The Civil Rights Act of 1871[4] did not create any new classes of protected individuals; instead it established the right to bring suit for monetary damages for a violation of civil rights by individuals acting under state or federal authority. The law is very rarely applied to private employers.

Civil Rights Act of 1964

The next major antidiscrimination act was the Civil Rights Act of 1964,[5] amended in 1991, that extended the basis for protection against discrimination to include religion and sex. Title VII of the Act, titled "Equal Employment Opportunity," governs most employment discrimination actions, including these:

- Prohibited employment practices
- Permissible employment practices
- Pregnancy discrimination
- Sexual discrimination
- Sex-based insurance rates

Title VII applies to any employer that regularly employs fifteen or more persons in an industry that affects interstate commerce—most employers in the U.S. Even a small store with sixteen employees can affect interstate commerce when, for example, an out-of-state customer purchases an item. The law also applies to labor organizations and employment agencies. Title VII does not apply to the U.S. government or to any corporation wholly owned by the U.S. It does not apply to any religious group regarding employment of individuals of a particular religion to perform work connected with the group's activities, including educational institutions associated with it. It also does not apply to bona fide not-for-profit private-membership organizations, other than labor organizations.

Although the Act permits exceptions based on BFOQ, such exceptions are very narrowly construed and difficult to prove. To defend a BFOQ exception, an employer must prove that an employment practice is directly based on a business necessity and that no less-restrictive alternative is available. Race or color is almost never considered a BFOQ.

The EEOC oversees compliance with Title VII. If a settlement is not reached within 180 days after a complaint has been filed with the EEOC (within the specified time limit for filing), the EEOC must issue a right-to-sue letter to the complainant, who may then bring suit within 90 days of receiving the letter.

Because Title VII does not preempt state law, many states have expanded the list of protected classes. Common additions prohibit discrimination on the basis of political affiliation, sexual preference, and physical characteristics such as weight.

A case of employment discrimination under Title VII may be based on either the **disparate treatment theory** or the **disparate impact theory**. See the exhibit "Employment Discrimination Legal Theories."

Disparate impact theory

A legal basis for an employment discrimination complaint requiring the plaintiff to establish that an apparently neutral employment practice or criterion, applied equally to all individuals, operated to exclude a disproportionate number of the protected class.

Disparate treatment theory

A legal basis for an employment discrimination complaint requiring the plaintiff to establish the employer's practice of intentionally treating individuals differently solely because of their sex, race, color, religion, or national origin.

Employment Discrimination Legal Theories

Disparate Treatment Theory

The disparate treatment theory requires the plaintiff to establish that the employer intended to unlawfully discriminate. An employment decision motivated in part by discrimination is also unlawful, even if other factors also motivated the decision (a "mixed motive" case). However, if the employer can show that the same decision would have been made without the discriminatory motivating factor, the court's judgment is limited to declaring the parties' rights, attorney fees, and costs to the plaintiff, and damages cannot be awarded.

Disparate Impact Theory

Under the disparate impact theory, the employer's intent is not an issue. The 1991 Civil Rights Act altered the litigants' respective burdens of proof in disparate impact cases. The act permits a plaintiff to challenge the disparate impact of the employer's entire decision-making process as one employment practice and places the burden to persuade a judge or jury on the employer to show that the challenged practice is job related and consistent with business necessity. Before the 1991 act, the plaintiff had to show specifically what practice of the employer led to the disparate impact and also had to prove that the employer did not have a legitimate business reason for the practice.

[DA06219]

Quid pro quo sexual harassment

A practice whereby an employer demands or expects sexual favors in exchange for continued employment, workplace advancement, or other job-related benefits.

Hostile work environment

An environment that exists when an employee is subjected to harassment that is so severe or pervasive that it alters the conditions of his or her employment and creates an abusive working environment.

The EEOC recognizes sexual harassment as a form of sex discrimination and, in 1980, developed rules to address claims of sexual harassment under Title VII. The EEOC defines sexual harassment as any unwelcome sexual advances, requests for sexual favors, or other verbal or physical conduct of a sexual nature when submission or rejection of such conduct would affect employment or the work environment. The two basic types of sexual harassment claims that have emerged under title VII are **quid pro quo sexual harassment** and **hostile work environment**. Along with civil rights remedies, a plaintiff claiming sexual harassment may also have a tort claim for such harassment under common law.

Civil Rights Act of 1991

The Civil Rights Act of 1991[6] enacted technical revisions to the following previously enacted antidiscrimination laws:

- The Civil Rights Act of 1866
- Title VII of the Civil Rights Act of 1964
- The Age Discrimination in Employment Act of 1967
- The Rehabilitation Act of 1973[7]

The 1991 Civil Rights Act included these changes:

- Broadened the scope of Section 1981 of the Civil Rights Act of 1866 to expressly apply to all aspects of the employment relationship, including hiring and termination. As a result, persons alleging unlawful intentional discrimination on the basis of race, color, ancestry, or ethnicity (but not sex or religion) can recover potentially unlimited compensatory and punitive damages.
- Amended Title VII and the Americans with Disabilities Act (ADA) to allow plaintiffs to recover compensatory and punitive damages in suits alleging intentional discrimination.
- Changed the law regarding the burden of proof placed on each litigant in disparate impact cases brought under Title VII and the ADA, making it easier for plaintiffs to prove their cases.
- Allowed for jury trials in cases in which the plaintiff seeks compensatory damages under Title VII or the ADA.

Executive Order 11246

Employers with federal government contracts are subject to the civil rights laws as well as to Executive Order 11246[8] of 1965, which also bans job discrimination on the basis of sex, race, color, religion, or national origin. The order applies to federal contractors and subcontractors who do more than $10,000 in business with the federal government in a one-year period.

Affirmative action plan
A written plan that the federal government requires of employers with federal contracts, detailing how the employer will meet hiring goals for groups the law protects from discrimination.

The Order originated both the terms "Equal Opportunity Employment" and **affirmative action plans**. It requires those with federal contracts of $50,000 or more to establish programs to affirmatively ensure nondiscrimination and to offer employment opportunities to minorities, women, and veterans. The Office of Federal Contract Compliance (OFCC) of the Labor Department oversees compliance with the Order. Penalties for noncompliance include cancellation of the federal contract and a ban on any future contracts.

Equal Pay Act

The Equal Pay Act (EPA)[9] of 1963 prohibits employers from paying lower wages to employees of one sex than it pays to those of the other sex for work requiring equal skill, effort, and responsibility and performed under similar working conditions. There are several affirmative defenses to the EPA. Wage differentials are acceptable if based on a seniority system; a merit system; a system that measures pay by quality or quantity; ability tests; or employees working in different locations, if such differences are not the result of an intention to discriminate because of sex, race, color, religion, or national origin. For example, an employer could legally base wage differentials on substantial differences in working conditions. To avoid conflict with the provisions of the Civil Rights Act of 1964, an amendment to the 1964 Act incorporated the defenses under Title VII.

Immigration Reform and Control Act of 1986

The Immigration Reform and Control Act (IRCA) of 1986[10] prohibits employers and employee-referral services from hiring, employing, or refer-ring aliens not authorized to work in the U.S. The act also bars employment discrimination based on national origin and citizenship status. Although an employer cannot legally hire a person not authorized to work in the U.S., the employer also cannot legally discriminate against aliens who have obtained appropriate authorization to work. The IRCA is enforced by the Special Counsel's Office of the Justice Department.

The IRCA requires employers to attest that they have verified the identi-ties of their employees and of their employees' right to work in the U.S. Employers can face civil penalties for record-keeping violations, even if per-sons hired are U.S. citizens.

Discrimination Based on Disability

Two significant federal laws prohibit discrimination based on disability; the Rehabilitation Act of 1973 and the American with Disabilities Act (ADA).

Rehabilitation Act of 1973

The Rehabilitation Act of 1973[11] prohibits employers with federal gov-ernment contracts exceeding $2,500 from discriminating against disabled persons who are otherwise qualified to fulfill the contract. An "otherwise qualified person" is one who can perform the essential functions of the job either unaided or with reasonable accommodations from the employer. Accommodations are considered unreasonable if they impose undue financial hardship on the employer or require a fundamental change to the nature of the job.

Employers with federal contracts that employ fifty or more individuals must also implement an affirmative action program. Compliance with the act falls under the jurisdiction of the OFCC of the Department of Labor.

Americans With Disabilities Act

The Americans with Disabilities Act[12] prohibits discrimination against qualified individuals with disabilities. The act applies to all aspects of the employment process, including job application procedures; hiring; advancement; termination; training; compensation; and other terms, conditions, and privileges of employment. The ADA applies to all employers with fifteen or more employees and engaged in a business affecting interstate commerce, governments and government agencies, employment agencies, and labor organizations. The act, passed in 1990, became effective for most businesses in 1992.

The ADA defines "disability" as "a physical or mental impairment that substantially limits one or more of the major life activities of such individual" and defines "qualified individual with a disability" as an individual who, with or without reasonable accommodation, can perform the essential functions of the job. Infectious and communicable diseases, mental illness, and drug addiction are all considered disabilities under the ADA. Some states, including California and Washington, have much broader definitions of "disability" that might require employers to accommodate a wider group of individuals.

The ADA requires employers to accommodate a disability unless doing so would impose undue hardship on the employer. Reasonable accommodations include job restructuring, modified work schedules, and equipment modification.

As provided by the 1991 Civil Rights Act amendments, plaintiffs seeking relief for intentional discrimination under the ADA may demand a jury trial and seek to recover compensatory and punitive damages. Reinstatement, back pay, and attorney fees are also remedies available to the plaintiff. An employer can avoid damages by showing that it made a good-faith effort, in consultation with the employee, to identify and make reasonable accommodations.

The Act was amended in 2008 to broaden the scope of protection in response to U.S. Supreme Court decisions that narrowed the scope and eliminated protection for many individuals whom Congress intended to protect. The amendment includes the requirement that the determination of whether an impairment substantially limits a major life activity shall be made without regard to the effects of mitigating measures, such as medication, prosthetics, or hearing aids.

Discrimination Based on Other Factors

Antidiscrimination laws protect employees in many situations. Federal law protects employees from discrimination based on factors such as military service, jury duty, and wage garnishment.

The Vietnam Era Veterans' Readjustment Assistance Act of 1974[13] prohibits employers from terminating employees because they leave employment to serve in the military and requires employers with federal contracts of $25,000 or more to implement an affirmative action plan for Vietnam-era veterans.

The Uniformed Services Employment and Reemployment Rights Act of 1994[14] (USERRA) is intended to ensure that persons who serve or have served in the Armed Forces, Reserves, National Guard, or other "uniformed services" do not experience a disadvantage in their civilian careers because of their service, are promptly reemployed in their civilian jobs upon return from active duty, and are not discriminated against in employment based on their military service.

Under the Jury Systems Improvement Act,[15] an employer may not discharge, threaten to discharge, intimidate, or coerce any employee who misses work due to jury duty.

The Consumer Credit Protection Act[16] prohibits termination due to an order of garnishment of any employee's wages.

LABOR-MANAGEMENT RELATIONS

There was a period in United States history when employees who united to demand better wages or working conditions could be tried for criminal conspiracy. Federal labor laws now protect workers by guaranteeing them the right to form associations or unions for negotiating with employers.

Labor unions are associations formed to negotiate with employers on behalf of employees, usually for wages, benefits, and better working conditions. The rise of labor unions in the U.S. can be traced back to the industrial revolution in the eighteenth and nineteenth centuries. In the 1930s, U.S. labor laws began establishing the conditions and terms for negotiations between labor unions, union members, and employers. There are three key areas of law regarding labor-management relations:

- Collective-bargaining relationships
- Collective-bargaining process
- Economic pressures

Collective-Bargaining Relationships

Collective bargaining

A process by which employees, represented collectively by a union, negotiate (bargain) with the employer on a labor contract dealing with wages, hours, and working conditions.

Collective bargaining stemmed from the belief that employees negotiating with an employer as a group were likely to have more influence than individual employees negotiating alone.

Norris-LaGuardia Act of 1932 and National Labor Relations Act (NLRA) of 1935

The first modern labor law was the Norris-LaGuardia Act of 1932.[17] Although this law did not require recognition of labor unions, it prohibited any federal district court from issuing an injunction in a labor dispute until all efforts to resolve the issue through negotiation were exhausted. The Norris-LaGuardia Act permits an injunction on a finding that unlawful acts may occur and may result in irreparable harm; however, the injunction is limited to the illegal activity. The act also prohibits employers from requiring an employee, as a condition of employment, to promise not to join a union.

The National Labor Relations Act (NLRA) of 1935[18] (also called the Wagner Act) was the first law to require recognition of labor unions and protected employees from economic retaliation based on union membership. The NLRA remains the primary law governing relations between unions, their members, and employers in the private sector. Federal government employees, agricultural workers, and employees of the airline and railroad industries are not covered under the scope of the act.

The NLRA grants employees the right to be represented by a union and to participate in collective bargaining. The NLRA is administered by the National Labor Relations Board (NLRB), created by Congress as part of the NLRA. The NLRB's purpose is twofold:

- To prevent and remedy unfair labor practices, whether conducted by labor organizations or employers
- To determine whether or not certain groups of employees desire labor organization representation, and their selection of a union, for collective-bargaining purpose

Exclusive Bargaining Agent

The NLRA rules provide that the union becomes the exclusive bargaining agent between employees and employer when a majority of employees in a "unit appropriate for such purposes" agrees to union representation. This selection process begins when the union, usually without the employer's knowledge, provides authorization cards to employees of the unit for their signature. The signed cards become, in essence, the employees' votes for representation.

In measuring the appropriateness of the unit, the NLRB considers the similarity or dissimilarity of the employees' skills, duties, working conditions, and interests. Determination of an appropriate "unit" is important to the success or failure of a unionization drive. For example, it is not sufficient to receive a majority of signatures from one department of a company if the entire company should appropriately be considered as the unit. On the other hand, one particular group of employees within a large manufacturing company (for example, electricians) may be a more appropriate unit than all employees. After employees return the authorization cards, the union has two alternatives:

- The union can make a direct request to the employer to initiate collective bargaining. If more than 50 percent of the employees have returned authorization cards agreeing to union representation, the employer frequently proceeds to collective bargaining. If the employer refuses to recognize the union, the union can file an unfair labor practice charge with the NLRB. As a defense to the charge, an employer may challenge whether the union actually represents a majority of the employees.
- The union can file a representation petition with the NLRB. The NLRB will then hold an election among the employees to certify the union as the authorized labor representative. The union must have cards signed by at least 30 percent of the employees before it can request an election.

Before an election, the employer can be expected to conduct a campaign to influence workers to reject union representation. The NLRA states that it is an unfair trade practice for employers to interfere with, restrain, or coerce employees while they exercise their rights of self-organization. It is unlawful for an employer to threaten reprisal, such as threatening to move a plant or discharge workers, or to confer benefits immediately before an election (for example, granting a pay raise or extra holidays). An employer is permitted to set forth any views, arguments, or opinions that are not threats of reprisal, intimidation, or promises of benefits.

If the employees elect union representation, the union is certified and will then proceed to collective bargaining with the employer, following mandated procedures. Once a majority of the workers vote for union representation, all workers become bound to the collective bargaining agreements negotiated by the union, including, in states where permitted, those workers who do not join the union.

Collective-Bargaining Process

The NLRA makes it an unfair labor practice for either an employer or a union to refuse to bargain collectively and imposes a duty to bargain in good faith. The law does not specify what constitutes a refusal to bargain; however, the NLRB and the courts have inferred a requirement that the representatives of both sides meet at reasonable times and confer in good faith regarding issues under negotiation. In determining whether a party has engaged in good-faith bargaining, the NLRB will first consider whether collective bargaining is mandatory by law for the issue or issues under dispute. The NLRB will then consider the totality of the actions taken, including the employer's past labor relations.

Collective bargaining is mandatory for "wages, hours and other terms of employment." Over the years, court decisions have sought to set standards to define the broad reference to mandatory issues. Any issue relating to an aspect of the relationship between the employer and employee is considered an issue requiring mandatory bargaining.[19] Issues such as vacation pay, bonuses, workload, seniority, insurance benefits, and grievance procedures are examples of mandatory issues. Refusal to engage in collective bargaining on mandatory issues is considered bad faith. See the exhibit "Examples of Bad Faith in Collective Bargaining."

Examples of Bad Faith in Collective Bargaining

- Refusal by either side to enter into negotiations on mandatory issues
- A take-it-or-leave it approach by the employer from the time of the first bargaining conference
- Participation in a lengthy series of bargaining conferences with no intention to enter into an agreement

---

[DA06211]

For those issues that are not mandatory for collective bargaining, either side may agree to collective bargaining; a refusal to do so will not constitute bad faith, and one party's request for bargaining does not require the other party to participate. Examples of subject matter for which collective bargaining is not mandatory include the right to subcontract work (unless it constitutes a departure from existing practices) and balloting procedures during labor negotiations.

The NLRA specifically prohibits bargaining over activities that are considered illegal under the act. For example, a union and an employer cannot negotiate terms of discrimination against nonunion members. Collective bargaining also may not result in any agreement that would violate other federal or state laws or regulations or that would waive obligations imposed by law. For example, a collective bargaining agreement may not eliminate rights granted to employees under antidiscrimination statutes or reduce safety protections required under law.

When the collective bargaining process results in a settlement of terms, members of the union must still accept or reject the settlement by majority vote. If a majority of employees accepts the agreement, the contract is ratified and becomes legally binding. If the majority of employees reject the settlement, the negotiation process begins again.

If the parties fail to reach an agreement, they may voluntarily agree to mediation. If an agreement still cannot be reached, the next step may be **arbitration**. Arbitration is usually agreed to voluntarily by the union and the employer; however, in rare occasions, arbitration may be mandated by the federal government.

Economic Pressure

If the union and the employer cannot agree on a contract after good-faith bargaining, each side can strengthen its position with tactics intended to exert economic pressure on the other party. The economic tactics of the union include a strike, boycott, or picketing. Employer tactics include employment of replacement workers or, under certain conditions, a lockout of employees.

Union Economic Tactics

Employees may vote to strike or cease work. The employees' right to strike, however, is not absolute. For example, sit-down strikes, in which employees seize and occupy a part of the plant, are illegal. Employees cannot be simultaneously at work and on strike; they must be either subject to the employer's authority or off the job on a total strike. Therefore, a refusal to work overtime or a work slowdown to protest a work condition are considered illegal.

Another tactic unions might use is boycott, or refusal to deal with an employer. A boycott can be either primary or secondary. A primary boycott occurs when customers or vendors are encouraged to stop doing business with the employer in support of the union's position. A boycott is often enforced by picketing as union members stand or protest outside the employer's premises.

A secondary boycott occurs when unionized employees apply a boycott against one employer to pressure that employer to stop doing business with another. Under a secondary boycott, the employees refuse to work on or with materials coming from or going to the second employer. The second employer either may be engaged in a labor dispute or may employ a nonunion workforce.

Similarly, a sympathy strike is a strike by union members, who have no grievance against their own employer, to support another union in a labor dispute. The Taft-Hartley Act of 1947[20] (also called the Labor-Management Relations Act) amended the NLRA and made both secondary boycotts and sympathy strikes illegal. The Landrum-Griffin Act of 1959[21] (also called the Labor Management Reporting and Disclosure Act) strengthened the Taft-Hartley Act by making it illegal for a union and an employer to evade the statutory prohibition against secondary boycotts by entering into an agreement under which the employer must refrain from using or transporting another employer's goods.

Arbitration

An alternative dispute resolution (ADR) method by which disputing parties use a neutral outside party to examine the issues and develop a settlement, which can be final and binding.

Employer Economic Tactics

An employer may not fire an employee for striking. However, the employer may apply economic pressure by using replacement employees. When a strike occurs because the parties have not been able to agree on labor contract terms, the employer can hire replacement employees and refuse to reinstate the striking employees. However, if the strike is wholly or partially due to unfair labor practices, the employer must reinstate all striking employees, even if doing so requires dismissing the replacements. A refusal to do so makes the employer liable for full back pay.

A lockout occurs when the employer withholds work from the employees. Generally, during bargaining negotiations, an employer cannot either lock out or threaten to lock out employees in order to gain a more favorable bargaining position. However, a lockout is permissible under certain circumstances. For example, an employer may lock out employees if the employer has reasonable grounds to believe that a strike is threatened or imminent, or if employees intend to stage a sit-down strike or to commit acts of sabotage.

EMPLOYEE WELFARE LAWS

Congress has enacted a number of laws intended to address employee welfare. Insurance professionals should be familiar with the various laws that, while protecting employees, create numerous liability exposures for employers.

The vast majority of workers today benefit from myriad laws intended to protect their safety and well-being. Employee welfare laws address several areas:

- Safety and health
- Wages and hours
- Family medical leave
- Privacy

Regulation of Employee Safety and Health

Occupational Safety and Health Act of 1970 (OSH Act)

An act passed by Congress in 1970 to ensure every employee a safe place to work by setting safety standards for employers and imposing penalties for violation of the standards.

The **Occupational Safety and Health Act of 1970 (OSH Act)** [22] is a comprehensive federal law that provides for safety and health standards in the workplace. Standards adopted under the law include specific requirements designed to protect employees against workplace hazards and cover subjects such as mandatory safety devices and equipment; training, protecting and medically examining employees; and warning of hazards. The standards also mandate how employees must do their jobs safely.

The OSH Act applies to all employers engaged in a business affecting interstate commerce, with some exceptions. The act essentially governs health and safety standards applicable to general industry, such as retail operations, offices, and factories. It does not directly apply to the United States or any state or political subdivision as an employer, but it requires federal agency heads to establish and maintain safety and health programs consistent with the standards applicable to the private sector. The act also does not cover self-employed workers, family farms, and workers in occupations covered by other federal laws (such as railroad workers). See the exhibit "Occupational Safety and Health Act General Duty Clause."

Occupational Safety and Health Act General Duty Clause

The OSH Act requires employers to comply with safety and health standards promulgated under the authority of the act covering workplace conditions and operations. Section 5 of the act, known as the general duty clause, imposes a general requirement on employers. This requirement applies to serious hazards not otherwise covered by a specific standard.

Section 5. Duties

(a) Each employer -

1. shall furnish to each of his employees employment and a place of employment which are free from recognized hazards that are causing or are likely to cause death or serious physical harm to his employees;

2. shall comply with occupational safety and health standards promulgated under this Act.

[DA06209]

Congress created the Occupational Safety and Health Administration (OSHA) to enforce the OSH Act. Under the jurisdiction of the Department of Labor, OSHA is responsible for issuing and modifying the occupational safety and health standards applicable to businesses. OSHA is also given the responsibility to conduct workplace inspections, to investigate complaints regarding working conditions, and to issue regulations requiring employers to record and report certain work-related injuries, illness, or deaths.

Under the OSH Act, a state may assume exclusive jurisdiction over the health and safety aspects of employees' working conditions by developing and enforcing programs that meet or exceed federal requirements. Before assuming jurisdiction over workplace health and safety, the state must obtain OSHA approval of its program; therefore, another responsibility of OSHA is to certify and monitor state programs.

The OSH Act is enforced through workplace inspections and investigations, typically conducted during regular working hours and without advance notice, by OSHA compliance officers. Violations of the act may result in civil and criminal penalties.

Regulation of Employee Wages and Hours

The Fair Labor Standards Act (FLSA)[23] establishes requirements relating to minimum wage, overtime compensation, child labor, and equal pay for men and women. States may also establish laws regarding wages and work hours, provided the requirements meet or exceed federal laws.

The FLSA applies to employers engaged in interstate commerce or in the production of goods for interstate commerce, broadly defined to include most employers with exceptions for very small businesses. The act also covers employees of local, state, and federal government.

Nonexempt employee
An employee who is paid by the hour and who receives hourly overtime pay.

Exempt employee
An employee who is paid a salary and who does not receive overtime pay.

The act's overtime pay and minimum wage requirements generally apply to all **nonexempt employees**. Simply because an employee is salaried and not hourly, however, does not necessarily mean that he or she is an **exempt employee** and will not fall under the overtime or wage requirements of the FLSA. Regulations issued by the Secretary of Labor[24] establish several characteristics that must apply to a particular employee's duties and specify a minimum weekly salary requirement to determine whether an employee is exempt in terms of the act's overtime requirements. Generally, the act's overtime provisions do not apply to certain job categories, including executives, administrative workers, learned or creative professionals, outside salespersons, and certain other workers as defined by the regulations.

Under the FLSA's overtime provisions, an employer must pay nonexempt employees one and one-half times (often called "time-and-a-half") the employee's basic rate for time worked in excess of forty hours per week. If the employee is at least sixteen years old, the act does not limit the number of hours or the number of days per week that an employee may be required to work or the number of overtime hours that may be required. For example, if a nonexempt employee works sixty hours one week and ten hours the next, the employer must pay time-and-a-half for twenty hours of overtime worked during the first week.

Despite regulations implementing the act, it is not always clear whether a worker falls under the act or whether a worker is subject to the law's overtime requirements. For example, whether an insurance claim representative is entitled to overtime pay has been an area of some dispute and controversy. In addition, independent contractors are not considered employees for the purpose of the act and therefore are not covered by overtime pay and minimum wage requirements; however, whether a worker is correctly classified as an independent contractor is sometimes a matter for the courts to decide.

In addition to the FLSA requirements, three other federal laws specifically address minimum wages for employees working on federally funded projects. The Davis-Bacon Act,[25] applicable to employers with federal contracts greater than $2,000, establishes the minimum rate of wages for laborers and mechanics. The Walsh-Healey Public Contracts Act[26] applies to government contracts of more than $10,000 to manufacture or supply materials and requires covered employers to pay the prevailing minimum wage, plus overtime for hours worked in excess of forty per week. The Service Contract Act of 1965[27] applicable to employers with government contracts in excess of $2,500 to furnish services, requires employers to notify employees of statutory wage rights and to pay not less than the federal minimum wage.

Family Medical Leave Act

The Family Medical Leave Act (FMLA)[28] requires employers to provide employees with unpaid leave time for circumstances covered under the act. Employers must offer eligible employees up to twelve weeks of unpaid leave in a twelve-month period, with no loss of any employment benefits accrued prior to leave. Covered absences include parental leave following a birth or an adoption; an employee's serious health condition; or a serious health condition of the employee's spouse, child, or parent. In some circumstances, the act permits employees to take intermittent leave or to work a reduced schedule. An employee is not required to invoke the term "FMLA" to receive protection under the act; employers bear the responsibility to decide whether an absence qualifies for FMLA.

The FMLA applies to employers and employees meeting very specific criteria:

- The employer has fifty or more employees (including full-time, part-time, and temporary workers) during at least twenty weeks in the current or preceding year, located within a seventy-five mile radius of the work location where the employee requests leave.
- The employee must have worked for an employer subject to FMLA requirements for at least twelve months (not necessarily consecutive) and for at least 1,250 hours during the twelve-month period preceding the leave.

Regulation of Employee Benefits

Congress has addressed protection of employee benefits through three key laws. The Employee Retirement Income Security Act (ERISA) is intended to safeguard employee pensions, while the Consolidated Omnibus Budget Reconciliation Act (COBRA) ensures that terminated employees may still have access to health insurance benefits. More recently, the Health Care and Education Reconciliation Act of 2010 places requirements on employers for the purpose of expanding the availability and affordability of healthcare coverage.

Employee Retirement Income Security Act (ERISA)

The Employee Retirement Income Security Act (ERISA)[29] of 1974 created fiduciary duties for pension and health benefit plan administrators, trustees, upper management, insurance brokers, and other parties with respect to how they invest and distribute plan funds. The act also requires plan administrators to notify participants of important information about benefit plans and their funding; and requires an appeals process for denied claims. Employers are not required to provide an employee benefit plan under ERISA. An employer's obligations under ERISA arise only when a benefit plan is in place.

The federal act replaced a maze of state laws that previously governed employee benefit plans and trusts. The act preempts all state laws relating to employee benefit plans, except state laws that regulate insurance, banking, and securities.

Consolidated Omnibus Budget Reconciliation Act (COBRA)

The Consolidated Omnibus Budget Reconciliation Act (COBRA)[30] of 1986 amends ERISA to require certain employers who sponsor group healthcare plans to offer employees and their dependents continuation of group health insurance for a period of time after a qualifying event, defined as a termination of employment for any reason other than gross misconduct, or a reduction in hours resulting in loss of coverage.

The act applies to group health insurance plans sponsored by employers that have twenty or more employees (including part-time workers) on at least fifty percent of working days during the preceding year. Plans sponsored by the federal government and religious organizations are exempt from COBRA.

Benefits under COBRA must be offered to qualified beneficiaries, meaning the employee, spouse, and dependent children, for a period of eighteen months. Benefits offered must be identical to those provided before the qualifying event; however, the employer is not required to continue any premium subsidies offered during employment. In the event of a second qualifying event during the eighteen months, such as death of the employee, the spouse or dependent children are entitled to an additional eighteen months of coverage under the group healthcare plan.

Health Care and Education Reconciliation Act of 2010

The Health Care and Education Reconciliation Act[31] of 2010 does not require employers to offer group healthcare plans, but includes financial penalties for those who do not. Effective in 2014, employers with fifty or more employees that do not offer group healthcare benefits, or do not offer "affordable" coverage, as defined by law, will be taxed "free-rider" penalties, up to $3,000 per employee annually. Also beginning in 2014, employers must provide "free choice vouchers" to certain qualified employees, allowing the employee to take the amount of the employer's contribution to healthcare coverage and apply that amount toward coverage in a state-sponsored healthcare exchange.

Employee Privacy

A number of federal laws protect specific aspects of employee privacy. Common law often provides broader protections with respect to privacy, and employees may also bring common law suits for invasion of privacy.

Privacy Statutes

Federal laws protect employee privacy regarding drug, alcohol, and polygraph testing, as well as searches and surveillance.

The Drug-Free Workplace Act[32] of 1988 requires federal contractors with contracts of $100,000 or more and all federal grantees to establish drug-prevention programs and to maintain a drug-free workplace in compliance with the act. Such employers are also required to track and report drug-related employee convictions resulting from workplace activity. Drug testing (testing employees for the presence of illegal substances) is not required under the act but is required by federal regulation for certain jobs.

Private employers are generally permitted to require drug testing in all but a few states; however, the courts have not upheld the right to do so in all cases. The Substance Abuse and Mental Health Services Administration (SAMHSA) within the U.S. Department of Health and Human Services (DHHS) established guidelines for federal workplace drug testing. Drug testing programs that follow the guidelines have been supported by the courts, and private employers are free to follow these guidelines as well.

The Employee Polygraph Protection Act[33] of 1988 prohibits most private-sector employers from requiring or even requesting employees or applicants to submit to lie detector tests, or from inquiring about or considering the results of any such test. The act provides limited exceptions to administer tests as part of an investigation into employee theft, embezzlement, or industrial espionage. The act does not cover government employees and does not prohibit the federal government from administering tests to contractors or for purposes of national defense and security.

Title III of the Omnibus Crime Control and Safe Streets Act[34] of 1968 and the Electronics Communications Privacy Act of 1986 prohibit interception of any wire or oral communication in a place of business engaged in interstate commerce. Interception of communication is permissible, however, if one of the parties to a conversation has consented to monitoring. An example is recording or monitoring a customer service representative's phone conversation in order to monitor appropriate communications with customers.

Employee background investigations present another area where privacy may be a concern. The federal Fair Credit Reporting Act (FCRA),[35] as well as numerous state federal credit reporting acts, govern permissible disclosure of background information collected by consumer reporting agencies and commonly used for employment prescreening. See the exhibit "Employee Actions."

Employee Actions

Usually Do Not Create Privacy Exposures	May Create Privacy Exposures
• Monitoring of employee e-mails	• Intrusion into employee's private affairs ("emotional sanctum")
• Monitoring of employee Internet usage	• Disclosure of private facts regarding employees
	• Potential defamation suits because of information given in employee references

[DA06210]

Health Insurance Portability and Accountability Act (HIPAA)

The Health Insurance Portability and Accountability Act[36] of 1996 (HIPAA) was enacted to improve the portability of health insurance coverage for workers in the event of job changes and unemployment. The law has had significant impact on medical record privacy and confidentiality by replacing inconsistent state laws and establishing national standards for handling and accessing medical records. Under HIPAA, healthcare providers, health plans, and other healthcare services must adhere to guidelines established by the statute. The Department of Health and Human Services (DHHS) administers the act.

The act grants all patients the right to see, copy, and request to amend their own medical records. Notice of privacy practices about how a patient's medical information is used and disclosed must be given to the patient by each medical professional or medical facility (typically by a notice given the first time the patient sees a medical professional for treatment). The notice must provide information on how to file a complaint with the healthcare provider or with the DHHS Office of Civil Rights.

Under HIPAA, healthcare providers must also account for disclosures of patients' health information, and a patient may learn the identity of those who have accessed their records for the prior six years, with exceptions.

Employers are not covered entities under HIPAA; they are defined as plan sponsors. Employers that require medical information about employees or others must protect that information, may not disclose information except as permitted by law, and must account for all disclosures. These HIPAA requirements create liability exposures for employers, as well as insurers, that have reason to obtain and possess confidential medical information.

CORPORATIONS: FORMATION

Business entities can be organized in a number of different ways. The structure of a business entity may affect every aspect of the insurance transaction, including underwriting, coverage considerations, and contractual issues.

Business entities can be organized as corporations, partnerships, sole proprietorships, or unincorporated associations. Corporations have a legal existence separate from their owners. Partnerships enable individuals to join together for a specific business purpose. Sole proprietorships allow individuals to conduct a business. Unincorporated associations allow volunteers to join together to work toward a common purpose.

Business owners may incorporate for a variety of reasons. These topics are key to understanding corporate structure:

- Advantages of incorporation
- Federal and state regulation of corporations
- Foreign corporations
- Incorporation process
- Corporate ownership

A corporation is a separate, legally recognized business entity organized under state law and entitled to the same rights as a person, distinct from its owners. A corporation can sue, be sued, own property, hire employees, and enter into contracts in its own name. As a separate legal entity, the corporation provides protection against liability to its owners. See the exhibit "Form of Organization and Insurer Considerations."

There are three main types of corporations:

1. Government corporations, such as cities, counties, and states
2. Charitable or not-for-profit corporations, such as colleges, universities, hospitals, and religious institutions
3. Business for-profit corporations

The corporation charter, also known as its articles of incorporation, defines the corporation's reason for existence and its powers. Corporate bylaws include more detail about the corporation's overall operations and determine how the organization will be managed.

Advantages of Incorporation

The primary advantage of incorporation is that it limits the owners' liability for the corporation's contracts and torts. For example, if the corporation goes bankrupt, or if a tort claim exhausts both the corporation's available insurance and assets, the owners (stockholders in a for-profit corporation) are generally not liable for any remaining debt. However, in closely held (privately owned) or family-owned corporations, loan contracts may be written to bypass

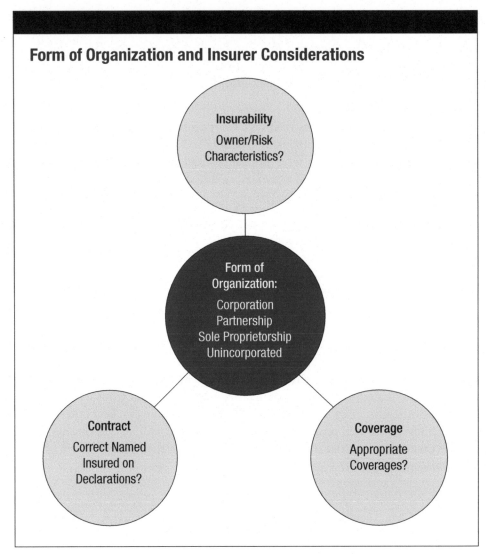

Form of Organization and Insurer Considerations

Insurability
Owner/Risk Characteristics?

Form of Organization:
Corporation
Partnership
Sole Proprietorship
Unincorporated

Contract
Correct Named Insured on Declarations?

Coverage
Appropriate Coverages?

[DA06212]

the stockholders' immunity from liability for corporate debts. Banks lending money to such corporations can demand from stockholders, as collateral, signed notes to secure the obligation with their credit, as well as with the corporation's credit.

Bypassing stockholders' immunity from tort liability is much more difficult than bypassing immunity from contractual liability. Therefore, a corporation, or even a private individual, may choose to incorporate a particularly hazardous business, or part of a business, separately to isolate loss exposures that might otherwise affect the main business.

Certain state laws may make exceptions to corporate owners' limited liability. For example, several states hold stockholders liable for employee wages and unemployment benefits earned but unpaid before a corporation's insolvency.

Courts may also make exceptions, or "**pierce the corporate veil**," for the corporation's wrongful acts. This typically occurs when a plaintiff alleges that a corporation is actually a sham—formed to advance the private interests of owners or to commit a fraud. Courts may also hold owners liable when the stockholders themselves ignore the separate identity of the corporation (for example, by commingling personal and business funds).

Finally, "thin financing" and inadequate capitalization can also defeat the limited liability of a corporation. "Thin financing" occurs when a corporation has inadequate equity capital and excessive loans. For example, investors may loan the corporation money for a start-up venture. In the event of insolvency, the loans of investors may be treated as investments rather than loans, meaning that outside creditors will have priority for repayment over the investors. Inadequate capitalization occurs when a corporation creates a subsidiary without sufficient capital to ensure success. In the event the subsidiary fails, the courts may overlook the separate identities of the parent corporation and the subsidiary, requiring the parent to respond to the subsidiary's debts.

In addition to the advantage of limited liability, other advantages are associated with incorporating, including these:

- Possible tax advantages
- Easier to sell or transfer ownership
- Easier to raise capital
- Perpetuity beyond the death of owners

Pierce the corporate veil

A court act of imposing personal liability on corporate officers, directors, and stockholders for the corporation's wrongful acts.

Federal and State Laws and Regulations

Federal law plays a large role in many corporate operations. The Commerce Clause in the United States Constitution provides Congress with the authority to regulate commerce among the states, and most corporations are involved in interstate commerce.

State law governs the formation of corporations. All states have general laws that authorize corporate formation for any lawful purpose, with the exception of certain businesses and the practice of a profession. The American Bar Association Revised Model Business Corporation Act (RMBCA) has been widely adopted by the states and is used as the reference point of this discussion. See the exhibit "Corporate Law Provisions."

General business corporation laws prohibit professionals such as doctors, lawyers, and accountants from incorporating because of the personal and confidential relationships required with their clients. However, many states have adopted specific laws to allow members of the same or associated professions to form professional corporations (PCs). In a professional corporation, the members are liable for their own malpractice, but they are not liable for the malpractice of other employees of the corporation. See the exhibit "Special Incorporation Laws."

Corporate Law Provisions

General state corporation law contains provisions about the following features and functions of a corporation:

- Formation
- Powers
- Principal office and agent
- Books
- Certificates

- Reports
- Officers
- Stock
- Dividends
- Meetings

- Elections
- Directors
- Amendments
- Mergers and consolidations
- Dissolution

[DA06213]

Special Incorporation Laws

Special incorporation laws apply to these businesses:

- Insurance
- Banking
- Railroads
- Telephone Companies
- Savings and Loans
- Not-for-Profit Corporations

[DA06214]

A corporation is a citizen of the state where it is chartered (incorporated), and that state is the corporation's domicile, or legal home. A corporation that confines its business to one state will usually find it advantageous to incorporate there. Choosing a different state might increase organizational and operational costs and taxes. For a corporation that operates in several states, the incorporators choose the state in which to incorporate. A business may choose a particular state of domicile for business reasons, often because of attractive laws regarding incorporation and taxation.

A corporation formed in one state is a foreign corporation in any other state, and a corporation chartered in another country is an alien corporation outside that country. A corporation may elect to maintain a principal place of business outside the state of domicile and may wish to do business in other states. However, a corporation is a legal entity only in the state of incorporation; no state can grant a corporation the right to operate in another state. If a corporation wants to do business in another state, it must comply with the other state's laws.

Foreign Corporations

Foreign corporations (those incorporated and domiciled in another state) must be admitted and recognized by a given state to do business in that state. For example, the RMBCA requires a foreign corporation to obtain a certificate of authority from the secretary of state before transacting business.[37]

A state can forbid or control the activities of a foreign corporation with respect to intrastate (within the state) commerce but has no jurisdiction over interstate (between the states) commerce of any corporation. Federal laws apply to activities defined as interstate commerce. Congress and federal courts have consistently broadened the definition of interstate commerce. Activities that may occur outside the state of incorporation but are not considered interstate commerce include holding stockholders' or directors' meetings; maintaining financial accounts; conducting isolated, short-term transactions; suing or being sued; and other transactions not completed for profit.

State laws governing insurance company admissions are stricter than those governing general business corporations. State laws may include requirements regarding deposits, reports, examinations, background checks on officers, and other requirements specific to insurance regulation. Out-of-state insurers generally apply to the state department of insurance rather than to the secretary of state for authority to conduct business.

States have enacted "long-arm" statutes that allow residents to sue, in their own state's courts, people or entities (including corporations) who are not physically present in the state but who have minimum contacts there. These laws provide jurisdiction to local courts over foreign (out-of-state) defendants. Long-arm statutes may apply to torts, contracts, or both.

To sue a person or business, a plaintiff must accomplish service of process—that is, physical delivery of a complaint and summons to a defendant. With respect to insurance, the majority of states have enacted the National Association of Insurance Commissioners' (NAIC's) model Unauthorized Insurers Process Act, which provides that service on a foreign insurer must be delivered to the state department of insurance.

Incorporation Process

A promoter is a person who creates a corporation. The promoter can be one or more persons, corporations, or paid organizations. For example, the promoter might be a shareholder in the organization being promoted. The promoter works to recruit interest, cooperation, and financing in forming the corporation and completes the legal and practical steps required to create the corporation.

State statute requires a minimum number of incorporators, or those who sign the formal articles of incorporation filed with the state. Most states require three incorporators, and the promoter can be, but is not required to be, one of the incorporators. Along with the articles of incorporation, states require appropriate filing fees, and some require proof of public notice via proof of publication in a newspaper or legal publication.

Under the RMBCA, a corporation's existence begins when the articles of incorporation are filed with the state.[38] In some states, however, the state issuance of the certificate of incorporation signifies corporate existence.

A corporation formed in compliance with the law is called a de jure (in law) corporation. If, however, despite a good-faith attempt to comply with the law, there was failure to meet some minor requirement, the corporation is a de facto (in fact) corporation. Only the state can legally challenge the existence of a *de facto* corporation.

If a corporation is neither *de jure* nor *de facto*, then it technically does not exist, and individuals engaged in the business and aware that the corporation does not exist can be held personally liable for the debts and contracts of the business. However, a third party that has dealt with those individuals as a valid corporation may not be able to legally deny its corporate existence.

After the certificate of incorporation is issued, the corporate organizational meeting is held. The corporate bylaws are the formal provisions for the corporation's structure, regulation, and operation. See the exhibit "Typical Corporate Bylaw Provisions."

Typical Corporate Bylaw Provisions

- Stockholders' meetings—date, place, conduct of elections, order of business
- Directors—term of office, compensation, meetings, loans, authority to elect officers
- Officers—names and functions, appointment, removal, authority to sign checks and enter contracts
- Indemnification of directors, officers, and agents of the corporation—provides for corporate reimbursement for individuals' liability
- Shares of stock—issuance, transfer, record date
- Corporate seal and officers' signatures
- Procedures for transfer or dissolution
- Future amendment of bylaws

[DA06215]

Corporate Ownership

Corporations raise funds by issuing two principal types of securities: debt securities and equity securities. A debt security, or **bond**, is a debt obligation. Equity securities are the corporation's capital stock and represent the stockholders' ownership of and equity, or financial interest, in the corporation. Bondholders are creditors of the corporation, while stockholders are owners of the corporation.

Stock

Common stock may be issued as different classes of stock, where voting rights differ according to the class. **Preferred stock** is an ownership interest that generally does not provide voting rights to the stockholder. If the corporation dissolves, preferred stockholders will receive preference in corporate assets and are entitled to the stock's **par value** (face value), plus any accrued dividends, after the corporation's debts have been paid. Stock certificates are evidence of the stockholder's interest in the corporation and are considered negotiable instruments under the Uniform Commercial Code (UCC). Thus, stockholders are subject to the rights and obligations provided under the UCC, and other federal and state laws, with respect to such instruments. See the exhibit "Stock Purchase Rights."

Stock Purchase Rights

- Stock Rights: Short-term options to purchase corporate shares. Often given to current stockholders to encourage purchase of a proportional quantity of new stock, often at less than market prices.

- Stock Warrants: Similar to stock rights, but evidenced by a negotiable instrument, typically issued with preferred stocks or bonds.

- Stock Options: Typically used to provide deferred compensation for corporate executives, they permit executives to purchase a certain number of shares at a stated price, relative to status or salary.

- Preemptive Rights: Rights, when given, of existing stockholders to purchase the portions of a new issue of stock relative to an individual stockholder's total outstanding shares of the same class of stock.

[DA06216]

Stated capital is the total amount of capital contributed by stockholders. If a stock sells for less than its par value amount stated in the articles of incorporation, the stock is said to be "watered" or "diluted," and the directors and stockholders are liable to unsatisfied creditors for the difference.

Capital surplus is the difference between the stock's purchase price and par value when stocks sell for more than par value. The difference is considered

Bond

A long-term debt instrument that requires the issuer to pay a set annual rate of interest and to repay the borrowed sum on a specified date.

Common stock

An ownership interest in a corporation that gives stockowners certain rights and privileges, such as the right to vote on important corporate matters and to receive dividends.

Preferred stock

Stock that is generally nonvoting but that has priority over common stock, usually regarding dividends and capital distribution if the corporation ends its existence.

Par value

An arbitrary dollar value that an organization assigns to its shares.

surplus for use against future liabilities. Capital surplus can be converted to stated capital by obtaining stockholder consent to amend the articles to increase the common share's par value to match the selling price.

A corporation may reacquire issued securities by repurchasing them. This reacquisition is known as redemption. The original agreements between the corporation and the purchasers of debt securities and preferred stock can include provisions to make the securities redeemable at the corporation's option, or to provide for a mandatory retirement of the security. This type of agreement allows the corporation to reshape its financial structure at will when needed. A corporation may also provide for redemption of nonvoting stock but cannot provide for the redemption of all common voting stock. A corporation can redeem stock only if its assets exceed its liabilities, including any obligations to preferred stockholders in the event of dissolution.

When a corporation with sufficient surplus buys its own shares in the market, it can either hold the stock without reissuing it or retire the shares. Stock issued as fully paid to a stockholder and subsequently reacquired, but not retired, by the corporation is called **treasury stock**. Treasury shares are considered authorized and issued, but not outstanding, and have no dividend or voting rights.

Treasury stock

A corporate stock issued as fully paid to a stockholder and subsequently reacquired by the corporation to use for business purposes.

Corporations may choose to repurchase stock for a number of reasons, including these:

- Reducing the number of issued shares may result in a stronger return on investment. If earnings are static, the earnings per share will increase with fewer outstanding shares.
- Repurchasing shares can make a corporation less attractive for a takeover. Stock repurchases can reduce accumulation of excessive cash in the corporation and increase the market value of remaining outstanding stock. Both are deterrents to a takeover.

In closely held (privately owned) or family-owned corporations, there is generally no market for trading shares. Ownership may be retained by a few persons or even one. Without the ability to trade stock, such corporations may have a more difficult time raising capital. However, closely held or family-owned corporations also have advantages. For example, they do not have to comply with securities laws and may be able to make business decisions more quickly.

Board of Directors

The corporation's board of directors makes two types of decisions: it decides the corporation's structure and form, and it determines business policy. The first requires stockholder approval, while the second does not. See the exhibit "Sarbanes-Oxley Act."

Sarbanes-Oxley Act

The 2002 Sarbanes-Oxley Act was enacted in response to a succession of corporate scandals that arose as a result of gimmickry or fraud in some companies' financial statements. The act's requirements are intended to ensure the credibility of financial requirements and include these provisions:

- Creation of the Public Company Accounting Oversight Board to establish and oversee standards for auditors of public companies

- Independence of the audit committee of a public company's board of directors

- Certification of corporate financial reports by the company's chief executive and chief financial officers

- Rapid, current, and transparent reporting

15 U.S.C. § 7241 [DA06217]

Board decisions that would change the terms of the contract between the corporation and its stockholders require stockholder approval. These are examples of such decisions:

- Amendments to the articles of incorporation, including capital structure, purpose, name, or preemptive right limitations

- Mergers or consolidation

- Dissolution of the corporation

Board decisions that do not require stockholder approval (providing they are not otherwise limited by the articles of incorporation) include these:

- Issuing stock or borrowing money

- Electing and assigning officer duties

- Declaring dividends

- Purchasing or selling property in the normal course of business

- Decisions concerning insurance coverage

- General policy decisions regarding company operations

State statutes may establish the minimum number of directors required, if a board is required at all. In some states, the articles specify the number of directors, while other states allow the articles of incorporation to state how the number will be set (for example, in the bylaws). Statutes may also specify whether directors must be stockholders or meet residency requirements.

Directors can be **inside directors** or **outside directors**. For example, an outside director might be a respected businessperson who can provide perspectives on the organization that are distinct from those of persons involved in the day-to-day operations of the business. Directors, whether inside or outside, have no legal right to act individually on behalf of the corporation and can make

Inside director

A corporate officer that serves on the corporation's board of directors.

Outside director

A member of a corporation's board of directors who is a corporate officer and who may not necessarily be connected with the corporation.

decisions only when acting together in a meeting. An exception may occur if all directors have consented in writing to a decision. Unanimous written consent has the same legal effect as a unanimous vote at a meeting.

While directors are concerned with corporate form and decisions relating to business policy, corporate officers, in turn, implement the policies determined by the board of directors. Officers of the company manage the corporation's internal affairs and deal with persons outside the organization. See the exhibit "Corporate Officers."

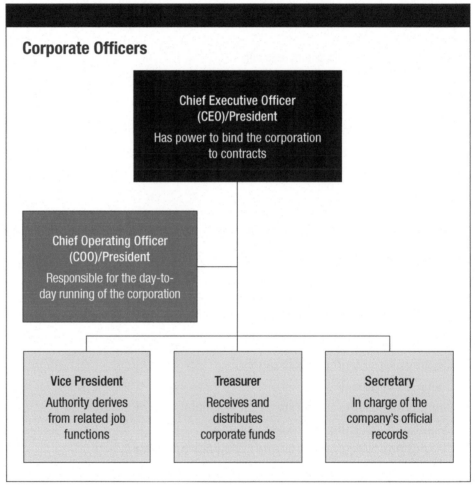

[DA06218]

CORPORATIONS: DUTIES AND OBLIGATIONS

An understanding of the various responsibilities of corporations, directors, officers, and stockholders is important to insurance professionals in assessing corporate risks.

Ownership and management of a corporation include numerous responsibilities that extend beyond business operations. Both common law and statutory or civil law address, directly or indirectly, numerous areas, including these:

- Corporate powers
- Liability for torts and crimes
- Duties of directors and officers
- Stockholders' powers and duties
- Dividends

Corporate Powers

State corporation statutes define and limit the powers of corporations. Laws require corporations to file corporate charters, also called articles of incorporation, which specify the type of business for which a corporation is being formed and the goals and objectives of the corporation. Traditionally, the charter stated the corporation's precise purpose; however, most states now permit the stated purpose to be written as "for any lawful purpose."

In addition to the powers given by law and those stated in the charter, corporations have implied powers to do all things necessary or convenient (and not in violation of law or regulation) to achieve the corporation's purpose. For example, a corporation has implied power to sue, purchase property, or invest funds. A corporation can exercise its powers, express or implied, only to further its primary purpose.

A corporation that exceeds its chartered powers acts **ultra vires** . Under corporate law, a contract entered into *ultra vires* is illegal. If a corporation has a restricted purpose per its articles of incorporation, stockholders can sue to enjoin (stop) the corporation's directors from engaging in *ultra vires* activities. For example, stockholders might sue if the corporation's charter states that business will be limited to book publication and the corporation subsequently begins to manufacture tires. Additionally, if the corporation loses money in an *ultra vires* activity, the directors who authorized the activity are personally liable for the loss. Today, the doctrine of *ultra vires* is rarely an issue for private corporations. This is because states now permit corporations to be chartered with broad, rather than specific, stated purposes. Corporations may also amend their charters, or articles of incorporation, as needed to recognize changes to their business. See the exhibit "Articles of Incorporation."

Ultra vires

An act of a corporation that exceeds its chartered powers.

Liability for Torts and Crimes

A corporation, its directors, and its officers can be liable for their actions under both tort and criminal law. Under tort law, a corporation is liable as a principal or an employer under the doctrine of *respondeat superior* ("let the master answer") for all torts committed by its agents or employees within the scope of their agency or employment. Corporate officers and directors,

---

Articles of Incorporation

Typical Items Included in Articles of Incorporation

- Corporate name
- Duration (usually perpetual)
- Purpose (usually broadly stated)
- Number, classes, and par (face) value of shares
- Provisions, if any, for the stockholders' right to purchase a proportionate share of newly issued stock
- Provisions, if any, restricting the transferability of shares
- Registered office or place of business and registered agent
- Number, names, and addresses of the initial board of directors
- Names and addresses of incorporators

[DA06220]

however, are not liable for any employee's or agent's tort. In addition to the corporation itself, the actual tortfeasor (employee or agent) is always liable.

Under criminal law, corporations can sometimes be found guilty of a crime even with no specific criminal intent. For such crimes, often called absolute liability crimes, lack of intent is immaterial. Crimes under this category include food and drug violations and participation in restraint of trade. The test of corporate criminal responsibility for absolute liability crimes is whether the responsible employee or agent acted within the scope of employment to benefit the corporation.

Other crimes, such as larceny, price-fixing, and obtaining money under false pretenses, require a specific criminal intent. The test for corporate liability is the same as that for absolute liability: whether the employee was acting within the scope of employment to benefit the corporation. A corporation can be held responsible for an employee's criminal activity if the corporation could have uncovered the activity through reasonably diligent supervision.

Officers and employees are personally responsible for their criminal acts. In addition, under statutes that impose criminal liability for unintentional acts, an officer can be criminally responsible for failure to ensure that subordinates comply with the statute.

Corporations may also have the right or the duty of indemnification to directors, officers, and other employees. Under corporate law, indemnification means reimbursement of expenses incurred in defending a lawsuit instituted or threatened against a person in his or her official capacity with a corporation. Defense expenses include attorneys' fees, judgments, fines, and settlement amounts. Some state statutes require indemnification only to directors and officers, while others extend the duty of indemnification to employees and agents. Some statutes permit reduction of the statutory right of indemnification if such is included in the articles of incorporation; others do not permit rights to be reduced.

All states require indemnification, unless denied by the article of incorporation, when a person is found not liable in a civil case or not guilty in a criminal case. If a court imposes civil liability, a corporation may choose to indemnify the person anyway, especially when the person acted in good faith and believed the action was in the best interest of the corporation.

Duties of Directors and Officers

Directors are not the corporation's agents, but the law imposes similar duties upon them. Officers are agents of the corporation and, as such, have the fiduciary duties of agent to the corporation (their principal).

Duties of Care and Loyalty

Directors and officers have a duty of care to the corporation. They must act honestly and in good faith and exercise a degree of care that a reasonable officer or director would exercise. They do not guarantee profitability of the business and are not required to have business skills. The law provides that a decision is proper if made within the range of reasonable "business judgment."

Directors and officers also owe a duty of loyalty to the corporation. The duty of loyalty exceeds the general duty not to defraud others. A fiduciary has not only a duty to avoid misrepresentation, but also an affirmative duty to disclose all material facts.

The Employee Retirement Income Security Act (ERISA) of 1974[39] also imposes duties on officers and directors. The act created fiduciary duties for pension and health benefit plan administrators, trustees, upper management, insurance brokers, and others with respect to how they invest and distribute plan funds and how they treat participants and beneficiaries. A director or an officer who exercises discretionary control in such a plan's management or over its assets, or who gives investment advice, is a fiduciary under ERISA with specific statutory duties and liabilities. Directors and officers have these duties under ERISA:

- To act solely in the plan participants' interest
- To exercise the care and skill of a reasonable person conducting a similar enterprise
- To diversify investments unless it is clearly unreasonable to do so
- To act in accordance with the plan documents

Transactions With the Corporation

In the course of business, directors and officers often enter into business transactions on behalf of the corporation. Sometimes, when beneficial, the corporation may enter into business with one of its own directors or with another corporation that shares some or all of the same directors (referred to as interlocking directors). State statutes generally provide that such contracts are valid, even if the director involved voted in favor of the contract, provided the material facts of the relationship were known and voted on by the board or the stockholders, and the contract is fair to the corporation.

Appropriation of a Corporate Business Opportunity

Directors and officers may not appropriate a business opportunity that belongs to the corporation for their own gain. For example, a director may not purchase a business that he or she knows the corporation is seeking to purchase. Similarly, a director or officer may not compete with the corporation.

Directors and officers are privy to confidential information about the corporation. Material information about a corporation's affairs that could, if made public, change the value of the corporation's stock, is called insider information. It is illegal for directors or officers of a corporation to use insider information to their own advantage, such as to buy or sell stock to profit or to avoid loss. If they do, stockholders from whom they purchased shares or to whom they sold shares can sue for damages.

In addition to the private right of action afforded to wronged stockholders, directors or officers who improperly use insider information for personal gain are also subject to stiff civil penalties. The Insider Trading Sanctions Act of 1984,[40] amended by the Insider Trading and Securities Fraud Enforcement Act of 1988,[41] imposes a civil penalty on anyone who deals in securities based on "material, nonpublic" information. This penalty is based not on a duty to the corporation's stockholders, but on a duty to the investing public. Information gained by legitimate research can be used freely in investment decisions. Information cannot be used that comes from such sources as a corporate insider, an investment firm entrusted with the information for business purposes, or a law firm representing the corporation.

Stockholders' Powers and Duties

Stockholders normally delegate management powers of the corporation to the board of directors. The board and the officers appointed by the board have the power to create and implement business policy. Stockholders have the power to make decisions on issues likely to fundamentally affect them. Stockholder decisions include these:

- Electing board members and, in many states, removing them without cause.
- Approving changes to the articles of incorporation.
- Making or amending bylaws.
- Approving loans to the corporation's directors, officers, or agents.

- Ratifying (approving) board actions. If a board explains specific actions and then obtains stockholder ratification, an approving stockholder cannot later sue the board regarding that action. If the stockholders have no knowledge of the board's actions, a blanket shareholder resolution approving a board's actions for the past year is ineffective.
- Suing directors for mismanagement. To exercise that right, stockholders may initiate a suit on behalf of the corporation, called a shareholder derivative suit.

Stockholders have a right to the corporation's financial statements, which they receive by mail or electronically, at least annually. Stockholders also have the right to inspect certain books or records, such as some types of financial records, minutes of stockholder meetings, and lists of stockholders' names and addresses.

Stockholders have no fiduciary relationship to the corporation and therefore can vote in their own best interests. However, majority stockholders may not manipulate corporate affairs to the disadvantage of minority stockholders.

Stockholders' Meetings

Stockholder meetings are held annually for the purpose of giving stockholders, as the corporation's owners, an opportunity to vote on corporate matters over which they have power. To determine which stockholders are eligible to vote, state laws permit the establishment of a cutoff date before the meeting. Only those stockholders owning stock with voting rights as of the cutoff date will be eligible.

Most state laws require an annual meeting but leave it to the bylaws to specify meeting details. If no annual meeting occurs within a statutory time limit, a stockholder can apply to the court to hold a meeting. In addition to annual meetings called by the corporation, holders of a certain percentage of the outstanding shares may also call special meetings, when permitted by statute, articles of incorporation, or the bylaws. The articles or bylaws may also permit other persons, such as the president, to call meetings.

Meeting notice is provided to stockholders in writing, along with information on specific board-proposed actions, such as amendments to the articles that require stockholder approval. A quorum, established by statute, articles, or bylaws, is needed to transact business lawfully at the meeting. In other words, the specified proportion of outstanding shares of voting stock must be represented, either in person or by proxy.

Stockholders' Actions

Derivative suit

A lawsuit brought by one or more shareholders in the name of the corporation.

Stockholders may file one of three types of civil lawsuits to pursue complaints: class action suits, derivative suits, and direct action suits. Stockholder suits are usually either class actions or **derivative suits**.

- Class actions—When a transaction damages many people, one or more damaged persons can file a representative suit, or class action, on behalf of all, thus avoiding multiple suits on the same factual and legal questions. A common example is a stockholder class action suit against directors and officers for damages for fraud, such as failure to make a full disclosure in connections with a public stock offering.

- Derivative actions—One or more stockholders may initiate a suit on behalf of the corporation for damages incurred by the corporation. For example, one or more stockholders might file a derivative suit if an outside auditing firm negligently audited the books of a corporation. Any recovery from the suit belongs to the corporation, because the corporation was directly injured, although successful plaintiffs may also be awarded reimbursement for litigation expenses.

- Direct actions—A stockholder might also file suit to seek remedy for direct harm. For example, a stockholder might file a direct action for harm sustained while engaged in company business.

Dividends

Dividends are shares of corporate profits paid to stockholders. To the stockholder, dividends are considered capital gains, or profits on owned stock. Therefore, some stockholders may prefer to invest profits back into the corporation, while others may prefer to receive dividends. Corporate management decides whether to declare dividends in good faith and for a corporate purpose. Directors can also defer (postpone) dividends or exercise bond call (redemption) provisions to provide expansion capital, build surplus, or accomplish other business goals. To force payment of dividends, stockholders must prove bad faith, which has rarely been found by the courts.

Dividends are usually paid in cash, but there are other types of dividends. Property dividends are shares of another corporation that the declaring corporation has acquired. Stock dividends are corporate profits issued in the form of additional shares of the issuing corporation and can be paid in treasury stock or from authorized but unissued shares. The board may also decide to issue an extra dividend, a dividend in addition to the usual and expected regular dividend. Distribution of assets during a corporate reorganization is often called a liquidating dividend; however, such a distribution is not a true dividend because a dividend comes from corporate profits.

Once the board formally declares a dividend, the stockholders become creditors of the corporation. If the corporation becomes insolvent before paying the dividend, the stockholders participate equally with other creditors to the extent of the dividend. Because declaration of the dividend creates a debtor-creditor relationship, the board cannot revoke a declared dividend.

CORPORATIONS: MERGERS, DISSOLUTION, AND REORGANIZATION

Corporations exist forever unless they merge, dissolve, or reorganize.

Corporations may cease to exist through merger, dissolution, or reorganization:

- Merger is the joining together of two or more corporations to become a new organization.
- Dissolution is a voluntary or involuntary termination of a corporation.
- Reorganization occurs when a corporation becomes bankrupt.

Merger

In a corporate merger, two or more corporations join to become a new, single corporation. The newly merged corporation owns all the assets and is subject to all the liabilities of the merging corporations. A true merger is considered a friendly transaction to which the boards of both (or all) merging organizations agree.

Before a merger, the board of directors of each corporate party to the merger must adopt a plan of merger. The stockholders of the "disappearing" corporations (those corporations that will be dissolved as a result of the merger) must approve the merger plan, but the stockholders of the new (or acquiring) corporation are required to approve the plan only if the number of voting or participating (sharing in corporate profits) shares increases substantially.[42]

Stockholders are entitled to dissent to a merger, a share exchange, or to the sale of all or substantially all of a corporation's assets that does not occur in the usual course of businesses. They are also entitled to an appraisal and to receive fair value for their shares in any merger that requires shareholder approval. If a stockholder files a written dissent to a merger before or during the stockholders' meeting, he or she must receive a written notice after the action giving rise to dissenters' rights that provides a time period and procedure to file a buyout demand.[43]

A corporation that owns at least 90 percent of another corporation's stock may merge that subsidiary corporation into itself without stockholder approval.[44] The corporation need only send the merger plan to the subsidiary's stockholders. Many insurance corporation statutes require 95 percent rather than 90 percent ownership of a subsidiary before such a merger can occur, along with approval from the state department of insurance.

Share Exchange and De Facto Mergers

In a share exchange merger, a corporation acquires all of another corporation's outstanding shares in return for shares of the acquiring corporation. A share exchange plan must be adopted by the board of directors of the "disappearing" corporation and approved by the stockholders of the corporation whose shares are being acquired, but it does not have to be approved by the stockholders of the acquiring corporation.

Another form of merger is one in which a corporation sells all or most of its assets to another corporation, in return for the purchasing corporation's shares for distribution to its stockholders. In this way, two organizations are merged, but not necessarily in accordance with the statutory requirements for a merger. This transaction is known as a *de facto* merger—a merger in fact, if not in law.

Under the American Bar Association Revised Model Business Corporation Act (RMBCA), widely adopted by the individual states, a sale of all or substantially all of a corporation's assets not in the usual course of business requires stockholders' approval in the manner of a statutory merger or consolidation.[45]

When a *de facto* merger meets the structural changes of a statutory merger, the new corporation assumes the liabilities of the predecessor organizations. The courts will not necessarily find the new organization responsible for the liabilities of the acquired corporation if the successor organization is not a continuation of the prior business. See the exhibit "Corporate Mergers."

Corporate Mergers

There are a number of reasons that one or more organizations may initiate a merger, including the desire to increase market share, achieve operational efficiencies, and expand marketing and distribution channels. These are the most common types of mergers:

Horizontal Merger—A merger between businesses that directly compete with each other.

Vertical Merger—A merger between an organization and a customer or supplier. An example is a merger between an ink company and a printer manufacturer.

Conglomerate Merger—A merger of two organizations that are not competitors or linked as customer and supplier. An example is a merger between a paint retailer and a carpeting retailer.

[DA06328]

Takeovers and Tender Offers

One corporation may wish to gain control of another corporation for various business purposes, such as increase in market share or acquisition of assets.

There are various methods a corporation may use to achieve a **takeover** of another corporation.

When one corporation wants to control or acquire a corporation against the will of that corporation's board, the acquiring company can attempt a hostile takeover. Often, a hostile takeover attempt subsequently becomes a friendly takeover when the terms offered by the acquiring corporation improve or the acquiring corporation gains the endorsement of the target corporation's board.

One corporation can gain control over another by bypassing the target corporation's board and acquiring sufficient proxies from the target's stockholders to elect its own board of directors or to vote for a merger. United States Securities and Exchange Commission (SEC) rules and regulations govern proxy solicitation in these situations.

Another method a corporation may use to acquire a corporation that is unwilling to merge is to purchase sufficient shares of the target corporation to become eligible to vote on its board of directors. To purchase shares, the prospective acquirer will make a **tender offer**. Federal law requires mandatory disclosure of certain information in a tender offer. Any person or group that acquires, or intends to acquire, more than 5 percent ownership of a class of securities registered with the SEC must file a statement with the SEC and send a copy of the statement to each offeree and to the issuing company. This information enables stockholders to make an informed decision about whether to sell their shares in the target company. See the exhibit "Insurance Company Mergers."

Dissolution

Dissolution, or termination, of a corporation can either be voluntary or involuntary. Each method follows a different procedure and has different repercussions for the parties involved.

Voluntary corporate dissolution begins with a board resolution to dissolve the corporation, approved by a majority of the stockholders. The corporation must also file a formal "statement of intent to dissolve" with the state. The corporation then proceeds with liquidation. The corporation can request court supervision for liquidation, if necessary.

Involuntary dissolution occurs when the state of incorporation, the stockholders, or corporate creditors file for involuntary dissolution proceedings. State proceedings are unusual and occur only in cases of gross abuse of the corporate privilege or fraudulent acquisition of the articles of incorporation. A state might hold such a proceeding when a corporation has allegedly defrauded the public repeatedly.

Stockholders can ask a court for involuntary dissolution on the basis of the right to protect stockholders. The court can then order liquidation of corporation assets and distribution of the proceeds, after payment of debts, to the

Takeover
The assumption of control by one corporation over another through merger, acquisition, or some other type of transaction.

Tender offer
A purchase offer made directly to the shareholders of the target, typically at an offer price greater than the current market price.

Insurance Company Mergers

Most states' insurance company merger laws mimic general corporation laws. However, there are also significant differences between insurance company mergers and general corporation mergers:

- Regulated corporations, such as insurance companies, can engage in only one type of business; insurers can merge only with companies in the same business.

- State departments of insurance must approve insurance company mergers.

Sometimes corporations with diverse interests wish to purchase controlling interests in insurance companies for investment purposes. Corporations that purchase controlling interests in other corporations are called holding companies. Merger laws do not apply in these situations because the insurance companies continue as separate corporations. Instead, every state and the District of Columbia have adopted the National Association of Insurance Commissioners (NAIC) Model Insurance Holding System Regulatory Act. The model act includes requirements that insurer subsidiaries file information with the state department of insurance relating to capital structure, ownership, financial condition, and general business operation. The act also limits dividend payments by insurance subsidiaries to holding companies.

Under the act, persons wishing to acquire control of, or merge with, an insurer are required to file a specific form (Form A, Statement Regarding the Acquisition or Control or Merger with a Domestic Insurer), which is analyzed by the state to determine whether to approve or disapprove the transaction. The filed form is also shared with other states.

[DA06329]

stockholders. The RMBCA provides that stockholders can file suits to dissolve the corporation on these grounds:[46]

- The directors are deadlocked, the stockholders cannot break the deadlock, and irreparable injury to the corporation either has occurred or might occur.

- The directors' or officers' acts are illegal, oppressive, or fraudulent.

- The stockholders are deadlocked in voting power and have failed to elect directors for two successive meetings.

- The corporate assets are being wasted or misapplied.

If a judgment for a creditor's claim is unsatisfied, or the corporation admits insolvency in writing, the creditor can sue for dissolution of the corporation. The corporation need not be bankrupt, with its liabilities exceeding its assets. Insolvency means only that the current liabilities (as opposed to total liabilities) exceed current assets. Thus, a corporation that cannot meet its current obligations is insolvent, even though its total liabilities are less than its total assets.

Because of the public interest in an insurance company's ability to pay its claims, the courts designate the state department of insurance as the receiver in an insurance company dissolution process.

Reorganization

Under Chapter 11 of the Bankruptcy Reform Act of 1978,[47] a corporation may be placed under federal bankruptcy court supervision for reorganization purposes. Chapter 11 proceedings may be voluntary or involuntary and may end in either a restructured organization or termination through bankruptcy liquidation.

Chapter 11 filings are the most common way for corporations to restructure debt. Corporations will typically restructure, that is, make changes to the ownership or operational structure of the organization in order to be more profitable. Under Chapter 11, the bankruptcy court must appoint a committee of creditors and also might appoint a committee of stockholders to work under its supervision. The court can permit the current managers to continue control of the business and may appoint an examiner to investigate and monitor the reorganization. The court can appoint a case trustee, separate from the U.S. Trustee, to take control of the business if it finds management guilty of fraud, dishonesty, incompetence, or gross mismanagement or if it finds that the appointment of a trustee is in the best interests of the creditors, stockholders, or other persons.

In the absence of a satisfactory reorganization or other plan, the bankruptcy court may convert the case to a regular bankruptcy liquidation proceeding under Chapter 7 of the federal bankruptcy laws.

PARTNERSHIPS

Formation of partnerships allows individuals to pool their resources and capital to pursue a business for profit. However, partnerships involve complex responsibilities and liability exposures for owners that vary depending on the type of partnership structure.

Partnerships, limited partnerships, limited liability partnerships, and limited liability companies are forms of business ownership that share some characteristics but differ with respect to the liability exposures of the owners. The insurance professional should have a basic understanding of these partnership characteristics:

- Partnership formation
- Partnership liability
- Partners' relationships to one another
- Relationship of partners to third parties
- Dissolution, winding up, and termination
- Limited partnerships and limited liability partnerships
- Limited liability companies

Partnership Formation

Partnership

A for-profit business entity jointly owned by two or more persons who share ownership and profits (or losses), although not necessarily on an equal basis.

A **partnership**, also called a general partnership, is a form of legal ownership of a business. The Uniform Partnership Act (UPA), a model law adopted by a majority of states, defines a partnership as "an association of two or more persons (legally defined as individuals, groups, companies, or corporations) to carry on as co-owners of a business for profit."[48] An advantage of forming a partnership is that income is taxable at each individual partner's tax rate rather than at a rate that would apply to a corporation.

Partnerships can arise by people's actions as partners, by oral agreement, or by written agreement. Two or more persons are presumed to be partners if they agree to work together in any line of activity and share the profits and losses, although not necessarily on an equal basis. To be considered a partnership, the enterprise need not have physical assets but must have profit as its goal.

Unlike corporations, formation of partnerships does not need government approval. However, if the partnership uses a fictitious name or any name other than all the partners' surnames, state laws require registration of the name in a public records office. See the exhibit "Joint Ventures."

Joint Ventures

A joint venture is an unincorporated association of two or more persons (legally defined as individuals, groups, companies, or corporation) established to conduct a single transaction or a series of related transactions, as compared with an ongoing business involving many diverse transactions. Examples include a business established to buy a single tract of land in order to subdivide it for sale to others or to drill for oil offshore.

The concepts of joint venture and partnership have virtually merged. Because a joint venture can range from an association for a single transaction to a complex, long-range association, joint ventures can differ more among themselves than they do from a partnership.

[DA06266]

Partnership Liability

Only a legal entity can be a party to a lawsuit, but under common law partnerships were not considered legal entities. Therefore, for a partnership to sue or be sued, all the partners had to be joined individually in legal actions by or against the partnership. A plaintiff suing a partnership would have to serve papers on each of the partners. Due to the burden of determining all the partners to a business, as well as the difficulties of serving papers on every party, some states passed **common name statutes**, permitting suits against the partnership in its name. Some state laws permit satisfaction of judgment only from the firm's assets and not from those of the individual partner who was served personally. Typically, when the partnership is the plaintiff, all partners must join in the suit.

Common name statute

A law that permits service of process on a partnership by serving any one of the partners.

In cases in which more than one person was at fault, the common law distinguished between contract and tort liability. If two or more persons, such as partners, were liable on a contract, the liability was joint, and a plaintiff had to sue all of those at fault. For tort cases, however, the liability was joint and several. The plaintiff could choose to sue all the partners or any number of them. Many states have adopted laws amending the common law rule so that liability on all obligations, both contract and tort, are joint and several.

The laws of agency govern liability of a partnership and of the individual partners for torts committed by one of the partners. If a partner's act or omission in the ordinary course of the partnership's business causes loss or injury to a third person, the partnership, that partner, and each of the other partners are liable, and the partners' private property can be used to satisfy the judgment. The acting partner is ultimately liable. If the partnership or any other partner is forced to respond in damages to the third party, theoretically the acting partner must reimburse the other partner or the partnership. In reality, however, insurance usually covers the liability.

A partnership is not usually responsible as a business entity for a crime; only a partner who has participated in a crime is held criminally responsible. Vicarious liability, or holding the partnership legally responsible for the actions of a partner, does not usually exist in criminal law.

Partners' Relationships to One Another

The partnership agreement, the UPA, and general principles of contract and agency law govern the relationship among partners. Unless contrary to public policy, the partnership agreement can deviate from UPA provisions.

Financial Relationship

Unless otherwise provided by the partnership agreement, each partner shares equally in profits, losses, and any surplus that remains on dissolution of the partnership (after satisfaction of all liabilities), even when the partners' capital or service contributions are unequal. See the exhibit "Example of a Partnership Financial Relationship."

The partnership indemnifies each partner for payments made or personal liabilities incurred in the business when a partner has acted within the scope of his or her authority. However, a partner who is guilty of gross negligence, fraud, or wanton misconduct that gives rise to damages is solely liable and is not entitled to indemnification.

Fiduciary Relationship

Every partner has a fiduciary relationship with the other partners and the firm, meaning each partner owes a duty of trust, loyalty, and good faith to the partnership, similar to the duty of an agent trustee. The fiduciary duties are implied in law, and cannot be waived by contract.

> ### Example of a Partnership Financial Relationship
>
> Assume that Anne and Bob form a partnership with start-up capital of $100,000, Anne contributes $90,000 in cash and Bob contributes $10,000 in cash. Bob also has a special skill the partnership will use.
>
> If the partnership makes a $10,000 profit in a given year, Anne and Bob are each, unless otherwise provided, entitled to $5,000.
>
> If the firm dissolves and $70,000 remains after all liabilities are paid, Anne and Bob must share the $30,000 loss unless the partnership agreement provides otherwise. How much would Anne and Bob receive?
>
> Anne is entitled to $75,000 ($90,000 − $15,000, her original contribution minus half of the $30,000 loss). Therefore, Bob must provide Anne with $5,000 ($10,000 − $15,000, his original contribution, minus his half of the $30,000 loss) to augment the partnership's remaining $70,000. Anne then receives the full $75,000, and Bob loses $5,000.

[DA06267]

A partner who derives any personal benefit from any transaction connected with the partnership without the other partners' consent must account to the partnership for the benefit and hold any profits for the partnership as a trustee.[49] For example, Nadia and Paul are partners in a dog grooming business. Paul's neighbor brings her West Highland terrier to receive grooming services from Paul, who keeps the payment for himself instead of putting it in with the business receipts. Nadia can demand that he turn the payment over to the partnership.

Partners are liable to the partnership for failing to render the services they originally agreed to perform. A partner is not liable to the partnership for ordinary negligence or for loss caused by errors in judgment. The partnership assumes the risk of ordinary poor judgment. However, a partner is liable for gross negligence, fraud, or wanton misconduct.

Partnerships' Books and Property

Unless otherwise provided, the partnership's books must be kept at its principal place of business. All partners have the right of access to the partnership's books for purposes related to the partnership.

Assignment of Partner's Interest in Partnership

A partner's transferable interest in the partnership is his or her share of the profits and losses and the right to receive distributions.[50] A partner can assign a financial interest in the partnership if agreed to by the other partners (either in the original partnership agreement or when the assignment occurs) but cannot assign the partnership status. Assignment of financial interest does not give the assignee any right to participate in management, to require information or an accounting, or to inspect the partnership's books. On dissolution, however, the assignee is entitled to the assignor's interest and can require an accounting from the date of the last accounting agreed to by all the partners.

Relationships of Partners to Third Parties

A partner has neither the right nor the power to bind the partnership by any contract with a third party that requires unanimous or majority consent of the partners. Third parties are at risk in dealing with partnerships if they are unaware of which partnership decisions require unanimous consent. However, any partner can make ordinary day-to-day contracts involving third parties.

Every partner is the partnership's agent for its business purposes,[51] so agency rules apply. A partner may have actual authority to bind the partnership (with express or implied authority or by ratification), but even without actual authority, a partner can bind a partnership under principles of estoppel.

Apparent Authority (Estoppel) of Partners

Apparent authority is also called authority by estoppel. See the exhibit "Partnership by Estoppel."

Partnership by Estoppel

The doctrine of partnership by estoppel protects innocent third parties who have relied on the appearance of a partnership. A partnership by estoppel results if three elements are present:

- A person who is not a partner purports to be a partner or permits others to think he or she is a partner.

- The third party deals with the entity in justifiable reliance on a belief that it is a partnership or that the person who purports to be a partner is actually a partner.

- The third party changes his or her legal position because of reliance on that belief, for example, entering into a contract.

Under these circumstances, the person who has permitted the appearance is liable to the third party to the same extent that an actual partner would be. In addition, the purported partner has the power to bind the partnership, just as an actual partner would. If all the partners consent to the representation, the apparent partner's transaction is a partnership act or obligation. If fewer than all the parties consent, the act is the joint obligation only of the consenting partners and not of the partnership itself.

Risk of partnership by estoppel may occur when a retired partner has not provided appropriate notice of the retirement to people who previously knew of the partnership.

[DA06268]

The existence of partnership itself creates the appearance that a partner has authority to act on behalf of the partnership. A third party might assume that all partners can act in the partnership's day-to-day business. If a partner lacks authority or has been denied authority to act, and a third party changes legal position because of the partner's actions, the partnership is estopped from denying that partner's authority.

For example, assume that Anne, Bob, and Carla are partners in the business of selling hunting and fishing equipment. Anne and Bob vote not to sell equipment for bow-and-arrow hunting, although Carla favors doing so. Other hunting and fishing equipment retailers in the area sell archery equipment. Carla, despite the partnership's policy, contracts to purchase a quantity of bows and arrows from a supplier who is unaware of the restriction. The partnership is bound because the third party could have reasonably assumed that this partnership also sells such equipment.

Acts Outside the Usual Scope of Business

The term "usual scope of business of the partnership" refers not only to what the partnership usually does, but also to what similar partnerships in the geographical area ordinarily do. These practices create appearances on which the third party might rely, thus estopping the partnership from denying liability. A partner's act outside the partnership's usual scope of business does not expose the partnership to liability because the partnership created no appearances. Instead, the third party merely relied on its own perceptions.

Referring to the example of Anne, Bob, and Carla, who sell hunting and fishing equipment, if Carla enters into a contract to purchase a line of guitars, the partnership would not be bound to the contract. Unless Anne and Bob had given Carla this actual authority, Carla, not the partnership, created the appearance of her authority, and the partnership therefore can deny Carla's binding authority. The third party could, however, sue Carla for breach of the implied warranty of authority (for giving the impression of authority where it did not exist) under the law of agency.

Ability to Convey Real Property

The real property belonging to a partnership is held in the name of the partners and the partnership, such as in the name of "Adams, Burns, and Cunningham, partners doing business as The Excelsior Company." In such a case, all the partners must sign a deed to transfer legal ownership to a purchaser.

Partnership property might also be titled in the name of one or more partners without naming the partnership. Those partners are the property's "apparent owners." If a purchaser of the property gives full value and does not know of the partnership's interest in the property, good title passes on principles of estoppel. The same principles apply to other types of property for which a written document indicates ownership, such as a bill of sale or an automobile title.

Dissolution, Winding Up, and Termination

A partnership dissolves whenever any partner ceases to be associated in carrying out the business, if it becomes unlawful to carry on the partnership, or if the partnership becomes bankrupt. Unless otherwise provided or agreed to, partnership affairs are then "wound up," or liquidated, and the partnership is terminated.

A partnership agreement can provide that the partnership will not dissolve on any partner's death but will continue with the surviving partners. In legal terms, the partnership dissolves but is reformed immediately with the surviving partners as the partners.

Rightful and Wrongful Dissolution

Partnerships may dissolve voluntarily, or the courts can declare dissolution. A partner can apply to the court for a decree of dissolution for certain situations, such as one partner becoming incapable of performing his or her part of the contract (for example, due to illness), or if a partner is guilty of conduct that harms the business.

A dissolution (also called dissociation) can be considered rightful or wrongful. A rightful dissolution is one that is in accordance with the partnership agreement and is not any partner's fault. On rightful dissolution, the partnership is liquidated. If the partnership is solvent at the time of dissolution, the parties share in any surplus remaining after payment of debts and partners' equity. If the partnership is insolvent, the partners share the losses.

These are examples of rightful dissolutions:

- The term of a partnership ends.
- A partnership without a term (a partnership at will) is dissolved by one or more partners.
- All the partners agree to dissolve even if the partnership has a term.
- A partner has been declared incompetent in any judicial proceeding or is shown to be of unsound mind.
- A partner has become incapable of performing his or her part of the partnership contract, for example, because of extended illness.
- The partnership business can continue only at a loss.

If dissolution is wrongful, the innocent partners can choose to either wind up the business and hold the at-fault partner liable for breach of contract damages or continue the business for the remainder of the partnership term. If they choose to continue, the remaining partners must pay the wrongful partner his or her share of the assets, less any damages the wrongful dissolution caused. Remaining innocent partners must then release the wrongful partner from all liability for existing debts.

Examples of wrongful dissolutions include the following:

- A partner becomes bankrupt.
- A partner is guilty of conduct that harms the operation of the business, such as competing with the partnership, embezzlement, or breach of the fiduciary relationship.
- A partner willfully or persistently breaches the partnership agreement.

Winding Up the Partnership Business

If the partnership dissolves, the business is liquidated. Remaining partners, or the last surviving partner's legal representative, must wind up the partnership affairs. If dissolution is by court decree, the court may either appoint an outside person, called a receiver, or designate one of the partners to wind up the business.

Unless the partnership agreement provides otherwise, upon dissolution the partnership's assets are distributed in this order:

1. Partnership creditors
2. Partners' advances
3. Each partner's capital (If partnership assets are insufficient, the loss of capital is deducted from each partner's capital contribution according to each partner's share of the profits.)
4. Surplus to the partners, divided in the same proportion as profits

If the partnership has sufficient assets to pay creditors, partners' advances, and partners' capital contributions, there are few problems. If the partnership is insolvent, the partners have unlimited liability for partnership debts.

If the partnership and all of the partners are insolvent, the case goes into a bankruptcy court in liquidation proceedings. Federal bankruptcy law permits partnership creditors to enter the full amount of their claims against both the partnership assets and each individual insolvent partner's assets. If one or more of the partners is solvent and their assets are sufficient to pay both their creditors and the partnership's outside creditors, they must do so.

Effect of Dissolution on Third Parties

Dissolution does not affect the rights of the partnership's existing creditors against the partnership, the partners, or the estates of deceased partners. If new contracts arise, such as those needed for orderly liquidation, the partnership, the partners, and the deceased partner's estate are all liable for these contracts.

A problem can arise if, after dissolution and without any authority, a partner enters into a completely new contract on the partnership's behalf. Even if the partner lacked actual authority to enter into the new contract, he or she might have had apparent authority. If, however, a third party has or should have had knowledge of dissolution, the contract cannot be enforced. For example, if a partnership dissolves because one partner has filed bankruptcy, third parties are held to have notice of such matters of public record.

If a partner knowing of dissolution enters into a new contract, the partnership and the other partners might be bound, but they have rights against the partner who entered the contract. If a contracting partner has no actual knowledge of dissolution, for example resulting from a partner's illness, but has received notice of dissolution (as in a letter left unopened) the partner is solely responsible for a contract he or she entered into after dissolution.

A partner who has retired remains liable to third parties for obligations incurred while a member of the firm. Even the continuing partners' agreement to relieve the retiring partner of prior obligations does not change a third-party creditor's rights. To be relieved of these obligations, the retiring partner must obtain the third-party creditor's agreement to obtain payment only from the remaining partners. The term "retiring partner" includes a deceased partner's personal representative.

Limited Partnerships and Limited Liability Partnerships

To form a **limited partnership**, the partners must comply with state statute and file a certificate of limited partnership with the appropriate public official. Limited partners receive a return on their investment as agreed upon in the partnership agreement.

> **Limited partnership**
>
> A form of partnership made up of one or more general partners, who have unlimited liability, and one or more limited partners, whose liability is limited to the amount of capital they have contributed to the partnership.

If a limited partner exercises any control over the management, the limited partner might face an unlimited liability exposure. The firm can employ a limited partner, but this practice can raise difficult questions concerning when the limited partner's advice or review of management decisions becomes actual participation in management.

A limited partnership can provide tax advantages to investing partners. Federal income tax laws treat a limited partnership as a partnership. The partnership itself is not taxed, and the income attributable to each partner is taxed at the partner's personal tax rate. However, in businesses with high up-front costs (such as theatrical productions) or with high depreciation allowances (such as some real estate developments), "paper losses" are attributable to each partner each taxable year. A paper loss is an unrealized loss. These paper losses are particularly valuable to high-bracket taxpayers who, under some circumstances, can use these losses to reduce their taxable income while the limited partnership develops its business.

Limited liability partnership

A partnership limiting each partner's personal liability for acts or omissions of other partners.

A **limited liability partnership (LLP)** differs from a limited partnership in that it limits liability for each partner. This limitation, however, does not apply in situations such as these:

- Individual acts of negligence or wrongful acts by a withdrawing partner
- Debts or obligations of the partnership for which a withdrawing partner has agreed to be liable
- Debts and obligations expressly undertaken in the partnership agreement

States differ with respect to the extent of liability protection recognized. Some states, referred to as "limited shield" states, significantly reduce liability protection for limited liability partnerships. In such states, partners have limited liability only with respect to actions of their partners, but still have unlimited personal liability in all other situations.

Limited Liability Companies

Limited liability company (LLC)

A form of business entity that provides its owners the limited liability of a corporation and the tax advantages of a partnership.

In a **limited liability company (LLC)**, owners are called members. The members appoint managers to conduct the LLC's business operations. Members may also serve as managers.

The limited liability structure is appealing to real estate firms, high-technology start-up companies, and other entrepreneurial businesses with small numbers of active investors. Not all businesses can operate as LLCs. State laws generally prohibit banking, trust, and insurance industry businesses from forming LLCs, and some states also prohibit professionals (such as doctors and accountants) from forming LLCs.

UNINCORPORATED ASSOCIATIONS

The First Amendment of the United States Constitution has been interpreted to protect freedom of association; thus, it protects the right of individuals to form unincorporated associations to accomplish a common legal purpose.

Unincorporated association

A voluntary association of individuals acting together under a common name to accomplish a lawful purpose.

Unincorporated associations share characteristics with both corporations and partnerships. Examples include trade associations, labor unions, religious organizations, and clubs.

These four areas provide a basic understanding of these organizations:

- Characteristics of unincorporated associations
- Formation and financing
- Liability of members to third parties
- Dissolution and winding up

Characteristics of Unincorporated Associations

An unincorporated association is sometimes called a voluntary association, a voluntary organization, or an association. Although defined as "voluntary," some associations may actually be involuntary. In such cases, membership is required by state law.

Associations are the most common organizational form of not-for-profit organizations, but associations can be organized as for-profit entities as well. Some corporations, particularly not-for-profit corporations, can be described as associations, and some state statutes provide for the incorporation of associations. For purposes of this discussion, the term "association" is used only in the sense of an unincorporated association.

Associations, although unincorporated, resemble corporations in their form and organization. The biggest difference between a corporation and an association is that, in common law, an association is not a legal entity separate from its members and managers. Corporations can sue and be sued in the corporate name, but in many jurisdictions, an association cannot. Because they are not legal entities, unincorporated associations also cannot hold or transfer property in the name of the association. Associations are formed under the common law right of contract, have no separate legal existence, and do not legally possess perpetual life.

Associations are not subject to franchise, transfer, and other taxes commonly levied on corporations. However, not-for-profit associations enjoy tax-exempt status similar to not-for-profit corporations. Unlike corporations, associations do not need to register in the states in which they do business or file various reports required of corporations; however, they may have to comply with fictitious name statutes.

An association resembles a partnership in that, because an association is not a separate legal entity like a corporation, its members may be individually liable for the association's activities.

Associations differ from partnerships in several ways:

- An association cannot usually hold title to real property or execute a lease in the association's name.
- A member's withdrawal does not cause dissolution.
- Any expense-sharing or profit-sharing in an association is frequently other than per capita.
- An association's individual members do not have authority to participate directly in its day-to-day management.

State Regulation

States have statutes concerning many aspects of associations. Some states have laws that address specific matters, such as suits by or against associations in the association's name. Associations such as labor unions, insurance organizations, and credit unions are also subject to any specific laws governing such operations.

State laws do not restrict the formation of associations for any legal purpose. The constitutional guarantee of freedom of assembly implies the right to form or join associations, and no legislation can eliminate that right. Any law affecting associations cannot unreasonably inhibit free speech or assembly; however, it may forbid activities that pose a clear and present danger to society.

The National Conference of Commissioners on Uniform State Laws (NCCUSL) adopted a model law in 1996, The Uniform Unincorporated Nonprofit Association Act (UUNAA), to address unincorporated not-for-profit associations. This act was revised in 2008 as the Revised Uniform Unincorporated Nonprofit Association Act (RUUNAA). The model act addresses tort and contractual liability of members, owning and conveying of property, and suits by and against an unincorporated nonprofit association. Additionally, the model law recognizes an unincorporated not-for-profit association as a separate legal entity, distinct from its members—meaning that it may own and transfer property and sue and be sued in its own name. The model also provides that liability stemming from contract or tort is solely the liability of the association and not of its members. Although the model law has been enacted in only a few states, it contains provisions similar to those found in most states' statutes.

Types of Associations

These are the six major types of unincorporated associations:

- Trade associations—The largest group of unincorporated associations is composed of more than 10,000 American trade associations. These organizations foster their members' interests by exchanging and compiling information, lobbying, setting standards, and issuing publicity. They include boards of trade, chambers of commerce, and other business organizations.

- Labor unions—The next largest group of associations is labor unions. Local unions, as well as national organizations representing multiple smaller unions, may be formed as associations. Any benefits, such as health insurance, provided by the union are regulated according to relevant state and federal law. Labor unions are also subject to applicable state and federal employment laws. The group liability of unions organized as associations is limited in most states.

- Benevolent and fraternal associations—Fraternal and benevolent societies have long taken the form of associations. If these organizations provide insurance or credit for their members, they must comply with state laws governing such issues. Some benevolent and fraternal associations are referred to as "secret societies," a term describing organizations that conceal their activities from nonmembers. Special statutes in many states regulate secret societies.

- Religious organizations—Religious associations may be unincorporated associations or may choose to incorporate.

- Clubs—A club is an association of persons for some common objective, such as social purposes or the pursuit of literature, science, or politics. For example, a local sports league or a club of antique auto owners may be structured as an unincorporated association. Clubs follow agency rather than partnership rules. A club member, therefore, is liable to pay money beyond the required subscription if that person expressly or impliedly authorizes a contract. The club's limitations on its agents bind third parties.

- Condominium owners' associations—Most states have statutes regulating condominium association activities. Some condominium associations are incorporated, although statutes do not require incorporation. State statutes usually specify limitations on the formation, powers, finance, and operation of condominium associations. All unit owners within the condominium are association members, and the association is responsible for the condominium's operation and the care and preservation of the common areas (the shared areas of the property).

Formation and Financing

Associations are generally defined as voluntary, formed by a group of individuals for some common lawful purpose and financed as they desire. However, involuntary associations may be established by statute or regulation. For example, assigned risk automobile insurance plans, Fair Access to Insurance Requirements (FAIR) plans, and insurance guaranty funds are involuntary associations because, by law, all insurers that write applicable lines of insurance in a given state must belong to that state's association. The statutes creating such involuntary associations frequently specify the means of formation, financing, and management, or they may specify that state regulation governs those aspects of the association.

Articles of Association and Bylaws

The contract of association is embodied in an instrument usually termed the "articles of association," "constitution," or "charter." Like a corporate charter, this instrument is the fundamental body of rules governing the association.

A voluntary association can adopt bylaws to serve as the rules of the association and provide regulations concerning discipline, doctrine, or internal policy. Association members are bound by the provisions of the bylaws.

The bylaws of an unincorporated association typically include provisions addressing these issues:

- Qualifications, selection, and terms of directors and trustees
- Meetings
- Qualifications for membership
- Acquisitions and transfer of property
- Rights and duties of members
- Dissolution

The association has the right to interpret and administer the bylaws and regulations. However, courts will not enforce them if they compel a person to lose rights in accumulated assets or to forgo basic constitutional rights, or if they are illegal, immoral, or against public policy.

Rights of Members in Association Property

Every voluntary association member has a property right in its assets. Because associations are not legal entities, any property that an association ostensibly holds belongs jointly to its members as tenants in common. Therefore, unless state statute provides otherwise, common law gives members the right to dispose of the property at their joint pleasure. The articles of association, however, can give the right to control and dispose of property solely to the board of directors. Unless the articles or bylaws state otherwise, members lose whatever interest they have when their membership ends.

Dues and assessments paid by members become the association's property, free from any individual right or claim. An individual member cannot prevent use of his or her dues for objectives to which a majority of the members agree.

Directors or Trustees

Individual members of the association normally do not participate in the day-to-day management of the association; that authority is usually given to the association's elected board of directors or trustees. Association directors and trustees have legal rights and duties almost identical to those of corporate directors. Association directors have no legal right to act individually on behalf of the association and can make decisions only as a group. One difference is that directors of not-for-profit associations do not have as high a standard of care as directors of corporations or associations engaged in business for profit. This is because their positions in not-for-profit associations are often part-time and uncompensated.[52] If they receive compensation, their standard of care is higher.

Liability of Members to Third Parties

Individual members can be liable for both torts and contracts arising from the association's activities. Association members are jointly and severally liable for torts committed by the association's agents and employees acting within the scope of their employment. However, under the Volunteer Protection Act,[53] those who provide voluntary services are immune from liability in many instances.

In common law, an unincorporated association is not liable for the actions of its members because it is not a separate legal entity and cannot be sued. Many state statutes now allow unincorporated associations to sue and be sued; however, the fact that an association might be sued in its own name does not eliminate the members' individual liability.

A member who has suffered damage to his or her person, property, or reputation through the tortious conduct of another member or an agent of the association cannot sue the association but can sue the other member or agent individually.

Absent statutes to the contrary, members of an association organized for trade or profit are individually liable for contracts made by an authorized officer or agent in the association's name or incurred in the course of business for which the association was organized. This liability exists even if the other party does not know the individual members' names.

Members of not-for-profit associations organized for social, moral, patriotic, political, or similar purposes and not for trade or profit do not have individual liability to third parties unless they join in authorizing a contract. In this situation, agency rules apply, and agency cannot be implied by the mere fact of association or paying dues.

Dissolution and Winding Up

Because no specific statutory provisions apply to the dissolution of associations, they can be dissolved in a variety of ways:

- By members' vote
- By the death or withdrawal of a majority of the members
- By court action on application of creditors or members, or for illegal conduct
- By the expiration of a period stated in the articles

The person authorized to wind up association affairs liquidates the assets and pays all debts and obligations. That person distributes the remaining assets pro rata (proportionately) among the members unless the articles provide otherwise. Sometimes, the articles state that the remainder of the liquidated assets will go to a charitable or benevolent purpose. See the exhibit "Unincorporated Associations Characteristics Summary."

Unincorporated Associations Characteristics Summary

- Formation—Voluntary: Group of individuals with common purpose. Involuntary: Established by statute or regulation.

- Ownership—Individual members have rights in the association assets.

- Liabilities—Individual members can be liable for both torts and contracts arising from the association's activities. Association members are jointly and severally liable for torts committed by the association's agents and employees acting within the scope of their employment.

- Termination—Unincorporated associations can terminate by membership vote, by the death or withdrawal of substantially all the members, by court action on application of creditors or members or for illegal conduct, or by the expiration of a period stated in the articles.

[DA04686]

SUMMARY

Under the doctrine of employment at will, an employer is free to terminate any employee at any time, for any reason or for no reason. Exceptions to the doctrine, intended to protect employees, have arisen through common law or statutory changes. The four major types of exceptions to the doctrine of employment at will are public policy, implied contract, covenant of good faith, and statutory.

While nearly every state recognizes the employment-at-will doctrine with respect to the employer-employee relationship, there are exceptions to the doctrine resulting from federal laws intended to protect workers against discrimination because of age; sex, race, color, religion, or national origin; disability; or other factors, including military service, jury duty, or wage garnishment.

The collective bargaining process allows unions to represent employees in labor contract negotiations with employers. Federal laws and oversight ensure that both parties to a labor dispute bargain in good faith. Labor-management relations include collective-bargaining relationships, the collective-bargaining process, and economic pressure.

Numerous laws protect employee welfare in the areas of safety and health, wages and hours, family medical leave, benefits, and privacy. These laws create numerous obligations and compliance issues for employers, as well as significant liability exposures.

The primary advantage of incorporation is that it limits the owners' liability for the corporation's contracts and torts. State law governs the formation of most corporations, and corporations may have to comply with the laws of the state of incorporation and every other state where it does business, as well as applicable federal laws. A corporation is a foreign corporation in states other than the one where it is domiciled. Stockholders share in the ownership of corporations and may have voting rights, including approval of some decisions made by the corporation's board of directors.

The powers of a corporation stem from statute and are delineated by the corporation's charter, or articles of incorporation, filed in accordance with the law. Corporations, directors, and officers can be liable for their actions under both tort and criminal law. Directors and officers have the power to manage the operations of the corporation, and they owe a care of duty to the corporation and must make decisions for the benefit of the organization. Directors and officers can be liable to the corporation's stockholders (owners) for their misdeeds or mismanagement. Stockholders have the power to elect board members and to approve board decisions that would fundamentally change the organization or otherwise affect stockholders. Stockholders may file suit on behalf of the corporation or themselves. Stockholders, as owners of the corporation, have the right to share in the profits of the organization, usually in the form of cash dividends.

In a corporate merger, two or more corporations join to become a new, single corporation. Companies may merge for a variety of reasons, but they typically merge to form a more competitive or efficient organization. Dissolution occurs when a corporation is terminated, either voluntarily or involuntarily, and ceases to do business. Reorganization occurs when a corporation becomes bankrupt. Reorganization may result in a restructured corporation, or in the complete dissolution of the corporation due to bankruptcy.

Partnerships, limited partnerships, limited liability partnerships, and limited liability companies are types of business ownership. These structures, although similar in many respects, differ in the liability of the partners. The Uniform Partnership Act sets forth rules governing the formation, relationships, rights, responsibilities, and dissolution of partnerships.

Unincorporated associations are a form of business ownership defined as a voluntary association of individuals acting together under a common name to accomplish a lawful purpose. Associations may also be involuntary; in such cases, the association is formed by statute or regulation, and membership is mandatory for a particular group (for example, automobile assigned risk plans). Associations are the most common organizational form of not-for-profit institutions, but associations can be organized as for-profit entities as well.

Individual members are bound by the terms of the bylaws of the association. Members do not have a say in the day-to-day management of the association, but elect directors or trustees to oversee management decisions. Association members are jointly and severally liable for torts committed by the association's agents and employees acting within the scope of their employment.

Unincorporated associations may terminate in a number of different ways. Upon dissolution, after liquidation of assets and payment of all debts and obligations, the remaining assets are distributed among members on a pro-rata basis.

ASSIGNMENT NOTES

1. 29 U.S.C., § 621.
2. 29 U.S.C., § 626.
3. 42 U.S.C., § 1981.
4. 42 U.S.C., § 1983.
5. 42 U.S.C., § 2000e.
6. 42 U.S.C., § 12101.
7. 29 U.S.C. § 794.
8. 30 F.R. 12319, September 16, 1965.
9. 29 U.S.C., § 2.6d.
10. 8 U.S.C., § 1324a-b.
11. 29 U.S.C. § 793-794.
12. 42 U.S.C. § 12101 et seq.
13. 38 U.S.C., § 2021.
14. 38. U.S.C., § 4301.
15. 28 U.S.C., §1875.
16. 15. U.S.C., §1601.
17. 29 U.S.C., § 101.
18. 29 U.S.C., § 151 et seq.
19. 29 U.S.C., § 158(d).
20. 29 U.S.C. § 141-197.
21. 29 U.S.C. § 401.
22. 29 U.S.C., § 651.
23. 29 U.S.C. § 201.
24. 29 C.F.R., § 541.0.
25. 40 U.S.C., § 276a.
26. 41 U.S.C., § 35.
27. 41 U.S.C., § 351.
28. 29 U.S.C., § 2601.
29. 29 U.S.C., § 1001.
30. Pub. L. Nos. 99-272–102-26 (codified as amended in sections of U.S.C.; see 42 U.S.C.§ 1395).
31. Pub. L. No. 111–152.
32. 41 U.S.C., § 701.
33. 29 U.S.C., § 2001.
34. Pub. L. Nos. 90-51–102-332 (codified as amended in various sections of U.S.C.).
35. 15 U.S.C., § 1681.
36. Pub. L. Nos. 104–191.
37. American Bar Association, Revised Model Business Corporation Act (RMBCA), 1984, Chapter 15.

38. American Bar Association, Revised Model Business Corporation Act (RMBCA), 1984, §2.03(a).

39. 29 U.S.C., § 1001.

40. 15 U.S.C., § 78a et seq.

41. 15 U.S.C., § 78u et seq.

42. Revised Model Business Corporation Act (RMBCA), Chapter 11.

43. RMBCA, § 13.02, 13.21, 13.22.

44. RMBCA, § 11.04.

45. RMBCA, § 12.02.

46. RMBCA, § 14.30.

47. 11 U.S.C., § 101 et. seq.

48. Uniform Partnership Act, revised (1997), § 101(6).

49. UPA, § 404.

50. UPA, § 502, 503.

51. UPA, § 301(1).

52. 42 U.S.C. §14503(a).

53. 42 U.S.C. §14503(a).

The International Legal Environment

Educational Objectives

After learning the content of this assignment, you should be able to:

▷ Describe each of the methods a company can use to engage in international business, including key issues involved in each method:

- Foreign trade
- Foreign contractual relationships
- Foreign direct investments

▷ Describe the characteristics of these predominant legal systems:

- Civil law (including Roman-French, German, and Scandinavian)
- Common law
- East Asian
- Hindu
- Islamic
- Socialist-Communist

▷ Distinguish between public international law and private international law.

▷ Summarize the roles and/or responsibilities of these multinational organizations and agreements in influencing the direction and development of world business:

- United Nations
- World Trade Organization
- The North American Free Trade Agreement
- European Union
- Association of Southeast Asian Nations
- Asia-Pacific Economic Cooperation

Outline

Methods of Engaging in International Business

Legal Systems

International Law

Multinational Organizations and Agreements

United States Laws Affecting International Business

Financial Considerations in International Business

Non-Legal Factors Affecting International Business

Summary

10

▶ Explain how a U.S. company's international business can be affected by these U.S. laws:

- Internal Revenue Code

- Foreign Corrupt Practices Act

- Patriot Act

▶ Explain how each of the following financial considerations can affect a company engaged in international business:

- Currency and foreign exchange markets

- Expropriation

- Accounting standards

- Taxation

- Tax havens

▶ Describe these factors affecting companies involved in international business:

- Language

- Culture

- Time differences

- Distance and space

- Types of government

The International Legal Environment

METHODS OF ENGAGING IN INTERNATIONAL BUSINESS

As more businesses seek to participate in international business, the insurance or risk management professional needs to know the different methods by which a company may get involved, as well as the key issues each method involves.

An organization can engage in international business through any of these methods, each of which involves different levels of investment and business risk:

- Foreign trade
- Foreign contractual relationships
- Foreign direct investments

Foreign Trade

Foreign trade is the importing and exporting of a product from one country to another. It is the most common method used to participate in international business, and, compared with other methods, is the one that requires the lowest level of investment and entails the least amount of **business risk**.

Key issues for organizations involved in foreign trade include both regulatory compliance and the formation of international sales contracts. Export and import controls imposed by the United States government are important regulatory concerns, while international sales contract concerns include terms of sale and methods of payment.

Business risk

Risk that is inherent in the operation of a particular organization, including the possibility of loss, no loss, or gain.

Export Controls

Any kind of good that is sent from the United States to another country is an export. The form of transfer—shipment by carrier, mail, airplane courier, or facsimile—is subject to governmental controls. Any item, even if it leaves the country only temporarily or is not for sale (for example, a gift), is subject to control.

Most exports do not require a license and are sent to other countries under the No License Required (NLR) designation. Some goods require a Commerce Export License, which must be obtained from the Bureau of

Industry and Security (BIS). BIS is responsible for implementing and enforcing the Export Administration Regulations (EAR), which regulate the export and re-export of most commercial items. These goods are often referred to as dual-use items, because they have both commercial and military applications.

Any goods may be subject to a classification system determined by the U.S. Department of Commerce. The Department of Commerce assigns a specific alphanumeric code to goods known as an Export Control Classification Number (ECCN); all ECCNs are listed in the Commerce Control List (CCL). The classification of the good determines its licensing requirements.

Once the classification is determined, the country of destination and end user are reviewed. Depending on the geopolitical climate, some classifications of goods may be prohibited from sale. Other types of goods are classified as EAR99, not subject to the CCL. Generally these items do not require a license in many situations.

The EAR does not control all goods, services, and technologies; other U.S. government agencies regulate more specialized items.[1] The Office of Foreign Assets Control (OFAC) of the U.S. Department of the Treasury administers and enforces economic and trade sanctions as determined by U.S. foreign policy and security objectives. OFAC operates under Presidential national emergency powers as well as authority granted by legislation. OFAC imposes controls on transactions and can freeze assets under U.S. jurisdiction.

OFAC may prohibit trade or financial transactions and other dealings by U.S. entities based on national policy and national security goals. Prohibitions vary and must be reviewed. OFAC may provide for a general license authorizing certain transactions, or it may provide a specific license on a case-by-case basis, depending on the circumstances.

Insurers participating in worldwide insurance markets through global insurance policies can insure global risks without violating U.S. sanctions law by inserting policy language that explicitly excludes risks violating U.S. sanction laws. For example, such a clause in an ocean marine cargo policy would read, "…whenever coverage provided by this policy would be in violation of any U.S. economic or trade sanctions, such coverage shall be null and void." This type of exclusion prevents OFAC compliance problems and ensures that insurance and risk assumption will not be extended to sanctioned countries, entities, or individuals.

If the insurer cannot use the exclusionary language, OFAC also allows for an insurer to apply for a specific OFAC license in order to compete in international insurance markets. A separate license is required for an insurer to pay claims arising under any authorized global policy. OFAC regulations supersede all state regulations, regulating an insurer's ability to decline policies, cancel policies, or withhold claim payments.

Import Controls

The U.S. regulates the import of goods by using one or a combination of four techniques:

- Tariffs
- Quotas
- Licenses
- Prohibited imports

Many goods are imported into the U.S. because it is cheaper to manufacture them in another country. Tariffs are a tax, or duty, assessed on goods imported into the U.S. The tariff is *ad valorem*, a percentage of the price added to the sales price of the goods. The tariff increases the item price for the U.S. consumer, which may make a similar good produced in the U.S. more attractive to the American consumer. The tariff helps to eliminate the cost advantage of the imported good, protecting its American manufacturers and distributors.

Import duties are collected by the U.S. Customs Service. Goods are unloaded from carriers and stored in warehouses until the shipments are examined. Formal entry into the U.S. is made through the presentation of documentation describing the goods for classification so that the correct import duties are assessed.

Quotas are limits on the amount of a good that may be imported into the U.S. Often the good can be manufactured or otherwise produced at a cheaper cost. The imported good, if brought into the U.S. for sale in the quantity American consumers would buy, may provide sufficient supply at a price that precludes American producers from competing. Limiting the amount of a good that is already made in the U.S. protects the American producer.

Licensing, the third method of control of imports, is granted by a country's government. By requiring a license to conduct business, the government ensures that a good will be imported into the country on more favorable terms than if domestic companies competed for the goods for use or resale.

Prohibited imports are goods that are illegal to be imported and sold in the U.S. Obvious examples of prohibited imports are marijuana and cocaine.

International Sales Contracts

International trade is facilitated by agreements between trading partner countries. The United Nations Convention of Contracts for the International Sale of Goods (CISG) provides for a uniform code for international contracts. Similar to the Uniform Commercial Code (UCC), which provides uniformity for commerce within the U.S., CISG provides rules for writing international contracts and transfer of goods under the contracts.

While the same sales contract may not be used by parties for all transactions, the contract terms should clearly define the venue by which any disputes would be decided (choice of law) and the method, timing, and currency of payment. The contract may define whether the goods are to be sold directly to consumers in the foreign country or whether any distributor(s) will be selected. Warranties for the goods may also be addressed in the contract.

Choice of law specified in the sales contract will address most issues regarding differences in contract law because the country, as well as the local jurisdiction (such as state, province, or municipality), is specified in the contract. The method of payment ensures compliance with import and export financial regulations. Timing determines cash flow and delivery dates. Choice of currency addresses the risk associated with inflation and currency fluctuations on the international market.

Often, international sales contracts will include a *force majeure* (French for "superior force") clause. Essentially, incorporating this clause in the international contract frees all parties from obligation when an extraordinary event or circumstance beyond the control of the parties (such as war, strike, riot, earthquake, or volcanic eruption) prevents one or both parties from fulfilling their obligations under the contract.

Selling Terms

The selling terms agreed to by the seller and buyer and referenced in the contract of sale are a key issue in foreign trade.

The selling terms in a contract of sale typically follow standards expressed in either the *Revised American Foreign Trade Definitions (RAFTD)* or the *Incoterms*. The *RAFTD* were adopted by a joint committee consisting of representatives of the Chamber of Commerce of the United States of America and other U.S. trade associations. The Incoterms, developed by the International Chamber of Commerce, are now more widely used in international trade than the *RAFTD*.

The details of all the various selling terms defined in the *RAFTD* and *Incoterms* are beyond the scope of this discussion. However, an example will illustrate how selling terms can affect the respective duties of the seller and buyer in an international sale of goods.

Assume that a French company purchases American-manufactured cloth-covered folding chairs. The chairs are shipped in a metal intermodal container carried on an oceangoing vessel from Philadelphia, Pennsylvania, to Le Havre, France. During the voyage, the goods are damaged by salt water when the container breaks because of a severe storm. The selling terms stipulated in the contract of sale will determine which party (the buyer or the seller) will bear the financial consequences of the loss.

If the selling terms are Free On Board (FOB) Philadelphia, the American firm (the seller) assumes all risk and costs incurred to place the goods safely aboard the vessel named by the buyer. Once the goods are on board the vessel, the French company (the buyer) assumes the risk of loss or damage and must both pay the transportation costs (freight) and obtain cargo insurance if it wishes to insure the shipment.

If, instead of FOB selling terms, the selling terms are Cost, Insurance, and Freight (CIF) Le Havre, the seller's and buyer's responsibilities for loss are essentially the same as under FOB terms. However, under CIF terms, the seller must arrange and pay for ocean transportation to the named port and purchase cargo insurance covering the goods until they reach their destination. Thus, in the example, the buyer would still bear the risk of loss during the ocean voyage, but the cargo insurance purchased by the seller would indemnify the buyer.

In addition to addressing who bears the risk of loss, who pays freight costs, and who pays for insurance, selling terms also address issues such as these:

- Seller's duty to provide the goods and the commercial invoice in conformity with the contract of sale
- Seller's duty to assist the buyer in obtaining an export license or other authorization needed to export the goods
- Seller's duty to place the goods at the disposal of the buyer at the named place of delivery or on board a vessel named by the buyer
- Buyer's duty to pay the price stated in the contract of sale
- Buyer's duty to obtain any import license or other authorization needed to import the goods
- Buyer's duty to take delivery of the goods as agreed

Methods of Payment

Despite the selling terms, the seller is actually exposed to loss until it receives the buyer's payment for the goods. The buyer might be unable to make its payment, or may refuse to pay because the goods are damaged or do not meet the specifications agreed upon. The seller usually will define the method of payment in the sales contract. These are four possible methods of payment:

- Cash in advance—Funds deposited prior to receipt of the goods. This is a double disadvantage to the buyer. First, the buyer loses the time advantage of the funds, which is the use of the funds for other investment opportunities. Second, if the seller fails to ship the goods, the buyer may have difficulty recovering the funds.
- Open account—A rotating charge account under which the buyer settles the account at determined intervals. An open account is usually established only if there is a long-term relationship between buyer and seller.
- Draft—A written order by a first party, called the "drawer" (the seller), to the second party, called the "drawee" (the buyer), to pay funds to a third party, called the "payee," or to the bearer of the draft. The seller uses the draft drawn on the customer and sells it to the bank; the bank then discounts the draft. In consideration of the discount charge, the bank uses its

money to finance the shipment. The seller is paid the discounted value of the sale and does not have working capital tied up waiting for payment. If the drawee (buyer) refuses to pay, the bank has recourse against the seller. So, until the buyer pays the draft, the seller is still exposed to loss if the goods are lost or damaged in transit.

- Letter of credit (LOC)—The buyer establishes credit with a local bank, which then contacts a bank in the seller's country, establishing a credit in favor of the seller. The seller then receives a letter of credit in confirmation of the credit. If the seller is domiciled in the U.S., the letter of credit is called an "export letter of credit." If the buyer is domiciled in the U.S., the letter of credit (in favor of the foreign seller) is called an "import letter of credit." The LOC specifies what the seller must do to access the credit. If the LOC requires an insurance certificate or policy, the certificate or policy must be prepared exactly as stipulated. When the seller comes to use the credit, the seller follows the same procedures as though drawing a draft on the buyer and presents the documents to the bank that issued the credit. The seller immediately receives money from this bank, and if the letter of credit is properly drawn, there is no recourse against the seller. Letters of credit that have this no-recourse feature are called "irrevocable letters of credit." Revocable letters of credit are rarely used. The revocable letter merely states the manner in which payment is to be made. It provides no protection for the seller because it can be canceled or amended without notice to the seller.

Foreign Contractual Relationships

A second method for conducting international business is through the use of foreign contractual relationships. In comparison with foreign trade, foreign contractual relationships increase business risk and resource commitment. Two main types of foreign contractual relationships are product licensing and franchising.

Product Licensing

Product licensing is permission granted by one company to another to manufacture its product or to use its distribution facilities or technology. The licensing of products between different countries can occur for three primary reasons:

- A company may decide that selling its product in the second country is economically unfeasible because of labor costs, transportation costs, or regulations.
- A company may decide that it does not have the time or resources to produce the product in another country.
- A company may lack sufficient knowledge about the country's legal, political, social, and business environments.

Licensing technology includes granting the right to use, under specified conditions, the company's intellectual property, such as copyright, trademark, or patents. For example, a common license agreement provides for licensing computer software. A company does not buy the software program in a legal sense, but buys the right to use the program and agrees to do so under set conditions.

Just as software firms are concerned about the illegal use of their products, one of the major considerations for any firm granting a license to a foreign firm is protecting its assets. Before entering into any agreement, the domestic company assesses the trustworthiness of the foreign company it is dealing with and the foreign company's ability to meet the financial requirements of the licensing agreement.

Thoroughly understanding the foreign legal environment regarding copyright, trademark, and patent protection is necessary. A company should consult a lawyer who is an expert in the intellectual property field about global intellectual property legal issues.

Franchising

Franchising occurs when one company assigns to another the right to supply its products or services within a market. A franchise is a contract entered into for a specific time period. The franchisee (who receives the franchise) pays a royalty to the franchisor (who grants the franchise) for the rights assigned, in addition to other possible considerations. The franchisor provides training, technical assistance, specialized equipment, advertising, and promotion as stated in the agreement.

In franchising, the company image and its name are the franchisor's assets. The franchisor allows the franchisee to use its image and certain assets.

An important aspect of franchising is the control over the use of the company's name and the quality of the product or service. For example, many franchisors retain control over all advertising and pricing of products in the markets. Some companies control the risk of improper use of the corporate name or the risk of poor product or service quality by withholding vital technology or required component products. For example, a hotel chain can maintain control of its reservation system, or a grocery cooperative can maintain control of all product distribution.

Foreign Direct Investment

A third method to conduct foreign trade is foreign direct investment, which occurs when a company in one country acquires control over assets located in another country. This type of investment also anticipates managerial control of the assets acquired in the foreign market. This arrangement contrasts with foreign portfolio investment, which occurs when a company purchases foreign stocks, bonds, or other financial instruments. Foreign direct investment usually takes one of two forms, known as subsidiaries and joint ventures.

Subsidiaries

A subsidiary is a company owned or controlled by another company. A subsidiary might be subject to the parent company's complete or partial control. Generally, a company is not a subsidiary unless another company controls 50 percent or more of its shares.

A distinguishing characteristic of a subsidiary, as opposed to a joint venture, is that a subsidiary issues stock. The stock can be 100 percent owned by the parent company, or some of the shares can be publicly traded in the foreign market. In fact, joint ventures are often subsidiaries in which the partners each own a percentage of the stock. In many foreign markets, the government requires a company to form a subsidiary to bring the parent firms and subsidiaries under the local laws of incorporation. These local laws can require both the subsidiary and the parents to comply with local financial reporting and disclosure.

The fully owned subsidiary provides a company with the highest level of control over operations, but presents the highest level of business risk, commitment of capital, and managerial control. With higher risk, a company expects to achieve higher returns. For a company experienced in international operations, this trade-off between risk and return can be acceptable and even desirable.

The time required for a company to enter a foreign market using a subsidiary varies, depending on the entry technique the company chooses or requires. Acquiring an existing company in the foreign market can usually occur relatively quickly. Conversely, if a company develops its subsidiary from the ground up, it might take years to become relevant in the foreign market. This latter approach probably gives the company the greatest control over its foreign affiliates, because the parent company would develop the local management, distribution channels, and product mix. However, this approach also requires a larger investment of resources and time.

Joint Ventures

In the international trade context, a joint venture involves shared ownership and control of a foreign operation. Joint ventures allow a company to enter either a geographic or product market and to acquire technology or revenue that would not otherwise be within reach.

The most common joint arrangement involves a company joining forces with a second company to operate a joint venture in the second company's country. Less common are joint ventures formed by companies from two different countries to operate in a third country. Additionally, companies rarely enter into joint ventures with more than three partners.

Like subsidiaries, joint ventures increase companies' business risk and commitment of resources. A company might have to invest substantial capital or share proprietary technology with its joint venture partners. However, the value of the joint venture can be greater than the sum of the individual partners' contributions.

In some joint ventures, partner companies divide capital expenses among themselves and share the costs, depending on the market and the partners' preferences. Additionally, engaging in a joint venture requires a company to commit substantial managerial resources and might require considerably more time to enter a foreign market than to enter a domestic joint venture or acquire a subsidiary.

Perhaps the single most important aspect of forming a joint venture is choosing the right partner or partners. This choice is important because the companies share resources, managerial responsibilities, technology, and profits, among other things.

A company may choose foreign direct investment over foreign trade for a number of reasons. Barriers to trade, both those occurring naturally (for example, transportation costs and language and cultural differences) and otherwise (for example, tariffs, quotas, or political issues) contribute to a company's need to gain direct access to markets through direct investment.

Companies seeking direct foreign investment fall into three general categories:

- Resource seekers—Companies that enter a foreign market seeking that country's resources, such as oil reserves, lower-cost labor, or technology
- Market seekers—Companies that enter a foreign market to acquire new customers outside their own countries' boundaries
- Market followers—Companies that follow their customers into foreign countries, a common trend in service industries such as insurance and banking

LEGAL SYSTEMS

Although no two countries have identical legal systems, many nations share legal approaches and concepts. Additionally, some countries classified within one system have incorporated legal concepts found traditionally within other systems. This section provides information about the development of different legal systems to give insurance professionals a basic understanding of the differences they might encounter in the international legal environment.

In a majority of countries, the legal systems fall into these two major categories:

- Civil-law system
- Common-law system

The civil-law tradition developed within these three distinct subsystems:

- Roman (and French)
- German
- Scandinavian (Nordic)

Other predominant legal systems include the East Asian, Hindu, Islamic, and Socialist-Communist systems.

Civil Law

Civil law, or Roman-Germanic law, uses comprehensive codes and statutes to form the backbone of a legal system. This system relies heavily on legal scholars to develop and interpret the law. The civil-law system is the most influential system in the world. More countries use its subsystems, in one form or another, than any other legal system.

It is the dominant legal system of western Europe, almost all of Latin America, and parts of Africa and Asia. Additionally, the civil-law system can be found in parts of some traditionally common-law countries (for example, Louisiana in the United States, Quebec in Canada, and Puerto Rico). However, these legal systems can vary a great deal from one country to another in their legal institutions, processes, and rules.

In the civil-law system, a judge is a civil servant whose function is to find the correct legislative provision within a written code of statutes and apply it to the facts presented in a case. Judges perform little interpretation of a code, and their opinions do not determine their thought processes on legal issues.

The civil-law courts usually are divided into two or more separate sets, each with its own jurisdiction over different issues, with a different hierarchy, judiciary, and procedures.

The typical civil-law case usually is divided into these three stages:

- The preliminary stage involves submission of pleadings and appointment of a hearing judge.
- At the evidence stage, a hearing judge takes evidence and prepares a written summary of the proceedings.
- At the decision stage, the presiding judge decides the case based on the record provided by the hearing judge, the counsels' briefs, and arguments.

The civil law system does not have the common-law system's jury trial; instead, a series of isolated meetings, written communications, motions, and rulings help decide the case. Civil-law countries have varying time frames for these events; some countries' procedures proceed very quickly, and others proceed very slowly.

Roman-French Law

The French civil code of 1804 consolidated the contrasting concepts of law by decree and law by custom. Although a magistrate is the final arbiter of a private law dispute, a court can rely on appointed experts, who have wide-ranging powers to investigate and present evidence to support an opinion rendered by a court. A magistrate usually will not reject an expert's opinion.

However, in France and Italy, a party can appeal a primary court's opinion, although courts in those countries tend to have extremely heavy backlogs. Under these circumstances, the examination of detailed factual or legal issues can be difficult because, with the passage of time, memories fade and some witnesses become difficult to find.

The French civil code was the basis for codes in the Netherlands, Italy, Portugal, and Spain. Haiti also adopted the French Code, and Bolivia and Chile adopted it for the most part. In turn, Ecuador, Uruguay, Argentina, and Colombia used the Chilean code as the model for their own legal systems. Puerto Rico and the Philippines used the Spanish code as their legal systems' model.

German Law

Germany's location in the center of Europe has greatly influenced its political and social history. Many scholars consider the German civil law system as the most developed and influential of all the civil-law subsystems.

The German private law, or *Bürgerliches Gesetzbuch* (BGB), is the civil code that took effect in 1900. Unlike the French code, which was designed for laypersons to read, the BGB was developed for legal professionals to read and was too technical for laypersons. The German civil law influenced the U.S. legal education system; the American Law Institute's (ALI) restatements, or authoritative treatises, on law; and the development of the Uniform Commercial Code (UCC).

The original German code emphasized the rights of people to enter into contracts freely and dealt with the enforceability of all kinds of contracts. Similarly, the German code requires a finding of fault on the part of a wrong-doer in a tort suit. Although some elements of those concepts still exist, the availability of insurance as a risk- and damage-spreading mechanism has caused the German code to expand individual obligations and potential culpability.

Compensation for damages without culpability has effectively created a "cradle-to-grave" safety net as part of a wide social compact in Germany. For example, German statutes grant compensation for certain types of accidents, regardless of culpability, including railway, traffic, aircraft, electrical, gas, and nuclear power station accidents.

The German and Swiss codes, along with the French code, influenced code developments in Brazil, Mexico, precommunist China, and Peru.

Additionally, Japan used the German code in the development of its own code, and Turkey used the similar Swiss code in developing its legal system.

Scandinavian Law

The Scandinavian (Nordic) legal system is both a civil-law system and an independent system. The legal systems in the Scandinavian countries are based neither on large bodies of codified regulations, like those of the French and German systems, nor on case (common) law.

The Scandinavian legal systems evolved from a long-established history of customary law. Elements of law by decree developed as a result of Germanic and Russian influences. Additionally, the Scandinavian countries have codified historical business practices as statutes. In tort law, as distinguished from contracts, damages contain a punitive element beyond just and fair compensation.

The development of a virtually distinct legal system in Scandinavian countries resulted from the historically close links among those countries. For example, Finland was part of Sweden for hundreds of years until it became part of Russia, then eventually gained independence. Norway, now independent, was part of Denmark.

Common Law

In the common-law legal system, a judge interprets the facts of a case, examines precedents (prior judicial rulings in similar cases), and makes a decision based on the facts in the current case. Precedents are guides, not rigid frameworks for all decisions. This system tends to be fact-intensive, relying on the judge's reasoning for a final decision.

England and most of the former British colonial countries, including Australia, Canada, India, and the U.S., use the common-law system. Japan's law combines the civil- and common-law systems, particularly relating to corporate law, which resulted from U.S. influence in post-World War II Japan. East Asian legal systems also influenced Japan's legal system. Other examples of blended common-law systems are Canada and the U.S. Both the province of Quebec and the state of Louisiana have state legal systems based on French civil law.

East Asian Law

East Asian countries have a common background profoundly influencing their legal developments over the centuries. China has a dominant presence in East Asia. Although both Korea and Japan have different legal systems, they both reflect the Chinese influence.

Until the 19th century, Japan's civil code was based on the developing German civil code. However, this imported legal code did not supplant the local customary law already existing in Japan. Even today, a tradition of informal compromise, contrasted with individual parties' asserting their rights in negotiations, remains a strong characteristic of the East Asian countries' approach to contract disputes. Japan today has relatively few attorneys, judges, and lawsuits.

Other Asian countries have relied on both civil and common law to varying degrees. French colonialism influenced the legal systems of the southeast Asian countries Laos, Cambodia, and Vietnam for many years. By contrast, England's common-law system influenced the legal systems of Singapore, Malaysia, and Brunei. U.S. influence was prevalent in post-World War II Japan and in the Philippines after the Spanish-American War.

Hindu Law

Hinduism provides religious and philosophical rules in India and some surrounding countries. The Hindu legal system is perhaps the oldest in the world. The customs and laws of Hinduism have applied separately and distinctly to the members of four major caste groups: Brahmans (priests), Kshatriyas (warriors), Vaishyas (tradesmen), and Sudras (servants and artisans). Movement from one caste to another historically was not permitted, even with professional or political success, although laws have attempted to eliminate the rigid caste system. Legislation in India has voided all the rules of the caste system when they conflict with social justice.

By the early 1800s, most of India was under the control of the British, whose policy in settling colonies was to retain existing law, allowing Hindu law to become the official system for the Hindu population. The effect of British rule on Hindu law was the development of legislation, the judiciary, and the legal education system. A statutory code of commercial, criminal, and civil procedure has replaced the Hindu law of contracts and property. However, India's legal system still reflects remnants of the caste system.

Islamic Law

The Islamic legal system is used in countries whose citizens are almost entirely followers of the Islamic religion. This legal system is based on the foundations of the *Book of the Qur'an* (*Koran*) and includes almost all of the countries of the Middle East and northern Africa, southern Asia, southeastern Europe, and parts of southeast Asia.

More Islamic countries are members of the United Nations than countries whose majorities follow any other religion. Islam is the second most prevalent religion in the world, with approximately 1.2 billion followers.

With the end of World War I and the collapse of the Ottoman Empire, Europeans regained control of most of the territories that Islamic warriors had captured in previous centuries. In the decades following World War II, many Islamic peoples attempted to gain their independence, often from European countries. Internal debates, still ongoing, centered on whether states should be theocracies or secular states that follow Islamic law.

The primary system of law within the Islamic countries is the *Shari'ah*, with a secondary system of jurisprudence called the *fiqh*. The *Shari'ah* consists of the two primary sources of Islamic law from which all legal principles derive, the *Qur'an* and the *Sunnah*. The *fiqh*, or Islamic jurisprudence, is the process of applying *Shari'ah* principles to both real or hypothetical cases.

The *Qur'an*, the highest source of law within Islam, gives followers of Islam the authority to make law and render opinions. The *Sunnah* forms a second tier of the *Shari'ah* and mandates the standard of conduct people are to follow to comply with the *Qur'an*.

The *Qur'an* is a religious book, not a legal code or book of law, but it serves as the foundation for the Islamic legal system. It contains specific precepts about ethics, crime, business transactions, domestic relations, inheritance, and war. The *Qur'an* differs from a code of law in that it does not mention the legal consequences of the disregard of its rules.

The *faqh* refers to the body of laws developed from the *Shari'ah*. Five schools of *faqh* (*faqh madhhabs*) exist today. Four are within the *Sunni* sect of Islam. The fifth school is within the *Shai* (*Shiite* or *Shiah*) sect of Islam. At times, conflict has divided the different *faqh madhhabs*. Identifying with a different school or attempting to change affiliation can be considered heresy. Additionally, at times judges prohibit intermarriage between the different *faqh madhhabs*.

Approximately 90 percent of all Muslims identify themselves as *Sunni*, with the balance being *Shai*. The *Shai* live primarily in Iran, southern Iraq, Syria, and Lebanon and believe that the leader of the Islamic religion should be a direct descendant of Muhammad. *Sunni* Muslims do not have this requirement. A significant difference between *Shai* and *Sunni* is that *Shais* also believe that individual reasoning (*ijtihad*) is a legitimate source of Islamic law.

Socialist-Communist Law

The socialist system originated with the Marxist overthrow of czarist Russia in the October Revolution in 1917, which created the Soviet Union. Before the revolution, Russia was a civil-law country.

The result of the Marxist takeover was the imposition of socialist ideology over the civil-law system that already existed. The central idea of the system was the emphasis on the state's interest over that of individuals. Russia developed new codes that reflected the Marxist ideas that the laws should serve the interests of socialism.

Private-sector business legal principles, such as contracts, commercial law, torts, property, and bankruptcy, are of little use within a socialist system. Public law replaces private-sector legal principles. For example, because the government owns all property and production, all contract law is public. In a socialist country, the socialist political party controls and influences the entire legal system, including the courts. All decisions from the courts, although independent in nature, are subject to party control or revision.

Western civil- and common-law systems heavily influenced the law in Russia. Asian socialist-communist countries discovered problems applying the Soviet-style legal principles in their societies. The communist People's Republic of China, for example, abandoned the legal principles introduced to them by the Soviets and developed a more informal system more similar to East Asian traditions.

With the fall of the Soviet bloc in the 1990s, former eastern European bloc countries abandoned the socialist-communist legal system in favor of a civil-law system. Many changes were profound, with legislatures endorsing basic free market principles. The actual changes varied by country. Today, Russia is a civil-law country. However, the Russian government often changes the legal applications of civil law with regard to individuals and businesses.

Several other communist-ruled or communist-influenced countries, such as Cuba, North Korea, Vietnam, and the People's Republic of China, still use the Soviet-based legal system. The People's Republic of China now permits a private economy and has adopted it as part of the Constitution of the People's Congress. China's dominant constitutional principles still require observance of socialist doctrine. China also has adopted civil-law type of codification, the General Principles of Civil Law, and is developing an ever more extensive codification.

INTERNATIONAL LAW

In any legal dispute arising between parties from different countries, public and private international law must be considered.

Those resolving international disputes between individuals or corporations first apply any applicable public international law, such as an international treaty, that governs the dispute. If no international treaty applies, then any relevant laws of the involved countries are applied to the dispute in accordance with the principles of private international law.

Public International Law

Public international law concerns the interrelation of nation states and is governed by treaties and other international agreements.

International treaties agreed to by a business's country of origin govern some international business transactions. These treaties may be between two countries, or they may be multilateral treaties among many countries.

Public international law

A law that concerns the interrelation of nation states and that is governed by treaties and other international agreements.

The North American Free Trade Agreement (NAFTA) is a trilateral treaty governing all business interactions involving Canada, Mexico, and the U.S. Other treaties, such as the World Trade Organization's General Agreement of Tariffs and Trade (GATT), involve more than one hundred countries as signatories.

These international agreements affect member countries by requiring that they amend their national laws to comply with the agreements' requirements. For example, countries that signed GATT agreed to adjust their tariff rates on imported goods from other GATT member countries. However, these agreements are not limited to trade and tariffs. For example, NAFTA includes investment provisions, and the World Trade Organization's Trade-Related Aspects of Intellectual Property Rights Agreement ensures that the laws of member countries set basic standards for the protection of intellectual property.

Private International Law

Private international law

A law that involves disputes between individuals or corporations in different countries.

Private international law involves disputes between individuals or corporations in different countries and is also referred to as conflicts of law. It involves questions about which laws apply in settling the disputes and how they apply. It determines which jurisdiction's law applies to the business transaction in question, which country's court hears a dispute, and whether other countries will enforce the foreign decision.

In any legal dispute arising between parties from different countries, these two issues must be considered:

- Whether a court in one country will recognize the decision of another country's court
- Whether a court has the right to hear the legal dispute

The first issue is referred to as comity, the practice by which one country recognizes, within its own territory or in its courts, another country's institutions. Comity can also apply to the rights and privileges acquired by a citizen in a country. Many experts believe that comity is the basis for all private international law.

The second issue is referred to as jurisdiction. Just as in domestic cases, one of the basic questions of international law is whether a court has the right (jurisdiction) to preside over a particular case.

More specifically, courts in international cases must determine whether they have jurisdiction over the person or entity (*in personam* jurisdiction) and over the subject matter (*in res* jurisdiction) and if they have jurisdiction to render the particular judgment in the case.

In international cases, personal jurisdiction is based on whether the person or entity is present in the country or has committed the act in question in that country.

A significant issue frequently arising in international law is whether one country's courts have jurisdiction over either another country's citizen or a corporation with its place of business in another country. Jurisdictional issues are increasing in importance and complexity as governments try to control the increase in international business.

For example, one country's jurisdiction over Internet commerce originating in another country raises complex jurisdictional questions. Other cases involving jurisdictional issues include the U.S.'s attempt to prevent U.S. residents from purchasing prescription drugs from other countries, China's claim to all Chinese-language domain names and its blocking of certain Web sites, and some European courts' claiming authority over Web sites from outside their countries' borders.

MULTINATIONAL ORGANIZATIONS AND AGREEMENTS

Several prominent international organizations and agreements affect practically all international business dealings. They also can influence the direction of world business developments.

The international organizations and agreements discussed here are these:

- United Nations (UN)
- World Trade Organization (WTO)
- The North American Free Trade Agreement (NAFTA)
- European Union (EU)
- Association of Southeast Asian Nations (ASEAN)
- Asia-Pacific Economic Cooperation (APEC)

United Nations (UN)

In 1944, representatives of China, the Soviet Union, the U.K., and the U.S. met to propose a new international organization, the United Nations (UN). They signed the UN Charter in 1945. Over the years, the number of UN member states has grown to 192 countries.

Under the UN Charter, the UN's purposes are as follows:

- To maintain international peace and security
- To develop friendly relations among nations
- To cooperate in solving international economic, social, cultural, and humanitarian problems
- To promote respect for human rights and fundamental freedoms
- To be a center for harmonizing the actions of nations in attaining these goals

Five principal UN bodies are currently active:

- General Assembly
- Security Council
- Economic and Social Council
- International Court of Justice
- Secretariat

The UN entity, however, is much larger than these five bodies, actually encompassing some fifteen agencies and several programs and bodies. The General Assembly is the UN's deliberating body and comprises representatives of all the member states. Decisions on important questions, such as those involving peace and security, the admission of new members, and budgetary matters, require a two-thirds majority vote for passage, while a simple majority vote can decide other matters.

General Assembly

Under the UN Charter, the functions and powers of the General Assembly include these:

- To consider and make recommendations on the principles of cooperation in the maintenance of international peace and security, including the principles governing disarmament and arms regulation
- To initiate studies and make recommendations to promote international political cooperation; the development and codification of international law; the realization of human rights and fundamental freedoms for all; and international collaboration in economic, social, cultural, educational, and health fields
- To elect, jointly with the Security Council, the judges of the International Court of Justice
- On the recommendation of the Security Council, to appoint the secretary-general

Security Council

The Security Council's primary responsibility is to maintain international peace and security. It functions continuously with representatives of each of its members present at all times at the UN Headquarters in New York City.

When a complaint concerning a threat to peace comes before it, the Security Council's first action usually is to recommend to the conflicting parties that they try to reach agreement by peaceful means and then, in some cases, to investigate and mediate.

When a dispute leads to armed conflict, the Security Council's first concern is to end it as soon as possible. The Security Council also authorizes the UN to send peacekeeping forces to help reduce tensions in troubled areas, keep opposing forces apart, and create calmer conditions in which peaceful settlements might result. The Security Council also can decide on other enforcement measures, economic sanctions, or collective military action.

The Security Council has five permanent members (China, France, Russia, the U.K., and the U.S.) and ten nonpermanent members elected by the General Assembly for two-year terms and not eligible for immediate reelection.

Economic and Social Council

The UN's Economic and Social Council (ECOSOC) is responsible for promoting higher standards of living, full employment, and economic and social progress through many other UN agencies. ECOSOC is also responsible for these tasks:

- Identifying solutions to international economic, social, and health problems.
- Facilitating international cultural and educational cooperation.
- Encouraging universal respect for human rights and fundamental freedoms ECOSOC's responsibility extends to over 70 percent of the human and financial resources of the UN organization system. In carrying out its mandate, ECOSOC consults with academicians, business sector representatives, and more than 2,100 registered non-governmental organizations (NGOs).

International Court of Justice

The International Court of Justice (ICJ), located at the Peace Palace in The Hague (Netherlands), is the UN's principal judicial organ. The ICJ has a dual role:

- To settle, in accordance with international law, the legal disputes that countries submit to it
- To give advisory opinions on legal questions that duly authorized international entities and agencies refer to it

The ICJ comprises fifteen judges elected to nine-year terms by the UN General Assembly and Security Council. The ICJ cannot include more than one judge of any nationality. Judicial elections take place every three years, for one-third of the seats, with rules allowing reelection of judges. ICJ judges do not represent their national governments but act as independent ICJ magistrates.

ICJ judges must have the qualifications required in their respective countries for appointment to the highest judicial offices or must be jurists of recognized competence in international law. The ICJ's composition also reflects the principal legal systems of the world. When the ICJ does not include a judge representing a country that is party to a case, that country can appoint a person to sit as an ad hoc judge only for that case.

The ICJ can hear disputes in one of the following ways when a concerned country has accepted jurisdiction:

- By the conclusion of a special agreement between parties to submit the dispute to the ICJ.

- By virtue of a jurisdictional clause, typically, when the countries in question are parties to a treaty.

- Through the reciprocal effects of declarations the countries have made under a law providing that each has accepted the jurisdiction of the ICJ as compulsory in the event of a dispute with another country that has made a similar declaration. More than sixty countries have such a declaration in force. However, a number of these declarations are subject to the exclusion of certain categories of dispute.

Secretariat

The Secretariat is the UN's international staff, working around the world to carry out the UN's daily operations. The General Assembly appoints the secretary general, who heads the Secretariat on the Security Council's recommendation for a renewable five-year term.

World Trade Organization (WTO)

The World Trade Organization (WTO) deals with trade rules among nations. The WTO's existence depends on agreements that most of the world's trading nations have negotiated and ratified. The WTO's goal is to help producers of goods and services, exporters, and importers conduct their business. The organization has over 150 members. The entire membership makes the WTO's decisions, by consensus.

WTO members operate a non-discriminatory trading system. Each country receives guarantees that its exports will receive fair and consistent treatment in other countries' markets, and each country promises to do the same for imports into its own market.

Approximately, three-quarters of the WTO member states are developing countries. The WTO system gives these countries longer time periods to implement agreements and commitments, opportunities to increase trade, and support to help them build an infrastructure for WTO work, handling disputes, and implementing technical standards.

In the WTO, no board of directors or WTO executive has power to run the organization. Members enforce all decisions and rules under agreed procedures that they themselves have negotiated, including the possibility of trade sanctions. Sanctions imposed are authorized by the membership as a whole. In this respect, the WTO is different from some other international organizations, such as the World Bank and International Monetary Fund (IMF), which have bureaucratic structures in place to enforce actions.

WTO agreements are the legal ground rules for most international commerce. They guarantee member countries important trading rights. The three primary WTO agreements include these:

- The General Agreement on Tariffs and Trade (GATT)
- The General Agreement on Trade in Services (GATS)
- The Agreement on Trade-Related Aspects of Intellectual Property Rights (TRIPS Agreement)

The General Agreement on Tariffs and Trade (GATT) began with trade in goods. From 1947 to 1994, GATT was the basis for negotiating lower customs duty rates and other trade barriers. Since 1995, the updated version of GATT has become the WTO's umbrella agreement for trade in all goods. It has annexed dealings with specific sectors, such as agriculture and textiles. It has also annexed dealings with specific issues, such as state trading, product standards, subsidies, and actions taken against **dumping**.

Dumping

The act of selling a large quantity of goods at less than fair value, including selling goods abroad at less than the market price at home.

The General Agreement on Trade in Services (GATS) sets forth the principles that allow service providers (such as banks, insurers, telecommunications companies, hotel chains, and transport companies) wanting to do business abroad to enjoy the same principles of free and fair trade that originally applied to trade in goods. WTO members have also made individual commitments under GATS, stating which of their services sectors they are willing to open to foreign competition and how open those markets will become.

The Agreement on Trade-related Aspects of Intellectual Property Rights (TRIPS), the WTO's intellectual property agreement, sets forth rules for trade and investment in ideas and creative work. TRIPS states how all intellectual property (such as copyrights, patents, and trade secrets) should be protected in international business and trade.

North American Free Trade Agreement (NAFTA)

The North American Free Trade Agreement (NAFTA) is a comprehensive regional trade and investment agreement that Canada, Mexico, and the U.S. entered into in 1994 to improve all aspects of doing business in the North American market.

The objectives of this agreement, as elaborated more specifically through its principles and rules, including national treatment, most-favored-nation treatment and transparency, are to perform these functions:

- Eliminate barriers to trade in, and facilitate the cross-border movement of, goods and services between the territories of the parties
- Promote conditions of fair competition in the free trade area

- Substantially increase investment opportunities in the territories of the parties
- Provide adequate and effective protection and enforcement of intellectual property rights in each party's territory
- Create effective procedures for the implementation and application of the agreement, for its joint administration, and for the resolution of disputes
- Establish a framework for further trilateral, regional, and multilateral cooperation to expand and enhance the benefits of this agreement

NAFTA eliminated nearly all tariffs between the U.S. and Canada by 1998 and nearly all tariffs between the U.S. and Mexico by 2008.

NAFTA also removes many of the non-tariff barriers, such as import licenses, that have helped to exclude U.S. goods from the other two markets, particularly Mexico. NAFTA ensures that restrictive government policies will not coerce investment and that U.S. investors receive treatment equal to domestic investors in Mexico and Canada. At the same time, NAFTA's extensive easing of cross-border services rules ensures that U.S. companies need not invest in another country to provide their services if they do not wish to do so.

NAFTA establishes a mechanism for settling disputes between NAFTA countries over the interpretation and application of the agreement. It also contains separate dispute resolution mechanisms for antidumping and countervailing duty matters, as well as for specific sectors, such as investment and financial services.

For a U.S. product to be eligible for lower tariff rates when entering Mexico or Canada, the product must be produced in the U.S. entirely of NAFTA component parts; or, if the product consists of foreign component parts, a substantive transformation from the foreign component part to the final product must have occurred. Between 1993 and 2007, trade among the three countries tripled.

European Union (EU)

The European Union (EU) is a group of European democratic countries committed to working together for peace and prosperity. The EU is unique in that each member state delegated some of its national sovereignty so that decisions could be made on specific matters of joint interest democratically.

The Treaty of Maastricht (1992) introduced new forms of cooperation between the EU member state governments; for example, on defense and in the area of "justice and home affairs." By adding this intergovernmental cooperation to the original "European Community" system, the Treaty of Maastricht created the European Union (EU). All EU decisions and procedures are based on EU treaties, to which all member countries agree.

In the early years, much of the cooperation among EU countries centered on trade and the economy, but now the EU also deals with other issues, such as citizens' rights; ensuring freedom, security, and justice; job creation; regional development; and environmental protection.

Five EU institutions play specific roles:

- The European Parliament, one of two legislative bodies in the EU, is elected by the people of the member states.
- The Council of the European Union, the other legislative body in the EU, represents the governments of the member states.
- The European Commission is the EU's executive body.
- The Court of Justice is the EU's judicial body.
- The Court of Auditors is an external investigatory agency whose primary role is to audit the EU budget.

These institutions are supplemented by the following five other important EU bodies:

- The European Economic and Social Committee, which makes recommendations relating to economic and social issues
- The Committee of the Regions, which represents regional and local authorities
- The European Central Bank, responsible for monetary policy and managing the common EU currency, the euro
- The European Ombudsman, who deals with citizens' complaints about administration by any EU institution or body
- The European Investment Bank, which finances EU investment projects

The member states over time removed all barriers to trade among them and turned their **Common Market** into a genuine single market in which goods, services, people, and capital could move freely across borders. The single market was formally completed at the end of 1992, though the EU countries still have more to accomplish to complete the Common Market, such as creation of a genuinely single market in financial services.

Common Market
The European Union's member countries' single, unified market in which goods, services, people, and capital can move freely across borders.

Additionally, in 1992, the EU decided to go forward with an economic and monetary union (EMU), involving the introduction of a single European currency, the euro, managed by the European Central Bank. The euro became a reality in 2002, when euro notes and coins replaced national currencies in twelve of the fifteen countries of the European Union. As of 2010, the euro is the official currency of sixteen of the EU's twenty-seven member states.

Association of Southeast Asian Nations (ASEAN)

Five member states (Indonesia, Malaysia, the Philippines, Singapore, and Thailand) established the Association of Southeast Asian Nations (ASEAN) in 1967. Later, Brunei, Cambodia, Laos, and Myanmar joined ASEAN.

ASEAN's purposes are twofold:

- Accelerating the economic growth, social progress, and cultural development in the region through joint endeavors in the spirit of equality and partnership to strengthen the foundation for a prosperous and peaceful community of Southeast Asian nations

- Promoting regional peace and stability through respect for justice and the rule of law in the relationship among countries in the region and adherence to the principles of the United Nations Charter

ASEAN members have made significant progress in lowering intraregional tariffs through the Common Effective Preferential Tariff (CEPT) Scheme of the ASEAN Free Trade Area (AFTA) agreement.

Asia-Pacific Economic Cooperation (APEC)

Asia-Pacific Economic Cooperation (APEC) began in 1989 as a loose organization of countries set around the Pacific Ocean. APEC has attempted to facilitate economic growth, cooperation, trade, and investment in the Asia-Pacific region. Since its inception, APEC has worked to reduce tariffs and other trade barriers across the Asia-Pacific region, creating efficient economies and increasing exports.

The key to achieving APEC's vision is what is referred to as the Bogor Goals (adopted in Bogor, Indonesia, in 1994), which call for free and open trade and investment. Member countries aim to achieve these goals by 2010, with developing country members achieving these goals by 2020.

APEC is the only inter-governmental body that operates on the basis of nonbinding commitments, open dialogue, and equal respect for the views of all participant countries. Unlike the WTO or other multilateral trade bodies, APEC has required no treaty obligations of its participants. APEC members reach all decisions by consensus and undertake commitments totally on a voluntary basis.

APEC has twenty-one member states, including, among others: Australia, Canada, Japan, the U.S., the People's Republic of China, Hong Kong, and Mexico.

UNITED STATES LAWS AFFECTING INTERNATIONAL BUSINESS

The international business operations of a company domiciled in the United States are affected not only by international law and the laws of other nations but also by various U.S. laws.

Important examples of U.S. federal laws influencing international business and foreign investment are the tax code (Internal Revenue Code), the

Foreign Corrupt Practices Act, and the Patriot Act. Each of these laws affects an organization's earnings and practices in relation to international trade and business.

Tax Code

Within the U.S. tax code (Internal Revenue Code, or IRC),[2] a number of sections specifically address international business and foreign investment.

These sections can either help or hinder international investment and trade. For example, the current IRC allows a U.S. company to claim a credit against its U.S. taxes for taxes paid in other countries. These credits help avoid the double taxation of earnings that arise from the U.S.'s worldwide tax system.

Foreign tax credits are limited to the U.S. corporate tax rate. The U.S. federal corporate income tax code contains six marginal rates ranging from 15 to 39 percent. The majority of corporate income is taxable at a 35 percent marginal tax rate. The marginal tax rate refers to the highest published tax rate at which a taxpayer's last dollar earned is taxable. With a corporate tax rate at this level in the U.S., many companies form subsidiaries in tax haven jurisdictions and even move their incorporation to another country.

Repatriation of earnings is the process by which a U.S. parent company moves earnings from its foreign-based affiliates back to the U.S. to the parent company or to its stockholders. In the U.S., the Internal Revenue Service (IRS) levies corporate income tax at the time earnings are repatriated. IRC Subpart F codifies the federal government's system of "anti-deferral" rules, which lead to the taxation of certain kinds of foreign-source income in the year the company earned it, even though the U.S. parent company did not repatriate those profits during the year.

Foreign Corrupt Practices Act

U.S. companies, including insurers, planning to do business in foreign markets must be familiar with the Foreign Corrupt Practices Act (FCPA).[3] In general, the FCPA prohibits payments to foreign officials to obtain or keep business.

Passage of the FCPA was a result of an SEC investigation in the mid-1970s in which more than 400 U.S. companies admitted making questionable or illegal payments to foreign government officials, politicians, and political parties to secure or maintain business. Congress enacted the FCPA to stop these acts and to restore public confidence in the integrity of the U.S. business system.

The FCPA also requires companies who list their securities in the U.S. to meet certain accounting provisions. These accounting provisions operate in tandem with the anti-bribery provisions, requiring a company to keep accounting records that accurately reflect all the company's transactions and to maintain an adequate system of internal accounting controls.

The FCPA has had a significant effect on how U.S. companies conduct international business. Several companies that paid bribes to foreign officials have been the subject of criminal and civil enforcement actions, resulting in large fines and suspensions and debarment from federal procurement contracting. Additionally, some of these companies' employees and officers have gone to prison.

Following the passage of the FCPA, Congress became aware that U.S. companies were operating at a strategic disadvantage to foreign companies that routinely paid bribes and that, in some countries, could even deduct the cost of these bribes as business expenses from their taxes. In 1988, Congress directed the Executive Branch to start negotiations in the Organization of Economic Cooperation and Development (OECD) to obtain agreements with the U.S.'s major trading partners to enact legislation similar to the FCPA. In 1997, the U.S. and thirty-three other countries signed the OECD Convention on Combating Bribery of Foreign Public Officials in International Business Transactions. Since 1998, the U.S. has also applied FCPA to foreign companies and individuals who perform any act to further a corrupt payment while in the U.S.

The U.S. Department of Justice is responsible for all criminal and civil enforcement of anti-bribery provisions regarding domestic and foreign companies and nationals. The SEC is responsible for civil enforcement of the anti-bribery provisions regarding issuers.

Any person or company violating the FCPA can be barred from doing business with the federal government, and an indictment alone can lead to suspension of the right to do business with the government. Furthermore, any conduct that violates the anti-bribery provisions of the FCPA also can create a private cause of action under the Racketeer Influenced and Corrupt Organizations Act (RICO Act) or under other federal or state laws.

The Patriot Act

Congress enacted The Patriot Act of 2001 as a reaction to the terrorist attacks on the World Trade Center in New York City and the Pentagon in Washington, D.C., on September 11, 2001. The law's stated purpose is "to deter and punish terrorist acts in the United States and around the world, to enhance law enforcement investigatory tools, and for other purposes." The Patriot Act increases the surveillance and investigative powers of U.S. law enforcement agencies in several ways.

The Patriot Act's implications for online privacy are considerable. It extends the government's ability to gain access to personal financial information and student information without any suspicion of wrongdoing, simply by certifying that the information likely to be obtained is relevant to an ongoing criminal investigation. Additionally, several sections of the law apply directly to business, including those that track and invest internationally. Here are some examples of such sections of the Patriot Act:

- Section 215 revises the Foreign Intelligence Surveillance Act (FISA) provisions governing access to business records for foreign intelligence and international terrorism investigations. The Patriot Act broadens the FBI's ability to obtain business records pursuant to a court order. Previously, Section 501 of FISA (50 U.S.C. section 1862) had subjected only common carriers, public accommodation facilities, physical storage facilities, and car rental facilities to FISA business record authority. The Patriot Act eliminates these categories and allows the FBI to issue subpoenas to any person, including Internet service providers, banks, and any other business within the reach of business record authority.

- Subtitle B (Sections 351-366) amends the banking and finance laws to permit the government access to information from banks that might relate to terrorism. Section 351 gives the institutions and their directors, officers, employees, and agents protection from liability for reporting suspicious activities. The section also applies to securities brokers and dealers regulated by the Securities and Exchange Act of 1934 and consumer reporting agencies governed by the Fair Credit Reporting Act.

- Additionally, Section 351 allows the Secretary of the Treasury to impose sanctions, including cutting off all dealings with U.S. financial institutions or banks in foreign nations whose bank secrecy laws deny information to U.S. agencies. Foreign banks maintaining correspondent accounts in U.S. banks must designate someone in the U.S. to receive subpoenas related to those accounts and their depositors. If those subpoenas are not answered, the accounts can be ordered closed.

- Section 352 prohibits financial institutions from knowingly becoming involved in unlawful financial transactions with suspected terrorists and requires that companies establish and maintain written, anti-money-laundering programs that, at a minimum, do the following: (1) incorporate internal policies, procedures, and controls based on the company's assessment of its money-laundering risks; (2) designate a compliance officer; and (3) establish ongoing employee-training programs as well as independent audit functions to test programs.

FINANCIAL CONSIDERATIONS IN INTERNATIONAL BUSINESS

An important reason, if not the most important reason, for an organization to enter the international market is to generate revenue. Possible financial risks and opportunities are, therefore, of concern.

Financial considerations in the international insurance market include:

- Currency and foreign exchange markets
- Expropriation
- Accounting issues
- Taxation issues
- Tax havens

Currency and Foreign Exchange Markets

A business operating in the international market must consider both currency and foreign exchange markets because sales, profits, or investment can increase or decrease in value based merely on the change in the value of the other country's currency.

A currency is a unit of exchange, facilitating the transfer of a good or service between individuals, companies, countries, or a combination of these entities. A country or region has a specific currency that is the dominant medium of exchange for goods and services. Exchange rates are prices at which currencies, goods, and services can be exchanged for each other, and they facilitate trade between countries.

Almost every country has a single currency. Some countries share the same name for their currencies. For example, Canada, Hong Kong, and the U.S. all name their currencies "the dollar." Some countries share the same currency (such as the euro), and some countries declare the currency of another country to be legal tender.

Pegged currency

A currency based on the fixed exchange rate of another country's currency.

If the value of the currency is **pegged currency**, the government in question maintains its value at a fixed rate relative to the other currency. For example, if Nation Y pegs its dollar to the U.S. dollar at an 8:1 ratio, this means that $8 in Nation Y's currency is equal to $1 U.S.

The exchange rate (foreign exchange rate or FX rate) between two currencies shows how much one currency is worth in terms of the other. For example, an exchange rate of 100 Japanese yen to the U.S. dollar means that ¥100 is worth the same as $1. If a country's currency is appreciating, it becomes more valuable, and the exchange rate increases. Conversely, if the country's currency is weakening, the exchange rate decreases.

Supply and Demand

If a country's currency is allowed to float freely, its exchange rate against other countries varies, and it changes constantly within the financial markets around the world. A currency tends to become more valuable whenever demand for it is greater than the available supply and less valuable whenever demand is less than available supply.

An increase in demand for a specific currency results from either an increase in transaction demands for currency or an increase in speculative demand for the currency.

The transaction demand for money is highly correlated to the country's level of business activity, gross domestic product (GDP), and employment levels. The greater the number of people who are unemployed, the less the public as a whole spends on goods and services.

Central banks typically have little difficulty adjusting the available money supply to accommodate changes in the demand for a currency resulting from business transactions. Speculative demand for money is much harder for central banks to accommodate. However, central banks try to accommodate this demand by adjusting domestic interest rates, thus allowing an investor to choose to buy a currency if the interest rate generates a high enough return for the investment. The higher a country's interest rates, the greater the demand for that currency.

International Assets

When a corporation is involved in international business, it must be concerned that its international assets will retain their value in the future. A company does not want investments or income that will devalue in the future.

A currency tends to lose value, relative to other currencies, if that country's inflation level is relatively high, if the country's level of output is expected to decline, or if a country is troubled by political uncertainty. In the foreign exchange markets, rate fluctuations usually are linked to the world economy or significant events in a specific national economy.

Expropriation

When dealing in another country, a business must be aware of the possibility that the government will expropriate its assets. Expropriation, in its legal sense, means a government's lawful acquisition of property without the owner's consent. The government acquires property rights, and the owner loses them. The term usually refers to a government's takeover of private property, often without fair compensation, but usually with a legal assertion that the government has a right to do so.

The power of eminent domain is a government's power to confiscate private property for public use. Most governments use eminent domain when they require property for the completion of a public project such as a road, and the owner of the property is unwilling to negotiate a price for its sale.

The exercise of eminent domain is not limited to real estate but can also involve personal property. Governments can also condemn the value in a contract, such as a franchise agreement. For this reason, many franchise agreements stipulate that, in condemnation proceedings, the franchise itself has no value. Owners' rights vary by country.

The U.S. Constitution requires payment of just compensation upon use of eminent domain. In France, the Declaration of the Rights of Man and of the Citizen mandates giving just and preliminary compensation to the property owner.

Accounting Standards

A demand for and supply of capital transcending national boundaries often drive international business transactions in today's capital markets. High-quality accounting standards are a necessary element of a sound capital-market system. Companies use different forms of accounting to determine their financial situations. However, with the increase in cross-border capital-raising and investment transactions comes an increasing demand for a set of high-quality international accounting standards that companies could use as a basis for financial reporting worldwide.

In the U.S., for example, domestic firms that are registered with the Securities and Exchange Commission (SEC) must file financial reports using U.S. generally accepted accounting principles (GAAP). Foreign firms filing with the SEC can use U.S. GAAP, their home country GAAP, or international standards. However, if they use their home country GAAP or international standards, foreign companies must provide a reconciliation to U.S. GAAP.

The Financial Accounting Standards Board (FASB) is the designated organization in the private sector for establishing standards of financial accounting and reporting in the U.S. Those standards govern the preparation of financial reports, and the SEC and the American Institute of Certified Public Accountants (AICPA) officially recognize them as authoritative. Such standards are essential to the economy's efficient functioning because investors, creditors, auditors, and others rely on credible, transparent, and comparable financial information.

The London-based International Accounting Standards Board (IASB), organized in 2001, is developing a single set of high-quality global accounting standards that require transparent and comparable information in general-purpose financial statements. The IASB receives funding from the major accounting firms, private financial institutions, industrial companies, central and development banks, and other international and professional organizations throughout the world.

In 2002, the FASB and the IASB issued the Norwalk Agreement, a memorandum of understanding that marked a significant step toward formalizing their commitments to the convergence of U.S. and international accounting standards. Work continues on the project. As of 2005, the European Union required that all EU-listed public companies prepare their consolidated financial statements using IASB Standards.

Taxation

Corporations involved in international business must deal with issues of taxation in their home country jurisdictions as well as in the foreign country in which they conduct business or invest.

In today's business environment, many countries seek to attract investment by offering a "tax holiday," ranging from a partial to a total exemption from corporate income tax to an exemption for a number of years. At the end of the tax exemption period, a normal corporate tax rate applies to the corporate earnings of the investment.

Some countries have placed conditions on tax holidays, requiring that the corporation agree not to close down operation at the expiration of the tax holiday. Countries impose this requirement because many corporations have discovered that it is profitable, at expiration of the tax holiday, to close operations and relocate to a different country, often a country offering another tax holiday.

Countries use different approaches, including these, to tax corporations' earnings in the context of international commerce:

- Territorial tax systems tax all companies only on the economic activity that occurs within the country's geographic boundaries, regardless of the location of the company's incorporation or operations. For example, Ireland does not tax an Irish company on profits earned through sales in the U.S. However, both U.S. and Irish firms pay taxes on profits they earn through the sale of products in Ireland.

- A worldwide tax system taxes domestically incorporated companies on their total earnings from both domestic and international activities. Foreign companies are taxed on their economic activity within the country's geographic boundaries. For example, a U.S. company pays taxes on profits earned through its sales in the U.S. and in Ireland. An Irish company pays taxes in the U.S. on profits it earns only on sales in the U.S.

- Border tax adjustments (BTAs), rebates on exports and taxes on imports, are instruments governments use to establish a "tax-neutral" setting for international trade and investment. The General Agreement on Tariffs and Trade (GATT), which defines the scope of international BTAs, recognizes only consumption taxes (taxes applying directly to goods and services) as eligible for BTAs. A Value Added Tax (VAT) is BTA-eligible, but corporate income taxes are not.

- Corporations can use several processes to reduce their tax liability relating to international commerce. Earnings stripping arrangements usually involve the extension of debt from one corporate affiliate to another. The debt accumulates within the corporation's high-tax jurisdiction, which allows it to deduct interest payments from its taxable income in the high-tax country.

- Inversion, or expatriation, or reincorporation is the process by which a corporate entity established in a low-tax country purchases the shares and/or assets of a domestic corporation. The domestic company's shareholders typically become the new foreign parent company's shareholders. This process allows the domestic company to change its legal location and become a foreign-based corporation. An inversion typically does not change the company's operational structure or physical location; however, it does change the parent company's tax structure. A corporation may accomplish an inversion by setting up a foreign company and then reverse-engineering a merger to move the company's legal location. Large companies calculate each of their divisions' profits and losses separately.

Transfer price

The price one part of a company charges for products and services it provides to another part of the same company.

Countries also have differing transfer pricing laws, a concern for all companies that do international business. The **transfer price** is the price one part of a company charges for products and services it provides to another part of the same company. Under transfer pricing laws, companies are required to charge another affiliate or division the same price it would demand in an "arm's-length transaction," that is, a transaction between two unrelated entities.

Many experts believe transfer pricing is the most important international tax issue facing multinational corporations. Most countries impose strict transfer pricing rules on international transactions. Noncompliance can lead to pricing adjustments and large penalties.

Tax Havens

Tax haven

A country whose regulations offer financial and business incentives encouraging organizations from other countries to do business there.

In many countries, regulation imposes high costs on domestic businesses. Consequently, many companies seek **tax havens**. To move a business or division of a corporation offshore to operate in a pro-business climate usually requires nothing more than forming an offshore corporation in a tax haven country and transferring assets from the domestic corporation.

One of the reasons companies "go offshore" is to reduce corporate taxes. Many tax havens impose few or no taxes on foreign companies and have strict privacy laws. Corporations' decisions about tax havens are based on the advantages for the particular international investment project.

A business should consider these factors when establishing a subsidiary in an offshore tax haven:

- The country's tax structure
- The country's level of enforcement of its privacy laws
- The country's language
- The type of judicial system the country has
- The country's political stability

- The country's independence from the parent company's home country
- The costs of establishing the new subsidiary in the country

Tax havens are typically countries that have no taxes of any kind, whether personal or corporate income tax, capital gains tax, foreign investment tax, withholding tax, estate tax, sales tax, value added tax, and so forth. They have no financial reporting requirements. Some examples of well-known tax havens are Antigua, the Bahamas, Belize, the British Virgin Islands, the Isle of Man, Luxembourg, Nevis and St. Kitts, and Turks and Caicos.

To understand the precise role of tax havens, it is important to distinguish between two types of income: return on labor and return on capital. Income from labor derives from work: salary, wages, fees for professional services, and the like. Income from return on capital is the return on an investment: dividends on shares of stock; interest on bank deposits, loans, and bonds; rental income; royalties on patents.

Most corporations seek to use tax haven benefits for income derived from the return on capital and income from an investment portfolio. When a corporation forms a subsidiary or a trust in a tax haven, return on capital can be almost tax free, or at least taxed at a very low rate.

Types of Corporate Tax Structures

A tax haven country may have one of these four types of corporate tax structures.

- *Low or minimum taxes.* Some tax haven countries impose low or minimal taxes on all corporate income, wherever earned. Many countries with this system have double-taxation agreements with the high-tax countries that might help reduce the withholding tax imposed on income derived from the high-tax countries by local corporations.

  Double taxation arises because of competing claims of tax authorities of a home corporation's home country and the country of the source of income. Generally, the income source country gives way to the home country, with exceptions.

- *No corporate taxes.* Some tax haven countries have no income, capital gains, or wealth (capital) taxes. They allow companies to incorporate and/ or form trusts. These countries primarily charge small fees when a corporation files incorporation documents, on issuing of shares, and on annual registration fees. Any income these governments derive from corporations is not related to corporate income.

- *No taxes on foreign income.* Some tax haven countries impose income taxes, both on individuals and corporations, but only on locally derived income. These countries exempt from tax any income earned from foreign sources that involve no local business activities. Often, these countries do not tax income derived from the export of locally manufactured products. The countries that have no tax on foreign income fall into two different groups. The first group consists of countries that allow a corporation to do business both internally and externally but that tax only the income derived from internal sources. The second group consists of countries that tax a corporation for income derived from local business but do not tax income derived from external business. Some companies would conduct only foreign business and thus be exempt from taxation.

- *Special tax concessions.* Some tax haven countries impose all or most of the usual taxes, but either provide concessions to special types of companies or permit some special corporate structure allowing for lower taxes. Some special tax haven countries give tax exemptions on shipping or to movie production companies, for example.

Information Privacy

Tax haven countries also offer corporations some advantages relating to privacy of stock information.

Bearer share

A corporate share that is owned by the holder of the share certificate and is not registered; therefore, ownership remains private.

These tax haven countries allow for the issuance of **bearer shares**, stocks that are owned by the holder, the one who has possession of the share certificate. No one but the bearer of the shares knows who owns stock in the corporation. The ownership remains private, and shares can be bought, sold, or exchanged in complete privacy.

In contrast, most jurisdictions (including the U.S., Canada, and Great Britain) require shares to be registered with a government agency. With **registered shares**, the government and other parties know who owns a corporation's shares and the selling and buying prices for the shares.

Registered share

A corporate share on which records are kept indicating the share's owner and its selling and buying price.

Another privacy advantage that tax havens offer to corporations results from their laws forbidding financial institutions (such as banks, brokerages, and insurance companies) and advisers (such as brokers, accountants, attorneys, and investment advisers) from divulging information about clients or accounts to any third party. These privacy laws apply to all third parties, including individuals, companies, and governments.

NON-LEGAL FACTORS AFFECTING INTERNATIONAL BUSINESS

In addition to dealing with applicable laws and financial considerations, a company engaged in international business faces challenges and barriers resulting from various other factors.

Companies involved in international business have different needs and requirements based on their type of business and the intended outcomes of their business transactions. Each company and each international transaction is affected by the following factors:

- Language
- Culture
- Time differences
- Distance and space
- Types of government

Language

A language barrier can be the first challenge to a company in an international transaction. Although English has become the language of international business, skills with other languages are still necessary in most international transactions. In an international investment or sale of a product to a foreign market, numerous foreign language issues can arise, including interpretation of contracts, advertising, packaging information, product instructions, and warranties, as well as language issues regarding legal and regulatory compliance.

In many countries, it is common to speak more than one language—a possible advantage for international business in those countries. The ability to speak multiple languages gives a businessperson an advantage, not only in direct business negotiations, but also in personal interactions. Language ability also prevents misunderstanding or mistranslation through a third-party translator.

Culture

Differences between cultures can be challenging to any business transaction. Many Asian and African cultures, for example, are very different from the U.S. culture. Differences in cultures can involve variations in manners, body language, religion, family life and gender roles, and many other aspects of culture.

For example, business travelers should consider interactions between business and family when planning business meetings and business socializing in some countries. Whether it is appropriate to invite a spouse to a business dinner or a family to a sporting event can vary by culture.

Time Differences

Time differences between countries can make conducting international business challenging. For example, when it is 3:00 p.m.—an appropriate time for a conference call—in Philadelphia, it is 8:00 p.m. in London. Further, for companies communicating across the International Date Line, it can be Monday in London and Tuesday in Sydney.

Additionally, different countries and cultures perceive time differently, and those perceptions can affect interactions within a business transaction. In many northern European countries, along with the U.S., people perceive time in a linear fashion. People at a business meeting in the U.S. might have a set agenda they follow closely, moving from one item to the next. In another country, such as Spain, people may perceive time less linearly and may tend to do many tasks at the same time. Some countries value the use, or quality expenditure, of time more highly than the quantity of time spent on any endeavor.

Distance and Space

The physical distance between locations limits contact between individuals and influences the culture of both individuals and companies.

New travel and communication technologies have helped to reduce some of the physical distance barriers to international transactions and have helped to unify the world into a single international market. Technology makes it possible to conduct international business around the world twenty-four hours a day.

Space also affects individuals and cultures. Each individual has a preferred personal space, and the size of a person's preferred personal space varies by culture. How people interact, as well as the circumstances under which they touch others, also differs within each culture. A kiss on the cheek is an appropriate greeting in some cultures, a handshake in others, and a bow in others.

Types of Government

Government structure is important to consider in all international business dealings. Changes in government can result in changes to the business and legal environment within a country. These changes can occur quickly or slowly, depending on the type of government in a country. Most countries have one of six basic systems of government:

- Democratic
- Military
- Monarchal
- Single-party
- Theocratic

Democracy takes many diverse forms, and the name of a government can be deceiving. For example, the Democratic People's Republic of Korea is the name of North Korea, a single-party communist dictatorship, and is not the name of South Korea, a democracy.

Democratic rule is rule by the people through elected representatives. Modern democratic governments take these forms:

- A **nonparty democracy** is a form of government in which elected representatives have no political party affiliation.

- A **parliamentary democracy** is ruled by a prime minister and an elected parliament. Approximately sixty countries have had parliamentary democracies in recent years.

- A **presidential democracy** is governed by a president directly elected by the citizens. Approximately sixty countries have had presidential democracies recently.

- A **multiparty democracy** is a form of government in which representatives may be elected from several or many political parties. Many multiparty democracies have balancing roles of a prime minister and a president. Approximately thirty-five countries have had multiparty democracies in recent years.

Military forms of government have occurred throughout history. Another term for these governments is **junta**. Military rule is commonly associated with single-party or transitional forms of government. **Martial law** is the means by which the military assumes control of a country, often because of a perceived need for military security or public safety.

A **monarchy** may be a kingdom or dynasty over which one person rules for life. Individual monarchs can have titles such as king, queen, prince, emperor, czar, or sultan, among others.

Two common forms of monarchy are absolute and constitutional. In an **absolute monarchy**, the leader rules alone and selects advisers for assistance. In a **constitutional monarchy**, a parliament, or democratic legislative body, replaces absolute monarchical rule.

Many of the world's remaining monarchical governments had ended by the mid-20th century. Some countries, such as Great Britain, the Netherlands, Sweden, and Spain, still have monarchs, but their powers are limited and often ceremonial, and democratically elected legislative bodies have the real power to govern.

A **single-party government** usually has a constitutional requirement that only a specific political party can exist. Although these governments are not military, theocratic, or monarchical, most arose from those forms of government.

A **theocratic government** is based on religious doctrine, and religious leaders may govern. Throughout history, theocratic governments have ruled countries such as Tibet and China and the Aztec, Incan, and Mayan empires in Latin America, as well as many Islamic countries. Examples of theocratic governments today include Iran and the Vatican City.

A country has a **transitional government** when it is rebuilding its government, usually as a result of war.

Democratic rule
A form of government by the people through elected representatives.

Nonparty democracy
A form of government in which elected representatives have no political party affiliation.

Parliamentary democracy
A form of government involving rule by a prime minister and an elected parliament.

Presidential democracy
A form of government in which the citizens directly elect a president.

Multiparty democracy
A form of government in which representatives may be elected from several or many political parties.

Junta
A form of government by a group of military officers governing a country after seizing power.

Martial law
The assumption of control of a country by the military.

Monarchy
A form of government led by a hereditary chief of state with powers varying from absolute to ceremonial.

Absolute monarchy
A form of government led by a single ruler who selects advisers for assistance.

Constitutional monarchy

A form of government with a parliament, or a democratic legislative body, but with a monarch as a formal or ceremonial head of state.

Single-party government

A form of government that constitutionally permits only one specific political party.

Theocratic government

A form of government based on a religious doctrine and often led by religious leaders.

Transitional government

A temporary form of government used when a country is rebuilding its government, usually as a result of war.

SUMMARY

Companies can engage in international business through foreign trade, foreign contractual relationships, or foreign direct investment. Foreign trade involves the import and/or export of goods. Foreign contractual relationships include product licensing and franchising. Direct foreign investment can occur through the use of subsidiaries or joint ventures.

Countries share legal approaches and concepts, which can be grouped into predominant families of law. In general, countries adopt legal systems that are either civil-law systems or common-law systems.

International law comprises public international law, which governs the interaction of nation states, and private international law, which governs disputes between individuals or corporations in different countries.

Practically all international business dealings are affected by these multinational organizations and agreements:

- The United Nations
- The World Trade Organization
- The North American Free Trade Agreement
- European Union
- Association of Southeast Asian Nations
- Asia-Pacific Economic Cooperation

Important examples of U.S. federal laws influencing international business and foreign investment are the Internal Revenue Code, the Foreign Corrupt Practices Act, and the U.S. Patriot Act.

A business operating in the international market must consider both currency and foreign exchange markets because sales, profits, or investment can increase or decrease in value based merely on the change in the value of the other country's currency. Expropriation is a government's lawful acquisition of property without the owner's consent. High-quality accounting standards are a necessary element of a sound capital-market system. Corporations involved in international business must deal with issues of taxation in their home country jurisdictions as well as in the foreign country in which they conduct business or invest. Many multinational corporations use offshore tax havens to reduce their taxes and increase their information privacy.

Any organization conducting international business must weigh potential challenges and barriers of such ventures according to the types of transactions the organization requires. These challenges and barriers include language, culture, time, distance and space, and types of government.

ASSIGNMENT NOTES

1. Additional information can be found at www.ustreas.gov/offices/enforcement/ ofac/faq/answer.shtml#global1.

2. U.S.C., Section 26 et seq.

3. U.S.C., Section 15 et seq.

Index

Page numbers in boldface refer to pages where the word or phrase is defined.

SYMBOLS

49 percent comparative negligence rule, **6.11**
50 percent comparative negligence rule, **6.11**

A

Ability to Convey Real Property, 9.50
Absolute monarchy, **10.39**
Acceptance, **2.10**, 4.5
Acceptance by Offeree, 2.10
Accession, **5.5**
Accomplishment of Purpose, 7.14
Accord and satisfaction, **2.22**
Accounting, 7.10
Accounting Standards, 10.32
Active negligence, **6.44**
Acts Constituting Waiver, 3.29
Acts Outside the Usual Scope of Business, 9.50
Actual authority, **7.6**, 8.5
Actual Injury or Damage, 6.7
Administrative act (discretionary act), **6.14**
Administrative Agencies, 1.16
Administrative Agency Procedures, 1.25
Administrative law, **1.16**
Advantages of Incorporation, 9.25
Adverse possession, **5.22**
Affirmative action plan, **9.10**
Age Discrimination in Employment Act (ADEA), 9.6
Agencies' Adjudicatory Function, 1.27
Agencies' Investigative Powers, 1.28
Agencies' Rulemaking Function, 1.26
Agency, **7.3**
Agency by estoppel, **7.4**
Agency Creation, 7.3
Agency Termination, 7.13
Agent, **7.3**
Agent's Authority, 7.6
Agent's Duties and Remedies, 7.7–7.8
Agent's Duties to Principal, 7.8
Agent's Liability for Own Torts, 7.23
Agent's Liability to a Third Party, 7.18
Agent's Remedies, 7.13
Agent's Rights Against a Third Party, 7.19
Agents, 8.3
Agreed-On Period of Employment, 7.11
Agreement, 3.9
Agreement of the Parties, 2.48
Allegation, **1.17**
Alternative Dispute Resolution, 1.23–1.24

Alternative dispute resolution (ADR), **1.23**
Alternative liability, **6.50**
Ambiguity, 2.41
Americans With Disabilities Act, 9.12
Answer, **1.17**
Anticipatory breach, **2.53**
Antidiscrimination Laws, 9.5–9.6
Apparent authority, **7.7**, 8.6
Apparent Authority (Estoppel) of Partners, 9.49
Appeals, **1.22**
Appellate courts, **1.14**
Appellate jurisdiction, **1.12**
Application, 3.32
Appointment, 7.3
Appointment of Subagents, 8.13
Appropriation of a Corporate Business Opportunity, 9.38
Arbitration, 1.23, **9.17**
Articles of Association and Bylaws, 9.57–9.58
Artificial Conditions, 6.18
Artificial Entities' Contracts, 2.17
Asia-Pacific Economic Cooperation (APEC), 10.26
Assault, **6.22**
Assignee, **2.42**
Assignee's Rights, 2.44
Assignment, **2.42**
Assignment of Partner's Interest in Partnership, 9.48–9.49
Assignor, **2.42**
Association of Southeast Asian Nations (ASEAN), 10.25–10.26
Assumption of risk, **6.44**
Assumption-of-risk defense, **6.10**
Attachment, 4.23
Attractive nuisance doctrine, **6.18**

B

Bad Faith, or Outrage, **2.56**, **6.29**
Bailee, **4.19**
Bailee's and Bailor's Rights and Duties, 5.7
Bailee's Duties, 5.8
Bailee's Rights, 5.8
Bailment, **4.19**, **5.7**
Bailments, 5.7
Bailor, **4.19**
Bailor's Rights and Duties, 5.9
Bankruptcy, 4.34
Bankruptcy law, **4.34**
Bargain-and-sale deed, **5.16**
Basic Concepts of Property Law, 5.3

Battery, **6.22**
Bearer share, **10.36**
Beneficiaries' Rights, 2.46
Bilateral and Unilateral Contracts, 2.3
Bilateral contract, **2.3**
Bilateral mistake, **2.32**
Bill of lading, **4.18**, 4.20
Binder, **3.11**, **8.12**
Binding Promise, 2.20
Blank endorsement (general endorsement), **4.17**
Board of Directors, 9.32
Bona fide occupational qualification (BFOQ), **9.6**
Bond, **9.31**
Border tax adjustments (BTAs), **10.33**
Breach of contract, **2.3**, 2.52–2.57
Breach of Duty, 6.4
Breach of Sales Contracts and Remedies, 4.10
Breach of Warranty, 6.40
Broker, **8.3**
Brokers, 8.3
Building codes, **5.27**
Business invitee, **6.19**
Business risk, **10.3**
"But for" rule, **6.6**
Buyer's Remedies, 4.13

C

CAF (cost and freight), **4.8**
Capacity to Contract, 2.13–2.14
Capital surplus, **9.31**
Carrier, **4.18**
Case Facts, 2.58
Cause of action, **1.17**
Certificate of deposit (CD), **4.15**
Certificate of incorporation, **9.30**
Changed Circumstances, 7.16
Characteristics of Beneficiary Contracts, 2.46
Characteristics of Unincorporated Associations, 9.55
Charitable immunity, **6.14**
Charitable Subscriptions, 2.23
Chattel, **4.22**
CIF (cost-insurance-freight, **4.8**
Civil law, **1.6**, 10.12
Civil Rights Act of 1964, 9.8
Civil Rights Act of 1991, 9.10
Civil Rights Acts of 1866 and 1871, 9.8
Civil Trial Procedures, 1.16–1.17
Civil-Law System, 1.3
Class action (class action lawsuit), **6.52**
Class Actions and Mass Tort Litigation, 6.52
Classification, 3.25
Classification as Criminal or Civil Law, 1.6
Classification as Substantive or Procedural Law, 1.7
Classification by Subject Matter, 1.7
Classifications of U.S. Law, 1.6
Clerical Errors and Omissions, 2.40
COD (collect on delivery), **4.8**
Collateral, **4.22**
Collateral estoppel, **1.22**
Collective bargaining, **9.14**

Collective-Bargaining Process, 9.15
Collective-Bargaining Relationships, 9.14
Commerce Clause, **1.10**
Commercial Speech, 6.25
Common carriers, **6.5**
Common Law, **6.3**, 10.14
Common Market, **10.25**
Common name statute, **9.46**
Common stock, **9.31**
Common-law system, 1.3, **9.5**
Communication to Offeree, 2.7
Community property, **5.13**
Comparative negligence, **6.10**
Compensation, 7.11
Compensatory damages, **2.54**, 6.46
Competence, **1.21**
Competent Parties, **2.14**
Complaint, **1.17**
Compromise and Release of Claims, 2.22
Concert of action, **6.50**
Concurrent causation (concurrent causation doctrine),
    6.7
Concurrent Estates, 5.11
Condemnation proceeding, **5.27**
Condition concurrent, **2.51**
Condition precedent, **2.38**
Condition subsequent, **2.51**
Conditional contract, **3.3**
Condominium, **5.14**
Condominium Ownership, 5.14
Conflicts of law, **1.15**
Conforming and Nonconforming Goods, 4.8
Confusion, **5.6**
Consequential damages, **2.54**
Consideration, **2.18**, 2.18–2.20, 3.28, 4.6
Consignee, **4.21**
Consignor, **4.21**
Consolidated Omnibus Budget Reconciliation Act
    (COBRA), 9.22
Conspiracy, **6.50**
Constitutional monarchy, **10.39**
Constitutions, 1.9
Construction of Representations, 3.24
Constructive eviction, **5.29**
Constructive notice, **4.24**
Consumer Credit Laws, 4.31
Consumer Protection Laws, 4.27
Contestable period, **3.6**
Contract, **2.3**
Contract Assignments, 2.42
Contract Interpretation, 2.38–2.39
Contract Involving Fortuitous Events and the Exchange
    of Unequal Amounts, 3.4
Contract of adhesion, **3.6**
Contract of indemnity, **3.7**
Contract of Utmost Good Faith, 3.4
Contracts Case Study, 2.58
Contracts Harmful to the Public Interest, 2.25
Contracts in Restraint of Marriage, 2.27
Contracts in Restraint of Trade, 2.28
Contracts to Commit Crimes or Torts, 2.24

Contracts to Transfer Liability for Negligence, 2.27
Contracts With Unlicensed Practitioners, 2.26
Contractual Conditions, 2.51
Contractual Rights and Liabilities, 7.16
Contradictory Terms, 2.40
Contribution, **6.49**
Contributory negligence, **6.10**
Conversion, **6.37**
Cooperative ownership, **5.13**
Copyrights, **5.4**
Corporate Ownership, 9.31
Corporate Powers, 9.35
Corporations: Duties and Obligations, 9.34
Corporations: Formation, 9.25
Corporations: Mergers, Dissolution, and Reorganization, 9.41
Counterclaim, **1.17**
Counteroffers, **2.9**
Courts, 1.12
Covenant-of-Good-Faith Exception, 9.5
Creation of Intellectual Property, 5.4
Creditor beneficiary, **2.45**
Criminal law, **1.6**
Cross-examination, **1.21**
Culture, 10.37
Currency and Foreign Exchange Markets, 10.30

D

Damages, 2.54, 6.29, 6.45
Damages for Wrongful Death, 6.47
Damages in Tort Suits, 6.45–6.47
De facto (in fact) corporation, **9.30**
De jure (in law) corporation, **9.30**
Death or Incapacity, 7.15
Deed, **5.15**
Defamation (Slander and Libel), **6.24**
Default, 4.26
Default judgment, **8.31**
Defendant, **6.3**
Defenses, 6.30, 6.44
Defenses Against Negligence Claims, 6.9
Defenses to Invasion of Privacy, 6.27
Definite Terms, 2.7
Delivery of Insurance Policies, 3.15
Delivery Order, 4.21
Delivery Terms, 4.7
Democratic rule, **10.39**
Deposition, **1.19**
Derivative suit, **9.40**
Direct examination, **1.21**
Direct Liability, 7.21
Direct-action statute, **3.18**
Directors or Trustees, 9.58
Disclosed principal, **7.17**
Discovery, **1.19**
Discrimination Based on Age, 9.6
Discrimination Based on Disability, 9.11
Discrimination Based on Other Factors, 9.13
Discrimination Based on Sex, Race, Color, Religion, or National Origin, 9.7

Disparate impact theory, **9.9**
Disparate treatment theory, **9.9**
Dissolution, 9.43
Dissolution and Winding Up, 9.59
Dissolution, Winding Up, and Termination, 9.51
Distance and Space, 10.38
Distinguishing Estoppel From Waiver, 3.30
Distraint, **5.29**
Diversity jurisdiction, **1.13**
Dividends, 9.40
Doctrine of stare decisis, **1.4**
Documents of Title, 4.18, 4.19
Donee, **5.6**
Donee beneficiary, **2.45**
Draft (check), **4.15**
Due Process Clause, **1.11**
Dumping, **10.23**
Duration and Termination, 2.8
Duress, **2.32**
Duties of Care and Loyalty, 9.37
Duties of Directors and Officers, 9.37
Duties of Loyalty and Accounting, 8.30
Duties to Those Who Enter the Land or Premises, 6.19
Duty to Ascertain Scope of Authority, 7.7
Duty to Disclose Risks, 8.28
Duty to Follow Instructions, 8.29
Duty to Transmit Information Properly, 8.31

E

Earnings stripping, **10.33**
Easement, **5.25**
Easements, 5.25
East Asian Law, 10.14
Economic and Social Council, 10.21
Economic Pressure, 9.17
Effect of Dissolution on Third Parties, 9.52–9.53
Effective Date, 3.11
Effectuation of Intent, 2.39
Election, **3.31**, 3.31–3.32
Electronic Fund Transfer Act, 4.33
Elements of a Contract of Sale, 5.15
Elements of Negligence, 6.3
Elements Required to Establish False Representation, 3.22
Eminent domain, **5.27**
Emotional distress, **6.46**
Employee, **7.20**
Employee Privacy, 9.23
Employee Retirement Income Security Act (ERISA), 9.21
Employee Welfare Laws, 9.18
Employer Economic Tactics, 9.18
Employment at will, **9.3**, **9.6**
Employment-at-Will Doctrine, 9.3
Endorsements, 4.16
Enforceability of a Contract, 2.29–2.31
Enterprise liability (industry-wide liability), **6.50**
Entire and Divisible Contracts, 2.39
Environmental law, **6.39**
Equal Credit Opportunity Act, 4.34
Equal Pay Act, 9.11

Equal Protection Clause, **1.11**
Equitable Remedies, 2.56–2.57
Equity, **1.5**
Escape of Toxic Substances, 6.39
Estate for years, **5.28**
Estate in Fee Simple, 5.11
Estoppel, **3.30**, 7.4
European Union (EU), 10.24–10.25
Evolution of Common Law, 1.5
Exceptions to the Consideration Requirement, 2.22
Exceptions to the Legal Purpose Requirement, 2.29
Exclusionary zoning, **5.26**
Exclusive Bargaining Agent, 9.14
Exclusive control, **6.8**
Exculpatory clause (exculpatory agreement), **2.27**
Excuses for Nonperformance, 4.12
Executed and Executory Contracts, 2.3
Executed contract, **2.3**
Executive Branches, 1.15
Executive Order 11246, 9.10
Executory contract, **2.3**
Exempt employee, **9.20**
Exhaustion of administrative remedies, **1.30**
Expanded Liability Concepts, 6.49–6.50
Export Controls, 10.3
Express and Implied Contracts, 2.4
Express and Implied Warranties, 4.9
Express authority, **7.6**
Express contract, **2.4**
Express license, **6.19**
Express warranty, **6.40**
Expropriation, 10.31
Extent of Producers' Authority, 8.7–8.9
Extracontractual damages, **2.56**

F

Factors Establishing Estoppel, 3.30
Fair Credit Reporting Act, 4.33
Fair Trade Laws, 4.28
False arrest, **6.22**
False imprisonment, **6.22**
False Imprisonment and False Arrest, 6.22
Family Medical Leave Act, 9.21
Family purpose doctrine, **6.51**
FAS (free alongside) vessel, **4.8**
Federal and State Laws and Regulations, 9.27
Federal Bankruptcy Act, 4.34
Federal Court System, 1.12
Federal Trade Commission Act, 4.28
Fee simple estate, **5.11**
Fiduciary Relationship, 9.47–9.48
Final order, **1.30**
Financial Considerations in International Business, 10.29–10.30
Financial Relationship, 9.47
FOB (free on board) place of destination, **4.8**
FOB (free on board) place of shipment, **4.8**
FOB (free on board) vessel, **4.8**
Forbearance, **2.12**, 2.19
Foreclosure, **5.19**

Foreign Contractual Relationships, 10.8
Foreign Corporations, 9.29
Foreign Corrupt Practices Act, 10.27
Foreign Direct Investment, 10.9
Foreign Trade, 10.3
Foreseeability rule, **6.7**
Formation and Financing, 9.57
Formation of Sales Contracts, 4.5
Forms of Assignment, 2.44
Forms of Collateral, 4.23
Forms of Secured Transactions, 4.22
Franchising, 10.9
Fraud, **2.30**, 6.28
Fraudulent Alteration, 2.51

G

General agent, **8.3**
General Assembly, 10.20
General damages, **6.46**
General jurisdiction, **1.12**
General verdict, **1.21**
General warranty deed, **5.15**
Genuine assent, **2.29**, 2.30
German Law, 10.13
Gift, **5.6**
Gifts, 5.6
Good consideration, **2.18**
Good Samaritan Issues, 6.51–6.52
Good Samaritan law, **6.52**
Government Controls, 5.26
Governmental function, **6.13**
Grantee, **5.15**
Grantor, **5.15**
Gratuitous promise, **2.19**
Gross negligence, **6.12**

H

Hardship variance, **5.27**
Health Care and Education Reconciliation Act of 2010, 9.22
Health Insurance Portability and Accountability Act (HIPAA), 9.24
Hearsay rule, **1.21**
Hindu Law, 10.15
Holder in due course, **4.17**, **4.25**
Holders in Due Course, 4.17
Holdover tenant, **5.28**
Hostile work environment, **9.9**
Hotel Guests and Tenants, 6.20

I

Immigration Reform and Control Act of 1986, 9.11
Immunity, **6.12**
Implied authority, **7.6**
Implied contract, **2.4**, **9.4**
Implied license, **6.19**
Implied Terms in Insurance Contracts, 3.14
Implied warranty, **6.40**

Implied warranty of fitness for a particular purpose, **4.10**
Implied warranty of merchantability, **4.10**
Implied warranty of title, **4.10**
Implied-Contract Exception, 9.4
Implied-in-fact contract, **2.4**
Implied-in-law contract, **2.4**, **9.5**
Import Controls, 10.5
Impossibility, 2.49
Improvements and betterments, **5.24**
In pari delicto agreement, **2.29**
Incidental beneficiary, **2.45**
Incidental Real Property Rights, 5.21
Incontestable clause, **3.6**
Incorporation Process, 9.29
Incorporeal Interests, **5.25**
Indemnity for Losses, 7.12
Independent contractor, **7.20**
Information, 7.10
Information Privacy, 10.36
Injunction, **2.57**
Injurious falsehood, **6.30**
Innocent Misrepresentation, 2.34
Insane Persons' Contracts, 2.16
Inside director, **9.33**
Inspection, 4.8
Insurable interest, **2.25**
Insurance agent, **8.3**
Insurance as Third-Party Beneficiary Contract, 3.17–3.18
Insurance Cases, 6.29
Insurance Company Designation, 3.15
Insurance Contract Formation, 3.9
Insurance Customer Failed to Read Policy, 8.25
Insurance Customer Was Partly at Fault, 8.25
Insurance Law and Estoppel, 3.30
Insurance Policy Content, 3.13
Insurance producer, **8.3**
Insurance Producer Classifications, 8.3
Insurance Was Not Available to the Customer, 8.26
Insured's Election, 3.32
Intellectual property rights, **5.4**
Intent to Contract, 2.5
Intentional infliction of emotional distress, **6.23**
Intentional nuisance, **6.36**
Intentional tort, **6.21**
Intentional Torts: Part 1 of 2, 6.21
Intentional Torts: Part 2 of 2, 6.28
Interference With Copyright, Patent, or Trademark, 6.33
Interference with employment, **6.32**
Interference With Family Relationships, 6.33
Interference With Relationships Between Others, 6.30
Interference With Right to Use One's Own Name in Business, 6.33
International Assets, 10.31
International Court of Justice, 10.21
International Law, 10.17
International Sales Contracts, 10.5
Interpretative rule, **1.26**
Interrogatories, **1.19**
Interspousal immunity, **6.14**

Intervening act, **6.7**
Intoxicated Persons' Contracts, 2.17
Intrafamilial Immunity, 6.14
Intrusion on Solitude or Seclusion, 6.26
Invasion of privacy, **6.26**
Invasion of the Right of Privacy, 6.26
Inversion, or expatriation, or reincorporation, **10.34**
Invitee, **6.19**
Invitees, 6.19
Is the Contract Enforceable?, 2.61–2.62
Islamic Law, 10.15

J

Joint and several liability, **7.21**
Joint tenancy, **5.12**
Joint tortfeasors, **6.48**
Joint Ventures, **6.50**, 10.10
Judicial Influence on Common Law, 1.4
Judicial Review, 1.30
Junta, **10.39**
Just Cause, 7.13

K

Knowledge Requirement, 3.28

L

Labor-Management Relations, 9.13–9.14
Land Contracts, **5.20**
Land Use Restrictions, 5.25–5.26
Landlord and Tenant Relationship, 5.27–5.29
Landlord's Remedies, 5.29
Landlord's Rights and Duties, 5.28
Language, 10.37
Lapse of Time, 2.8, 7.14
Last clear chance doctrine, **6.10**
Lateral support, **5.23**
Lease Interests, 3.20
Legal and Fair Interpretation, 2.42
Legal duty, **6.3**
Legal Purpose of a Contract, 2.23–2.24
Legal Systems, 10.11
Legislative Bodies, 1.11
Legislative rule, **1.26**
Lessening Warranty Effects, 3.26
Liability Concepts Affecting Tort Claims, 6.48–6.49
Liability for Agent's Misrepresentations, 7.22
Liability for Independent Contractor's Torts, 7.22
Liability for Torts and Crimes, 9.35
Liability in Extraordinary Circumstances, 6.37
Liability of Landowners or Occupiers of Land, 6.17
Liability of Members to Third Parties, 9.58
Libel, **6.24**, 6.25
License, **5.26**
Licensees, **6.19**
Licenses, 5.26
Lien, **4.25**
Life estate, **5.11**
Life Estates, 3.20
Limited Interests in Realty, 3.20

Limited Liability Companies, **9.54**
Limited liability partnership, **9.54**
Limited partnership, **9.53**
Limited Partnerships and Limited Liability Partnerships,
    9.53
Liquidated damages, **2.56**
Liquidation Proceedings, 4.35
Loss of wages and earnings, **6.46**
Loyalty, 7.8

M

Magnuson-Moss Warranty Act, 4.30
Malice, **6.31**
Malicious abuse of process, **6.35**
Malicious interference with prospective economic
    advantage, **6.31**
Malicious prosecution, **6.35**
Market share liability, **6.50**
Martial law, **10.39**
Mass tort litigation, **6.52**
Material Breach, 2.53–2.54
Material breach of contract, **2.53**
Material fact, **2.30**
Materiality, **1.21**
Mechanic's lien, **5.20**
Mechanics' Liens on Real Property, 5.20
Mediation, **1.24**
Merger, 9.41
Methods of Engaging in International Business, 10.3
Methods of Payment, 10.7
Ministerial act, **6.14**
Ministerial duties, **7.9**
Minors' Contracts, 2.14
Misrepresentation, **3.5**, 6.40
Mistake, **2.31**
Misuse of Legal Process, 6.34–6.35
Mitigation of damages, **2.56**
Monarchy, **10.39**
Mortgagee, **5.18**
Mortgages, 5.17
Mortgagor, **5.18**
Mortgagor's and Mortgagee's Interests, 3.19
Motion, **1.17**
Motion for summary judgment, **1.17**
Motion to dismiss, **1.17**
Multinational Organizations and Agreements, 10.19
Multiparty democracy, **10.39**

N

National Association of Insurance Commissioners
    (NAIC), **1.12**
Natural Conditions, 6.17
Necessary Terms in Insurance Contracts, 3.14
Negligence, **2.27**, 6.3
Negligence per se, **6.8**
Negligent entrustment, **6.51**
Negligent infliction of emotional distress, **6.23**
Negligent supervision, **6.51**
Negotiable Instruments, 4.13
Negotiation, 1.24

Noncompete agreement, **2.28**
Nonconforming use, **5.27**
Nonexempt employee, **9.20**
Non-Legal Factors Affecting International Business,
    10.36–10.38
Nonparty democracy, **10.39**
Nontransferable Contract, 3.8–3.9
Nonwaiver Agreements, **3.35**–3.36
Nonwaiver Agreements and Reservation of Rights
    Letters, 3.34–3.37
Norris-LaGuardia Act of 1932 and National Labor
    Relations Act (NLRA) of 1935, 9.14
North American Free Trade Agreement (NAFTA), 10.23
Notice of Assignment, 2.44
Novation, **2.48**
Nuisance, **6.18**, 6.36
Nuisance per se, **6.36**

O

Obedience, 7.9
Occupational Safety and Health Act of 1970 (OSH Act),
    9.18
Offer, **2.5**, 4.5
Offer and Acceptance, 3.10
Offeree, **2.5**
Offeree's Communication of Acceptance, 2.12
Offeree's Rejection, 2.9
Offeror, **2.5**
Offeror's Revocation, 2.9
Older Workers Benefit Protection Act (OWBPA), 9.7
Operation of Law, 2.8
Original jurisdiction, **1.12**
Outside director, **9.33**
Ownership, **5.3**
Ownership and/or Possession of Animals, 6.38
Ownership and Possession of Personal Property, 5.3
Ownership of Fixtures, 5.24

P

Pain and suffering, **6.46**
Par value, **9.31**
Parent-child immunity, **6.14**
Parliamentary democracy, **10.39**
Parol evidence rule, 2.36, **2.41**, 3.29
Partially disclosed principal, **7.17**
Parties' Own Interpretation, 2.41
Parties Protected, 6.43
Partners' Relationships to One Another, 9.47
Partnership, **9.46**
Partnership Formation, 9.46
Partnership Liability, 9.46–9.47
Partnerships, 9.45–9.50
Partnerships' Books and Property, 9.48
Passive negligence, **6.44**
Past Consideration, 2.21
Patent, **5.5**
Patents, 5.5
Patriot Act, 10.28
Pegged currency, **10.30**
Perfected security interest, **4.24**

Perfecting a Security Interest, 4.24
Performance, 2.47, 4.7
Periodic tenancy, **5.28**
Personal defense, **4.18**
Personal property, **5.3, 6.35**
Physical Invasion, 6.27
Pierce the corporate veil, **9.27**
Plain Meaning, 2.38
Plaintiff, **1.17, 6.3**
Pleading, **1.17**
Pledge, **4.22**
Policy Provisions, 3.29
Possession, **5.4**
Possessory lien, **5.8**
Potentially Liable Parties, 6.43
Power of attorney, **7.3**
Preferred stock, **9.31**
Present and Future Consideration, 2.19
Presidential democracy, **10.39**
Pretrial Procedure, 1.17
Primary and Secondary Liability, 4.16
Primary liability, **4.16**
Principal, **7.3**
Principal's Duties to Agent, 7.11
Principal's Liability for Agent's Torts, 7.20
Principal's Remedies, 7.11
Principal's Rights Against a Third Party, 7.17
Principle of indemnity, **3.8**
Priorities for Mechanics' Liens, 5.21
Privacy Statutes, 9.23
Private international law, **10.18**
Private nuisance, **6.36**
Privity of contract, **2.3**
Probable cause, **6.35**
Procedural law, **1.7**
Procedural rule, **1.26**
Producer Assumed No Duty to Customer, 8.24
Producer Did Not Breach Duty to Customer, 8.24
Producer's Duty to Advise, 8.21
Producer's Duty to Follow Instructions, 8.16
Producer's Duty to Maintain Coverage, 8.17
Producer's Duty to Place Insurance With a Solvent
    Insurer, 8.19
Producer's Duty to Procure Insurance, 8.17
Producers' Authority, 8.4–8.5
Producers' Authority to Bind Coverage, 8.10
Producers' Defenses to Liability, 8.22–8.24
Producers' Duties and Liabilities, 8.15
Producers' Duties and Liabilities to Third Parties, 8.27
Producers' Duties and Liability to Insurance Customers,
    8.16
Producers' Duties and Liability to Insurer, 8.28
Producers' Notice and Knowledge, 8.9
Producers' Status as General Agents, Special Agents, or
    Brokers, 8.7
Product disparagement, or trade libel, **6.26**
Product Licensing, 10.8
Products liability, **6.39**, 6.39–6.40
Profits à prendre, **5.25**
Promise to Perform an Existing Obligation, 2.22
Promisee, **2.3**

Promisor, **2.3**
Promissory estoppel, **2.23**
Promissory note, **4.15**
Property, **5.3**
Proprietary function, **6.13**
Provisions Relevant to Insurance, 1.10
Proximate cause, **6.5**
Public international law, **10.17**
Public invitee, **6.19**
Public nuisance, **6.36**
Public Official Immunity, 6.14
Public Policy Exception, 9.4
Publication, **6.24**
Punitive Damages, **2.54**, 6.46
Pure comparative negligence rule, **6.10**

Q

Qualified endorsement, **4.17**
Quid pro quo sexual harassment, **9.9**
Quit-claim deed, **5.16**

R

Ratification, **7.5**
Real defense, **4.18**
Real Estate Sellers and Buyers, 3.18
Real property, **2.35, 5.3**
Real Property Ownership, 5.10–5.11
Real Property Sales, 5.14–5.16
Real Property Security Interests and Liens, 5.17
Realty, **5.3**
Reasonable Care, 7.9
Reasonable person test, **6.4**
Recording Deeds, 5.17
Registered share, **10.36**
Regulation of Employee Benefits, 9.21
Regulation of Employee Safety and Health, 9.18
Regulation of Employee Wages and Hours, 9.20
Rehabilitation Act of 1973, 9.11
Reimbursement for Expenses, 7.12
Relationships of Partners to Third Parties, 9.49–9.50
Release, **6.12**
Releases and Exculpatory Clauses, 6.12
Relevance, **1.21**
Remedies for Breach, 2.54
Renunciation, 7.15
Reorganization, 9.45
Representation, **2.30**
Representations, 3.21
Representations and Warranties in Insurance,
    3.21–3.22
Repudiation, **2.52**
Required Proof of Negligence, 6.7
Requirements for Nonwaiver Agreements and
    Reservation of Rights Letters, 3.36
Requirements of an Offer, 2.5
Requirements of a Valid Acceptance, 2.10
Requirements That Deeds Must Meet, 5.16
Res ipsa loquitur, **6.8**
Res judicata, **1.22**
Rescission, **2.30**

Reservation of Rights Letters, **3.35**, 3.36
Respondeat superior, **7.21**
Respondeat Superior Liability, 7.21
Restitution, **2.14**
Restrictive, or collection endorsement, **4.17**
Revocation, 7.14
Revocation of Acceptance, 4.11
Rightful and Wrongful Dissolution, 9.51
Rights Assignable, 2.43
Rights Not Assignable, 2.43
Rights of Members in Association Property, 9.58
Rights of Perfected and Unperfected Security Interests, 4.25
Rights to Lateral and Subjacent Support, 5.23
Rights Under, Above, and on the Land's Surface, 5.22
Risk, **4.7**
Role of Administrative Agencies, 1.25
Roman-French Law, 10.13

S

Sales Contracts, 4.3
Satisfaction of a Secured Debt, 4.25
Scandinavian Law, 10.14
Scope of Authority, 7.6
Secondary liability, **4.16**
Secretariat, 10.22
Secured Transactions, 4.21
Security Council, 10.20
Security deposit, **5.29**
Security interest, **4.22**
Seller's Remedies, 4.12
Seller's Restrictions on Land Use, 5.25
Selling terms, **10.6**
Separation of Powers, 1.9
Severable contract, **2.29**
Share Exchange and De Facto Mergers, 9.42
Silence or Delay, 3.11
Single-party government, **10.39**
Slander, **6.24**
Slight versus gross rule, **6.12**
Socialist-Communist Law, 10.16
Soliciting agent, **8.3**
Sources of U.S. Law, 1.8–1.9
Sovereign, or Governmental, Immunity, **6.13**
Special agent, **8.3**
Special Characteristics of Insurance Contracts, 3.3
Special damages, **6.46**
Special endorsement, **4.17**
Special exception, **5.26**
Special verdict, **1.21**
Special warranty deed, **5.16**
Specific performance, **2.57**
Spot zoning, **5.26**
Standing to sue, **1.30**
State Court Systems, 1.14
State Regulation, 9.55
State Unfair Trade Practices Acts, 4.29
Stated capital, **9.31**
Statute, **6.3**
Statute of frauds, **2.34**, 4.6

Statute of Frauds and Parol Evidence Rule, 2.34
Statute of limitations, **6.15**
Statute of repose, **6.15**
Statutes of fraud, **4.6**
Statutes of Limitations and Repose, 6.15
Statutory Approaches to Misrepresentation, 3.23
Statutory Exception, 9.5
Stock, 9.31
Stockholders' Actions, 9.40
Stockholders' Meetings, 9.39
Stockholders' Powers and Duties, 9.38
Strict liability (absolute liability), **6.37**
Strict Liability and Negligence, 6.40
Subjacent support, **5.23**
Subpoena, **1.19**
Subsidiaries, 10.10
Substantial factor rule, **6.6**
Substantial performance, **2.12**
Substantive law, **1.7**
Substitution, 2.48
Supply and Demand, 10.30
Survival statute, **6.47**

T

Takeover, **9.43**
Takeovers and Tender Offers, 9.42
Tax Code, 10.27
Tax Havens, **10.34**
Taxation, 10.33
Tenancy, **5.11**
Tenancy at will, **5.28**
Tenancy by the entirety, **5.12**
Tenancy in common, **5.12**
Tenant at sufferance, **5.28**
Tenant's Rights and Duties, 5.29
Tender, **2.47**
Tender offer, **9.43**
Termination of a Contract, 2.46–2.48
Termination of Producer Authority, 8.14–8.15
Territorial tax systems, **10.33**
Theocratic government, **10.39**
Third Party's Rights Against a Principal, 7.17
Third-party beneficiary contract, **2.45**
Third-Party Beneficiaries, **2.3**, 2.45
Third-Party Contractual Rights, 2.42
Third-Party Interests in Liability Insurance, 3.18
Time Differences, 10.37
Time for Delivery, 4.8
Title, **5.4**
Title and Risk of Loss, 4.7
Tort, **6.3**
Tort Liability of Principal and Agent, 7.20
Tortfeasor, **6.3**
Tortfeasor's Capacity, 6.16
Torts Involving Use or Disclosure of Information, 6.27
Toxic tort, **6.39**
Trade acceptance, **4.15**
Trade fixtures, **5.24**
Trade Usage, Course of Dealings, and Performance, 2.42

Transactions With the Corporation, 9.37
Transfer, 4.16
Transfer price, **10.34**
Transitional government, **10.39**
Treasury stock, **9.32**
Trespass, **6.35**
Trespassers, **6.18**, 6.20
Trial Procedure, 1.19
Trust Deeds, **5.19**
Truth in Lending Act, 4.31
Types of Associations, 9.56
Types of Breach, 2.52
Types of Commercial Paper, 4.14–4.15
Types of Consideration, 2.18
Types of Contracts, 2.3
Types of Corporate Tax Structures, 10.35
Types of Deeds, 5.15
Types of Government, 10.38
Types of Illegal Contracts, 2.24
Types of Landlord-Tenant Estates, 5.28
Types of Product Defects, 6.41–6.42
Types of Sales Contracts, 4.4
Types of Third-Party Beneficiaries, 2.45

U

UCC Article 2, 4.3
UCC Article 3, 4.14
UCC Article 7, 4.18
UCC Article 9, 4.22
Ultra vires, **9.35**
Ultrahazardous Activities, **6.37**
Unconditional and Unequivocal Acceptance, 2.11
Unconscionable Bargains, 2.28
Undue influence, **2.33**
Unfair competition, **6.31**
Uniform Commercial Code (UCC), **2.36**
Unilateral contract, **2.3**
Unilateral mistake, **2.32**
Unincorporated association, **9.54**
Unincorporated Associations, 9.54–9.55
Union Economic Tactics, 9.17
United Nations (UN), 10.19
United States Laws Affecting International Business, 10.26
Unqualified endorsement, **4.17**
U.S. Legal System, 1.3
Use of Nonwaiver Agreements and Reservation of Rights Letters, 3.35
Use of Waivers, 3.27
Use variance, **5.27**
Usury, **2.26**
Usury Contracts, 2.26
Utmost good faith, **3.4**

V

Valuable consideration, **2.18**
Valued policy, **3.8**
Variance, **5.27**
Vendee, **5.15**
Vendor, **5.15**

Vicarious liability, **6.51**
Void contract, **2.4**
Voidable contract, **2.4**
Voidable Contracts and Void Contracts, 2.4

W

Wagering Contracts, 2.26
Waiver, **3.27**
Waiver of Lien, 5.21
Waiver, Estoppel, and Election, 3.27
Warehouse receipt, **4.18**, 4.19
Warranties, 3.24
Warranties Distinguished From Representation, 3.25
Was a Contract Formed?, 2.60–2.61
Was the Contract Breached, and, if so, What Is the Remedy?, 2.62–2.66
Water Rights, 5.23
What Is Not Valid Consideration?, 2.21
Winding Up the Partnership Business, 9.52
World Trade Organization (WTO), 10.22
Worldwide tax system, **10.33**
Writ of certiorari, **1.14**
Written Versus Oral and Informal Written Contracts, 3.13
Wrongful death action, **6.47**
Wrongful discharge, **9.4**
Wrongful-life action, **6.34**
Wrongful-pregnancy action (wrongful-conception action), **6.34**

Z

Zoning, **5.26**